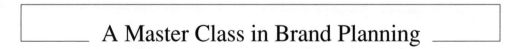
A Master Class in Brand Planning

A Master Class in Brand Planning

The Timeless Works of Stephen King

Edited by
Judie Lannon
Merry Baskin

John Wiley & Sons, Ltd

Other Wiley Editorial Offices

John Wiley & Sons Inc., 111 River Street, Hoboken, NJ 07030, USA

Jossey-Bass, 989 Market Street, San Francisco, CA 94103-1741, USA

Wiley-VCH Verlag GmbH, Boschstr. 12, D-69469 Weinheim, Germany

John Wiley & Sons Australia Ltd, 42 McDougall Street, Milton, Queensland 4064, Australia

John Wiley & Sons (Asia) Pte Ltd, 2 Clementi Loop #02-01, Jin Xing Distripark, Singapore 129809

John Wiley & Sons Canada Ltd, 6045 Freemont Blvd, Mississauga, Ontario, L5R 4J3, Canada

Wiley also publishes its books in a variety of electronic formats. Some content that appears
in print may not be available in electronic books.

Anniversary Logo Design: Richard J. Pacifico

Library of Congress Cataloging-in-Publication Data

King, Stephen, 1931-
    A master class in brand planning / The timeless works of Stephen King;
[edited by] Judie Lannon, Merry Baskin.
        p. cm.
    A selection of King's papers published during the past 30 years, with commentaries by current
marketing practitioners.
    Includes bibliographical references and index.
    ISBN 978-0-470-51791-8 (cloth : alk. paper)
    1. Branding (Marketing)—Management.   2. New products.   3. Brand name products.
4. Advertising—Management.   5. Marketing research.   I. Lannon, Judie.   II. Baskin, Merry.   III. Title.
    HF5415.1255.K56 2007
    658.8′27—dc22

                                                                                    2007035534

British Library Cataloguing in Publication Data

A catalogue record for this book is available from the British Library

ISBN 978-0-470-51791-8 (H/B)

Typeset in 10/12pt Times by Aptara, New Delhi, India
Printed and bound in Great Britain by Antony Rowe Ltd, Chippenham, Wiltshire

For Sally, Sam, Matt and Sophy.

Contents

Introduction

By Jeremy Bullmore

It's impossible to accept that one's grandparents were ever young. Rationally, we know they must have been, but all personal experience suggests otherwise. I'd certainly never attempt to persuade my own grandchildren that I was once a frisky teenager: they'd look at me very strangely.

In this book, a number of respected and current marketing practitioners have written excellent commentaries on selections of Stephen King's most perceptive articles. He's consistently described as prescient, intellectually rigorous and possessed of great clarity of thought and expression: a theoretician whose theories were all intensely practical, a giant in the world of marketing and advertising. All absolutely true. As the co-inventor of account planning as a distinct discipline, his benign influence has touched tens of thousands of people he'd never met. He was widely held in awe, no more so than in India, where they think more intelligently about advertising than just about anywhere else in the world. An invitation to hear him speak to the Delhi Advertising Club in 1992 reads in part, "... advertising has many gurus, many professors, many geniuses and many mavericks. But only one King."

When you read his collected articles in this book, you'll agree that every tribute has been well earned. He's all the things they claim for him. The only thing that's missing – and inevitably so – is more than a glimpse of the man himself. Just as we find it impossible to believe that our grandparents were ever teenagers, so the weight of Stephen's reputation and the richness of his legacy incline us to picture some austere, aesthetic figure, permanently late middle-aged and not a lot of laughs to be around. (How else do you imagine a Visiting Professor of Marketing Communications at the Cranfield School of Management to be?)

In the pages that follow, you'll find all the evidence you need of his professional achievements. And on page 341, there's a curriculum vitae that charts the skeleton of his life and works. But for now, I'd like to try to fill in with a bit of frivolous but all-important detail.

Improbably, we knew each other for more than 60 years. He turned up at school about a year after I did. We were in different Houses but went to the same French classes. (When, 50 years later, we were both summoned to have dinner with David Ogilvy in Paris it was clear that we'd either learned very little or forgotten a lot.) I remember him as small and wiry: it seems he didn't start growing till he was 15. He was good at games, was an ace squash player and dabbled (as I did) in theatricals.

Then we both, separately, did our National Service. As he left the Army, he wrote what may have been his only advertisement. It was for his 1936 Fiat – "Condition of body, shocking" – and was headlined "A RATTLING GOOD BARGAIN". It was marked down from "Any bids over £65?" To "£5 or near offer". I knew most of his cars after that and they were all neglected.

Then we both went to Oxford. Stephen, unlike me, lasted the full term – in his case, four years – and got a degree in Greats (philosophy and ancient history). We saw each other regularly but were never part of each other's inner circle. He played squash and tennis for the university and continued to dabble (as I did) in theatricals. He was in an Edinburgh Festival production of *Ralph Roister Doister* and there are records of an OUDS touring production of *Twelfth Night*. Stephen played Feste but couldn't sing the songs. Viola was played by Maggie Smith.

I joined J. Walter Thompson London in 1954. Stephen, for reasons I never fathomed, joined Mond Nickel (a business as far removed from the consumer as it's possible to imagine) and worked in their publicity department where he came into contact with their advertising agency. They offered him a job. Prompted by this, he decided to look around – and knowing that I was having an extremely agreeable time at JWT, he got in touch. I don't remember doing so but, according to Stephen, I fixed for him to have an interview – and in 1957, he joined. We worked together there for the next 30 years.

Stephen and JWT suited each other perfectly (it even provided him with a wife, Sally: a JWT copywriter). The agency traditionally honoured intellect (the old "University of Advertising" tag had been earned in New York before the Second World War) and had been the first agency to make serious use of consumer research through its wholly owned subsidiary The British Market Research Bureau. It was, however, in need of a new infusion. It was also fun: an irresistible combination. There was as much for Stephen to build on as there was for him to be irreverent about. He was good at irreverence.

An account director once called us all together and solemnly gave us a new Unilever brief. We were to invent new product opportunities for them. Blue-sky thinking was urged upon us: we should in no way be constrained by existing manufacturing capabilities or practical considerations of any other kind.

A ponderous person would have drafted a two-page memorandum pointing out the point-lessness of such a project. Stephen responded with an instant list of new product breakthroughs. The two I remember with the greatest affection were Spray-on Socks and Bed-Making Fluid. Nothing much was said about this project from then on – but it was to be a familiar King tactic. He could use wit and parody with telling effect.

When preparing a client presentation on the dangers of greed in brand positioning, he and I invented a brave new niche product for the dog food market. It was formulated exclusively for bitches and was called *Good Girl*. After three rounds of fictional but accurately simulated research, the fictional client realized that the brand had little appeal to 50% of the dog market and lost his nerve. The launch ad was amended accordingly – and the strapline now read: "Good Girl's Good for Boy Dogs, Too!" The real client absorbed the moral with grace and gratitude.

Nothing incensed him more than marketing people who thought that marketing's job was nothing more than somehow to get rid of stuff. He called it Thrust Marketing and invented a marketing director called Colin Thrust to personify it. For one industry presentation, Colin developed his all-purpose 10-Point Marketing Plan, which went as follows:

1. Up weight 10p-off flash packs to 80 % of throughput.
2. Increase over-riders to selected major multiples and cash-and-carries.

3. Re-motivate sales force with incremental incentive-linked sales targets.
4. Initiate tailor-made in-store merchandising with dealer-loaders, individualized gondolas and shelf-wobblers.
5. Upgrade pack design, to dramatically improve visibility and shelf-appeal.
6. Widen distribution to include discount stores and garden centres.
7. Increase stock levels to create product push.
8. Implement a country-wide back-to-back coupon drop to create consumer pull.
9. Draw up a 5-year PR plan.
10. Launch a massive consumer promotion to up-rate brand awareness and share of mind.

At no point, of course, was it evident what the actual product was or what purpose it had. At no point was it even considered that product quality might usefully be examined. Half his audience went away properly mortified but a great deal wiser. The other half just took notes.

As in his 10-Point Plan, his only use of jargon was to mock it. Once, just a couple of years ago, I asked him, for a piece I was writing, to select any speech from Shakespeare and give it the treatment. He chose the Polonius speech from *Hamlet*, "Neither a borrower or a lender be . . ."

> In overseas assignments it is essential to keep an appropriate and sustainably balanced credit/debit ratio. Unsecured loans may be irrecoverable and can endanger potentially profitable relationships, while sporadic borrowing inflows can conceal the underlying reality of cash flow projections.

Stephen's writings share many qualities but the rarest is this: when you've read them, and absorbed them, you know exactly what you have to do. His familiar criticism of vacuous corporate advertising – "why are they telling me all this?" – could never be applied to his own papers: they are all intensely practical. And so was he. He may never have bothered to clean his cars, but he could re-fit the entire inside of a house on his own – and so indeed he did: woodwork, cabling, plumbing, the lot. He called his internal JWT manual *The Account Planner's Toolkit* – and that's exactly what it is.

Had his dress sense been as immaculate as his thinking, he'd have been intolerable.

SOME THINGS YOU SHOULD KNOW

Stephen's wife, Sally, has been behind this book from the beginning. She welcomed our offer to make it happen and has given the two editors, Judie Lannon and Merry Baskin, endless help in tracing papers and filling in with facts and background.

In prospect, the task seemed simple enough. In reality, the amount of work involved has been immense. Judie and Merry have undertaken it all with a dedicated commitment – fuelled by their huge enthusiasm for the project.

All of the distinguished contributors, whose words preface the King articles, have given their services for nothing: they haven't been paid for what they've so thoughtfully written and they'll benefit not at all from any royalties that may accrue. We are deeply grateful to them.

All costs incurred in preparing the book for publication have been generously absorbed by our three sponsors: APG (the Account Planning Group), JWT and WPP.

All author's royalties from this book will go to Sally King. Stephen's work forms a priceless legacy and it's entirely right that Sally should inherit it.

And finally: beware, throughout this book, of the word "advertising". Today it's often used, very restrictively, to mean advertisements in mass media and nothing much else. Almost invariably, Stephen uses the word advertising to cover all forms of brand communication.

About the Book: How it Happened

The collected wisdom of Stephen King already exists – but not in one piece. If no-one steps forward to perform the task of publishing the Stephen King Collection it will be the ultimate proof that ours is a truly trivial trade.

Campaign, 24 February 2006

Stephen King had a very big idea, and that very big idea changed the way advertising agencies were structured, how they thought, and even what they produced. He changed our lives and the lives and careers of many others both in the UK and around the world where the idea of account planning has been adopted. Although Stanley Pollitt of BMP had a similar idea about the same time, Stephen did the most to codify and explain what this new discipline was and how it worked.

Like many original thinkers, he documented his ideas as they evolved in a number of articles and books published over a 30-year period – a total of about 40 or so. When he died in February 2006, there was, naturally, a flurry of talk about re-publishing his work to make it available to a wider and younger audience.

We felt we should do more to make the ideas described in his work relevant to today. After all, much has changed in the media, marketing and consumer environments over the last decade, never mind a 30-year period.

The solution was to choose a range of his articles that seemed to offer most guidance to readers today. For each, we chose an eminent practitioner to comment on what has changed in the intervening years and how the thoughts and principles apply now.

As testament to Stephen's breadth of interest, the articles and contributions cover four separate but related areas:

1. The origins of account planning: its ideas and structure
2. The account planner's craft skills
3. The use (and misuse) of research
4. The wider marketing world.

The hype, flimflam and promise of certainties that surround so much marketing and advertising writing are conspicuously absent in these articles. The writing is transparently honest, reflecting a great integrity; a mind searching for a way to bring order out of chaos.

The articles are not so much about *what* to think, but aim at teaching that most precious skill of all, *how* to think. The collection in this book of Stephen's work, along with the thoughts and ideas of today's practitioners, represents a treasure trove of insights, principles and guides to thinking that anyone in the world of marketing communications will find immensely valuable.

These principles were uniquely valuable in a simpler age and are even more valuable and necessary now.

Judie Lannon
Merry Baskin

Acknowledgements

Many people have contributed to this book and we are heartily grateful for the time, effort, advice and encouragement we have been given. In addition to the contributors and Sally King, our thanks go to the many people who helped along the way: from WPP, Sir Martin Sorrell, Jeremy Bullmore, Marie Capes, Vanessa Bryant; from JWT, Bob Jeffrey, Claudine Heinimann, Louise Hinchliffe, David Faulkner, John Furr; from WARC, Mike Waterson, Matthew Coombs, James Aitchison; from APG, Steve Martin; from John Wiley & Sons, Claire Plimmer; and our freelance typists, Hilary Watson and Janet Barbour.

About the Contributors

JEREMY BULLMORE
WPP

Born 1929. First job, trainee copywriter with J. Walter Thompson in London, where he stayed until retirement in 1987. Successively writer/producer, creative group head and head of television; 1964 to 1975, head of the creative department; 1976 to 1987, chairman. Chairman of the Advertising Association, 1981 to 1987.

1988 to 2001, non-executive director of the Guardian Media Group; 1988 to 2004, Non-Executive Director of WPP. Currently member WPP Advisory Board. Past President of NABS, and current President of the Market Research Society. Columnist for *Campaign, Management Today, Market Leader* and *The Guardian.* Awarded CBE in 1985.

Publications: *Another Bad Day at the Office?* Penguin, 2001; *Behind the Scenes in Advertising Mark III (More Bull More)* WARC, 2003; *Ask Jeremy,* Haymarket, 2004; *Apples, Insights and Mad Inventors,* John Wiley & Sons, 2006.

MERRY BASKIN
Planning Consultant, Baskin Shark

Merry has spent most of her 30-year career as an account planner, but started out as an international market researcher. Her resumé includes stints at blue chip firms such as BMRB, Saatchi & Saatchi, Chiat/Day and J. Walter Thompson, and over the years she has worked in London, Paris, New York, Stockholm and Brussels.

In 2000, Merry launched her own planning consultancy, Baskin Shark (Where Brands Move Forward or Die!), which offers strategic communications planning as well as planning craft skills training.

Her client experience extends from classic fmcg (Kellogg, Kraft, Unilever) to travel (British Airways, Avis) to financial (Visa Europe, Goldman Sachs) to retail (Argos, Subway, IKEA, Boots). She admits to being an Advert Tweaker and aspires to Grand Strategist, but is probably happiest as a brand planner.

Industry credits include APG chair 1998/99, MRS conference committee and Best Paper winner (2001), IPA Effectiveness Awards winner and judge, and winner of several US Effies.

TIM BROADBENT
Regional Effectiveness Director and Regional Planning Director Ogilvy & Mather Asia Pacific

Tim is the Regional Effectiveness Director and Regional Planning Director of Ogilvy & Mather Asia Pacific, based in Beijing, China. He is the only person to have won two Grand Prix in the IPA Effectiveness Awards, was Convenor of Judges of the Effectiveness Awards, and served as Chairman of the IPA Value of Advertising Committee. He has been an account planner since the 1970s, starting at BMP. Most recently he was Planning Director and Managing Partner of Young & Rubicam, and then Chief Strategic Officer of the Bates Group EMEA region. He is a Fellow of the IPA and Visiting Professor of Marketing of The University of The Arts London.

HUGH BURKITT
Chief Executive, Marketing Society

Hugh Burkitt is Chief Executive of the Marketing Society – the leading network for senior marketers in the UK. He has been responsible for the launch of the Society's *Manifesto for Marketing,* introduced the *Marketing Leaders Programme* for potential marketing directors and established the *Panoramic Group* – a new forum where all the UK's marketing organizations have agreed to work together to promote marketing.

He began his career as a Unilever trainee at Birds Eye Foods and progressed via the Manchester Business School to Collett Dickenson Pearce in 1972. He spent the next 30 years in advertising, founding the agency Burkitt Weinreich Bryant in 1986, and leaving in 2002 as Chairman of Burkitt DDB.

He is co-author with John Zealley of *Marketing Excellence*: *Winning Companies Reveal the Secrets of their Success*, John Wiley & Sons, 2006 (a review of the lessons to be learned from the winning companies in the *Marketing Society's Awards for Excellence*).

STEPHEN CARTER
Chief of Strategy and Principal Advisor to the Prime Minister

In January 2008, Stephen Carter was appointed Chief of Strategy and Principal Advisor to the Prime Minister, Gordon Brown. Previously, he was Group Chief Executive of Brunswick Group LLP, a UK based, privately PR advisory firm operating in 12 countries. Prior to this Stephen was the founding Chief Executive of Ofcom, and before that Chief Operating Officer of NTL UK & Ireland, and Managing Director and Chief Executive at J. Walter Thompson UK Limited.

He is an Honours graduate in law from Aberdeen University and also a graduate of the Harvard Business School's AMP programme.

He is an ex-Chairman of the Marketing Group of Great Britain, and is currently a Non Executive Director of Travis Perkins plc, a Governor of the Ashridge Business School, a Vice President of UNICEF.

Stephen was awarded a CBE in the 2007 New Years Honours list for services to the Communications Industry.

NEIL CASSIE
The Cassie Partnership

Neil is the Founding Partner of The Cassie Partnership (tcp), which helps clients like Visa Europe and Diageo to close the gap between the vision of the company and the behaviour of its key people.

Neil was previously Director of Brand Planning, Worldwide at Leo Burnett. He wrote the company's new global positioning and methodology "The Brand Belief System". This incorporated a core brand competence in organizational design and management, which is the foundation of the work his company undertakes today.

Prior to his global role Neil was the Deputy Chairman of Burnett's London agency.

While Head of Planning at GGT, Neil was a member of the APG committee and was responsible for training for three years.

Neil learned his trade at Halls in Edinburgh and then Ogilvy & Mather in London.

SIMON CLEMMOW
Clemmow Hornby Inge

Simon has worked in advertising for 25 years. He has always been based in London, and has always been an account planner, except for a short spell as CEO at TBWA. He is currently planning partner at his second successful start-up agency, Clemmow Hornby Inge.

Simon worked first at Benton & Bowles, and quickly moved on to Gold Greenlees Trott in 1983. He co-founded Simons Palmer Denton Clemmow & Johnson in 1988. The agency won accounts like Nike and Sony PlayStation and produced outstanding creative work, before selling to Omnicom and merging with TBWA in 1997. Simon co-founded Clemmow Hornby Inge in 2001. In 2004 the agency was British Television Advertising's Agency of the Year, and *Marketing* magazine's Creative Agency of the Year.

RITA CLIFTON
Chairman, Interbrand

Rita graduated from Cambridge and began her career in advertising. She worked at Saatchi & Saatchi for 12 years, becoming Vice Chairman and Executive Planning Director in 1995.

In 1997 she joined Interbrand, the world's leading brand consultancy, as Chief Executive in London; in January 2002 she became Chairman. She is in demand as a speaker and media commentator on all areas of brands, reputation, marketing and communications around the world. Her writing has included the book *The Future of Brands* and The Economist book *Brands and Branding*.

She is a Non-Executive Director of DSG International plc (formerly Dixons Store Group plc) and Emap plc. She also chairs Populus, the opinion pollster to *The Times* and is a Visiting Professor at Henley Management College. Other advisory boards have included the Government's Sustainable Development Commission, the Judge Business School at Cambridge University, BP's carbon offset programme and the Duke of Edinburgh's Award.

MARTIN DEBOO
City Analyst, Investec Securities

Martin Deboo is a City Analyst at Investec Securities in London, where he follows the fortunes of major consumer goods firms including Cadbury, Unilever and Reckitt Benckiser.

Martin is rather unique within the City in that he began his career not in finance or accounting, but as an account planner in advertising, with BMP and Publicis. Following an MBA at the London Business School he spent 12 years in strategic management consulting with OC&C, the last five as head of their Consumer Goods practice.

Martin speaks and writes extensively on the financial and economic aspects of marketing and retains an active involvement with London Business School, where he serves as a Governor.

TOM DOCTOROFF
JWT, Northeast Asia Area Director, Greater China CEO

Tom, born and bred in America's Detroit and educated in Chicago, somehow took a detour to Hong Kong in 1994 and never quite made it back to the States. In the meantime, he has become one of Asia's most respected advertising minds. Having started his advertising career at Leo Burnett (Chicago) in 1989, Tom jumped ship and joined JWT Chicago in 1992. In 1994, Tom moved to Hong Kong as Regional Business Director, managing several of JWT's largest multinational clients across Asia Pacific. Further promotions followed, and in 2002, he was appointed Northeast Asia Area Director (China, Taiwan, Hong Kong and Korea) and Greater China CEO. In 2003, Tom was named Regional Agency Head of the Year by the region's leading marketing and advertising publication, *Media Magazine*. He is also the author of *Billions: Selling to the New Chinese Consumer*, published by Palgrave Macmillan in January 2006.

WILLIAM ECCLESHARE
Chairman and CEO, BBDO Europe

After reading History at Cambridge University, William joined J. Walter Thompson as a trainee in 1978. He became Managing Director of JWT London in 1990 and moved to Amsterdam as CEO PPGH/JWT in 1993. He joined JWT's Worldwide Board in 1995 as Director of Global Strategy.

In 1996 William joined Ammirati Puris Lintas (Interpublic Group) as UK CEO and subsequently became regional director for Northern Europe and UK Chairman.

In 2000 he joined McKinsey & Company as a partner and leader of the European Branding Practice. He led major assignments in media, technology and mining sectors. He returned to the advertising industry and WPP in 2002, joining Young & Rubicam/Wunderman as European Chairman and CEO.

In 2006 he joined BBDO as Chairman and CEO for Europe, Middle East and Africa with responsibility for all advertising, CRM, interactive and consulting businesses in the region.

William is a Non-Executive Director of Hays plc and a governor of University College School, London.

PAUL FELDWICK

Paul Feldwick was an account planner for over 30 years at the agency that morphed from Boase Massimi Pollitt into DDB. He helped to found DDB University, and was convenor of judges for the IPA Effectiveness Awards from 1988–90. He is a former Chair of the AQR and of the APG, a Fellow of the MRS and of the IPA. He has written and lectured extensively on how ads work, including a book *What is Brand Equity, Anyway?* (WARC, 2002). He now pursues his continuing interest into the nature of communication and creativity as a freelance consultant and teacher. He is also a poet and a singer, and keen to explore ways of bringing creative arts into the workplace. He has an MA from Oxford in English Literature and an MSc from the University of Bath in Responsibility and Business Practice.

CHRIS FORREST
Partner, The Nursery

From 1982 to 1986 Chris was a qualitative researcher working for top dogs like Roy Langmaid and Roddy Glen.

From 1986 to 1991 he was at Ogilvy & Mather where he became their youngest board director.

Then from 1991 to 1997 he was Planning Director Duckworth Finn Grubb Waters where he won APG and IPA Effectiveness Awards and during this period was Vice Chair of the APG.

Chris is currently a partner in The Nursery, specializing in creative development research for advertising and brand communications.

MIKE HALL
Hall & Partners

Mike Hall is the founder of Hall & Partners, the specialist brand and communications research agency, which he set up in 1992 after developing the new theory about four models of how advertising works in different ways to affect brand relationships.

This theory, which changed the face of advertising and brand research, was developed after his experience at BMRB, BBDO and Leagas Delaney. Everyone used to say that "we know that advertising works in different ways but we don't what they are", so he simply resolved to work it out.

Three years after he set up Hall & Partners he opened in New York and his agency spread to LA and Chicago. After Hall & Partners joined the Omnicom Group in 2003, Mike developed further models of how the other communications disciplines work, culminating in a model of integrated communications that was launched in 2005.

JUDIE LANNON
Editor, *Market Leader*

Judie Lannon is a consultant in market research and marketing communications strategy. She was born in the United States and her advertising career began at Leo Burnett in Chicago. But the majority of her career was in the London Office of JWT where she was initially hired by Stephen King to set up JWT's creative research unit, which was part of the original Account Planning Department. Latterly she was Director of Research and Planning for JWT Europe.

She established her own planning and research consultancy in 1991. In addition to this consultancy work, Judie designs senior management courses in marketing communications, brand positioning and market research. Judie is also a recognized writer, editor and speaker in the field of marketing communications. She is Editor of the strategic marketing journal *Market Leader* (the Journal of the Marketing Society, Great Britain) and is on the editorial board of the *International Journal of Advertising*.

CREENAGH LODGE
Co-Chairman, Corporate Edge

Creenagh Lodge is co-Chairman of Corporate Edge, specialists in all forms of design, branding and innovation. Having originally intended to be an archaeologist, she abandoned this for social anthropology, which naturally led to market research, which in turn led to new product development, with a spell of advertising in between. She has written, lectured and broadcast a good deal on new product development; and can testify to the acute pleasure of seeing a new product, which one has helped to develop, succeed in the market place.

KEVIN McLEAN
Wardle McLean

Kevin started in research in 1984 at Market Behaviour Ltd and within six months was on a plane to West Africa thinking, "this is the job for me".

He moved to Strategic Research Group and trained under Roddy Glen and Barry Ross and stayed until he was made MD.

In 1996 he started Wardle McLean Strategic Research Consultancy with Judith Wardle.

Kevin has written many articles and conference papers on advertising, websites and research (MRS, Admap, AQR, QRCA), the latest being "Conversations, a new model for qualitative research" (QRCA, Atlanta, September 2006).

He is currently Chair of the annual MRS Conference. He was elected a Fellow of the Market Research Society in 2006.

TY MONTAGUE
Co-President, Chief Creative Officer, JWT New York

Ty has an impressive track record in building world-class brands for such New York agencies as Ogilvy & Mather, Weiden + Kennedy, Bartle Bogle Hegarty and Chiat/Day. He has created national and global campaigns for such clients as Reebok, Mercedes Benz, Coca-Cola, Volvo, Everlast and MTV.

Ty joined JWT New York in 2005 where he is known for "changing the channel": questioning the ways in which the advertising industry thinks, particularly beyond the traditional 30-second TV spot.

Throughout his career, Ty's work has received many major creative accolades, including The One Show, Cannes, Communication Arts, AICP, MOMA and The Clios. Most recently, *Advertising Age* magazine named him one of the Top 10 Creative Directors in America.

GUY MURPHY
Worldwide Planning Director, JWT

Guy joined JWT in January 2007 as Worldwide Planning Director. His primary role is to lead a world-class planning function at the agency that jointly invented Account Planning. The role also involves developing the agency's strategy to achieve outstanding creativity in the new communications era.

Prior to JWT, Guy worked for 14 years at BBH where he occupied a series of strategic roles; Regional Planning Director for Asia Pacific, Head of Planning for Europe, and lastly Deputy Chairman. In that final role he helped the agency to two consecutive Campaign Agency of the Year awards.

His career began as a trainee planner at BMP in London.

Guy is a published author on the subjects of effectiveness and communication strategy, and has received numerous industry awards for his work. He is currently the Chairman of the IPA Strategy Group.

MARCO RIMINI
MindShare

Having graduated from Oxford University with a degree in Politics, Philosophy and Economics in 1985, Marco spent several years as an account planner before becoming Head of Account Planning for Euro RSCG.

He joined CIA Media as Head of Planning and became deputy MD and member of the UK group board. He worked across a range of clients including Unilever, LloydsTSB and the launch of Daewoo.

His most recent position prior to MindShare was as Director of Strategy and Development at JWT London, where he was responsible for all the account planners and the knowledge centre. He worked across the range of JWT business including Kraft, Kellogg, Vodafone, Shell and Bandq as well as being the strategic lead on the WPP HSBC assignment.

He joined MindShare in July to develop the communications planning practice by reuniting the craft skills of account and media planning and applying them to the digital age.

ROSEMARIE RYAN
President, JWT New York

Rosemarie Ryan joined JWT as President of its New York headquarters in 2004. Prior to joining JWT, Rosemarie spent eight years as President of Kirshenbaum Bond + Partners, also in New York. Rosemarie began her advertising career at BBDO London, and was among the first wave of British imports to the account planning discipline in the United States in the late 1980s, when she joined Chiat/Day.

With roots in account planning, Rosemarie's strategic acumen and critical thinking have helped to launch, position and reposition countless brands, including Snapple, JetBlue and the Diamond Trading Company.

ANDREW SETH

Andrew Seth worked as a worldwide manager for Lever/ Unilever for more than 30 years in the UK, Europe, Mexico, Japan and twice in USA. He retired early as Chairman of Lever Brothers UK in 1995. Since then he has been Chairman of the Added Value group, and a Non-Executive Director of Tempus plc, Richmond Events and Ingram. He is Chairman of Plum Baby, Susie Willis's innovative new baby-foods company.

Andrew has been a Board member of the Consumers' Association, of the Royal Shakespeare Theatre Company, and of Dulwich College. He was Pro-Chancellor of Kingston University for eight years. He now represents Dulwich College Enterprises as its Board member in China.

Andrew has specialized in grocery retailing as a subject since leaving Unilever, co-authoring *The Grocers* (1999 and 2001/Kogan Page) and *Supermarket Wars* (2005/Palgrave Macmillan) with long-time Oxford college friend Geoffrey Randall.

DAVID SMITH
Director, DVL Smith Group

David Smith is Director of DVL Smith Group, and a Professor at the University of Hertfordshire Business School.

He is a Fellow, and former Chairman, of the UK Market Research Society and holds the Society's Silver Medal. He has won numerous awards from the Market Research Society, ESOMAR and other bodies.

David is also a Fellow of both the UK Chartered Institute of Marketing, and a member of the UK Institute of Management Consultants.

He is the author of *Inside Information – Making Sense of Marketing Data* and *The Art & Science of Interpreting Market Research Evidence*.

RORY SUTHERLAND
Ogilvy Group UK, Vice-Chairman

Rory Sutherland joined OgilvyOne as a graduate trainee in September 1988 and has worked there ever since. However, what at first glance may seem a dull career path has been ... well, the very word "path" is an overclaim.

After a year as the world's worst account man (in a last remedial effort he was booked on a time management course, but got the date wrong) Rory was moved to the Planning Department. From there he was fired in early 1990. After two weeks unemployed, Rory joined the agency's creative department as a junior copywriter. He was promoted to Head of Copy in 1995 and Creative Director in 1997. By happy coincidence he was also an early Internet user and so became an early advocate of Ogilvy's pioneering new media arm.

In 2005 he was made Vice-Chairman of the Ogilvy Group in the UK in recognition of his improved timekeeping.

MALCOLM WHITE
krow

Malcolm is one of the four founders of krow, an agency that believes it has a duty to create communications that trigger people to do something. Since its launch in September 2005, the agency has acquired clients such as FIAT, Thomson and the Elmlea assignment from Unilever.

Malcolm has been a planner since 1987 at agencies such as Yellowhammer, BMP DDB, Partners BDDH and Euro RSCG.

Career highlights include winning an IPA Effectiveness Award for Strepsils, helping the Labour Party back into power while at BMP, and leading Partners BDDH to a Grand Prix win in The Account Planning Group (APG) Creative Planning Awards in 2001.

He is the current Chairman of APG, and in 2006 invented and chaired The Battle Of Big Thinking – a new kind of conference celebrating the latest and best thinking in marketing, communications, planning and research.

Part I
Planning: Role and Structure

The articles in this section give a very vivid flavour of the London advertising world in the 1970s. It is the definitive account of where the new discipline of account planning came from and what it aimed to do at a time when all advertising agencies were modelled on the typical structure of American agencies. The multinational agencies were relatively large and coherent entities in the sense that all the disciplines lived under the same roof.

The value of this historical perspective to readers in the fragmented world of communications planning today is enormous. Why? Because the job to be done is exactly the same in our more complex world as it was in what seems a much more orderly past.

The bitty, fractious media and agency environment together with the distractions of technology and social change often obscure this fact. Yet the intellectual logic that binds the whole process together is the same now as it was then and the themes in this section have important lessons for today.

1

Who Do You Think You Are?

By Malcolm White, Planning Partner, krow

An introduction to:

1.1   The Anatomy of Account Planning
1.2   The Origins of Account Planning
1.3   How I Started Account Planning in Agencies

Of the articles presented in this wonderful book, 91% were written by Stephen King. The remaining 9% (or two articles) were written by the late John Treasure, formerly of JWT, and the late Stanley Pollitt, formerly of Boase Massimi Pollitt. Both these articles are collected here along with Stephen King's account of the birth of account planning.

These three articles are quite different from the others in this collection. They are not directly concerned with marketing, brands or budget setting, nor with technical subjects like pre-testing. Nor are they theoretical or obviously polemical.

Instead, all the articles are concerned with events that happened almost 40 years ago. They are the story of something extraordinary that happened when three people who are sadly no longer with us, and a host of other individuals who are much less well known than these three authors, started thinking along similar lines. The extraordinary something was the development and introduction of account planning in agencies.

The story each article tells from slightly different perspectives is played out in a world that seems very different from our own: it is a world that is sketched out in the articles. Advertising agencies have marketing departments that plan new product development, that analyse the sales data for clients and present the results to them at their board meetings. Account men are called "representatives" (or at least they were at JWT), and we come across a roll-call of agencies that no longer exist or have probably been swallowed up by one mega-merger after another: Pritchard Wood and Partners, DPBS, OBM and Beagle, Bargle, D'Annunzio, Twigg and Privet (the last of these is a favourite Stephen King joke: a spoof on the raft of small agencies that began springing up in the 1980s characterized by the name of virtually every employee on the door).

In short, these articles are firmly rooted in the past. They are history. Why then should the modern young planner in these time-pressed times give these articles the 30 minutes required to read them? The simple answer is that they will tell the modern young planner in these time-pressed times who they are, and what they should be.

Reading each of these articles is like coming across a box of old family photographs hidden in a dusty attic. And I don't just mean that these articles, like the old photographs, aren't looked at very often. The background and settings in the articles are certainly different from today, like the background and settings of years gone by in old family photographs. Many of the people mentioned in these articles aren't well known today; they are the equivalent of a shadowy figure in the back row of a formal family portrait.

But despite the obvious, superficial, differences between past and present there is a deep echo from the past in these articles that is slightly surprising but helps to explain why we are the way that we are, and even helps to explain the interests and preoccupations we have. A bit like spotting a family resemblance between yourself and a great, great aunt.

Have Planners Lost Touch with their Roots?

Planning has certainly changed and developed from the planning defined and practised by Stephen King, John Treasure and Stanley Pollitt. A certain amount of change is inevitable, but I think in the process many planners have drifted away from, and lost touch with, their roots, not always to the benefit of themselves, their agencies or their clients. I even suspect, from the conversations that I have, that today's planners under the age of 30 have little awareness of where they (and their job title) come from.

Reading these papers is at very least a comforting reconnection with the past and a return to roots. But there is something rather unsettling about these articles. They make me think that some of us are denying our roots, like someone from a working-class background in the North East who has succeeded in London and is slightly ashamed of his or her humble background. I think this because there are three clear lessons to be drawn from these three articles. They may surprise at least a few of the younger planning community.

1. Planning Was Never Intended to be Just about Imaginative Leaps or Just about Lateral Thinking

When attention has been paid to the story of the birth of planning over the last 40 years, too much of that attention has been focused on the differences in approach between the two agencies that could claim to have invented it. Reading the story of the development of planning at JWT (as told by Stephen King and John Treasure) and at BMP (as told by Stanley Pollitt), I was not only struck by the broad similarities but by the emphasis that both agencies put on thorough and rigorous planning, grounded in facts and realities.

JWT's approach was grounded in client marketing realities and its Planning Department sprang from their Marketing Department. BMP's approach was anchored by the reality of the consumer:

> All creative work – and we mean all creative work – at BMP is checked out qualitatively with a tightly defined target market... To give some idea of scale we conducted some 1,200 groups last year which arguably makes us the largest qualitative research company in the country. (Pollitt)

This all feels quite different from current practice. So much of what I see in the planning of today (including in our own APG Planning Awards) is more about interesting ideas than it is about the right idea (or even *a* right idea). These three articles remind us that great planning isn't creativity; it is grounded creativity. Great planners are those who can flip between logical analysis and lateral flights of fancy, or as Jeremy Bullmore put it: "We need to be intuitive, instinctive, scared and lucky AND we need to be rigorous, disciplined, logical and deductive" (Bullmore, 1991).

I think we need more of these sorts of people and less of those who are just "interesting". For the planning species to thrive and prosper, it has to reject the specious.

> *2. Planning today is too concerned with downstream creative interventions at the expense of big, strategic thinking which happens upstream*

Stephen King refers to his famous typology of planners in *The Anatomy of Account Planning*:

> I believe in fact that the most fundamental scale on which to judge account planners is one that runs from Grand Strategists to Advert Tweakers. And that nowadays there are rather too many agencies whose planners' skills are much too near the the advert-tweaking end of the scale.

Paul Feldwick (2007) has observed that "it would be fair to see JWT as closer to the former and BMP (at least by the 1980s) to the latter, though the choice is clearly somewhat loaded!" What Stephen King meant by "grand" at the extreme is clear from a later paper where he describes grand strategists as people who are "intellectual, aim to see the big picture, are a little bit above the fray, almost economists" (King, 1988). From my personal perspective, being "grand" by that definition is every bit as bad as being a tweaker. Also, more importantly, as marketing departments and consultants grew in number and in confidence, they tended to play this role.

Nevertheless, it seems to me that both agencies and planners have increasingly retrenched to the ad-tweaking end of the scale, even if few would call it that, and Stephen's criticisms are even truer today.

Because of all this, I think we need to reassert the role of the planner in developing big, strategic upstream thoughts. Thoughts like "Dirt is good" for Persil and Dove's "Campaign For Real Beauty", for example, are big upstream thoughts. They neither belong to the camp of the Grand Strategist, nor to the party of the Ad Tweakers.

They are much more like the idea of the "strategic concept" that John Treasure defines in his article:

> Such strategic thinking and planning is especially valuable for the advertiser who is financially unable to match forces (or dollars) with a strongly established competitor. And it will be seen here that CREATIVE thinking may be even more valuable than in the area of messages, where most of the talk about "creativity" in advertising is focused.

To encourage us all to strive more often for these big upstream strategic concepts, we at The Account Planning Group will be unveiling a small, but important change to our biennial awards: from 2007 they will be called The APG Creative *Strategy* Awards (rather than Creative Planning Awards as they are today).

> *3. Planning was, and is, a force for changing advertising and communications, and the way agencies think and behave*

Stephen King linked the futures of account planning and advertising in his article, and of course the stories that the three authors tell in their three articles is about the impact of planning on two agencies and on the world of advertising generally. Stanley Pollitt emphasizes that planning requires a particular agency environment in which to flourish, and he points out that the basic ground rules of advertising and how it is developed were also changed by planning.

In recent years there has been too much debate on the role and skills of account planners, and far too much emphasis on the planner as an inspired individual. This runs the risk of separating the planner from the process, the agencies and the clients.

To celebrate this broader role of planning we are creating a new award for our 2007 APG Strategy Awards. This award will be called The Stephen King Strategy Agency of the Year

Award, and will award not an individual but the collective efforts of the planners in the agency that has done best in the awards.

But What a Brilliant Idea Account Planning was

Reading these articles brings home a point that I think has too often been obscured by the shadows of history, by our contemporary obsession with the future, and by always moving forward. The three articles illuminate, with the flash of a firework exploding in the pitch black sky, what a brilliant idea account planning was. It was as big an idea in the narrow context of 1960s advertising as Darwin's idea of evolution was for the Victorian world.

To steal the words of the American philosopher David Dennett – meant for Darwin and his theory of evolution, I believe, and reading these three articles reminds me of this belief – account planning is *"the single best idea anyone has ever had"* (quoted in Dupre, 2003).

Let's not forget that.

And Finally ... the Challenge to Planners in 2007

Forty years on from the invention of account planning in agencies, most of us are quite familiar with planning. Reading these articles makes this familiar thing – planning – strange and wonderful again.

They challenge all planners to take a long, hard look at themselves and what they do, and ask some searching questions:

- How does what you do as a planner, measure up to the vision of Stephen King and Stanley Pollitt?
- Ask yourself when was the last time you were rigorous, deductive and logical rather than just intuitive and lateral?
- When was the last time your interesting ideas were really grounded in facts, realities and data?
- When was the last time you came up with a big strategic concept for a brand?

The correct answer to the last three, by the way, is: "Just last week, thank you very much".

REFERENCES

Bullmore, J. (1991) *Behind the Scenes in Advertising*. NTC Publications.
Dupre, J. (2003) *Darwin's Legacy: What Evolution Means Today*. Oxford University Press.
Feldwick, P. (2007) "Account planning: Its history, and its significance for ad agencies", in Ambler, T. and Tellis, G. (eds), *The Sage Handbook of Advertising*.
King, S. (1988) *The Strategic Development of Brands* – from an APG one-day event.

1.1

The Anatomy of Account Planning*

By Stephen King

Tracking account planning is rather like counting a mixed batch of tropical fish. You think you see patterns, but they've all changed by the time you've finished counting.

There's little enough doubt about its growth. Today most of the top UK agencies have planning departments and most of the recent new UK agency Weves have them built into the letter heading (at least one of Beagle, Bargle, D'Annunzio, Twigg and Privet will be a planner).

Yet the current approach of agencies varies between the integral and the non-existent. It's impossible to imagine Boase Massimi Pollitt without account planners. At the same time it's been recently announced, in suitably crude language and to no one's great surprise, that there's no room at all for account planning at McCann's.

I don't think one should just throw up the hands at all this diversity. It seems to me that the future of account planning, and maybe indeed of advertising agencies themselves, depends on our teasing out correctly the historical strands – three in particular.

HOW ACCOUNT PLANNING STARTED

The first strand is how it all started. Advertising has always been planned and campaigns have always been post-rationalized. People like James Webb Young, Claude Hopkins, Rosser Reeves, David Ogilvy and Bill Bernbach were all superb planners. What is relatively new is the existence in an agency of a *separate department* whose prime responsibility is planning advertising strategy and evaluating campaigns against it. Such departments are older than we sometimes think. To quote from a 1938 JWT London brochure: "*Bright ideas must survive sharpshooters in the marketing department and snipers on the Plan Board, before they stand a chance of being seen by the client.*" Despite the rather negative role of sharpshooting, it seems that there was a department that aimed to apply marketing thinking to advertising ideas. (This was not a research department. BMRB had been set up as a separate research company five years before.)

When I joined JWT's marketing department in 1957, there were about 25 people in it allocated to accounts – as described in some detail by John Treasure (1985). What we did for each of our clients included analysing marketing data and published statistics, writing marketing plans, recommending more research, and planning new product/brand development. Our marketing plans were a bit naive – strong on the broad view, but a touch vague on logistics and usually in the dark about profits; but somebody had to write them. Not surprisingly, they went into most detail on advertising strategy and expenditure. They were of course the basis for the agency's creative work.

*Published in *Admap*, November 1989. Reproduced with permission.

Then clients gradually started to build up proper marketing departments, who wrote their own plans. We tried to influence the strategic part of these plans by getting in first with our own blue book recommendations (with some relief abandoning any pretence of knowing much about distribution, journey cycles and case rates). Increasingly we concentrated more directly on our own expertise, the advertising strategy. We also set up four very small specialist groups – an advertising research unit and a media research unit in 1964, a new product development unit and an operations research unit in 1965.

In a sense therefore, when JWT disbanded the marketing department and set up its account planning department on 1 November 1968, it was more a reorganization and renaming than a radical change. Perhaps the biggest change came from recognizing that many of the senior media planners were analysing exactly the same data in exactly the same way as the people in the marketing department, as a basis for making the main inter-media recommendations (Jones, 1968; King, 1969).

The first written proposals to the management for the new department came on 8 April, the final blueprint on 23 August. It was all worked out in a series of meetings and away-days of the new group heads. At one of these (on 15 July) we finally settled the name: we'd tried target planner (too narrow and obscure), campaign planner (too competitive with what creative people did) and brand planner (too much restricted in people's minds to packaged groceries). Tony Stead suggested account planner and it stuck. Meanwhile a very similar gradualist development was happening at what turned into BMP. There was one important difference: the basis there was research rather than marketing. By 1964 at Pritchard Wood there was a media research unit, a marketing research unit (mainly doing desk research), a qualitative research unit and a research department (mainly commissioning quantitative research). Some 25 people in all, but not allocated to accounts, and too fragmented to have a very powerful voice in the agency. When Stanley Pollitt took over the research and media functions, he made the crucial change of putting *"a trained researcher alongside the account man on every account"*. He quickly found that a great many trained researchers were more concerned with technique than with the green-fingered interpretation and use of research; and so moved on to finding and developing specialist advertising planners, with Peter Jones as the first.

When BMP was formed in June 1968 account planning was built in from the start, and Stanley Pollitt became the first head of it in an agency (though the name was in fact later borrowed from JWT). The basis was the Cadbury Schweppes account group, whose members carried on their existing working practices.

While the start of it all at BMP was thus equally gradualist, there were some differences from JWT's approach. The ratio of planners to account managers was much higher – it has varied from one-to-one to one-to-two, whereas JWT has always had about one-to-four. Partly because of this and partly maybe because of their origins in research, BMP's planners have been far more *directly* involved in qualitative research. As David Cowan put it in 1981: *"A central part of the planner's job is to conduct the qualitative pre-testing research."* JWT's view was always that the gains this brought in involvement and direct contact with consumers would be more than offset by the loss in objectivity and that it was better to use specialist qualitative researchers.

Whatever the differences between the two pioneer agencies, the similarities were very much greater. Both recognized that the key innovation was the development of professional planning skills and of their integration into the process of producing advertising. It was a fundamental change in the internal balance of power and influence. As I wrote in 1969:

> What we have set up is a system whereby a project group of three skills (account management, creative and account planning) is the norm for the planning of advertising campaigns.

Or as BMP put it in their offer document of 1983:

> The main new element introduced into its structure by BMP was called the account planner. The planner brings not simply research, but also the use of data, into every stage of advertising development as a third partner for the account handler and creative team.

The rush by other agencies to follow this lead was muted. For several years nothing at all seemed to happen. By 1979 only six other agencies in the top 20 had planning departments (CDP, DDB, Dorlands, DPBS, FCB and OBM) and maybe a dozen of the smaller agencies. After 1979, maybe spurred on by the formation of new agencies and of the Account Planning Group, it all accelerated rapidly.

The speed of recent growth has had one unfortunate result, in my view. Many managements have copied the most overt element of BMP's account planning, without fully understanding the depth of skill and breadth of interest involved, the very high ratio of planners to account managers and the great commitment to training. All they have seen, in fact, is account planners running group discussions. As a result a large number of qualitative researchers have found themselves, after four years or so of slogging away at group discussions, translated overnight into instant agency Account Planning Directors. It was so much easier to find them than people with a thorough grounding in all aspects of brand building.

I believe in fact that the most fundamental scale on which to judge account planners is one that runs from Grand Strategists to Advert Tweakers. And that nowadays there are rather too many agencies whose planners' skills and experience are much too near the advert-tweaking end of the scale.

VIEWS ON "HOW ADVERTISING WORKS"

A second strand that affects differences in account planning is that of the brand personalities of the agencies themselves. This issue was richly and convincingly discussed by Charles Channon (1981) in "Agency thinking and agencies as brands."

His key thesis was that differences in agencies and their output "in the end reflect different ways of thinking about how ads work and consequently different approaches to planning ads which do so". He picked out "argument" as the essence of Masius' thinking, "imagery" for JWT, "rhetoric" for BMP, "aesthetic" for CDP.

It's certainly true that the development of account planning and of ideas about how advertising works have supported each other. For JWT, 1964 was a critical year. Its new advertising research unit, faced by off-the-peg quantitative ad-testing methods imported from the US, had got stuck. We felt that the only sensible approach was to measure whether ads achieved their specific objectives, but creative strategy was being set as a "consumer proposition". What on earth could be meant by "achieving a consumer proposition"?

This puzzle led eventually to a new approach to planning advertising, called the T-Plan. It was based not on what ought to *go into* the advertising, but on what ought to be the consumer's *responses* to the brand as a result. Other ideas about how advertising works – like reinforcement rather than conversion (King, 1967), brand personality, the direct/indirect scale of responses

(King, 1975) and the consumer's buying system – have all moulded the precise way in which account planning has developed at JWT.

One valuable addition to account planners' views on how advertising works was described most clearly by Rod Meadows in "They consume advertising too" (Meadows, 1983). He argued that people actively consume advertising in its own right; they're experts in what it's trying to do; they judge brands as much on the quality of their advertising as its content. These "advertising literate" people expect advertising to be original enough to get their attention, in a form that stimulates them, entertains them and recognizes their interest. Such views among planners have done much to support the distinctive form of UK advertising.

THE AGENCY ENVIRONMENT

The third formative strand has been that of external changes. Almost all business has become more competitive over the 25 years and has had to respond more rapidly to events. For instance, the pressures on package goods marketers from retailers and the "crisis in branding" in the mid-1970s led to a noticeable shortening of vision; it's hard to devote a lot of attention to strategic planning if Sainsbury's is threatening to delist you tomorrow.

The agency world has changed a lot too. Agencies used to be professional partnerships, often somewhat dozily managed. Quite suddenly, led by Saatchi and Saatchi, they become businesses in their own right, often facing all the financial pressures put on a public company. The trade tabloids started getting their stories and comments from financial analysts, rather than from people with a direct understanding of the business. Some managers of agencies inevitably become a little affected by some of the traditional "City values" (such as short-termism, greed, self-absorption and hysteria). They stopped worrying about the clients and the layouts and started worrying about convertible deleveraging ratios and fully diluted negative net worth.

There are other ways in which agencies may have been becoming more inward-looking. The recognition of consumers' advertising literacy has been wholly good for UK advertising, with its stress on the need for original ideas and vivid expressions of them. But it's not too difficult to slide from that to believing that the creative people in an agency and the creative work are the *only* elements that matter; that creative people alone are fit to judge the merit of campaigns; that the account manager's job is simply to sell the resulting great work to the unsophisticated client. While the extremes of such views are no doubt rare, I think there have been subtle changes in the balance of power and influence within some agencies; and certainly in the way that the trade press has presented them.

Any trends towards short-termism and self-absorption are bound, I think, somewhat to diminish the role of account planners. Their skills lie in the outside world and the longer term, trying to match clients' abilities and brand personalities with consumers' aspirations. On the whole, the agency environment has tended over time to push planners towards the advert-tweaking end of the scale.

SO WHERE WILL IT ALL GO NEXT, THEN?

It seems to me that the future of account planning will continue to depend on the same three strands and in particular on the role that advertising agencies decide to play in future.

Marketing companies today are increasingly changing their view-points. They recognize that rapid response in the marketplace needs to be matched with a clear strategic vision. The need for well-planned brand building is very pressing.

At the same time they see changes in ways of communicating with their more diverse audiences. They're increasingly experimenting with non-advertising methods. Some are uneasily aware that these different methods are being managed by different people in the organization to different principles; they may well be presenting conflicting impressions of the company and its brands. It all needs to be pulled together.

I think that an increasing number of them would like some outside help in tackling these problems, and some have already demonstrated that they're prepared to pay respectable sums for it. The job seems ideally suited to the strategic end of the best account-planning skills. The question is whether these clients will want to get such help from an advertising agency.

If agencies move further towards an inward-looking obsession with their profits or their creative awards and a narrow-minded view of advertising as a *competitor* to other communication media, I'm not sure that they will. The work will go, as it is already starting to go, to a wide variety of specialists, management and marketing consultants, public relations advisers, corporate identity designers, and so on.

However, advertising agencies do have a few powerful advantages in this area. Most outside observers believe that the quality of account-planning and brand-building skills and people is higher in agencies than elsewhere. They have made more progress on how communications work (though on a rather narrow front). They have pioneered the use of some valuable technical tools, such as market modelling. They have the immense advantage of continuous relationships with clients. If the will is there, it could be done.

What agencies, and the account planners in them, would have to do is above all, *demonstrate* that they have the breadth of vision and objectivity to do the job; apply "how marketing communications work" thinking and R&D to a much wider area; probably bring in more outside talent, from marketing companies or other fields of communication; make more efforts to "go to the top" in client contact (the one great advantage of the various specialists); and make sure that they get paid handsomely for the work. I very much hope that this can happen – I wouldn't like to think of the best strategic planners leaving for the other sorts of company or of agency planners shifting wholly to advert-tweaking.

I trust too that *Admap* will continue to plot how all this goes in the future as it has for the last 25 years. Its contribution has been enormous; most of the new ideas about advertising and how it works have emerged and been argued on its pages. It uniquely bridges the gap between *"D'Annunzio set to quit in Twigg, Privet image turmoil"* and *"Conjoint analysis of extrinsic benefit appeals: a magnitude estimation approach"*. Account planners have been constantly stimulated, infuriated and enlightened by *Admap*. They know that its particular flavour has been largely the work of two people. I know that the innate modesty of the publisher and consultant editor will not allow them to be named, but from all account planners I'd just like to say thank you.

REFERENCES

Channon, C. (1981) "Agency thinking and agencies as brands", *Admap*, March.
Jones, R. (1968) "Are media departments out of date?", *Admap*, September.
King, S. (1967) "Can research evaluate the creative content of advertising?", *Admap*, June.
King, S. (1969) "Inter-media decisions", *Admap*, October.
King, S. (1975) "Practical progress from a theory of advertisements", *Admap*, October.
Meadows, R. (1983) "They consume advertising too", *Admap*, July/August.
Treasure, J. (1985) "The origins of account planning", *Admap*, March.

1.2

The Origins of Account Planning*

By John Treasure

Planning Before 1968

In June 1960, at the request of the then managing director of JWT (Tom Sutton), I transferred from BMRB, where I had been managing director for the previous three-and-a-half years, to join the Board of J. Walter Thompson with the title of director of research and marketing.

In June 1960 the marketing department was organized in four groups under the leadership of four very experienced people. There were 22 executives in these four groups which meant that the department employed in total 27 executives. There were, in addition, a large number of secretaries, a charting department and sundry trainees, making in all a department of some 60 people. (The ravages of inflation are obvious from the fact that the annual salary bill for the 22 executives (i.e. excluding the group heads and myself) amounted to £26,450. The highest salary was £1,650 and the lowest £650.)

In the next few years (under my inspiring leadership!), the marketing department increased considerably in size. In November 1962 there were 42 executives in the department and the salary bill had risen to £69,150.

What did all these people do with their time? I can certainly remember that they were all very busy but it is difficult even for me now to understand (given the size of JWT at that time) why we needed so many people. I suppose one explanation must be that many clients relied on us to do the analysis of their market data for them.

Another reason why they were all so busy was that account executives (or "representatives" in Thompson language) at that time used the marketing executives working on their accounts to do all their donkey work for them. There was undoubtedly, also, a tendency for meetings with clients or suppliers to be attended by quite a lot of people, with the result that a good deal of executive time got used up with perhaps no great benefit to the agency.

However, there is equally no doubt that one of the more important jobs done by these marketing executives was planning. The creation of an advertising plan for the brand, which defined objectives and strategies and suggested ways of measuring effectiveness, was clearly understood to be the job of the senior marketing executive, who was a full member of the account group. It was not always done well but then it is not always done well today!

During this period, I can remember feeling very irritated that we did not have a system of analysing markets which defined target groups correctly. A system was developed in due course in 1964 and became known as the T-Plan. (Incidentally, the T in T-Plan does not stand for the Thompson Plan or the Treasure Plan but for the Target Plan.)

The very name T-Plan with the implication that planning is an agency responsibility shows that by the early 1960s the importance of planning as an integrative process was clearly

*This is an edited version of the article published in *Admap*, March 1985.

and explicitly accepted. I cannot do better than to quote a passage from the introduction from the T-Plan (as written by Stephen King in 1964) which makes the point very clearly indeed:

> I think the main requirement for a new system of setting creative strategy is that it should be more in terms of the consumer. <u>Our objective must be a certain state of mind in the potential buyer, not a certain type of advertisement. . . . It must be essentially a consumer system because advertisements are means, not ends</u>. Until we know more about how they work and what sort work best, strategy should be about ends.
>
> We can only get a comprehensive system of objectives in terms of the consumer's mind. It is the one thing in common to product design, marketing strategy, creative strategy, media strategy, testing effectiveness. Most advertising aims to intensify or lessen people's existing predispositions. It is not trying to drive something new into their brains.
>
> Modern psychological theory shows that what is put into an advertisement can be very different from what is got out of it. It is the response that concerns us.
>
> Setting creative strategy in consumer terms can eliminate ambiguous advertising jargon (brand image, copy platform, etc.). This sort of system is far less constricting to creative people.

I hope I have said enough about planning at JWT in the 1960s to demonstrate (a) that planning was firmly accepted at that time as the specific responsibility of the marketing executive and (b) that planning had reached a respectable level of sophistication, proof of which is the creation of the T-Plan in 1964.

This means, among other things, that the late Stanley Pollitt was writing without a full knowledge of the facts when he published his article in 1979 entitled "How I started Account Planning in Agencies". In this article, Pollitt said that a paradox developed in the 1960s – as more and more data relevant to sharper advertising planning was becoming available more and more of the agency researchers, who were competent to deal with the information, were leaving the agencies to join research companies. He went on to say:

> At this point in 1965, I found myself suddenly acquiring responsibility for research and media at the then Pritchard Wood and Partners: I had a free hand to try to resolve the paradox and this was how the idea of planning and planners emerged.

First, he says, he tried to convert his agency researchers into planners but this proved to be disappointing – they had grown cosy in their back rooms. So they decided to breed planners themselves from numerate, but broad-minded, graduates.

Clearly, Stanley Pollitt was developing his ideas along very similar lines to Stephen King and others in JWT at that time. However, if only for the record, it is a fact that the use of numerate and broad-minded graduates in a planning function was well established in JWT in the form of the marketing department long before 1965. It is true that it was not until some years later, in fact in 1968, that the term "account planning" was invented to describe this particular job function but Pollitt, of course, acknowledged in his article that he borrowed the term "account planning" from JWT.

The Birth of Account Planning

I was recently given a print-out of the membership of the Account Planning Group. I went through this list and, according to my calculations, there were 262 account planners working in agencies. (The last two words are redundant, of course, because account planners can only exist in agencies.) However, given that there may be agencies with account planners who do not belong to the APG, that some of the people listed in the print-out may not actually be performing the job of account planner, and that I know that APG membership went up quite a lot after the date of the print-out, it is probably wise to say that there are now around 300 account planners employed by advertising agencies in this country.

This figure came as quite a shock to me. The massive change in the organization of British advertising agencies – and it is still very much a British innovation – has taken place in 16 short years. I can be as positive as this about the period of time because I have been able, with Stephen King's help, to find documentary evidence of the actual date on which the name "account planning" was, for the first time, agreed and the first account planning department established.

The evidence is a minute of a meeting held at the Londonderry House Hotel on 15 July 1968 (see below). This date, 15 July 1968, can properly be regarded as the birthday of account planning.

Minutes of meeting held at Londonderry House Hotel 15th July, 1968
1. Name: The name Account Planning was agreed as a reasonable description of our functions – and the title Account Planning Group Head was also agreed. In the minutes hereunder the short term A/P will be used.

I can clearly remember the ferment of discussion that took place about this new idea. It was very much Stephen King's idea, and without his authority and determination nothing would have happened. However, I would like to say that Christopher Higham, who was then JWT's media director, also played a very important part in the birth of the account planning department in the sense that though its creation was politically damaging to his department, because he lost all his media planners, he was one of the most enthusiastic supporters of the need to make a change. Credit should also be given to Tony Stead for inventing the name "account planning".

It was, even at this distance in time, a staggering change to make in the organization of the agency. It involved taking a large number of people from the marketing department and the media department and welding them into a new department with novel responsibilities. There were, in the new account planning department, seven groups, each consisting of a group head and two assistants, i.e. 21 planners in all. In addition, we set up an advertising research unit (under Judie Lannon), a media research unit, a new product development unit and a marketing consultancy unit as a separate subsidiary company. The repercussions on people's careers of making so many sweeping changes on such a large scale were enormous.

I have re-read four documents, all written in 1968, which were concerned with the need to set up an account planning department and to identify the problems which its setting-up would create.

The need to set up a new department to replace the marketing department (and to take over the media planning functions of the media department) was seen at the time to have been created by two factors. These were:

- the increasing marketing skills of clients which made part of the job of the marketing department redundant and
- the increased availability of data and improved methods of planning – e.g. the T-Plan – which made it desirable for someone in the account group to specialize on advertising planning.

Perhaps a series of quotations from the documents will help to communicate the flavour of what was being argued about at that time.

April 1968: The skills of administration and personal relations that most reps have are not really technical enough to count as skills; in any case, they are fine for a going concern but not all that valuable in a crisis or to avoid a crisis. The crucial skill of strategic planning is nearly always missing, largely through lack of practice.

April 1968: The media/marketing planner would essentially be concerned with tactical planning (although in the early stages no doubt reps/backstops will lean on them for longer-term strategic planning). Essentially, the work would involve starting with the raw material of published and private research and ending with a T-Plan creative strategy and a T-Plan media strategy.

May 1968: The general response (to Stephen King's memo about account planning) seemed to be that it made sense, many pointing out that it is not really a very radical change...

May 1968: This change in particular will affect the account planning group – the basic project group of our business. Today it is a group of four people – rep, creative, media and marketing. In future it will be a group of three – rep, creative and target planner. We are sure that this will be a more effective working group...

July 1968: The account planning function.... was advertising rather than marketing strategy.

There are two themes which recur in these documents. One is the concept of the group of three with the account planner as the third man (or third woman) being the essential planning unit of the agency within which the three elements of practicality, imagination and intellect are functionally represented and fused through group interaction.

The other main theme is the importance of strategic planning. I cannot resist the temptation to go back to James Webb Young's little book *How to Become an Advertising Man*, published in 1963, to see what he has to say on the subject of strategic planning.

> Finding the one best opportunity in the market for the particular advertiser, and shaping his advertising to exploit that opportunity, is one of the greatest contributions the Advertising Man can make to his client. And his chances of making that contribution, I repeat, will depend upon his penetration into the real facts and nuances of that advertiser's situation.

When the California raisin growers were suffering from a heavy over-production, and a quick expansion in raisin consumption was needed, a strategic concept did the trick. This was to direct the advertising, not towards an "Eat More Raisins" programme, but towards increasing the consumption of the greatest single carrier of raisins, namely raisin bread. This was based on the observation that the consumption of any food is higher where there has been established a fixed time or day for serving it – as with fish on Friday, baked beans in New England on Saturday, hot cross buns at Easter, etc. So a campaign devised in cooperation with bakers to feature "Fresh Raisin Bread on Wednesday" (normally a low day in bread sales) raised consumption of this item 600% in one year; and of raisins used for that purpose proportionately. A strategic concept.

This is of special significance at this time when so much effort is expended by account planners on the use of qualitative research to support, reject or improve the advertisements which the agency has recommended or is in the process of recommending. It would be a pity if all this work became the modern substitute for the labour of marketing executives in the 1960s – the dreary digesting of Nielsen reports, for example – so that the essential and truly valuable contribution which the account planner can make, i.e. strategic thinking – gets elbowed out by the pressure of day-to-day account servicing.

This does not mean that I am opposed to the user of qualitative research in the "pre-testing" (if that is the right word) of advertisements. There is a passage in the T-Plan which says that "we have found small-scale, evaluative research much the most useful method for pre-testing". This view was quite controversial in those days but the passionate advocacy it has received from Stephen King, Jeremy Bullmore, Judie Lannon and many others made it, in the course of time, a quite respectable position to adopt.

It was, therefore, with entire agreement but some mild surprise that I read David Cowan's article "Advertising research – qualitative or quantitative?" (*Admap*, November 1984). I found nothing to disagree with in what Mr Cowan said, but I am surprised that it is still necessary to say these things in 1984. I thought they had all been said and more or less accepted 10 or more years ago. However, since the argument is an important one, perhaps it is desirable that each generation of advertising thinkers should restate the eternal verities.

I should like to make two other points about the development of account planning if only for the sake of historical accuracy.

Don Cowley in his introduction to the IPA booklet on account planning, published in 1981, says that it is interesting to note that the chief focus of interest in the late 1960s, when account planning departments were first being set up, was the way that account planners would help in inter-media decisions. This is quite incorrect, at least as far as JWT was concerned. The primary focus of interest in setting up the account planning department in 1968 was to improve advertising planning, particularly in relation to:

(a) setting of objectives
(b) contributing to creative development and
(c) improving the methods used to evaluate, the effectiveness of advertising campaigns.

John Bartle, in an article in *Admap*, April 1980, said that account planning departments emerged in the 1960s as a reaction to general economic pressures. This was certainly not the case in JWT in 1968. The motivation was quite simply a desire to improve the ability of the agency to keep its clients and to obtain new business. The thought that this was a way to save money was not in our minds at all.

Summary

There are many other issues involved in the development of account planning over the past 25 years that deserve mention. For example, it is strange and sad that account planners, with a few honourable exceptions, have so markedly neglected econometrics as a weapon in their professional armoury. However, the theme of this article has been the origins of account planning. I have no doubt that these origins lie in the ideas and personalities of a number of people who were working in JWT in the early 1960s and, of these, the one person who can rightly be regarded as the founder of account planning is Stephen King.

1.3
How I Started Account Planning in Agencies*

By Stanley Pollitt

"Account planning" and the "account planners" have become part of agency jargon over recent years. I have been able to track down about 10 agencies currently using them. There is even a new pressure group called the Account Planning Group. Unfortunately there is considerable confusion over what the terms mean, making discussion of the subject frustrating. It is worth tracing how the terms came to be introduced in 1965, how planning has evolved and what it means at BMP.

Market research in agencies has changed substantially over the past few years. Planning emerged as a particular way of dealing with this. In the 1950s, advertising agencies were the main pioneers for market research. Except for a few of the very largest advertisers, it was the advertising agency that devised total market research programmes, often from budgets in the advertising appropriation. Main agencies had either large research departments or research subsidiaries like BMRB and Research Services. It was a reflection of the broader consultancy role advertising agencies played. They were partly torchbearers for a new marketing perspective on business.

In the 1960s this changed dramatically and rapidly. More consumer goods companies were restructured along marketing lines. Included within this new "marketing" function was a closer responsibility for market research. Companies set up their own market research departments, devised their own research programmes and commissioned research themselves. They looked to their agencies for more specialist research advice on specifically advertising matters. This again was part of a wider – and I believe, a healthier – trend. Agencies were moving out of general consultancy and concentrating more on the professional development of ads. This meant a substantial reduction in agencies' revenue from market research – especially from commissioning major surveys. Agencies cut the number of market research people they had. The old research subsidiaries and some new subsidiaries formed out of separate departments became increasingly separated from their agency parents. They had to fight, competitively, for general research work in the open market and worked more for non-agency clients, thus losing any previous connections with and interests in advertising. A small rump of researchers stayed in the agency to cope with the diminishing number of clients still wanting a total research service and provide some advice for other departments. This is still largely the case with most agencies today, and leaves something of a research vacuum there.

At just this time there was a considerable increase in the quality and quantity of data that was relevant to more professionally planned advertising such as company statistics, available

*This is an edited version of an article that originally appeared as Pollitt, S. (1979) "How I started account planning in agencies", *Campaign*, April. The headline was *Campaign's*

consumer and retailer panel data, and so on. Also, facilities for analysing data were becoming more sophisticated and more cheaply accessible. This posed a paradox: as more data, relevant to sharper advertising planning was coming in, more and more people qualified to handle it were leaving the agencies.

At this point in 1965 I found myself, essentially an account director, suddenly acquiring responsibility for research and media at the then Pritchard Wood Partners. I had a free hand to try to resolve the paradox. And this was how the idea of "planning" and "planners" emerged. It seemed wrong to me that it should be the account man who decided what data should be applied to ad planning and whether or not research was needed. Partly because account men were rarely competent to do this – but more dangerously, because as my own account man experience had shown – clients on the one hand and creative directors on the other, made one permanently tempted to be expedient. Too much data could be uncomfortable. I decided, therefore, that a trained researcher should be put alongside the account man on every account. He should be there as of right, with equal status as a working partner.

He was charged with ensuring that all the data relevant to key advertising decisions should be properly analysed, complemented with new research and brought to bear on judgements of the creative strategy and how the campaign should be appraised. Obviously all this was decided in close consultation with account man and client.

This new researcher – or account man's "conscience" – was to be called the "planner". I felt existing researchers in the agency – the rump – were being misused. They were closeted in their own little backrooms, called on at the account man's whim, dusted down and asked to express some technical view about an unfamiliar client's problem.

PWP was not an untypical agency. It had a separate media research unit where researchers were beavering away to determine how many response functions would fit on the head of a pin; a market information unit that sent market analyses through the internal post, which if read were never systematically applied to solving the main advertising problems; a general researcher, who was called in, spasmodically and inevitably superficially, to give instant advice on particular research problems; and finally a creative researcher who would occasionally be called in to conduct creative research to resolve political problems, either within the agency or between agency and client. He would usually be called in too late, when a great deal of money and personal reputations had already been committed to finished films or when the commercials were already on air.

It seemed to me that these researchers should be taken out of their backrooms and converted to being an active part of the group involved with the central issues of advertising strategy. They were to be the new "planners".

 This experiment proved disappointing. I found that the existing agency researchers had grown cosy in their backrooms. They did not want mainstream agency activity. They had grown too familiar with relying on techniques as a crutch, rather than thinking out more direct ways of solving problems. They had grown too accustomed to being academic to know how to be practical and pragmatic. They mostly disappeared into research agencies.

As my first planning manager, I chose Bob Jones who had precisely the pragmatic but thorough base we wanted. We decided the only way to find this new type of researcher was to breed them ourselves from numerate but broad-minded graduates. Peter Jones, first planning director at BMP, and David Cowan, our current director of planning, were the first mutations at PWP. Since then we have "bred" from 22 trainees – 15 are still with us – and adapted five agency or company researchers – three are still with us.

That was the first phase of "planning". Difficult to define precisely, but it was concerned with making sure that research was a central part of the way all the main decisions were taken. Planners were people who were willing and able to take up this central role. People who were practical, pragmatic, confident and more concerned with solving problems than selling techniques.

When we set up BMP in 1968 we were already able to structure this on the account manager/account planner team basis. (JWT had adopted the planning idea in 1967 and coined the term "account planner". I borrowed it from them.)

From the outset at BMP we added an important new dimension to the planner's role which has almost come to be the dominant one. In addition to the development of advertising strategy and campaign appraisal we started to involve planners more closely in the development of creative ideas.

It is impossible for anyone not directly brought up in advertising agencies to understand the immense importance a good agency can attach to getting the advertising content right. It can become a mission and a never-ending struggle for standards of excellence. At BMP the way we have aimed to get it right is through a sensitive balance between the most important ingredient – the intuition of talented creative people – with the experience of good account people and clients and with an early indication of consumer response which the planner is there to extract.

Traditional market researchers are heavy-handed when trying to deal with creative work. The nightmare world of sixties advertising when a number of now discredited mechanistic techniques were being used is a good reminder of this. What we set out to do was to guide account planners to be able to be honest and clear about consumer response without stifling creativity.

All creative work – and we mean *all* creative work – at BMP is checked out qualitatively with a tightly defined target market. Commercials are checked out in rough animatic form, typically with four discussion groups of about eight respondents each. Press advertisements are checked out in individual in-depth interviews with some two respondents. Target market samples are recruited by our own network of 80 recruiters – the majority outside London. Account planners are the moderators of the groups or depths. To give some idea of scale, we conducted some 1200 groups last year, which arguably makes us the largest qualitative research company in the country.

This may not sound particularly unusual. To have some elements of qualitative research on rough and finished creative work is commonplace in most agencies. But I would argue that the scope and thoroughness of account planning at BMP makes it not readily – or maybe sensibly – transplantable to other agencies. It does require a particular agency environment with a number of elements present at the same time.

First, it requires a total agency management commitment to getting the advertising content *right* at all costs. Getting it right being more important than maximizing agency profits, more important than keep clients happy, or building an agency shop window for distinctive-looking advertising. It means a commitment and a belief that you can only make thoroughly professional judgements about advertising content with some early indication of consumer response. I would guess a majority of, not only creative directors, but also account directors, would find this hard to swallow. For planning to work it needs the willing acceptance of its findings by strong creative people.

John Webster and his creative people have grown up with this system. John would say that "planning" is very far from perfect – but like "democracy" it is better than the alternatives. If advertising is to be rejected or modified it is better that this should be the result of response from the target market than the second-guessing of account men or clients.

Second, it means a commitment by agency management to "planning" absorbing an important part of agency resources. For a "planner" to be properly effective both in marshalling all the data relevant to advertising strategy, and in carrying out the necessary qualitative research, he can only work on some three or four brands.

You need as many "planners" as "account men". It is interesting to compare some industry figures in this respect – in the top eight agencies billing between £35m and £65m the average number of researchers involved in advertising and creative planning is about eight. In the next 12 – billing between £15m and £30m (excluding BMP) – the average number is four. It involves a financial commitment and the even more difficult commitment to find and train qualified people.

Third, it means changing some of the basic ground rules. Once consumer response becomes the most important element in making final advertising judgements, it makes many of the more conventional means of judgement sound hollow. You cannot combine within the same environment decisions to run advertisements because account directors or creative directors "like" them, or because US management believes that UK consumers respond in some way that the hard research evidence contradicts.

This obviously limits the territory in which the agency can operate. Evidence of consumer response can act as too much of a constraint on some clients and agency people. If it helps to limit the territory for the agency to operate in, it also helps to establish a clear identity and a remarkably consistent sense of purpose within the agency. This second phase of account planning has involved it more directly in the sensitive and rightly carefully guarded area of creative ideas development.

Politically fraught, a minefield though this is, account planners at BMP seem to be coming through it well. "Account planning" described in this way is very much a central part of the agency. As such it is not a simple task to convert to it. Although I am sure we will be hearing the terms "account planning" and "account planners" more widely used, I doubt whether they will carry the significance and meaning that they carry at BMP. "Bolt-on" planning, as *Campaign* rather unkindly referred to one recent change in an agency, is not a really practical exercise.

How Brands and the Skills of Branding have Flowered

By Rita Clifton, Chairman and Chief Executive, Interbrand

An introduction to:

2.1   What is a Brand?

I freely admit that I was in total awe of Stephen King when I was at J. Walter Thompson in the mid-1980s and had very little primary contact with him. And yet, much later, I realized that what he thought, what he did and who he was had a profound influence on the way my career developed.

He was a prolific writer on the subject of brands and advertising, but the publication of most influence for me was the booklet *What is a Brand?* It was professionally printed and liberally available around the agency at the time, and it contained important elements of the Andrex case history, one of my key responsibilities. At the time, I remember being impressed by data showing how quality advertising investment had made Andrex more valued by its consumers and had helped to see off its significant rival at the time, Delsey. I remember the importance he attached to the consistent tone, style and message of Andrex advertising.

What has Changed and What has Not

So much, so familiar and so back to the future. What has been even more interesting for me is looking again at *What is a Brand?* after almost 20 years, and seeing what has changed and what has not.

Like most great thinkers, you get a spooky sense of familiarity from Stephen's writing, even if some of the vocabulary we now take for granted had not yet been invented. For instance, in discussing the future pressure on retailers, he refers to "competition of other forms of selling such as discount stores, mail order and direct selling".

If the word "internet" had been available, it would have belonged here, and Stephen clearly understood that "retailing" was not always going to be about physical shops, but about all the channels through which people might want to buy. In this age, we have seen that, in a blurring on- and off-line world, anything and anyone can be a power retailer and a powerful medium, if they can build strong enough brand and consumer relationships – a subject about which Stephen was also exercised.

He also predicted that "retailers will concentrate still more" (and how they have), although the internet has extended the boundaries and definitions of retail in an intriguing way. And how about "retailers will undoubtedly pass on their pressures to manufacturers, and the fourth, fifth and sixth brands in any market will find it increasingly tough going?" Make that third, fourth and sometimes even second brands in some markets today, particularly in competition with retailer own label which now consists of sub-brands up, down and across the range of consumer segmentation in so many categories.

Taking that further, it is tempting to see Stephen's thinking about brands being very focused on boxes and bottles and packets and cans; very fmcg and housewife oriented. And it is true that, 20 or 30 years ago, when you said the word "brand," these associations are what would come to the vast majority of people's minds.

Today, the term "brand" has truly become a modern concept that can be accurately applied to utilities, charities, football teams and even individuals. In fact, any organization that wishes to add value to day-to-day process and cost needs to think of itself as a brand if it is to generate sustainable wealth and value. However, many business leaders even today who should recognize this still rather coyly talk about their "reputation", or "values" or "proposition" rather than their brand. It is unfortunate that the word has been contaminated by mischievous or ignorant commentary on corporate renaming exercises, or by its traditional roots in soap powder.

Nevertheless, whatever people might wish to call the process of creating a property that combines tangible and intangible attributes, can be symbolized in a trademark that creates influence and value if properly managed.... Well, that is branding by any other name.

Brands Beyond FMCG

Related to the point about fmcg, Stephen actually refers to several other categories of brands in his work here, and rightly applies the same principles and challenges to, for example, refrigerators, packaged travel and machine tools. What is so interesting today is that retail brands such as Tesco are creating the same competitive environment for categories like financial services, energy and mobile telephony as that enjoyed by more traditional manufacturers.

With the strength that Tesco has now built into its own brand and consumer relationships, it requires many companies across sectors to "white label" their products and services, for instance in the area of financial services (where the Royal Bank of Scotland provide the service under the Tesco brand), mobile telephony, energy provision and yes, travel, too. For some companies now, their main "consumers" are actually Tesco and Tesco buyers, and more money is invested in creating relationships with this trade audience than the end consumer. And retail buyers are not the most loving or rewarding of consumers to deal with.

Sadly, the relationship will always be doomed to one of inequality unless the supplier has a strong brand (as Stephen points out so clearly in his original paper), and it not surprising that so many find themselves in the frustrating Catch-22 situation.

However, all this goes to prove the point that the future will be much more about the battle of the brands wherever they exist – regardless of sector, since so many successful brands now cross at will into new sectors and categories and take their customer loyalty with them. No brand is now sacred in its marketplace and yes, above all, the winner is the brand that is most valuable to, and valued by, its consumers.

It all Starts with Organization

One of the areas covered by Stephen's booklet which I had forgotten about until my recent reading was his analysis of the organizational structure of so many companies, and how often this can get in the way of successful brand building. In fact, I noticed that many of the questions he posed of organizations, such as, "Are all top management involved deeply enough in the nature of their brands?", "Do they realize fully enough that it is from the success of their brands . . . that profits will come?", or indeed. "Do they fully understand the nature of brands?" are, astonishingly, just as relevant today as they were when this booklet was written. They are all questions I have put to clients in the past year.

Around a third of the total financial value of stock markets today can be accounted for by brands, making them the most important single asset. It makes logical sense that the brand should be the organizing principle by which competitive advantage is stitched into everything an organization does – in products and services, in people and behaviour, in environments and channels and, of course, in communications. Now, more than ever, the brand should be the central organizing principle to generate maximum sustainable value, but this is also where Stephen highlighted a major problem so many years ago. Very few organizations are structured and geared to this principle. He describes the need as "blending", to reflect the needs for special "blends" in creating distinctive brand personalities, and asks "Who is going to do the blending?" – particularly when most organizations are in silos.

If Brands are so Important, Why isn't Marketing More Central in Companies?

This question and debate echoes the internal debate the marketing industry is having vigorously even today. Why isn't marketing as central to business as it should be, and shouldn't marketing be the facilitator and manager of the brand with authority across an organization, responsible for all the brand levers like service, people, product development, and so on?

Marketing as a discipline has its own issues, particularly in terms of not being seen as commercial or financially aware, as it needs to be when the language of the Boardroom is finance. And, of course, as many CEOs come up through the financial and operational route, structuring the business around brands doesn't come naturally.

With the glorious benefit of hindsight, it might well be that the terms Stephen used like "brand personality" and "appeal to the senses" sounded too soft for Boardroom ears, even though he also talked very vigorously about the profit delivery of brands. In more recent times, we have found that expressing the value of brands in the language of other corporate valuations has been useful in getting the brand debate to centre stage of the Board in most companies, where it belongs.

Also, the central importance of traditional advertising to the success of brands has blurred over time to embrace all touchpoints and experiences. Even though Stephen expressed the importance of all these aspects, this was not something an advertising agency was able and willing to implement for clients, and hence the development of specialized brand consultancies and the spectrum of specialist agencies over the past 20 years.

Whatever the changes, the wisdom and perspective provided by his original booklet is both a testament to Stephen's leading thinking at the time, and to identifying many of the critical issues with which we still struggle today. All of us in the brand and related businesses owe Stephen so much.

2.1

What is a Brand?*

By Stephen King

INTRODUCTION

The programme for the Advertising Association's 1970 conference started with a survey of advertisers, to get an idea of what they wanted to discuss. Several themes emerged. In particular, through unease at the growing power of retailers, those of discounts, below-the-line and private label. In fact, all the chosen themes converged on one point – that is, the role and future of the manufacturer's brand. How can the brand yield ever-increasing profits in face of retailer pressure and private label? What sort of advertising can help the brand? How can we use research to control and measure this advertising?

Usually when we discuss such difficult and controversial topics, we rush in and start to argue about techniques. So often we try to solve problems without working out the theory of the thing first. So here I want to stand back a little and consider:

- First: What can we learn from the economic history of brands?
- Secondly: What makes a brand successful? What role does advertising play?
- Thirdly: Where does this mean we should sharpen up, and how?

I shall be looking at this from the manufacturer's point of view. Of course, I realize that different industries have different problems and are at different stages of development. After all, the brand is crucial to most, whether it's a brand of soap or a brand of refrigerator or a brand of packaged travel or a brand of machine tool.

HOW BRANDS GREW UP

First, then, let us look briefly at the development of the brand over the past 100 years. I think that the manufacturer/distributor relationship tends to move in cycles, and there is a lot to be learned here from the past.

By the late nineteenth century, when brands started to emerge, wholesalers had become the dominating force in the marketing of manufactured goods. These wholesalers were more than just a link between buyers and sellers. Retailers chose from what the wholesaler had in stock, and the wholesaler specified what the manufacturers should make – a position of some power. *eroding wholesaler power base* In this situation of competitive tender the manufacturer's profit depended mostly on sheer production efficiency. There was little scope for building up margins by providing a unique product. It was nearer to commodity marketing. Then, as manufactured products became more complicated and as the benefits of large-scale production became apparent, the need arose to invest in expensive plant. But this was very risky in the competitive tender situation.

*Published by JWT London, 1971. Reproduced with permission.

Manufacturers got over the problem gradually through the use of patents. And gradually brand names spread to non-patented goods. This was, of course, opposed fiercely by the wholesalers, but their position was weakening somewhat through competition among themselves.

The next step was to safeguard the manufacturer's position by applying pressure on the wholesaler from the other end; hence advertising – the direct link with the buying public. The point is that at this time the basic motive for advertising was to *stabilize* demand, thus allowing regular large-scale production, free from the whims of the wholesaler. Partly because of this the advertising tended to be based on the idea of reliability and guaranteed quality. (It was, of course, partly because reliable quality was still rather rare.)

The next stage developed from the first breaking of the chains – a period of manufacturer domination that lasted from about 1900 to 1960. It was a period of great concentration in numbers of manufacturers – from hundreds or even thousands in some product fields to the oligopoly situation we see so often today. The brand was used to concentrate demand on a relatively small number of lines, and the basis of growing profits became *economies of scale* – in production, raw material purchasing, distribution, investment capital, and so on. In keeping with this, the role of advertising was now seen as one of promoting growth – regular increases in sales volume. The old role of stabilizing demand became rather taken for granted. A key factor in the domination was that manufacturers could control their consumer prices, with the full backing of the law. Wholesalers became reduced more to distributing agents. At the same time, retailers' profit margins came under increasing pressure, with manufacturers more or less able to dictate both their buying and selling prices.

Then in the 1960s this manufacturer domination began to wane, and retailers began to redress the balance of power. They got new management who saw the profit opportunities and themselves started using economies of scale – in buying, warehousing, store size and location, self-service. They started taking initiatives as entrepreneurs – branding goods like cheese, meat and vegetables; and introducing new products like delicatessen. Of course, a key factor in all this was the ending of Resale Price Maintenance. One effect was that of increasing the concentration within the retail trade, as marginal or specialist retailers were forced out of business. And, of course, more immediately the retailer gained much greater control over buying and selling prices – a means of applying his increased power.

So is today a return to the situation the manufacturer was in during the period of wholesaler domination in the late nineteenth century? In many ways it is. I think it is clear that in the 1970s retailers will concentrate still more. There will be more big mergers. There will be increasing pressure on retailers' margins, through conventional competition, through retailers' margins, through conventional competition, through the competition of other forms of selling, such as discount stores, mail order and direct selling, through rising costs in an inevitably labour-intensive business, and so on. Retailers will undoubtedly pass on these pressures to manufacturers, and the fourth, fifth and sixth brands in any market will find it increasingly tough going. Ultimately some balance will be reached. The public will demand more variety. There might ultimately be legislation, but it seems more likely to be a Monopolies Commission type restricting the growth of an individual chain than anything on the lines of Robinson Patman. In fact, I think it will be the retailers themselves who will set the limit. After all, they need strong brands. The problem for manufacturers is that they do not need very many strong brands.

In other words, I think one must see the 1970s as being a continuation of the trends in the 1960s. The question the manufacturer must ask is not how to stop them, but how to exploit them. This is where it is useful to look at history. The manufacturer broke away from wholesale domination before. Can he do it again? I believe that he can, and that the principles by which he did it can be applied again. But there are certain crucial changes in the context which mean that the approach will have to be rather different from the nineteenth-century approach and very different from the approach in recent years.

NEW APPROACH FOR THE 1970S

First, I cannot see increased economies of scale helping the manufacturer as much as in the first half of the century. This is not to say that all factories have fully exploited economies of scale or that there will be no totally new production process. But on the whole, in most industries, production has already reached the size where plant utilization matters more to profits than scale per se. Secondly, the manufacturer's link with the consumer in the nineteenth century was based on product reliability, guaranteed quality. Today I think that this is largely taken for granted by the public, even with private label goods. Consumer protection legislation will make it more so. And thirdly, I doubt if there is any real prospect of the manufacturer regaining the direct control of prices that he had up to the 1960s.

So in these changed circumstances how will he break away from middleman-domination, as he did before? How is he going to sustain and increase his profits? The two methods that were most potent for him in the past are not, I think, going to be so potent in the future. Obviously, production efficiency and sheer volume will continue to be vital to profits – but they are unlikely to offer the means for sustained *growth*. Unless the manufacturer can retain and increase his control of margins *indirectly*, pressure from retailers will attack his profits in a way that simply building sales volume will not be able to offset.

This is really a new situation which has been creeping up on manufacturers over the last 10 years. In fact, I think that they have often been able to ignore it by the device of putting special discounts as a lump sum into the marketing budget, as if they were a form of marketing expenditure, like advertising or competitions. This may be an administrative convenience, but I think it is a totally false way of looking at them and one that is potentially very dangerous. *The truth is that discounts are not expenditure at all. They are income forgone.* They are purely a notional way of expressing the fact that the manufacturer's selling price is no longer fixed, that the price he can get from a big customer is less than from a small one. This may seem a rather theoretical point, but I believe that it is very important indeed. It has led to many false diagnoses. The real truth is that, when special discounts have to be made bigger and bigger, the brand is simply *not valuable enough* in the retailer's eyes. And yet so often the manufacturer's solution has been to cut back on those very things that would make the brand more valuable. And so he goes into a vicious spiral. It is a vicious spiral that could be critically dangerous in the economic conditions of the early 1970s.

So how do we improve margins indirectly? I think this new situation means a new role for marketing and advertising.

The key to it must be, as before, the link with the consumer. In the current situation, the only leverage the manufacturer can apply to the retailer is his relationship with the consumer. And the main element in profit growth is going to have to lie in making his brand more valuable to the retailer, through its being more valuable to the consumer. And that means his brand must be unique, it must have no adequate direct substitutes – because it is in this, after all, that value lies. Sustained profit growth will only come if his brand has unique added values. So how do brands become like that?

Let us look at one market in particular – that of toilet paper – and consider the fortunes of Andrex and Delsey. This is not because I want to tell the conventional sort of success

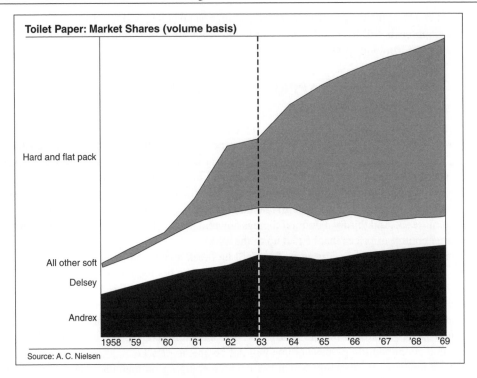

Figure 2.1 Toilet paper: market shares (volume basis)

story, which is usually oversimplified and untrue to life. But I think we can see a number of pointers from the history of this market. It is a market where there has been a great deal of price-cutting, many minor brands introduced and a lot of private label. Indeed it looks like the sort of near-commodity market where private label thrives best.

First, let us consider market shares up to 1963. You can see that Andrex and Delsey together steadily built up the soft toilet paper market, against the old type of hard paper. Andrex led the way, but Delsey was not all that far behind. In 1961, soft paper sales looked attractive enough to tempt in other manufacturers, who grew fairly rapidly up to 1963 – and became a real threat to Bowater-Scott (see Figure 2.1) and Kimberley Clark. So, of course, was the growing pressure from retailers which accompanied these smaller cheaper brands. But from this point the two major manufacturers diverged in their response.

Figure 2.2 shows that one general effect of retailer pressure was to reduce media advertising as funds were switched to discounts and promotions. Or, as I have suggested we should think of it, to price-cutting and promotions; that is, the manufacturers' margins decreased (or, to put it another way, the net sales value per roll decreased) and they made up for it by cutting their marketing budgets. But there was a great difference between Andrex and Delsey. By the end of 1964, Delsey had virtually given up trying to speak directly to the consumer through advertising and was concentrating more on discounting. Andrex kept a balance between the two.

You can see what happened. The "all other soft" category – in which of course Bowater-Scott are strongly represented – gained share more rapidly. Andrex continued to grow. Delsey slipped

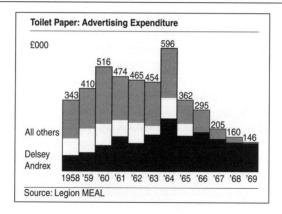

Figure 2.2   Toilet Paper: Advertising Expenditure

back a lot. But in a sense this is not the most important result. I think it is more significant that by 1969 Andrex reached a 30% share of market value, by taking a positive approach and not a defensive one. What has made it a profitable brand in recent years has not been so much a spectacular growth in market share as that Andrex has been formed into a brand that is *valued highly* by consumers.

We can see from the Advertising Planning Index how people's ideas of the relative values of Andrex and Delsey have changed. Figure 2.3 shows the percentage of people attributing the qualities of strength and softness to Andrex and Delsey over the past five years. You can see that up to 1966 the two brands were advancing at much the same rate; but since then Andrex has continued to go ahead and Delsey has dropped back. Not only are less people mentioning Delsey at all, but more people are saying "not so strong" and "not so soft" about it.

Now, I do not think that objectively the standards of the two physical products have diverged all that much. They have both always been of very high quality. Nor do I think people have

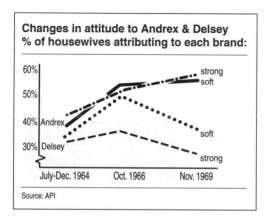

Figure 2.3   Changes in attitude to Andrex and Delsey

suddenly thought to themselves "Delsey isn't as soft as it was". What has happened is that, relative to Andrex, people simply value Delsey a little less highly than they did, as a brand. These words are simply their way of expressing Delsey's lower value and Andrex's higher value to them. So where does this added value come from?

I think that pretty clearly the success of Andrex has been due to a blend of a lot of things. First of all, consistently high product quality and efficient marketing; then Andrex's early leadership in soft toilet paper and its leadership in innovations and product improvements – the positive approach. But the added values – the factor that allows Andrex to command a proper price – must certainly depend a good deal on the way in which the company has used advertising. Or to broaden that a little, the consistent way in which Andrex and its values have been presented to the public *as a brand*. Andrex has been very much a brand, not an object. And it is in this that I am sure the difference lies. Let me try to illustrate the point by looking at some of the Andrex advertising over the past 12 years.

Below are some fairly different campaigns created by a lot of different people, approved and modified by a lot of different people. Superficially they vary quite a lot, and yet there is quite a consistency. I think this is because they are dominated by the personality of Andrex itself. What runs through them all is not any unique product claim or unique feature or functional description. It is a sort of attitude of mind and values and tone of voice that belong to Andrex. Andrex the brand emerges as a clear personality. She is reliable, dainty, clean-living, domesticated, family-centred, radiating confidence in her ability to manage. It is this that makes Andrex, as it were, a nice person to have about the house.

What I am saying, in fact, is that Andrex succeeds as a profit-earner because, in addition to its values as a product, the brand has values beyond the physical and functional ones. And that these added values contribute to a brand personality. People choose their brands as they choose their friends. You choose friends not usually because of specific skills or physical attributes (though of course these come into it) but simply because you like them as people. It is the total person you choose, not a compendium of virtues and vices.

This might perhaps be thought a rather fanciful way of describing why one brand is valued more than another. But it is not too hard to find evidence to support it. For instance, blind versus named product tests. Figure 2.4 gives one example. You can see that when the two

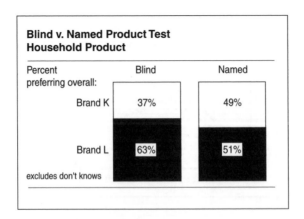

Figure 2.4   Blind v. Named Product Test – House Product

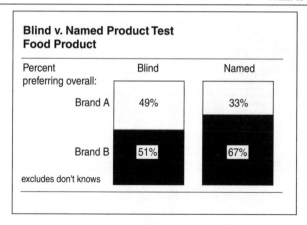

Figure 2.5   Blind v. Named Product Test – Food Product

brands are tested against each other blind, Brand L is an easy winner. When the two brands are names, they come out about even. Quite clearly there is something in Brand K *as a brand* which raises its value to that of Brand L. It cannot be a physical or functional thing – since that would presumably have arisen in the blind test. Brand K clearly has more added values – non-functional values – than Brand L. Another example is shown in Figure 2.5, where Brands A and B appear to be level on physical, functional performance, but Brand B has considerably more added values.

One could add of course a lot of evidence from outside marketing to demonstrate the power of these non-functional values. For instance, the well-known placebo effect in medicine, whereby an inert substance will cure the patient if the patient thinks it will. Or the Hawthorne experiments, which showed how productivity was put up among a group of workers, not by the actual changes in working conditions but through the emotional rewards of having the management take an interest in them. Not only are people influenced by such values, but I think that as they become better off, they will get more and more of their rewards in life from the non-functional. They will require style as much as performance. They will value brands for *who they are* as much as for *what they do*.

I think that in the advertising business we may all have been slow to recognize this because there is still a Puritan streak in us which says that it is wicked for people to have non-functional values, that they ought to buy brands for function and performance only. I cannot really see any reason why we should have this feeling. If we are really honest with ourselves, we must surely admit that on the whole the non-functional pleasures that we ourselves get are more intense and meaningful than the functional.

Fortunately, consumers, who know a lot more about brands than manufacturers or advertising agencies, do not get too bogged down in the Puritanism. They can and do see brands as personalities – in some cases, the personalities are more vivid than the product. Here are some comments that housewives made in a recent series of interviews, in which they were simply asked to imagine certain brands as people – what sort of personalities would they have? (See Figure 2.6).

Figure 2.6   Andrex advertisements

Washing Powders

Interviewer: "What kind of a person would you think Fairy Snow would be?"

Housewife A: "Well, I think it would be somebody older . . . somebody whose outlook on life was a little slower, most probably her children would be growing up, she would be a married woman again, I should imagine. Generally doing a slower run of life than would Mrs Ariel".

Interviewer: "Tell me more about Mrs Ariel."

Housewife A: "I think she would be the sort of person who has got to get everything done, though very well and very efficiently, to have rather a good social life at the same time. Very sparkling, and would be the sort who would always have a baby-sitter at the ready, to go out in the evening and take good care of herself; and who likes to keep young and follow trends."

Interviewer: "What would Mrs Fairy Snow do in the evenings?"

Housewife A: "Well, just sort of sit by the fire and watch television."

Interviewer: "And what about Tide? What sort of personality would Tide have?"

Housewife B: "A very gruff old man, very fierce. Ex-army type."

Interviewer: "What about Tide, if Tide became a person?"

Housewife C: "A little nearer a Mrs Ariel sort of person. She would be a little more with it, more mini-skirted, more Americanized, I would think. The sort of person who tends to buy the frozen foods and have a rather flashy car. It matters to her – social things matter to her, I would think, rather than with Mrs Surf. I don't think it matters too much if *she* doesn't keep up the Joneses."

Soups – Heinz

Interviewer: "What about Heinz, if that became a person?"

Housewife C: "Oh, she's rather like Mrs Persil."

Housewife B: "I think the older person; by older I mean 60–65. A woman who hasn't got a lot of money, perhaps a pensioner. Oh, very sweet, very understanding, but a little bit narrow."

Toilet Soaps – Lifebuoy

Interviewer: "What about Lifebuoy, if that became a person?"

Housewife D: "That's an older man, about fiftyish, somebody whose children are growing up, a very steady job and looking to retirement."

Housewife A: "I think the sporty type of man, who is always on the tennis courts."

Housewife E: "A male worker in his twenties – dirty job, mining or something."

Interviewer: "What would he be like as a neighbour?"

Housewife E: "Oh, I should think he would be very good, but people might take him wrongly because he was so abrupt. But underneath it all he was kind-hearted."

Toilet Soaps – Camay

Interviewer: "What about Camay toilet soap as a person?"

Housewife F: Fresh, bright young girl of about 18 or 19, very bright and very clean. She likes to wash her hair at least twice a week – and of course have a bath every day – and look after herself and her bedroom, very tidy."

Housewife A: "A single person, a model, I would think. You know, very tall and very slim and very, very careful about her make-up and the toilet things she uses."

Interviewer: "What sort of boyfriends does she have?"

Housewife A: "Oh, I should think very go-ahead boyfriends, you know, sort of salesmen and people like this."

Housewife E: "She might be a bit like that to everybody and sort of underneath a bit catty perhaps; but she's warm to everyone. But secretly she might be thinking differently about you."

Interviewer: What would she be like as a neighbour?"

Housewife G: "A neighbour? Oh, I should think she would be terribly hard to live next door to."

From all the experimental research that we have done on this, it seems pretty clear that brands do have personalities. And they tend to be consistent, though what is one person's praise is another's condemnation. For instance, Persil is seen by some as happy and contented; by others as dull and lacking in ambition. Two facets of the same person. One can often trace the sources of a brand personality – here it is the advertising, there the pack, somewhere else some physical element of the product. Of course, the personality is clearest and strongest when all the elements are consistent.

WHAT MAKES A BRAND SUCCESSFUL?

I think that from all this evidence we can get a fairly clear theory of what it is that will make a brand successful in today's and tomorrow's marketing conditions. By successful I mean able to bring in worthwhile profits over a long period.

First, it has to be a coherent totality, not a lot of bits. The physical product, the pack and all the elements of communication – name, style, advertising, pricing, promotions, and so on – must be blended into a single brand personality. Secondly, it has to be unique, and constantly developing to stay unique, because it is through its uniqueness that the brand can offer sustained profit margins. And the uniqueness will depend on both functional and non-functional values – appeals to the senses, the reason and the emotions. The added values beyond the functional may become increasingly important. Thirdly, this blend of appeals must clearly be relevant to people's needs and desires, and immediate and salient. It must constantly stand out from the crowd; it must spring to mind. This will not of course be a static thing. It will constantly have to develop and to take the initiative to avoid me-tooism.

If the brand can have these three sets of attributes it will succeed, because retailers will need it as much as the public does. It will get its due distribution and display and be valued highly enough to build a good profit margin.

One advantage, I think, of looking at the brand in this way is that it makes it easier to pick out the contribution that advertising can make. It can operate in all three of these areas – but perhaps most particularly in expressing and synthesizing the brand's personality. In fact, you can judge the value of advertising or a promotion or a product improvement or a price adjustment or any other marketing action by asking yourself about its contribution to the brand in these terms:

- Does it enhance the brand's total personality?
- Does it contribute to the blend of appeals to the senses, the reason and the emotions?
- Does it bring the brand to the front of the mind?

And if it does not do any of these things, what *is* it for?

WHERE SHOULD WE SHARPEN UP?

Let me try to summarize briefly where the argument has led us so far.

- Like it or not, we are entering a period of greater power for the retailer. The successful manufacturer will be the one who can make the best of it.
- Sustained profits for the manufacturer in the future are going to depend much more than they have done on improving and holding margins, much less than they have done on sheer size and growth.
- The only way to improve margins will be by developing and building brands that are more valuable to consumers than competitive brands, brands that have added values. And that will mean a positive approach, with frequent brand improvements.
- These added values will tend increasingly to be non-functional values. But they will only work if they are blended with the physical and functional values to form an integrated brand personality.
- Advertising has a crucial and changing role to play today. It will of course continue to have a role in increasing volume sales, but its main task will be to improve profits. Not only is it an important element within the added values, but it is also a primary means of expressing the total personality of the brand.

If all this is true, where do we need to sharpen up? There seem to me to be four main areas we should consider, from the manufacturer's point of view.

Organization

First, organization and management. I wonder whether all top managements are involved deeply enough in the nature of their brands. Do they realize fully enough that it is from the success of brands rather than as products that the profits will come? Do they fully understand the nature of brands? Do they set company objectives in terms of brand positioning or simply in financial terms? Or is the responsibility for brand positioning delegated to the junior brand manager?

We can ask too whether the company organization is ideally suited to making profits from brands. I think it would be fair to say that many companies have the structure shown in Figure 2.7 with neat hierarchies and departmental barriers. Yet everything that emerges from

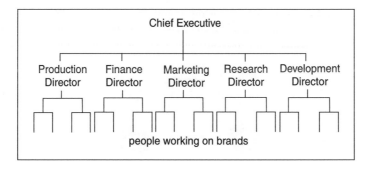

Figure 2.7   Chief Executive Organogram

any consideration of successful brands is that they are a *blend* of elements. We face today this new factor of the variable selling price, so the blending becomes more complex – involving R&D, production, finance, investment, plant utilization, product improvement, selling, advertising and so on. Is the sort of organization we see here the right one for producing such a blend? Can it be done effectively without a project team type or organization? And then, who is going to do the blending? I think we are going to have to do something about our ambivalence over the term "marketing". All the textbooks suggest that marketing is a total planning function with the aim of satisfying consumer demand at a profit. But is the marketing director in Figure 2.7 in any position to do this? He can certainly control the distribution mix, but has he the authority or the influence to control planning of the brand?

Planning

Then there is the whole approach to planning. There is an element to this which springs from the organizational problem. In some cases, I suspect manufacturers are doing very little long-term planning because there is no organization for doing it. Divisional directors are very involved in their functional responsibilities, and the board meetings have to cover a lot of ground – from the shareholders to the bicycle shed. Long-term planning can easily be left out. I think we have seen this very clearly in the tendency of some manufacturers to treat the "retailer problems" as a short-term, direct salesforce problem – requiring short-term solutions. Whereas I hope I have shown that it is a long-term thing.

Sharpening up on planning methods is going to be necessary too in improving a going brand or developing a new one. It can be like the sad parable of the man rich enough to have an entirely custom-made car. He decided that nothing but the best would do, so he went to the best people regardless of expense. He himself was very keen on speeding up the M6, so he went to Jaguar (Figure 2.8) for the engine.

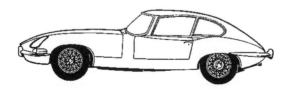

Figure 2.8   Picture of a Jaguar

He knew his wife found parking a bit of a problem, so Fiat seemed the best people to go to for the chassis (Figure 2.9).

Figure 2.9   Picture of a Fiat

Figure 2.10   Picture of a Volvo

And he felt that Volvo could deal best with accommodating his three children, two retrievers, au pair girl and beagle in the back; so they did the bodywork (Figure 2.10).

The curious thing was that when the car was assembled (Figure 2.11), it never seemed to work very well. And when in the end he decided to sell it, he had quite a lot of trouble finding a buyer at all.

Figure 2.11   Picture of a Combined Jaguar/Fiat/Volvo car

But isn't this happening quite a lot with the planning of brands? Experts are hired to construct all the bits – a production unit in the north midlands, some basic research people from High Wycombe, an advertising agency in W1, a packaging boutique just off the Tottenham Court Road, some merchandising experts from Soho; and in some office suburb someone choosing a name by sticking a pin into a computer print-out.

Research

Then there is the way we use research. There seems to me endless scope for sharpening up here.

To keep it short, I will stick to just one point. And that is that <u>we will never use research to the full unless we start from a carefully worked out theory of what the brand is, why it is successful or not, and what advertising can contribute</u>. For instance, consider what follows from the theory I have been outlining:

- If a brand is a complex blend of elements, with the relationships between them as important as the elements themselves, can it really make sense to test the elements in isolation? Can a name test in isolation mean anything? Or a pack test in isolation?
- If advertising works mainly by giving added values to a brand in the long run, what can we learn from a single exposure advertisement test whose results are based on short-term brand switching?
- If brands seem to consumers almost living things with personalities, are we learning anything by getting people to choose between phrases printed on a bit of card?

- Again, if brands have personalities, with all the subtleties of people, are we using the right balance of qualitative and quantitative research? Once you have heard people describing Lifebuoy as rather abrupt, Tide as gruff and ex-army, Camay as a bit catty, will you be content to rely solely on the sort of research that gets people to put crosses on a seven-point scale running from "kind to the hands" to "not so kind to the hands"?

And so on. Once the theory is there, the questions about our current use of research come pretty easily.

Advertising

And finally, we can of course sharpen up on our approach to advertising. First, we can recognize that in the 1970s it may well have a different role from the past. Added values and their effects on profits will become more important – the direct effect on sales volume increase rather less. We can sharpen up by following through the implications of this role.

Secondly, we can improve our methods of setting advertising objectives, by thinking of them in terms of the advertising's contribution to the added values of the brand – how it can contribute to the brand's appeal to the senses, and to the reason and to the emotions.

And thirdly, we can recognize that advertising itself is a totality. A campaign, like a brand, is not just a number of bits put together – a claim here, a pack shot there, a reason why somewhere else. If we try to produce it by the atomistic approach, we will end up with a sort of Identikit brand. It will be a perfect description of the structure of the brand, as the Identikit can describe the contours of the face. But it won't be the same thing. The brand will never come to life.

CONCLUSION

This is only a short list. But there seems to be quite a lot to do. Today's pressures from the retailer are not altogether pleasant for the manufacturer. But if they can discipline and stimulate us to sharpen up in these four areas, then in a few years' time I think we will be able to look back with a certain feeling of gratitude.

3
The Price of Freedom is
Eternal Vigilance

By Rory Sutherland, Executive Creative Director and Vice-Chairman, OgilvyOne London; Vice-Chairman, Ogilvy Group UK

An introduction to:

3.1   Advertising: Art and Science

You know those passages in the memoirs of the pre-war rich? Colonial civil servants who describe how "Six hours later I awoke to discover that both my houseboys had scarpered into the bush, leaving me to make my own breakfast." Or Cabinet Ministers who have "always loathed summer in Portofino, not least because the *Daily Telegraph* arrives two days late" .

Although the writer is hoping for your sympathy, your reaction is more along the lines of "And you think you've got problems, mate?"

Well, I had a little of the same reaction reading this glorious piece from 1982. Because, while everything King says is absolutely right and true, and though his points are even more relevant now than then, I still can't help sneakily envying his problems. It seems to me that, writing in 1982, King couldn't imagine how much worse things were going to get.

Asked to speak about whether advertising was art or science, King characteristically, turned the question around, producing a brilliant analysis of why advertising is both art and science. But here's the point: what kind of science? What he called "Old Science" (deductive, logical and useless) was contrasted to "New Science", which is creative and harnessed to innovation.

Our Business Today is Almost Completely in Thrall to Old Science

Or, put less kindly, to Bad Science. And why is this?

We have all heard the adage about people who "use research as a drunk uses a lamppost – for support rather than illumination". And in our current backside-covering age this is endemic. People everywhere are always on the lookout for some semi-scientific methodology to lend apparent cohesion and justification to their every action and cost. Yet, for all this methodology, they aren't really blessed with a scientist's *mentality*: a mind motivated by a spirit of enquiry – the continuous urge to ask new questions and test new theories in an open-minded and open-ended quest for progress.

Real science often is more mentality than methodology. Newton was not the first man to have an apple land on his head – he was simply the first person to wonder why. Einstein never conducted a single experiment. Many other advances in science (Archimedes, Roentgen, Fleming, Mendel) have simply been the result of an insightful mind presented with a lucky break. Darwin, as King observes, probably attributed to process what was really due to insight.

This love of methodology comes not only from backside-covering instincts, but also from that overpowering human urge to create a sequential narrative around any series of events – especially when presenting a business case study. The demands of narrative require that you depict any series of events as though they arose in logical order: *post hoc* and *propter hoc*. In reality, this is as likely to be a post-rationalization of events. (Isn't it interesting, by the way, that there is no such phrase as "pre-rationalization"?).

You'll observe this phenomenon in most descriptions of battles, wherein victory is usually attributed (especially by the victors) to a few early strategic decisions made by the most senior people on the field. It simply doesn't do to say that Agincourt was the result of an unusually muddy field and some opportunistic Welshmen with big mallets.

And it is an absolute must in any agency pitch, where the secret of success is to mug the audience with an irrefutable sequence of logic – even though every single person in the room knows that things will almost never turn out that way.

This obsession with sequence has been further exacerbated by a few technical "advances" – not least the ubiquity of PowerPoint which was no more than a sinister gleam in Bill Gates's eye in 1982. It is a format that imposes a kind of spurious narrative on any information it carries.

But the absence of PowerPoint was only one of the advantages the scientific minds of JWT's planning department enjoyed back in 1982.

Life was Easier then

First of all, they did not have to contend with anyone beyond the simple agency–client relationship. No brand identity firm had earlier developed a brand onion (or brand avocado or whatever) for After Eights (the brand described in the speech) with which the hapless JWT planner was forced to work. He had a relatively clean sheet.

Furthermore, they were party to all available knowledge and background. They understood that a brand (Andrex, After Eight, Mr Kipling) was the product of a whole number of variables. They enjoyed partial control over many of these variables and had an understanding of the rest.

Today's planner is perhaps attempting to fly a brand with far fewer instruments and just using the pedals.

By contrast the agency of that time was responsible for the packaging and the naming – so there was a small chance of getting those two ducks in a row – aligned with the main idea for the brand. Some bright spark could even add the line MINI-MENTHES ENROBÉES DE CHOCOLAT NOIR on the packaging – a lovely touch. Today, by the time you had conceived the idea of creating an upmarket post-prandial wafer-thin mint, you would probably be presented with luminous orange packaging for "Rowntrees All-Day Mints" by a client desperate not to limit the consumption opportunities to evenings only. And the packaging would be bilingual – but in English and Arabic.

Better still, the planners of that day were free to conceive a fairly simple role for the product – as a sophisticated after-dinner treat. This was the idea for the product. It wasn't felt necessary for the planner to embellish a simple idea with a whole bunch of pseudo-science about 'commensality' or 'post-prandial bonding' or whatnot – which planners are fairly prone to do nowadays.

Best of all, this was before the arrival of the media independent. Today, if the creative agency were to suggest advertising in *Vogue* (and, never mind the reach, this is not a wholly absurd way to launch an upmarket brand) they would almost certainly discover (generally after the work had been developed as full-page ads) that the media agency had bought small spaces in *Bella* and *OK* instead – either to satisfy some arcane deal with a media owner or simply to scotch the notion that a media suggestion by a creative agency could have any value whatsoever.

And – just a few more things – the JWT of 1982 probably had a client who would be around long enough to allow for a little to-ing and fro-ing before the After Eight brand took final shape. And they were probably remunerated in a way that did not (as payment by the hour often does) force them to deploy talent in narrow silos and in sequence rather than in parallel – an order of engagement based on the wholly bogus pretence, to use the words of an Ogilvy planner, John Shaw, "that you can make distillation precede fermentation".

Why does all this matter so very much?

The Pretence of Creativity as a Sequential Process

At one level, it matters to me as a creative person because, in maintaining the pretence that our business works through a rational and sequential process, I feel we are perpetrating a minor fraud. And the victim of this fraud is creativity itself. Because in suggesting in our case studies that we arrived at success through process, we are falsely paying to logic a debt that we really owe to magic. The magic of imagination, or insight. And, as a result, we are causing the left-brain to be overvalued at the expense of the right.

But, to any agency paid by the hour, process is so wonderfully time-consuming, isn't it?

This debate also matters because I sincerely believe that a relentless application of sequential logic untempered by imagination is responsible for the greatest absurdities and extravagances we see in business and government. The 3G auction; NHS target setting; the ERM debacle; obsessive punctuality targets for trains – all have been perpetrated by people following the relentless dictates of logic without an imaginative grasp of the alternatives. And logic – unlike creativity – is allowed to go unpoliced.

Sutherland's first law states that "All creative people must submit their thinking for appraisal by more rational people". The second law states that "This does not apply the other way round". No one engaged in the 3G auction thought to ask what else you could do with £16 billion – such as installing public wifi in every hamlet in Britain. No one spending £6 billion on the Channel Tunnel Fast Link asked whether £6 billion might improve the lot of passengers if spent some other way than by marginally accelerating the trains. They already had their formulae, thanks very much.

The Tyranny of Metrics and Scores

Earlier in this piece, I mentioned the example of the drunk and the lamppost. Yet there is a better story about drunks and lampposts that David Ogilvy used to tell. A drunk had lost his keys on the street and was frantically searching for them under a streetlamp. "Where did you drop them?" asked a concerned passer by. "Over there" he replied, indicating a spot 30 yards away. "So why are you looking here under the lamp?" "The light's better here," he explained.

With its obsession with following established processes and metrics, Old Science causes us to commit this same absurd mistake – making absurd decisions simply to satisfy the demands of metrics and measurement.

The survival of media metrics – an obsession with reach and frequency at the expense of impact or relevance – are a case in point. Never mind the death of the 30-second commercial – it was the death of the 40-second commercial that was the real disaster.

As any new scientist will tell you, most forms of measurement are proxies – they only apply until a better one comes along. Old scientists need the old measures – for the light is so much better there.

Some Suggested Remedies....

1. James Webb Young and Claude Hopkins both predicted years ago that it would soon be impossible to work in advertising without a background in mathematics. Yet, since then, the problem has worsened. Advertising is at risk of becoming a place for arts graduates with rich parents. This won't do us any favours in fighting our cause against Bad Science. We should aim predominantly to hire graduates with scientific backgrounds. Interestingly two of the best planners I have ever come across are geneticists.
2. As an industry, we need to fight the overwhelming influence of Bad Science in its most influential manifestations. These include Management Consultants and Financial Analysts. These have absorbed all the methodology and linearity of science untempered by any capacity for imagination. The influence they exert is pernicious, and far worse than the influence of Procurement folk – who do actually understand the distinction between price and value.
3. Creative agencies should do a 10% job swap every year with media agencies. The moronic separation of these two inseparable disciplines has worsened the two-cultures rift within our business.
4. We must recapture a culture of measurement and testing within agencies. Why? Because if we do not do so, other people will do the measurement and testing; and these other people won't necessarily know what to measure or test.
5. We must also become more American, by which I mean that advertising must aspire to be the arty end of the business world, as in the USA, rather than being the greedy end of the arts world, as in the UK. The creative community in the UK has surrendered so much ground in 20 years as to become a generation of proposition-gilders rather than problem-solvers.
6. The phrase "Give us the freedom of a tight brief" is simply wrong for our times. "Give us the freedom of a well-defined problem" is more like it. Furthermore, that whole planner story about the brief for painting of the Sistine Chapel ceiling (used by planners as yet one more land grab against the creative community) is a complete lie: Michelangelo completely rewrote the brief, as he was quite right to do, knowing rather more about painting than some syphilitic pontiff.
7. We must find some new kind of remuneration to replace payment by the hour that allows us to deploy resource against our problems as we choose, not according to some contractual arrangement. But we should abandon the idea that we should charge solely for ideas – Tim Berners-Lee had the biggest idea in 100 years but Gates/Jobs/Page/Brin/Yang/Clarke made all the money.

3.1

Advertising: Art and Science*

By Stephen King

One of the very few things I know is that India is the land of paradox because everyone here has told me that. But even so, I was slightly startled at the daring and wit of the organizers in providing the final paradox in this Congress. Here you are with a Congress on economic growth, and you're ending with a speaker from a nation which has been in continuous relative economic decline since 1857. I suppose what we are hoping to do is learn something from the UK about how not to do it, while there is still a little bit of warmth in the ashes.

One of the commonsense assumptions in this conference has been that economic growth will come as individual managements of companies and institutions move from being amateur to being professional or, if you like, as the methods move from those based on Art to those based on Science.

And yet, in the United States, after three decades of management science, a few nagging doubts are just beginning to arise. People are beginning to ask: How much Science should there be? Is Science forcing Art out? Is Art forcing science out? How much of each should there be? There is seen to be an inevitable conflict between the two.

The brief I received asked: How far is advertising a Science? How far could it become a Science? So I want to cover today how this conflict between Art and Science has gone in the UK – first of all, looking at economic growth in general, then looking at the development of new brands and finally looking at advertising.

Let me start in the broadest terms, economic growth in general. At the peak of Britain's economic power at the end of the nineteenth century, businesses tended to be led by inventor-businessmen and inventor-engineers. There was great excitement in the technology of the industrial revolution and there was a certain amount of encouragement for lunatic inspiration. People made functional things, but they also made functional things aimed to satisfy the soul. They were, if you like, artists; they worked on the whole by hunch, by the seat of the pants, by untutored judgement. The only research they did, if they did any at all, was to ask their wife, or mother, or boyfriend, according to taste. But gradually, as organizations grew, these sorts of people became very awkward to fit in. They often had very unpleasant and difficult habits. They didn't clock in on time; they were rude and arrogant, and they dressed in a difficult way. They began to be seen as pretty irresponsible, and so gradually there was a move towards professionalism. Management science came in. People started going to MIT and the Harvard Business School. They got their MBAs and they started talking about, even thinking about, things like discounted cash flow, management by objectives, linear programming, critical path analysis, economics and so on. And finally, computers and micro-computers have been sprouting in offices like pot plants.

*Presented at the 13th Asian Advertising Congress, New Delhi, 1982. Reproduced with permission.

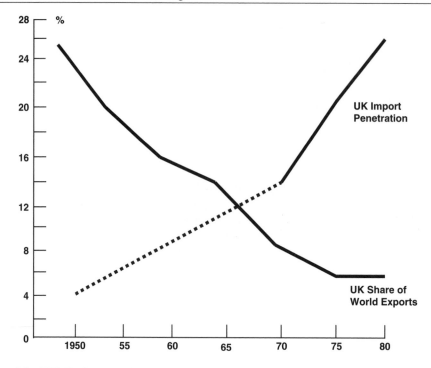

Figure 3.1   U.K. Trade – Manufactured Goods
Source: Dept of Trade

In the 1950s marketing came into the UK from the USA. And from then on, the whole thing has become a great deal more responsible and a great deal more scientific.

The results of this move to professionalism in UK management have been really quite dramatic (see Figure 3.1).

Our share of world exports of manufactured goods has dropped like a stone. Import penetration has risen like a bird. (I suppose whatever the national bird of Japan is.) Now why is this? There are a great many causes – functional, historical, social and so on, not the least of which is a very deep psychological resistance to change which I suspect is not entirely unknown in other countries. But there is one factor which stands out again and again. Let me give you a couple of examples of what I mean, one from heavy industry and one from light.

The first one is textile machinery. The UK used to dominate textile machinery in the world and had something like 60 to 70% of the world's trade at the end of the nineteenth century, with still about one-third of the world market in the 1950s. But over the last 30 years our share has dropped from 30% to 12%, and leadership has been taken over by the Germans.

One of the theories about why this was so was that the British were being priced out of the market by all those cheap imports. This theory took a little bit of a knock when it was found that the German machines were about one-third more expensive than the British ones. But they were cheating; not only were they one-third more expensive, they were more modern, they worked better.

The real reason why our share declined is, I think, very clear from a survey that was done on British textile manufacturers who were users of imported textile machinery. They were simply asked why they were doing so. No less than 45% of the reasons given were that the imported machines worked better. They had a more advanced design. The second main reason: 38% said no UK machines were meeting their particular needs. Price really hardly came into it at all – making up only 4% of mentions.

In other words, it was sheer lack of innovation and modernization. Somehow or other, in the move from Art to Science, some of the inspiration, some of the vision, had gone out of the door.

Let us consider the other end of the scale: packaged goods. There was a recent analysis in the UK of 585 new food brands launched in the eight years from 1969 to 1976. Two years after the end of that period, by 1978, 53% of those new brands were dead, taken off the market; and 43% could be categorized as the "walking wounded" – they were still on the market, but their sales were under £4m at retail selling price – in other words, under the level that's necessary to run a respectable business. Just 4% remained on the market with sales of over £4m, just 21 brands out of those 585; and about half of those were really more line extensions than new brands. It's a pitiful analysis of a pitiful situation. But the reasons for it are terribly clear.

There have been dozens of different analyses of why new brands fail. And they all come to basically the same conclusions. There is one particular analysis which I've always found very helpful, by Hugh Davidson (*Harvard Business Review*, 54, 2, 1976). In it, he compared 50 successful new brands with 50 failures, on three main dimensions. keys to success:

You can see from Figure 3.2 that <u>price isn't a terribly critical discriminator between success</u> price: no <u>and failure. The successes were just as likely as the failures to be more expensive in the market</u> <u>place than</u> the competition.

However, when he looked at performance it was a very different picture. By performance performance: I mean doing better in blind product tests than the brands on the market already. Having a yes <u>good performance was quite clearly linked with success. Some three-quarters of the brands</u> <u>with the same or worse performance failed; three-quarters of those with a better performance</u> succeeded.

<u>Exactly</u> the same was true about distinctiveness: <u>70% of those brands that weren't very</u> distinctive: <u>different from the competition failed and 70% of those that were very different succeeded.</u> yes

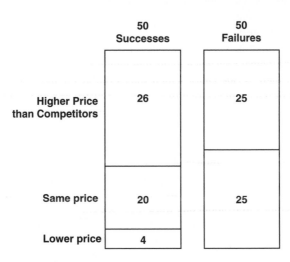

Figure 3.2   What Works for New Brands?

So the rule ends up – and always ends up – as: be better and be different. It is a marvellous, straightforward, simple rule. It is, of course, very difficult to comply with; but the rule is very simple.

The reason for the very high rate of new brand failure in the UK, and for the drain on company resources of the "walking wounded", is simply that they weren't better enough and different enough from what there was already. In particular, they tended to underestimate the public's taste and the public's sophistication and intelligence. What was required was a great deal more innovation, and I think we can conclude quite easily that one of the main reasons for poor economic growth in the UK and loss of share in world markets is simple lack of inventiveness, lack of vision and courage. It's really the converse of the Japanese approach.

So we have to ask, has management science failed? Well, I don't think any Japanese would say so. I think the truth of it is a great deal more subtle than that.

It seems to me that there are two fundamentally different concepts of science, which I shall call the Old Science and New Science. What has gone wrong in Britain is that on the whole we have chosen the wrong one. It seems to me quite critical for any country which is hoping to have economic growth to choose the right sort of science.

The father of the Old Science in the UK was Francis Bacon. He said in effect that there was a four-stage process of discovery, of the scientific development of knowledge. You start off with controlled observation, you observe everything madly in all directions. Then, secondly, you accumulate data; you gather facts together and then, thirdly, by analysis, some general laws emerge. Fourthly, you do some more observations to verify these general laws and if you do that you end up with knowledge. In other words, it's a step-by-step brick-by-brick approach. Truth is built up to by an inductive process in a totally logical way.

For instance, the scientist Karl Pearson in a book called *The Grammar of Science* in 1892, wrote, "The classification of facts and recognition of their sequence and relative significance is the function of science". Just collect the facts, put them together and that's it.

The danger is, of course, that raw observations, naked facts, may give you a very incomplete picture. For instance, you can look in the wrong place or you can look with inadequate instruments. In fact, I think, by definition, instruments at any point of time are always inadequate for what you really want to find out. The whole history of science has been one of laws which turn out to be not quite true.

The most vivid example is Newton's physics, which were regarded as an immutable truth for two centuries before Einstein came along. No less a person than Charles Darwin wrote (talking about *The Origin of Species*): "I worked on true Baconian principles and without any theory collected facts on a wholesale scale." In other words this is a sort of "playing safe" science. Don't risk anything by guessing or having a theory, just collect a lot of facts. And maybe this playing-safe element is why it has appealed so much to corporate man. Happily, of course, as you know, Darwin didn't practise what he preached. He was an arch-theorizer. I think he belongs much more to the New Science.

To me the best describer of the New Science was Karl Popper. He seemed to turn the whole Baconian process upside down. He thought of Science as a spiritual adventure. He said the main needs in Science and in scientists are vision and creativity. He pointed out that Archimedes and Copernicus and Galileo and Einstein had all been visionaries, had all been creative artists. They worked by challenging the accepted ideas and this is very similar to the great painters. The Impressionists, the Cubists, Picasso, Matisse, were all challenging the accepted ideas of the time.

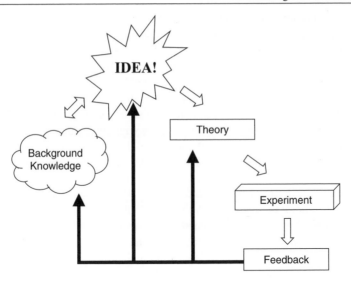

Figure 3.3   How Innovation Happens

I think one of the critical things that Popper has said about this is: you don't start with observations. You start with what he calls a trial solution, what we might call an idea. He wrote, in fact: "Observations are always interpretation of the facts observed. They are interpretations in the light of theories." In other words you can't make any sense of facts until you've had an idea, or as Einstein put it, "Theory cannot be fabricated out of the results of observation – it can only be invented." That seems to be the fundamental difference between the Old Science and the New Science.

The Old Science is saying: build it up gradually, step-by-step, brick-by-brick; and the New Science is saying that what you have to do is invent a solution right from the beginning, even if it is wrong. It seems to me that the process of invention according to the New Science is somewhat like Figure 3.3.

You start off with background knowledge. You have to understand the issues, understand your subject, understand people and their motivations and lives very thoroughly. You start with a dissatisfaction with the existing theories, dissatisfaction with the status quo, and that leads to working out the right problem to solve. Often the right problem to solve comes from a challenge to the existing conventions.

Next you have to have an idea. You have to have a vision of this trial solution. This is a non-logical process. It's an unconscious process, an extremely messy process. I suppose it should have a dotted relationship rather than that firm arrow, even if it does go both ways; the idea does arise from the background knowledge in a sense, but it's not related to it in any sort of formal way. I think that Gordon's synectics, the brainstormings that we all do, Edward de Bono's lateral thinking, all these are attempts to set up a deliberate interruption to the whole process of logical step-by-step thinking which we are all too familiar with.

James Webb Young said all the right things about advertising (very irritating – you think you have an idea and you go back to Jim Young only to find that he said it 40 years ago). He wrote in "A Technique for Producing Ideas" that what you should do at this stage is: drop the subject altogether. Drop it altogether and then, he said, out of nowhere the idea will come. It will come to you when you're least expecting it.

The third stage, I think, is in two parts. First of all what you have to do is pat the idea into shape, make it into a coherent theory – form a hypothesis, with sentences that start off "I wonder if...". "I wonder if we did so and so what would happen?" And secondly, the implications have to be worked out into some sort of practical form. The idea has to be worked up into something which is capable of being tested and tried out.

The next stage is experiments, and here was one of Popper's main innovations. He said that the critical thing here is deliberately to attempt to disprove your ideas. The Old Science had always been: "Collect a few more examples to verify your law". Popper said: "Have this idea and deliberately set out to disprove it," and pointed out that this can be a very exciting process. "It is part of the greatness and the beauty of science that we can learn, through our own critical investigations, that the world is utterly different from what we ever imagine."

The final stage in the invention process is feedback . . . two sorts of feedback. One – the more obvious one – into improving the idea. (We've done our experiment; it didn't quite work, so let's improve the idea.) Secondly – and something we do all too little – is going back to modify the problem. Very often it is impossible to understand the problem we ought to be solving until we've tried out a solution. And this is something that the Old Science, I think, wouldn't tolerate; but the New Science actively encourages it. It stresses that innovation is a continuous cycle with no final solution.

To me there are three things about Popper and the New Science that are fundamentally different from the Old Science. First of all there is this emphasis on inventing the right problem to solve, the dissatisfaction with the status quo. Secondly, the critical and early role of vision in it all – absolute importance and exhilaration of anarchy at the idea stage. And thirdly, having the confidence – and, in our case, having clients and agencies working together closely enough to have the confidence – to set out to disprove our theories and to enjoy disproving them; be pleased we've disproved them and therefore can learn.

If you look at the New Science this way it seems to me that the processes are very similar to those of Art. After all Art, the process of Art, is in just the same way understanding, followed by an idea, followed by an experiment. What's missing perhaps, is the feedback, the purposive part of it. But if you think of Science as purposive art, I don't think there can be any conflict between Art and the New Science.

I've gone into this in some detail because it seems to me that in planning new product development and in planning advertising the difference between success and failure lies critically in whether we tend to be using the Old Science or the New Science.

Let me look first at new product development. Now you well know, as I do, that most existing new product development systems – and there are plenty of them – are based on the Old Science. They are nearly all variations of what you might call the funnel or hopper system. What you are supposed to do is get a lot of little bits, pat each one into shape and chuck them all into the hopper. Then if the bits are all right, they will work through the system step-by-step and you'll come up with The Ideal Brand. That seems to me rather like saying that if each brick is properly shaped we will inevitably produce great architecture. So often these patent systems are trying to invent without vision, without ideas and without anarchy; and I think they tend to fail for that very reason.

One example of the techniques of Old Science is Gap Analysis, which is an attempt to invent by deduction; to get new products untouched by human mind. Figure 3.4 shows a hypothetical example.

Brands of shampoo are plotted on two scales – a strong/gentle scale and a medicated/cosmetic scale. You can see that there are three brands seen by people as strong and medicated, four

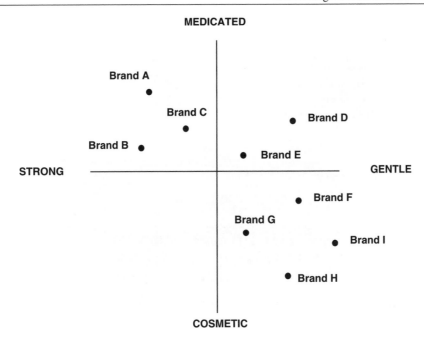

Figure 3.4   Gap Analysis Shampoos

as gentle and cosmetic, one as gentle and medicated and one more or less in the middle. But there are none in the strong and cosmetic sector; therefore, says Gap Analysis, that is your opportunity. But it seems to me that however much this is all dressed up with phrases like "*n*-dimensional concept space", the main reason for most of these gaps is that no one actually wants something in that combination. If we are not careful, Gap Analysis is a very elaborate machinery for saying that if there is already a market for hot coffee and a market for iced coffee, the gap for us is in selling warm coffee. There are many systems written up in those ghastly, unreadable American marketing magazines, full of unpublishable PhD theses, and they all set out to take the risk and the mess and the uncertainty from new product development. I think they fail because they are, in doing so, removing an absolutely essential element from invention – and they fail because they are rooted in the Old Science.

By contrast I'd like to take you briefly through a real case history. This isn't the usual sort of agency case history in which our immaculate heroes proceed, without hesitation, from brilliant analysis to startling conclusion and in the final frames stride into the sunset pursued by pathetic bleats of gratitude from their half-witted clients. I'd like to try to tell you what really happened. This one started off with a man from Rowntrees finding some chocolate peppermint creams in the USA and, being a wise man, he said, "Ah, those look nice" and he brought some home. It didn't start off with a multistage stratified segmentation analysis of something called the Peppermint Cream Market; it started off with a nice piece of luck. I think if the company had then used the Old Science, the step-by-step approach, they could have ended up with a safe, modest, me-too brand which would have been something of a failure. In fact, after an enormous amount of muddle, antagonism, argument, bad ideas, liquor, threats, creative walkouts, tears, lies – you know, the normal life of an agency – a slightly bolder idea emerged, as After Eight Thin Mints (Figure 3.5).

Figure 3.5   After Eight

The theory was that this particular product could be very exclusive, rather expensive, for a limited number of very classy customers. Rowntrees were hardly very happy with this suggestion, because all their skills and distribution were in mass-market goods. But in the end they accepted this limitation, and the mints were wrapped up in little envelopes for elegance and daintiness, to appeal to these classy customers. The first press advertisement that ran in 1962 was headlined: "'Every woman loves temptation. That's the secret of After Eight' says Mrs Roy Boulting" (wife of the chic film producer).

One hypothesis was that this brand could be a range of products: a bar of chocolate, chocolate assortments and thin mints. That hypothesis turned out to be wrong, because the first two failed almost immediately. Another hypothesis was that since this was an extremely exclusive brand, we should only use very upmarket press: the first advertisement, in fact appeared in the high fashion magazine *Vogue*. Wrong again. The third thing that was wrong was the sales projection; and that actually turned out to be better for the mints than anyone expected. So the agency said "Why not try out TV in an area?" and the client said "This is one of your tricks to get the appropriation up. Let's have none of it. Anyhow," he said, as a second line of defence, "it's ridiculous to try to put a minority upper class product on a mass-market working-class medium like television." So the agency went away and sulked for a bit and tried going round behind his back to his boss and so on. Eventually a television treatment emerged, or the eighth television treatment emerged, and was taken along to the client. It was absolutely way over the top for a popular medium, using extremely classy settings, because, of course, this was a high-class product.

So there were some group discussions to try to test this extreme creative treatment. To a person, the people in the group's discussions said about the test commercial "Silly! It's just silly!" They have continued to say that ever since. But it was a bold hypothesis, and, after the usual arguments and tears, the whole thing actually went on the air in a small test area.

The first commercial was of a dinner party, set on a terrace of a clearly exclusive house. The guests were all in evening dress, beautiful people of the most overpoweringly aristocratic class, animatedly impressing each other, amid the shimmering of Georgian silver and cut glass. The perfection of their butler-studded meal was only brought to its final fruition by the After Eight Thin Mints – "unashamed luxury". And this, with variations, was the basis of all television for After Eight for the following 20 years.

Today, that brand is a very successful mass-market line – considerably more people buy After Eight than buy any other boxed chocolate. The social class of the core of its market, the most frequent buyers, is exactly the same as that of all people who buy boxed chocolates. It didn't turn out, after all, to be an exclusive brand, but it did turn out to be an extremely profitable brand. And that is because it was designed to appeal to a *feeling* for the associations of exclusivity in a wide range of people.

So you can see that this brand was produced by a fair amount of muddle, a great deal of anarchy, a great deal of luck. Most of the hypotheses on which we were working were wrong, but there was also a certain degree of vision, of boldness about it all; there was a great deal of making mistakes and learning from them. In other words, it was not too different from the processes of the New Science. And in general I think the New Science usually does work in new product development.

It seems to me, too, that advertising has progressed in very much the same sort of way. When mass advertising started in the UK in the late nineteenth century, it was based very much on an intuitive approach – and often that intuitive approach was very inspired. Then, in came market research and with it management science. But I think that all too often in the UK it was the Old Science – the step-by-step inductive approach. You can tell this by looking at the sort of models that people have of how advertising works. Let me just go into two of them, because I think they have been particularly pervasive, certainly in the Western world.

The first one is Rosser Reeves' Unique Selling Proposition. The USP, as interpreted by Rosser Reeves' followers, has all too often been about knocking prepared phrases into people's brains. What it seems to say is: get the bits right, get this wedge of fact right, and then hit it into people's heads – and if you fail, hit it harder, hit it more often, or get a bigger hammer. Now this all seems a lovely, safe, careful, logical approach, but it fails because it is treating the receiver's mind as an inert, passive receptacle. Theories based on the empty mind are opposed to the work of all philosophers since Aristotle, all psychologists, all communications researchers – and common sense, which is perhaps better still. The consumer's mind is simply *not* a passive receptacle into which one can hit prepared phrases.

A second very pervasive model, derived in my view from the Old Science, is based on re-search methods – those of Daniel Starch particularly and our old friends AIDA and DAGMAR. The whole thing is based on a step-by-step approach. The advertising pushes the consumer from ignorance, through recognition to awareness, comprehension and (with mounting excite-ment) conviction and then... action! – she buys the brand. Now when you start looking at this in detail, there are some snags which arise. For instance, if you buy, are you allowed to stay on the top step or have you got to go down to the bottom and start all over again? Are you allowed to go up two steps at a time? Can you miss out recognition and comprehension, or is that cheating? If it's a competitive market, where you buy lots of brands, are you on lots of different steps for different brands – which may be awkward anatomically as well as psychologically? Most of all, I think the snag is that this whole model is based on the idea of advertising working by rational argument, logic, conviction.

But if you think of all the big decisions and issues in your lives – religion, sex, marriage, children, houses, education, politics, prejudice, lifestyle, patriotism – all these are spurred mainly by emotional feelings. Emotion is much the largest element in making those decisions, and I can't for the life of me see why, if all the important decisions are based on emotion, one should suddenly go all rational about soap powder. The real problem is that all these old models of advertising are still the Old Science. They are looking for a logical, deductive system for how advertising works. They are all about what ought to go into ads, about what ads do to people. I think the New Science started coming to advertising when we started to realize that this was starting at the wrong end. The planning should start not with what ads do to people, but with what people do with ads. Not what goes in, but what people get out. How they might respond. In other words, Popper's trial solution. I think that this was a very fundamental change. I find it very sad (and I've heard it at this conference) that still so much of the language of discussions about advertising, particularly in the USA, is based on the Old Science. I can't help feeling that it is what lies behind all those commercials that treat me as if I were a mentally defective three-year-old.

So many of the discussions are about those sterile, arid classifications of types of commercials (like slice-of-life, reason-why, product demonstration and so on) and rules about what should go into advertisements. The discussions ought to be about people, their motivations and their responses. We've found it, ourselves, very helpful over the years to concentrate on people's responses. People have different sorts of responses to anything – to a brand, to an idea, to an advertisement – in different combinations and in different proportions for different situations. You can have responses from the senses; you can respond to appeals of taste, of aesthetics, of design. Then there are rational and logical responses, to appeals of function, performance, content and price; they play a part in almost any choice. But I think the most important sorts of responses to any form of communication are probably the emotional responses, to appeals of style, personality and associations.

Gradually the best marketing companies have, I think, moved from the Old Science towards the New Science, but I have to say that the progress has not always been fast or universal. Let me give you an example from the washing powder market in the UK.

In recent years Persil commercials have been a branch of high-class showbiz. They have eminently hummable popular music of the sort that gets into the charts, well-filmed quick-cut shots of people and families enjoying themselves in a wide variety of activities, from getting up in the morning to pole-vaulting. There is an air of brightness, with vivid colours; life is energetic and pursued with zeal. Persil and its use in washing machines are an element in this life: not its central purpose. The commercials are all about getting housewives to respond to Persil with pleasure, like greeting an old friend.

By contrast, Procter and Gamble stick to "classic" washing powder advertising formulae. There tends to be a spokesman, who tells one rather loudly about the benefits of the brand. For some reason, he often seems to repeat himself, feeling that we may not be bright enough to get the point the first time; or there are those amazing stilted conversations between two ladies in a kitchen, in which one persuades the other to change her brand by tearing shirts in half. The commercials are all about feeding information into housewives and they seem to assume that washing clothes is the abiding passion of the female population.

You may possibly detect a modicum of bias in me. To avoid any possible suspicion, let me quote a little bit from some experimental research about the effects of such commercials on people. We showed housewives one commercial for Lever's Persil Automatic and one for P & G's Ariel, each of the sort that I have described. And to get under the skin a little bit, we asked people: "What would the maker of those commercials be like?" The sort of thing they said about the maker of Ariel was:

1. "Staid, probably thinks of women as humdrum, kitchen-sink women."
2. "He just cons them."
3. "He just thinks that this is a soap which will dissolve the grease, and just works from there."

In other words, a male chauvinist who's thinking of him, not us. When it came to asking about the maker of Persil they said things like:

1. "Has a much better outlook on women as being equals rather than tied to the kitchen sink, and I like that idea."
2. "I got a feeling it could be a woman who made it." That's high praise.
3. "They've realized at long last that not every woman works in that way of comparing what results she's getting."

In other words, he, or possibly she, is one of us. I can't help feeling that's a slightly healthier response to get and that it has played some part in the relatively greater success in the market place of Persil Automatic. The results are very much related to the difference between an input philosophy – which I think Procter and Gamble still impose on their agencies – and a response philosophy.

The full implications of Popper's invention process seem to me to be very significant indeed for advertising. Three points: I think, first of all, it makes it clear that ideas simply cannot come directly from facts. You can't bludgeon creative people into ideas by giving them ever-tighter and more logical briefs. And if creative people, at times, seem irresponsible and anarchic, maybe that's because they're more scientific than you are.

Secondly, you have to start with the solution – you have to start with the idea, and then be bold and meticulous in trying it out, especially in the market place. I think we shouldn't try to deceive ourselves into thinking that so-called pre-testing and many of these intermediate measures can actually help us very much. The important thing is to be experimental and to hope to learn from our attempts to disprove.

And the third point, of course, is that the whole process of advertising is not a safe, cautious, step-by-step build-up, because that would inevitably lead to me-too advertising for me-too brands.

I think the whole idea of the New Science has been very liberating indeed – liberating, for instance, about setting creative strategies. Creative strategies tended in the past to be in terms of 198 things which had to go into the ad. Now they can be set as a testable hypothesis about the sort of responses that might work and that we might want to get. For instance, one might want to get this type of response: "Great, I'll buy that right now!" The hypothesis here, of course, is that the ad can be a direct stimulus to purchase. You can see that in direct response advertising, which is very much the sort of advertising that Claude Hopkins was writing about and David Ogilvy was talking about. All the rules that have been established by experiment over the years make sense in this sort of advertising. It's very easy to see how to set up an experiment and how to test it. You put a keyed coupon into the ad, then you can do a split run or you can try different ads at different times or in different areas. The whole idea of the experimental feedback process is very obvious in direct response advertising.

Or, you might be looking for responses rather more like: "What a good idea!" or "That's just the thing for me." The hypothesis here is that advertising doesn't work and can't work absolutely directly for this brand. This is more particularly the response we are trying to get to ads for new brands; for instance, the response the early Walkman ads were trying to get. It's asking people to relate the brand to their own lives, their own needs, their own desires. The test is again pretty obvious. Indeed, how to measure advertising and its effect is not terribly hard if you work out in advance what sort of response you are trying to get, because the basic question then is: Are we getting that response? You start by asking: When they saw the ad, did people in fact relate it to their way of life? Did they say, or think, "Oh, look, what a good idea?" Then of course the real test is trying it out in the market place. The question then is: Did enough people think "What a good idea" strongly enough to buy it?

Another sort of response you might be trying to get is "Mmm, yes, that's just what it's like." The hypothesis here might be: you have an old, familiar brand which everyone has tried and bought again and again. There's nothing new to learn about it. There's no startling discovery, no new need to meet, its simply reinforcing the pleasures that people got from using the brand the last time. Getting them, as it were, to lick their lips in anticipation – adding the values to the brand. This is obviously much harder to test. Maybe you have to test it in the market place by how much the brand really is valued, how much people are prepared to pay for it, how much (if you like) the demand curve has been pushed to the right by the advertising. And it struck me, thinking about yesterday's Walkman presentation: Walkman are selling in the UK at the moment for £64, which is about $28\frac{1}{2}$ thousand Yen, which is rather less than the "crazy" chairman suggested. It may well be that the proper advertising strategy for Sony in the UK is now not to get a "What a good idea" response, but an "I'm right to buy/respect Sony" response. In other words, they should be aiming not to demonstrate the benefits of the Walkman, but to reinforce the quality values of the Sony company. Otherwise, they will be forced by cheaper competition to reduce their prices and margins; they could end up successful but broke.

I think, above all, the New Science liberates and encourages us to do bold and original creative work and not play safe: the fact is that only brands that are perceived as original and different will survive in a competitive market place.

For instance, when some years back all the US cars were producing ads with ever more frantic competitive boasting, DDB were right, I think, to produce their famous ad for Volkswagen – a huge area of empty space with that curious shape crouching in the corner and the simple headline: "Think small." That brand, in one advertisement like that, immediately becomes totally original, totally distinctive. It's obviously based on the thing itself – on what it offers, but what an original way, in that circumstance, of showing the car.

In the UK, when all beers appeared to have the same taste and all the commercials appeared to be based on manly, good-hearted, young (but not too young), loud, noisy (but good-humoured) people in pubs talking to each other in a jovial way, Collett, Dickinson, Pearce produced a very strange commercial for Heineken. The camera panned along a row of morose-looking policemen. They were without socks and shoes, and their trousers were rolled up to the knee. The story was simple: these policemen had lost the use of their feet through lack of foot refreshment. A simple test – giving them a glass of Heineken – demonstrated that they could be given back the use of their toes and that "Heineken refreshes the parts that other beers cannot reach". With one bound, Heineken was free: free from the restraints of beer advertising conventions. Heineken went on tasting like all the other beers, but it immediately was set apart from all the others.

I think those two brands have gained enormously from the sheer invention of those ads, and it paid off at the till.

Let me give you, finally, a quick glimpse of the whole system at work, based, I think, on the New Science. And that is for a brand of toilet paper called Andrex. Andrex had, as so often

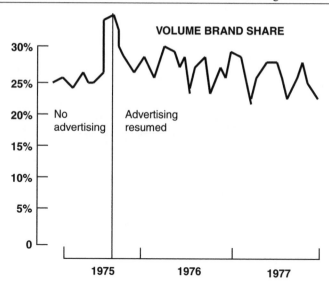

Figure 3.6   Andrex (volume)
Advertising/No advertising experiment

happens, an accidental experiment. In 1975 – for various reasons which are too boring to go into – it had no advertising for a whole year and then that situation came to an end and it could start advertising again. The marketing hypothesis then was: if we have a minor product improvement and new advertising we can add value to that brand, we can make it seem to be worth paying its full price for and thus rebuild our profits. The hypothesis for the advertising was, we're trying to get this sort of response: "I was righter than I thought to buy Andrex." The hypothesis in fact was that advertising would reinforce old-established but temporarily forgotten values in people's minds. It wasn't a matter of introducing the product improvement in a "New, Now, At Last, Three Ways Better" type of advertisement but simply aimed quietly to congratulate buyers for going on buying the best brand that there was. With this hypothesis as the strategy, the experiment, the commercial was based on using a puppy as a symbol of the softness, strength and sheer "niceness" of the brand.

Now, I don't think that any amount of pre-testing could have told us the payoff for using that commercial. The feedback, of course, comes in the market place, and Figure 3.6 shows the chart of volume brand shares when there was no advertising and when advertising started up again.

You can see that there was virtually no change in volume brand share when the advertising resumed. However, there was a marked change in relative price: in other words, the price that people were prepared to pay for this brand compared with other brands in the market.

There was less need for price-cutting for Andrex in order to retain its volume share. And by doing market modelling, using regression analysis, it was possible to build a model of advertising and at various prices (Figure 3.7).

Thus it was possible to work out an estimate of return on investment for that advertising, which, as it happened, for this brand, at this time, in those circumstances, worked out to be very profitable. And so the brand now went on to the next stage of the cycle, to new experiments. For Andrex it was a drip versus burst media experiment and experiments using different advertising

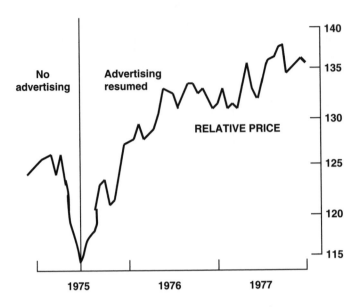

Figure 3.7   Andrex (price)
Advertising/No advertising experiment

weights. The aim has always been to try to learn something, to put forward new hypotheses which might be proved wrong or might fortunately not be proved wrong.

So where do we stand on the main question of Art versus Science? First, it seems to me clear that economic growth does need innovation and this means that it has to be based on the New Science. Secondly, I can't see that there is the slightest degree of conflict between Art and Science. As Bryan Magee wrote in his book about Popper:

> If Popper is right, there are not two cultures but one. The scientist and the artist, far from being engaged in opposed or incompatible activities, are both trying to extend our understanding of experience by the use of creative imagination subjected to critical control.

Not a bad line for us – creative imagination subjected to critical control.

The Market's Evolved, Why Hasn't Planning?

By Merry Baskin, Brand Planning Consultant, Baskin Shark Ltd

An introduction to:

4.1 Strategic Development of Brands

What's in a Name?

Quick, what's the difference between a "neologism" and an "aphorism" – terms that have recently featured in planner blogs?[1]

Although he would probably have despised the idea of his thinking being reduced to an '–ism', the man who helped to invent account planning (both the name and the discipline) gave us plenty of both, and his anniversary speech offers up at least three memorable and noteworthy examples.

The paper you are about to read, therefore, has many merits: historical context, planning lore, witty apothegms and visionary wisdom – a King classic in fact. For one thing, it lays to rest the mythology surrounding the choice of title for our discipline – one of the most obfuscating and unhelpful ones ever invented. For the record:

> Tony Stead thought of the name "Account Planner". We started by not knowing what on earth to call it. We thought of "Brand Planner" and we used that as a code name for quite a while. Then people said that "brand" suggests that we were only involved in small packaged things[2] so Tony said "Why don't you call them Account Planners?" And that was that. That was at a meeting of one of our Away Days in July '68. There was a lot of discussion going on and by the time it had emerged we had a department of 23 people. It was very easy to cast because it was taking people from the Marketing Department and a very few key people from the Media Department. Some of the Reps[3] felt a bit threatened by the new Department, but Reps always feel threatened, it's part of their job description. We had a pretty bad first six months with Planners – who are inclined to gloom at the best of times – feeling that it was all a disaster. But it picked up . . . Planning seems to have lasted rather well.
>
> (Stephen King interview, *Fifty in 40, the unofficial history of JWT London*, Tom Rayfield, December 1996)

Delivered with characteristic understatement, planning has indeed lasted rather well, in spite of its unhelpful name. All the fledgling departments struggling to justify their agencies' investment in account planners should take heart.

---

[1] A neologism is the introduction or use of new words or new senses of existing words; an aphorism is a terse saying embodying a general truth, or astute observation.

[2] Hard to imagine now, but back in the 1960's the word "brand" only applied to fmcg. Banks and hotels and shops were all considered services, not brands.

[3] What JWT used to call their account handlers: account representatives.

Some Background

> *I hope that the coming anniversary of account planning isn't going to mean another orgy of "who first started it?" articles. There wasn't an It, it's impossible to tell and it's about the least interesting element of the whole thing.*
>
> E-mail from Stephen King to Jeremy Bullmore in 1998

Back in July 1988, there were 250 (pretty much the entire APG membership in those days) planners who flocked to hear Stephen King speak at this conference convened to celebrate two decades of planning and the first decade of the APG. The list of speakers and the APG organizing committee reads like a list of the UK Planning's Hall of Fame so it's a shame that more of the "Whither Planning?" proceedings have not survived.

It was at this conference that Stephen's famous (but faintly pejorative) continuum for defining different planning styles was first described, with "Grand Strategists" (JWT) at one end and "Advert Tweakers" (Stanley Pollitt's BMP) at the other. If you have never asked yourself which end you (or your planner) lean towards, now might be a good time.

I was very much in the camp of the "Advert Tweakers" for about seven years, following US agency Chiat/Day's wholesale importation of the BMP model of planner as creative qualitative researcher. I subsequently returned to the UK, joined J. Walter Thompson for nine years and became, if not a "grand" strategist, at least more a brand strategist, working on brands the agency had been building for decades, getting involved in portfolio management, NPD, as well as creative communication ideas midwifery. Not for nothing has the Andrex puppy been running around for nearly 30 years at JWT's behest. Since I've worked and trained as a planner from both perspectives, I particularly wanted to comment on this speech.

A Few Observations on What you are About to Read

The market's evolved – why hasn't planning?

Stephen King was a fine futurologist (although he would also have scoffed at that word). A lot of the developments barely perceptible in 1988 have come to pass: the rise of the importance of the brand on the balance sheet; the pressures on marketing to deliver organic growth; the spread of the Brand Idea beyond fmcg; increased consumer power; technological leapfrogging; and brand globalization.

Stephen saw how these developments represented wonderful opportunities for strategic thinkers – provided they were able to be a lot more insightful and analytical than merely being the "consumer representative" (one of the weaker definitions of the planner's role). He paints a very enticing role for a planner in today's communications environment: to help to generate organic growth for our clients via brand building and product/service innovation rather than simply providing consumer research fodder for the agency's creative department.

Yet, 20 years on, planning in advertising agencies hasn't really changed that much. Sadly, it has, if anything, gone down the food chain rather than up. The reasons for this are not immediately obvious. Despite the never-ending demand for senior planners in communications agencies worldwide, despite the high salaries even inexperienced ones can command, despite the clamour for decent training, and despite the challenges represented by the changes listed earlier, planning is still generally considered to be an expensive and difficult to justify overhead in some places. (There is certain circularity here – at the time of this speech, McCann Erickson

London had just famously disbanded its entire planning department; declaring them all "dead from the neck up". They subsequently changed their minds.)

Is it the fault of the ad agencies or their marketing clients?

Is it because planning's future has always been too intrinsically linked to the traditional ad agency structure, which has itself fundamentally failed to evolve? Since the media department splintered off, too many ad agencies have failed to adapt to the new media scene and have been reduced to merely making the pictures and posting them.

Is it down to the advertising industry's own inherent barriers and problems – self absorption, creative obsession, inability to evolve its business model, backing executional short termism over brand-building idea-based strategies and integrated campaigns?

Or is it due to the squeezing of margins, thanks to the heavy hand of the client's procurement manager or the network's chief accountant?

Whichever way, this decreasing status of the advertising agency in general has resulted in a great deal of strategic thinking and other added value services being given away free; in planners being spread too thin over too many accounts to really dig deep into their brand's development *and* have the time to become the eclectic generalists they need to be.

Concern about the demise of strategic input at the top and the diminishing role of the planner has rumbled on for some time now. The irony is that, in these much more value conscious times, it should be (one of) the planner's job(s) to justify the potential impact and effectiveness of the agency's work to an increasingly activist CFO or purchasing consultant. Planners should be more valuable, not less.

So What's the Solution?

As marketing clients tend to work with more and more specialist communications agencies across a plethora of different media formats but ultimately reach similar audiences, the skills of the planner should be being applied to weaving the teams together, breaking down the silos and egos, spotting opportunities, ferreting out insights and nurturing business building ideas into multi-faceted, full blown existence.

Stephen talked about the possible evolution of the name Brand Planner to Brand Designer (also suggested in the last chapter in this book, *Brand Building in the 1990's*). The big question now has to be: Who is designing the brand at an organizational level? As one of the key inventors of Mr. Kipling's cakes for Rank Hovis McDougal (RHM), Stephen had already demonstrated what a "Brand Designer" actually does.

Surely this role for planners, devised and practised by Stephen himself, is an idea whose time has come.

Planning is (literally) about thinking ahead, moving things forward, embracing change. Good planners are also natural facilitators, intuitive and empathetic, rigorous and disciplined, experienced in researching, evolving and gauging ideas (sometimes even creating them). For some reason, however, too many agency planners seem to be static – some even going backwards.

Having set up the function for us, in this paper Stephen was challenging us to build on his original idea by "adapting to the changing environment". This meant shaping and building the brands we are responsible for within a much wider context. We owe it to him, and the career that he generously gave us, to crack on and do just that. If necessary, doing so without waiting for the advertising agencies to catch up. Maybe even switching sides and going client side. Or, heaven forbid, going freelance and doing it with everyone.

Things to do Next

Consider your role re-imagined as a brand planner – or even a brand designer – as defined by Stephen. What would you stop doing? What would you need to start doing differently? Do you have the required craft skills and diversity of general experience? (If not, start acquiring some.)

Think more about your clients' business and the role played by (any or all) communications ideas in building it. Think less about how extrinsically creative and award-winning your agency's creative output might be. How can you genuinely contribute to organic growth by helping to grow your brand(s)? Learn to talk to the CFO without mumbling. Explain value to the Procurement Officer – he or she will understand.

Those of you who are running group discussions on creative work/doing vox pops/hanging out in malls and chat rooms/running quick/dirty/cheap internet surveys all the time; stop it. By all means keep in regular contact with your target audiences – talk to them, listen, observe. But don't make "doing consumer research" your core skill or primary activity. Think, read, write, debate, persuade the others as well.

Further Reading

Every planner should have a decent library/list of favourite websites/hoard of other people's papers to refer to or crib from.

To make things really simple, there's a suggested reading list for planners on http://plannersphere.pbwiki.com/Books%20for%20Planners, the blog run by former APG Chair Russell Davies.

But also look out for books or papers by any of the following: Jeremy Bullmore, Wendy Gordon, Judie Lannon, Mark Earls, Leslie Butterfield, Simon Anholt, Professor Andrew Ehrenberg, Patrick Barwise, Paul Feldwick, Robert Heath. Then make up your own mind.

Any (or all) of the IPA Advertising Works volumes of effectiveness case histories.

Visit www.apg.org.uk – a site run by planners for planners – full of smart and savvy thinking and planning tips and techniques. Plus APG publications such as:

- *How to Plan Advertising*, 2nd edition, Cassell, 1997
- *APG Creative Planning Awards 1997–2005* – inspiring and informative volumes of winning creative strategy case histories.
- *The Pollitt Papers*, edited by Paul Feldwick, contains Stanley's other two papers.

Plus: A downloadable pdf of Alan Hedges' *Testing to Destruction*.

4.1

Strategic Development of Brands*

By Stephen King

As this year's Event celebrates, Account Planning has just had its twentieth birthday. The name was finally agreed at a meeting at the Londonderry House Hotel on 15 July 1968. We had argued a good deal about the title and very nearly decided to call ourselves Brand Planners. In a sense, what I'll be talking about today is wondering whether we got it right.

From the very start there were two rather different approaches to the job, and the range has widened since then. It's useful to think of account planners as positioned on this scale shown in Figure 4.1.

At one extreme, there are the "grand strategists", who are intellectual, aim to see the big picture, are a little bit above the fray, and almost economists. At the other are the "advert tweakers", who peer myopically at advertisements, conduct group discussions, justify creative work to sceptical clients, and are almost qualitative researchers. Most agencies lie somewhere in the middle, veering around as agencies do. Of the founders of account planning, BMP started from a research department and so tended to be right of centre; JWT started from a marketing department, and so tended to be left of centre. You can still see the tendencies in their entries to the IPA Advertising Effectiveness Awards. BMP's are rattling good yarns, but sometimes a teeny bit cursory on the statistics; JWT's are inexorably argued, but sometimes a touch short on fun. They both win a lot of awards, but BMP is apt to charm the judges into acquiescence while JWT forces them into submission.

All the many changes in marketing over the past 20 years have pushed account planners one way or the other on this scale. On the whole the external forces of clients' needs have moved them towards the strategic end and the internal changes in the advertising business to the tweaking end.

First, of the external changes, the squeeze of the marketing department from the glories of the 1960s – the disillusion with the inflated promises of "Management Science" (success untouched by human imagination), the ratchet effect of retailer pressures, the 1970s crisis in branding, the decimation of budgets and staff. The marketing department turned out to need outside strategic and brand-building help after all.

Secondly, the new converts to marketing. In 1970, 53% of press and television advertising expenditure went on the traditional repeat-purchase goods; by 1987 it was down to 39%. The new big spenders – corporations, financial services, government departments, cars, durables and leisure goods companies – tended to have come rather late to marketing and often didn't really think of themselves as brands. Promotions attracted them because of the effect on volume

*Speech at the 20th Anniversary of the founding of Account Planning. APG One Day Event, July 1988. Reproduced with permission.

Figure 4.1

sales. This was a great opportunity for account planners to demonstrate to these converts the values of strategic branding in building margins.

Thirdly, technological leapfrog. When the new product that you've slaved for two years to develop is copied and undercut in the marketplace in two months and outdated from Taiwan in six, how do you recover your development costs? When the sheer speed of change overwhelms, how does the now under-staffed marketing department cope? The only answer is added values through strategic branding; and, again, there's a need for outside strategic help and advice.

Fourthly, retailers discovered branding. Nearly all the most exciting strategic branding ideas in the 1980s have come from them. Led by Habitat, Laura Ashley, The Body Shop, Next, etc.; now increasingly followed by bigger retailers – M&S Foods, for instance, or Sainsbury's Homebase or the new plans for Safeway. If manufacturers' brands were to flourish in this context, no amount of tweaking would be enough. Account planners, to be really useful to clients, had to offer something at the strategic end of the scale.

Fifthly, consumers themselves, as they moved from the new individualism of the 1970s to the Designer Everything of the 1980s. What people came to want, in almost everything, was both variety and style. A company like Hi-Tec meets this by making some 200 different styles of shoe – a manufacturing triumph but a bit of a problem for marketing and distribution. A clear need for the account planner's classic role of strategic simplifier.

But if external changes were drawing planners to the left, two changes within the advertising business were pulling them to the right, to a much more exclusive concern with advertisements. The first was the recognition that, today, consumers know about and willingly participate in the game of marketing. They had come to value a company for the style of its advertising, not just the contents or the arguments. The Benson & Hedges Gold ads became collectors' pieces not just for advertising people but for everyone. Account planners became much more involved in the fine tuning of creative execution. They ran group discussions, listened to the nuances of consumers' responses to rough ads and then justified what was often "difficult" advertising to the clients. (Some of the clients were very keen on creativity as long as it didn't contain anything new or disturbing.)

Then the change in structure of agencies built on this newly respectable creativity. Suddenly, led by Saatchi, agencies moved from being professional partnerships to being businesses in their own right. Competition between them increased. Priorities, time frames and values changed somewhat; the advertising business started to look inwards a lot more. The new businesslike vigour stimulated many new agencies, who came in waves called Beagle, Bargle, D'Annunzio, Twigg and Privet. Most of them were based on creative people, and their high creative standards set the agenda for all agencies. While the resulting British advertising is widely admired, there is a danger lurking of an inward-looking circularity – a belief that great ads are ads thought great by great advertising people. (One is disturbingly reminded of the analogy of architects, who tend to believe that great architecture is architecture that is thought to be great by great architects – and to hell with the people who have to live in their buildings.) Again, account planners moved to the right on the scale, because they were increasingly judged by their success in contributing to and selling the most creative campaigns.

It seems to me that in the 1990s all these marketing pressures are going to continue, the external ones pulling planners to the left and the internal ones pulling them to the right. But I think there are two further issues that broaden the question to one of the whole future of communication services.

By far the most important change of the last 10 years has been the "new radical economics". The British do genuinely seem to have turned away from making charming apologies for industrial failure and moved towards a zeal for success. There is a sort of national recognition that competition is here to stay and that it's anyhow quite stimulating. It's hard to see any political party today wishing to lead us back to non-competitive economic fudge.

The first part of the process has gone quite well; there undoubtedly has been a big improvement in manufacturing efficiency. But of course you can play that trick only once. You can move from having 11 factories working at 30% capacity to four factories working at 83% capacity, just once. It's absolutely necessary to do it, to keep improving efficiency, to be a low-cost producer, but it's not sufficient; it's merely the entry fee.

The harder part of the economic miracle is yet to come, but there are some signs that the issues are being recognized. There seems to be a dawning acceptance that long-term profits and success – even survival – for companies, whether they are manufacturers or services or institutions, will depend on the *depth and quality of their brands*. That is, on having something to offer that is "better and different"; that has a unique combination of physical, functional and stylistic values; and that has a clear brand personality, expressed in every aspect of performance and communications.

It's still early days: the word "brand" is still associated mainly with packaged groceries. But there are signs of hope. In the dark recesses of the human mind, in the city and among accountants, it is becoming apparent that the traditional balance sheet is giving a very partial view of a company's worth. Most dramatically, Rowntree's 1987 accounts gave the group's gross tangible assets (land, buildings, plant and machinery before depreciation) as about £700 million. Even if one makes every possible allowance for current assets and for the traditional conservatism of such calculations, the real value of the company as a going concern (that is, what the highest bidder in a competitive situation was prepared to pay for it) was more than twice as much. The brands which made up over half the value of the company did not appear in the balance sheet at all. To more and more people it is beginning to seem ludicrous to refer to Kit Kat and Black Magic as intangible or to suggest that around £1.5 billion of Rowntree's value is "goodwill" – as if the company's success came from a vague benevolence on the part of the public, rather than from a lot of investment in the invention of brands and a lot of imaginative work by many people over many years.

All of us in marketing and advertising need to do more to widen this little chink in the minds of the financial establishment and to evangelize the cause of brands and the constant inventiveness that they need. But we will have to do it more strategically than we have in the past. In the 1970s all too often the praise and prizes have gone to minor tweakings – countless new Identikit instant custards or frozen pizzas. The genuine strategic brand building is less instant and maybe less dramatic, but it is a lot more comprehensive and lasts a lot longer. Take, for instance, the building of Mr Kipling Cakes. The development process itself took about two years, from an idea that germinated five years before that. The strategic brand design included examining the company's strengths and weaknesses, modifying corporate strategy, the key decision to concentrate on small cakes, analysis of trends in production machinery and processes, questions of bakery numbers and location, the choice of the range, naming, packaging, pricing strategy, advertising, merchandising materials, leaflets, van livery, salesmen's uniforms and all the consumer research that helped the decisions.

Outside packaged goods markets, the Japanese companies stand out for their strategic brand design – in cameras, cars, copiers and electronic equipment. When one reflects that within living memory Japanese goods used to have a reputation for being cheap and shoddy, it is amazing that their strategy of imagination, innovation, high quality and branding is not yet today's received wisdom in all manufacturing and services companies.

Another remarkable transformation has been that of Ford. At the end of the 1970s Ford cars still tended to be the traditional box with additions, most of which you had to pay extra for. By the late 1970s they have real brand designs, with aerodynamic shapes and the whole brand thought through. Strategic brand design seems to have changed the whole face and success of the company.

The logical outcome of the new radical economics is a need, in all types of company, for strategic imagination on the grand scale, building up the long-lasting range of added values that makes up any brand. A splendid opportunity for the right sort of outside adviser.

The second major issue of the 1990s is the increasing complexity of marketing. There will be more services, always harder to standardize and control. The cosy demarcations are going within retailers and financial services. Technology will go on changing, maybe even faster. Consumers will demand more variety and more designer everything. Retailers will move more and more into branding. There will be more international marketing, but more account taken of regional and tribal styles. There will be more need to communicate beyond consumers – to retailers, employees, institutions, pressure groups, bureaucrats and governments. Media will be increasingly fragmented, with more opportunities for one-to-one interactive marketing.

With all this complexity it will get harder to coordinate everything and make sure that a company speaks with one voice, and that all aspects of its brands add up to consistent and unique brand personalities.

But it goes further than mere coordination. Consistency will not be enough. Brands will have to be constantly inventive in all aspects of their design and communications. "New product development" won't be an optional extra, hived off to junior specialists: it will be the essence of any successful business and a prime responsibility of the chief executive. One of the most important and demanding questions that he will face is simply how to manage innovation and imagination.

In the 1970s a company's brand building and communications may involve using up to 10 specialist skills provided by different outside services (not to mention the complexities of doing it in many different cultures and languages). These are almost bound to come from *different* companies, simply because the people with the best talents will always want to work in quite small units of like-minded specialists; only the second-rate will be willing to be collectivized under one roof.

Managing the highest level of imagination is going to require a radical change in many company cultures – a point spelled out in detail in the recent NEDO booklet *Design for Corporate Culture*. But I think it goes well beyond culture – it's a matter of organization too.

At the moment, it's quite likely that these brand-building services are paid for out of half-a-dozen budgets run by half-a-dozen (competing) managers. Many of the decisions which affect brands are being made too low down the organization, with the people making them too isolated from each other. The traditional hierarchical family-tree organization, with its well-ordered layers and functional separations, seems wholly unsuitable for imaginative brand building.

Strategic brand design needs a management structure which is small, flexible and interactive. It must involve, in an overlapping way, the key skills of production/R&D and marketing/communication and general management/finance. The Japanese management systems seem nearer to this sort of permanent working group. Equally the retailers who have got their strategic brand design right tend to have had one dynamic leader who has embodied these skills – like Terence Conran or George Davies or Anita Roddick. Larger companies have simply got to develop a group leadership that acts as if it were one person obsessed with the brand. Maybe the time has come too to have someone within this top management group with the specific role of Brand Designer – using the word "design" in its broadest sense.

If (maybe, when) companies do have their strategic brand designers, who are they going to talk to outside? They could talk separately to their specialists – industrial designers, advertising agency, PR company, pack designers, direct mail people, exhibition people, sponsorship people, market researchers and so on. Or, because they're likely to need a second opinion who talks their own language, they could talk first to just one outside specialist in brand design – someone one might call a *brand planner.*

A key question is where such brand planners are going to be working. Agency account planners will increasingly face a dilemma. They are crucially important to well-directed advertising, but the more the internal pressures of the business push them to the tweaking end of the scale, the less credibility they'll have for the broader brand-designing job. Much the same is true for planners in packaging, new product development or corporate consultancies, while the traditional management consultants have never been too expert in the communications side of branding.

I suspect that it will be a different sort of organization from any of these. Account planning skills are certainly a good basis for the new brand planners, but I think they're more likely to be working in specialist groups of their own, linked to the growing marketing and communication services groups. Wherever they are, I'm sure that the job could be one of the most attractive opportunities of the 1990s.

5
Learning and Improvement, Not Proof and Magic Solutions

By William Eccleshare, Chairman and Chief Executive, BBDO Europe

An introduction to:

5.1 Improving Advertising Decisions

Stephen was that rarest of combinations – a great intellect and a great simplifier. Never was this more clearly expressed than in the Planning Cycle which so many JWT people used – and still use – as the basic framework for their thinking. As explained in this article, the Cycle forces its user to recognize that we are engaged in a continual process, not a one-off exercise. That in itself is a basic lesson that is so frequently ignored in a world where instant ROI has become the mantra for the increasingly beleaguered Marketing Director or CMO. ("Chief Marketing Officer". How Stephen would have enjoyed that particular linguistic confection!)

What stands out in this nearly 30-year-old article is Stephen's lucid prose. Brilliantly direct, never polysyllabic if a plain word could be found, and always straight to the point. Stephen's resistance to jargon – even when writing, as here, in an erudite publication such as *Admap* – is palpable. His facility with words makes him a joy to read, and re-read: "The first straw contributes as much as the last to the breakage of the camel." Marvellous.

But beyond the prose one is struck by the absolute and continuing relevance of the thinking. The core message here is that a planner's job is never done: The planning process is "one of learning and improvement, not of proof and magic solutions". If that was true in 1977 it is even more the case in 2007. So often we see clients and their agencies being guilty of using research to prove that they are right, rather than learning to make better decisions going forward. The use of research as an analytical tool, not a crutch or a stick with which to beat someone, was a message that Stephen was always at pains to emphasize.

The Problem is the Thinking not the Data

One is struck throughout this piece by how much rigour has seeped away from our business over time. Almost all the research (consumer and market data, not ad testing) cited here is quantitative and there is a strong underlying assumption that agency people will have access to and a good grasp of all the information necessary to reach a judgement.

Would that this were so. My first years in this business were marked by bi-monthly sessions in a windowless room in York, listening to Nielsen presentations and making detailed notes on sales of bagged, boiled-sugar self-lines in Tyne Tees. Recently I asked a marketing director why our people were no longer invited to such sessions. "No point," she said, "we never felt the data was being used and never saw any value back."

But the article clearly recognizes that lack of information is not the real problem we face. Stephen writes, "I suspect that our weakness ... is more often a failure to analyse the data we've got than failure to buy enough data." Manufacturers and their agencies have really failed to spot the true power of good analysis, and even now mighty retailers have spent many years drowning in store card data before learning how to use it effectively.

It seems to me that it is really only comparatively recently that the intelligent use of information has been properly identified as a source of real differentiation for marketers.

Although strong in its commitment to the proper use of quantitative research, the article is highly critical of "off-the-peg" "advertisement testing methods" going on to suggest, pithily, that "anyone thinking of using one should spend some money testing the tests". An over-reliance on black boxes, the Link Test and its close relatives has become a major issue for agencies and one to which we have conspicuously failed to respond intelligently. It seems from reading this that Stephen foresaw such dependence, and I know he spent much time in later years trying to help demystify and provide intelligent interpretation rather than the knee-jerk reactions we sometimes see from today's time-pressed managers.

Old Rules Still Ignored

This paper was written three years before the first IPA Effectiveness Awards and it's interesting how the quest for proof of our industry's worth has become a global phenomenon. Effies are now developing a currency almost as great as creative awards and that's clearly a very good thing indeed. Having been a judge a few years ago, however, I only wish that the writer of every submission had been made to read, and put into practice, much of what Stephen writes in this piece.

He writes of "the old rule about correlation not being causation" and refers to it being the root of most of our practical problems. It is indeed, and although it may be an "*old rule*" it is one that has clearly not been learned by generations since. So often one reads or hears agency people, of any discipline, blithely reporting that "our campaign resulted in a sales increase of 30%" without any real attempt to isolate the specific contribution or remove the impact of any other factors.

The increasing trend for beleaguered plc CEOs to point to their shiny new ad campaign as having helped their turnaround may be gratifying for our industry and certainly provides good copy for lazy journalists, but it falls far short of the rigorous standards laid out in "Improving advertising decisions".

All Decisions can be Improved, not just Advertising

The only real way in which this piece has dated is in its inevitable concentration on traditional advertising. One can't help feeling how much Stephen King would have enjoyed the challenges of evaluating the impact of digital and interactive media with their seductive "certainties" of click-thru rates and the almost total loss of brand valuation measures in so much of what is now being done in the name of efficiency testing.

It would be most un-King-like to speculate on how he might have responded to the challenges posed by evaluating the effectiveness of on-line brand communications. I suspect, however, that he would have been wary of over-reliance on spurious "facts" about efficacy and might well have flinched at the profligacy with numbers that has led to some of the more spectacular booms and busts of the internet era.

Improving our advertising decisions is something that all good practitioners try to do every day. Recognizing that we need to do so is the first stage, and understanding that there is a simple series of steps that can help us will get us a long way down the road. The Planning Cycle's five questions are as relevant today as they ever were and this article's exposition of the hard work needed to answer those questions properly is a much-needed reminder that while intuition is a wonderful thing, there's no substitute for serious analysis if we are to have a more than average chance of getting it right.

Some Suggestions to Sharpen Your Thinking

1. Read *Advertising Works*, the bi-annual collection of winning IPA Effectiveness papers. Start with the most recent and work your way back to the first volume from 1980. These papers give an invaluable insight into research methodology and planning excellence. They are truly essential reading.
2. Go out and observe your clients' customers in real situations. Spend time loitering in supermarkets, bank queues, car showrooms or airports. Find some real families, surround yourself with children and see how they consume media during a normal evening at home. Intelligent first-hand observation is worth hundreds of focus groups.

5.1

Improving Advertising Decisions*

By Stephen King

Starting off the Market Research Society seminar, "The Proof of Advertising Value", was a good excuse for calling for a return to basics, particularly as one of the seminar's objectives was to integrate the various "modes of evaluating advertising". It's probably time to return to basics anyhow. We've always had periodic offerings of magic solutions to the problems of measuring advertising effectiveness. They are nearly always stimulating and lead to progress, but we also have to remind ourselves periodically *why* the magic solution approach won't work. Perhaps more important, research budgets have come under great pressure in the last couple of years and it's necessary to remind ourselves why research short-cuts don't work either. So no apologies for covering very familiar ground here.

THREE OBSTRUCTIONS TO THOUGHT

As much as anything, sloppy use of language is getting in our way, and three examples seem to me particularly to affect this issue. (The first was provocatively built into the title of the seminar, no doubt through fears that the seminar's subject-matter and structure would not provoke enough argument.)

"The proof of advertising value." The very use of words like "proof" or "test" and analogies from Euclidian mathematics or engineering can mislead us about the nature of marketing and advertising. (We should get our analogies from history or the social rather than the physical sciences.) The planning and execution of marketing and advertising are surely a process of continuous learning and adaptation, in a competitive environment, where the norm is uncertainty and change. The proper approach is a cycle of analysis, theory, experiment, feedback, new theory, and so on. "Proof", with all its implication of final solutions, doesn't really belong here.

Even if we could, we don't simply want to prove whether we were right or wrong in the past, but to learn how to do better in the conditions of the future. We need to *understand*, in order to make better judgements. We need to know not just whether advertising worked, but *how* and *why*. We should judge research by whether it helps in this whole process, whether it *improves* our decisions.

"The sales effect of advertising." Though gritty and purposive, this is a particularly dangerous phrase. There's a tendency to use it through fear of being accused of not being interested in "what really matters".

The implication of the phrase is that there is some direct relationship between advertising and sales. But I find it impossible to imagine any sort of advertisement that could work without

*This article, which appeared in *Admap*, 13(4), 1977, is based on a presentation made at the opening session of the Market Research Society's seminar, "The Proof of Advertising Value", Broadway, November 1966. Reproduced with permission.

first drawing some sort of mental response from consumers. It is the individual who turns the mental response into physical action, and it is the individual's physical action which leads to sales. To ignore the middle bit – the individual's responses – is deliberately to abandon hope of finding out *how* the advertisement works (and maybe whether it works too). And the phrase is more dangerous even than that, because it has often been used narrowly to mean something like "the variation in month-to-month advertising expenditure" – again implying that this is the only effect of advertising that is worth bothering about.

In any case, "the sales effect of advertising" is far too limiting a concept. Advertising is not all for fast-moving grocery products – quite apart from other types of product, it is increasingly concerned with the communication of ideas: for instance, reports on company performance, metrication, saving fuel, banking services, pleas for fair treatment by the Government, and so on. And there are other objectives than sales – supporting profit margins, increasing saleability, giving information, getting contacts, getting applications, introducing salesmen, and many more.

What all these variations in advertisements and objectives have in common is that they are all trying, as a first stage, to get some sort of *mental* response from a lot of individuals. No one would deny that, in most cases, the ultimate aim is sales, but uncritical use of "the sales effect of advertising" can easily lead to our ignoring that vital first stage. (We should obviously pay attention to all the stages in the process.) We should try to make the phrase as rare as "the sales effect of management training" or "the sales effect of R&D expenditure".

"Advertising research." Marketing and advertising decisions are very complex. Competitors, like fish, refuse to stand still while being counted. Many factors affecting the decisions are not measured at all, and some of the measurements that are used are extremely dodgy. There is a huge number of options, and quite clearly many of them are interrelated. Decisions on advertising expenditure, pricing policies, creative treatment, media choice and degree of product improvement cannot really be taken separately. Or on creative treatment, length of spot and desired number of TV ratings.

The term "advertising research" can imply that there are specialist forms of research that can get the decisions about appropriation, content, media choice and timing of advertisements all sorted out without our having to worry about the interrelationship with other aspects of marketing. Once again, the name gets in the way of the proper approach.

So what is the proper approach? It seems to me that it is first to establish a much clearer framework for decision making than we usually do, and choose research methods to fit the framework. We have to ask:

1. What are the processes and stages of making marketing decisions (including advertising decisions)?
2. How do these stages interrelate?
3. What roles can research play at each stage?
4. So what sort of research (interrelated in what way) is needed?

A FRAMEWORK FOR MARKETING PLANNING

We have found the planning cycle shown in Figure 5.1 to be a useful, if perhaps a little over-simple, framework for making decisions about advertising. And of course it applies equally to other aspects of marketing. Being a series of questions, it is particularly helpful to deciding about research.

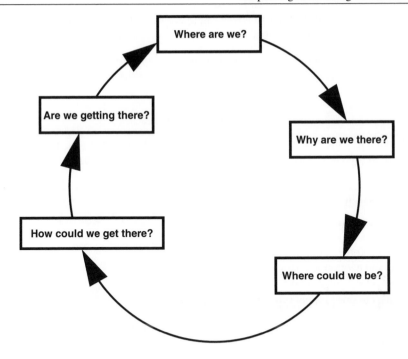

Figure 5.1   The Planning Cycle

1. *Where are we?* Where is our brand or service or activity now – in the general context of goods/services, in its own particular market, in people's minds? Where has it come from, and where does it look as if it's going?

2. *Why are we there?* What is the combination of factors, over what period of time, that has affected our position, direction and rate of change?

3. *Where could we be?* In our market, in people's minds? How soon?
   This is the first of a series of creative or judgemental decisions. It is a combination of: where would we like to be? and where do we think that, in practice, we could get to?

4. *How could we get there?* What combinations of actions, in the circumstances, would get us to where we want to be?
   This is where the first important feedback comes. It is clearly impossible to decide how to get there without reaching a decision on where to be. But equally we cannot be firm about where to be without considering whether it is possible to get there (and indeed why we did not get there in the past – Question 2).
   In fact, at the end of this stage what we should have is two mutually compatible hypotheses, which do not conflict with what we've learnt about the past.

5. *Are we getting there?* This can be asked both before and after taking the actions. That is, we can look at sub-systems and ask of each: Is it likely that this action would help us get there? (Which is where "pre-testing" fits in.) And we can measure progress in real life, after taking the marketing actions, against objectives.

This of course brings us back to : *Now where are we?*, and a new cycle starts – we hope, from a better position than the first.

Let us look at the roles for research and research methods in helping to answer each of the five questions.

WHERE ARE WE?

This is the area in which the roles for research are most obvious, the research methods most familiar and, in my view, the dangers of skimping on research the greatest.

Roles for Research

There are three fairly distinct, but overlapping roles:

1. Background knowledge:
   - Social and economic change.
   - Value systems in general.
   - Attitudes to our product type and its substitutes.

This is covering the whole context into which our brand fits. For instance, the recent redistribution of incomes and increases in older married women at work; the development under pressure of new buying skills and consumers' increasing antagonism to bigness; attitudes to, say, whisky as a product class and to its changing relationships with vodka, rum and vermouth.

Research methods are too well known to mention here, but I think there is far too little "semi-structured" research – with samples of a few hundred and a fair number of open-ended questions.

2. *Comparative map – Our brand v. competitors*:
   - Market shares, buying patterns, attitudes, awareness, knowledge, product comparisons, profitability.

The key marketing decision is very often one about the right balance between capitalizing on relative strengths and repairing relative weaknesses. It can't be made sensibly without knowing what those relative strengths and weaknesses are. Again, familiar research methods: retail audits, consumer panels, qualitative and quantitative attitude research, product tests, introspection. I suspect that our weakness in this area is more often failure to analyse fully the data we've got than failure to buy enough data.

3. *"Norms"*: Generalized patterns of buying, attitude, attitude change, distribution and so on.

The function of "norms" is to illuminate the abnormal in our brand. Is it behaving like a "normal" brand? If not, in what way? This is an area in which marketing men are rather short of information. The exception of course is Andrew Ehrenberg's (1972) wide-ranging and very fully-documented analyses of consumer panel data (possibly most honoured in the breach, because they deal mainly with people aggregated in a rather unfamiliar way). Beyond that, Nielsen, Attwood and AGB (Parfitt and Collins, 1967; Peckham, 1975) have produced some generalized data, but it is disappointing that there is so little (or maybe that the demand is so weak).

WHY ARE WE THERE?

The second question asks: What combination of name, pack, product, price, distribution, advertising, promotions, history, external events, etc., seems to have caused the current situation and trends? If our brand is "abnormal", what has caused it? Over what period of time?

All these factors have to be looked at from the point-of-view of both our brand and competitive brands or substitutes. Most factors have to be split into amount, structure, timing and style (e.g. advertising expenditure, use of media, scheduling and creative content). There is clearly unlikely to be any simple solution.

Roles for Research

Research can help us to *understand* what is the relative importance of the factors affecting our current situation, and occasionally to *eliminate* something that couldn't have caused it. Again, there is both a general and a specific role.

1. *"Causal norms"*
   - Generalized research which suggests (not proves) a "normal" causal effect.

We are on even shakier ground here than with other "norms", partly because of lack of data and partly because of the difficulty of ever establishing any causal effect with any confidence (outside the laboratory). Various attempts to link share of advertising expenditure with share of market (e.g. Moroney's Dynamic Difference model or some of Nielsen's findings) suggest a causal relationship, but neither would claim more than mild tendencies from them. (And I would discount any "laws" that may have been put forward on the basis of half a dozen carefully selected and interpreted case histories.)

"Within-person" analyses can obviously get closer to causal findings. The most obvious example is direct-response advertising, and it was the basis of many early attempts to provide rules and norms (Hopkins, 1923). The only research I know that has looked at the relationship of exposure to advertising and purchasing of brands in a large number of product fields, on a within-person basis, is the JWT/BMRB Diary Study, which at an experimental level produced a lot of useful ideas (Barnes, 1971; King, 1975; McDonald, 1969).

The data on "causal norms" do not go further than background for forming hypotheses, but they are very valuable for that. In particular, they are useful for *eliminating* theories – "whatever it is that caused our situation, it doesn't look as if it would have been *that*".

2. *Specific research – experiments or relationships:*
   - *Experiments.* In theory, the controlled experiment should be the best way of establishing causal relationships, as it is in the laboratory. In practice, as we all know, for marketing experiments there are terrible problems of both control and measurement, and the arguments against them are well known. I have certainly known far more market experiments with inconclusive than conclusive results; but I still think they are always worth doing. The ones with clear-cut results can be very rewarding, and it is very rare to learn nothing at all from the others. I feel sure that the relative infrequency with which marketing companies mount area experiments of advertising or promotions comes more from a lack of sympathy with the principle of experiments than from a belief that they cannot be measured or that they would be too expensive (though I would accept that the expense of an AdLab capable of measuring "significant" results is its main snag).

• *Relationships*. Analysis of internal relationships – particularly in continuous research – is perhaps the main way in which we try to decide about causes and understand the dynamics of markets. That can cover everything from simple cross-analyses to the complexities of econometrics and model building.

Since there is currently some controversy about the use of such relationships to establish causal effects, it is important to be clear that such methods cannot yield more than *hypotheses*. Correlations alone can never prove that A has caused B, or that it will do so in future.

There are several well-known reasons for this. First, the results of any analysis of this sort can be no better than the assumptions built into it, and particularly assumptions about the interaction or non-interaction of factors. Let us take five recent forecasts for changes in consumers' expenditure in 1977 compared with 1976:

NIESR (Aug '76)	LBS (Aug '76)	Henley (Oct '76)	Hoare Govett (Oct '76)	Phillips & Drew (Nov '76)
+ 0.5%	+1.5%	+3.2%	-0.3%	+0.1%

Why the divergence? (It might seem small, but in only 7 of the last 20 years has the change in consumption fallen outside these limits. The average of the last 20 years' figures would be bound to be nearer the truth than at least one of these forecasts.) It is not because some of these eminent forecasters were using different data or had econometricians of poor quality: it is simply that their models used different assumptions (and indeed that the assumptions changed between August and November).

Secondly, the data in marketing are of variable quality. It has been shown that conclusions about the effects of advertising tend to be dependent on the frequency of the measurements (Clarke, 1975). AGB, in their Prices Audit, have shown that *similar* average prices found for a brand in two different chains conceal radically different *distributions* – which could be very important if it is price thresholds that matter. Some things are barely measurable at all (advertising content, for instance). And so on.

Thirdly, the "solutions" from such models are always approximate. But it is very easy to slip into talking about a mild tendency, based on a "best-fit solution", as if it were a Universal Law. Andrew Ehrenberg's article (1976), "How good is best?", distributed at the seminar, was a magnificent corrective to this sort of thinking.

And fourthly, there is the old rule about correlation not being causation – which is at the root of most of our practical problems. To take a specific example, Figure 5.2 shows, first, annual consumption of branded food drinks, taken from the National Food Survey. There are considerable variations. Why?

Plotted against these figures are continuous data, from the Registrar General, for deaths from bronchitis and flu. A pretty close fit. But relatively few of us would conclude from this that the consumption of branded food drinks so weakened people that they were easy prey to bronchitis, or that death itself inclined the survivors to step up their consumption of branded food drinks. We might hypothesize that people thought branded food drinks were good for warding off flu in an epidemic. Or that cold weather was the cause of both sets of fluctuations. Or cold weather and changes in disposable income. The point is that the figures by themselves cannot tell us which, if any, of these hypotheses is correct.

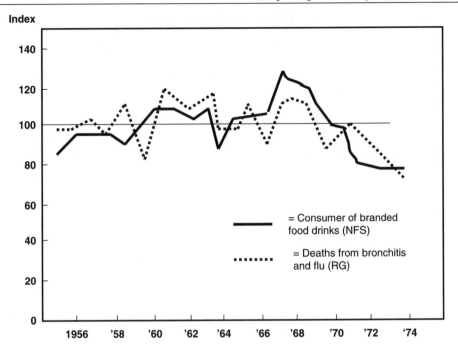

Figure 5.2 "Explaining" sales (Index: 100 = average for period)
Source: Admap April 1977.

Even if we could establish such causal relationships, there is another problem. The "explanations" we have considered so far are of the *variations* only. And in this case, it is clear that the variations are relatively small compared with the base (over 20 years the average variation from the "norm" – indexed at 100 – is less than 15%). It is easy when asking what caused the variations to forget to ask what caused the base. "Why are we here?" means what it says – not just "Why have we moved from where we were last time?" We must avoid the danger of "explaining" the trivial while ignoring the important.

I am wholeheartedly in favour of using the full range of continuous data (consumer panels, advertising expenditure, attitude measures, prices paid, promotions taken up, etc.) and of developing better methods of analysis to help us form better *hypotheses* of why we are here. But I think we should work to a set of rules. For instance:

- assumptions of the model to be made clear;
- the data used, and their limitations, to be open for inspection;
- the mathematical methods and their margins of error to be spelled out (even if not clear to all).

And we must all be aware of Causal Slippage – the "best-fit solution" that becomes "the" solution or the cluster which, given a name by the researcher, develops an identity of its own.

WHERE COULD WE BE?

The answer to this question – hypothetical as it is – has to be put, in the marketing plan, in very specific terms. Those of sales, market share, profits, profit margins, consumer attitudes and so on. All related to the figures for where each of those things are now, and often related to estimates of where competitors will be; over what time scale.

In the best-regulated companies the question is a little less terrifying than it sounds, since corporate strategy will have set some limits. For instance, is the company aiming to grow in this market or to milk existing brands? Is the aim to have a few big brands, maybe only one, or a series of quick fashion brands?

But however clear the limits are, the decision will still be creative, judgemental, hypothetical. How can research help?

Roles for Research

There are two rather different roles:

1. Stimulus – help in making these judgements and creative leaps

Research can give the decision-maker ideas, just as much as endless meetings in smoke-filled rooms can. What sort of research may depend more on the nature of the decision maker than on anything else. Some find quantitative research stimulating, others qualitative, others both, others neither.

2. "Norms" – as boundaries to ambition

"Norms" are extremely useful to help one avoid setting meaningless and unattainable targets, simply out of bravado. Some of these "norms" can be based on very simple analyses – either of data in a specific market or generalized data. For instance, Figure 5.3 shows the distribution of annual changes in the number of people holding a specific belief about a brand.

Bearing in mind that the bigger positive changes shown here were for new and rapidly growing brands, there would have to be some very special reason for answering "where could we be?" for an established brand by proposing a gain of 6 percentage points in the number thinking our brand is efficient.

The "norms" here are the same as those mentioned under "Where are we?" – mainly Andrew Ehrenberg's with a little from AGB, Attwood and Nielsen. It is no use *thoughtlessly* setting a target of "increasing the percentage of our users who are heavy buyers", if the "norm" suggests that in virtually all cases this percentage is entirely predictable and thus probably immovable.

There is perhaps one point that should be made (again) here, in relation to penetration ("getting new users") *versus* rate of use ("getting users to use more frequently") – because those are phrases we all use rather imprecisely and because the Ehrenberg findings are so constantly misinterpreted. The fact is that unless a time-period is specified, the terms are hardly meaningful; and there is a sense in which they come to the same thing.

Try this simple test. Table 5.1 shows the purchases of Brand X made by four people over four periods. Sales in Period 3 and 4 are up by 50% over Periods 1 and 2. Was it increased penetration or increased frequency of purchasing per buyer?

If you take the periods separately, you'll say it was increased penetration. If you consider Periods 1 and 2 *versus* Periods 3 and 4, you'll say it was increased frequency. (I'm not saying that this necessarily reflects how people do buy, but that we ought to be clear what we're talking about.)

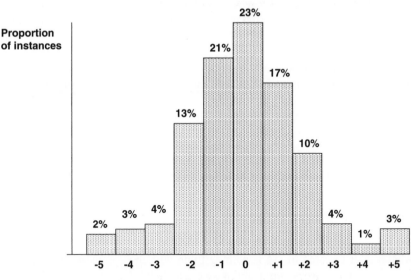

**Distribution of annual changes in the percentage
of people who hold a specific belief about a brand**

Figure 5.3   How Fast do Beliefs Change?

Table 5.1   Purchase of Brand X

Buyers	Period			
	1	2	3	4
A	X		X	X
B	X			X
C		X	X	X
D		X	X	
Total	2	2	3	3

HOW COULD WE GET THERE?

This is a horribly complex question. It involves deciding about the:

role,
amount,
type,
timing and
interaction of changes in

product, range, pack, pricing, sales methods, distribution methods, promotions and advertising.

It is not surprising, especially under the pressures of the last two years, that there's a yearning for simple numbers, or for a sort of deductive, accountant's way of reaching the right decisions. This is the sort of temptation that leaves us with the advertising budget as what's left when the cost of everything else, plus desired profits, is subtracted from a fairly arbitrarily set sales target.

The proper approach is clearly much harder – a constant feedback to "Where could we be?" with a great deal of judgement – a series of successive approximations until there is an internally consistent plan. Since by their very nature many of the "ways of getting there" will be novel, there can be no "proof" of what their effects will be, from past data. The means of achieving the objectives have to be *invented*.

Roles for Research

So the role for research is to help people to invent and help them to decide whether the inventions are likely to work.

1. Stimulus – as before, an aid to invention

This is the role for which advertising agencies particularly use group discussions. The decision about what sort of research to use is nothing to do with those earnest arguments about the relative merits of qualitative *versus* quantitative research. It is largely a question of what sort of research is most stimulating to the people who have the job of inventing the advertisements. On the whole, they find that the richness and interactions of group discussions are more stimulating than single interviews or books of figures. (The stimulus is of course set against the backcloth of all the research available from the first stage, much of which *is* quantitative.)

2. Trying out hypotheses – implications of all the research of the "Why are we there?" stage

That is, this is much more a re-examining of previous research and analyses than collecting new data. In effect, we are asking of both the experiments and the relationships of the past: "What happened last time? What seemed to cause our previous situation? Would it do so again – bearing in mind that today's objectives are a little different, and so are today's circumstances?"

We cannot assume that the causal relationships we identified at the second stage will remain the same for ever, but they must be the starting point. Having had some new ideas, we are trying them out in principle against the lessons that we thought we learned in the past.

To make this link between new ideas and old findings, and to make all the research *practical*, it is helpful to have some broad framework for expressing "how advertising works". Hence the Rosser Reeves' USP theory or the David Ogilvy brand image theory or the idea of a direct/indirect scale of desired responses (King, 1975). I think these frameworks are valuable not for describing how all advertising works (they are far too simple for that), but as a language for translating the rather abstract "This is how we should get there" into "This is what this advertisement has to do".

Short-term versus Long-term Effects

The question of whether advertising works in the short term or the long term fits into this area. "How do we get there?" implies "and how long will it take?". And a general theory of *when* and *for how long* advertising has its effects is very much one of these useful languages, as well as having specific implications for measurement.

One of the values to me of the MRS seminar was in making it clear that here too was an area in which we have all been using terms rather imprecisely. It is possible, by means of a combative spirit and selective use of a pair or scissors, to present a picture of a great schism between believers in short-term effects and believers in long-term effects. In fact, when the language is sorted out, I doubt if there is a great deal of disagreement about the principles (though there might be about implications for research). No one who has thought at all about direct response advertisements, classified advertisements or retailer advertising could deny the existence of short-term effects. Equally, anyone who believes that there was no lasting effect from 40-odd years of "Guinness is good for you" (last used in advertising nearly 20 years ago) has clearly not listened to older Guinness drinkers talking.

The imprecision comes in the use of "long-term effect". It is partly that some people use the word "effect" to mean "variation in sales between one month and the next", which rather begs the question. And partly that "long-term" is used to mean both "long-range" and "lasting". "Long-range" models might be of the time-bomb, howitzer or ferret variety: the critical action is taken (clock started, cord pulled, ferret put down rabbit-hole), there is then a long gap in which nothing very much seems to happen, and then suddenly there's an effect (explosion, crater or emergence of ferret with rabbit between teeth). "Lasting" models are more of the camel or slow puncture variety. The first straw contributes as much as the last to the breakage of the camel. Regular pumping of the tyre with the slow puncture keeps it at a satisfactory pressure and you can't really tell how long the effect of each individual bit of pumping lasts (i.e. which pieces of air have leaked). All you know for sure is that each new bit of pumping has an immediate effect, and that at any time you can measure the *cumulative* effect of all pumping, less leakage.

It seems to me that many of the doubts cast on the long-term effects of advertising (for instance, by Derek Bloom, 1976) are on the grounds that "long-range" effects are implausible (with which most of us would agree). However, the proponents of long-term effects tend to be thinking in terms of "lasting" effects. The common ground appears to be that an advertisement which works draws an immediate response from people, and that this response decays over time. The real question is *how far* it decays. Does it automatically go back to zero – so that, as far as the individual is concerned, after a time it's as if the advertisement had never been? Or could it return to a point marginally above datum – so that the response to the next advertisement starts from a marginally higher base? If the latter is possible, the cumulative effect of a series of advertisements could be bigger than the immediate effect of each one, even though for a single advertisement the residual effect after decay might be too small to measure.

For instance, one of the most striking changes in attitude to a brand that I know was that of its *users* to Oxo cubes – a change that most people have attributed to advertising. On one particular dimension the results were:

Of all Oxo users mentioning the brand, % who named it as:	July 1961	Jan 1971
used by good cooks	66%	81%
used by poor cooks	34%	19%
	100%	100%

Source: API

Over time, that change in the base of attitudes to Oxo was large and was judged to have been important; there clearly was a cumulative effect. But it represented an average rate of change of 0.13 percentage points per month and so a much smaller change per advertisement. In other words, the change in the base was not measurable in the short run by conventional methods, though certain immediate effects of advertisements were.

It seems to me quite reasonable to suggest that the main *immediate* effect of Oxo advertisements has been to increase the brand's salience or people's responses to buying it; which are relatively easily measurable. And that the main *lasting* or *cumulative* effect has been to increase Oxo's value or people's response to the brand itself; and that is barely measurable at all in the short run and only by hindsight and inference in the long run. Both effects are important, and they are clearly interrelated – the base from which the immediate effects happen being dependent on the success of the lasting effects.

If in broad terms that is true (however oversimplified), there are no problems as long as the sort of advertising that is best for increasing short-term salience is also best for building the base of lasting brand value. We simply measure what's easy to measure, and forget the difficult bits. But that is hardly satisfactory if, as seems much more likely, the two objectives are not necessarily best achieved by the same sort of advertising – indeed, if there may be some conflict between the two, as it has been suggested there is between advertising and promotions (Leman, 1969). Certainly over the years it has seemed that there has been a cycle of priorities for Oxo's advertising, in terms of the answers to "How do we get there?" They have gone from modify attitudes to reinforce new attitudes to increase salience to reaffirm basic values. And this seems to be true for many old-established brands with strong and clear-cut values – like Persil, Horlicks, Rice Krispies or Black Magic.

ARE WE GETTING THERE?

Essentially, at this stage we are completing the first cycle of a sequence of theory–experiment–feedback, and the object is to get help in improving advertising for the next cycle.

Roles for Research

1. *Pre-campaign exposure*

I think there is a limit to what we can expect to discover before advertisements appear in the media. Certainly not much about decisions on advertising expenditure, timing or use of media.

Creative content can be checked for internal consistency and against the communication objectives set at the previous stage. It is relatively easy to discover whether the ideas have been received by people as intended, and both qualitative and quantitative research are successfully used. Perhaps single unstructured interviews are the best way of getting a reasonable depth of response from reasonable numbers, but for certain product fields group discussions can be more sensitive. Since the object is much more to see if anything might be wrong than to "prove" that everything is all right, there seems little point in piling up numbers for this sort of research – particularly if there is a loss of sensitivity.

It is when pre-exposure research purports to predict not the mental response to an advertisement but the behavioural response arising from the mental response that we run into trouble. And the degree of trouble seems likely to depend on the degree to which any "pre-test" simulation of the market place differs from the reality of it. It is easier to imagine a valid predictor of the effect of advertising aimed at first trial of a new flavour of potato crisp or ice lolly than a valid predictor of advertising aiming to establish a subtle new position for a brand of lager or washing powder.

The record of most off-the-peg advertisement testing methods has been pretty bad, and I think that anyone thinking of using one should spend some money on testing the tests. It can be done very elaborately, as with the huge Printed Advertising Rating Methods survey in the USA, or quite simply, as JWT tested Schwerin tests. (Briefly, our experiments demonstrated that the spread of scores for different commercials was no greater than that for one commercial tested many times.)

2. *Post-campaign exposure*

Once the campaign goes into the market place, the role for research and the methods are much the same as at the first stage. We are asking "Now where are we?" and "How does that compare with where we said we wanted to be?"

This particularly emphasizes the importance of *continuous* research for the role of providing a comparative map. And the values of market experiments, however often they may disappoint. The occasional clear-cut answers to area tests are usually visible to the naked eye, and of great value. Where there seem no differences at all, it is likely that the experiments have not been bold enough, and that is useful to know. And in the middle ground new methods of analysis like Beechams' AMTES (which seems to me to stick splendidly to my rules of openly stating assumptions, methods and data, while presenting results with proper humility) may well turn answers from the dubious to the likely (Bloom *et al.*, 1976).

The whole problem of immediate versus lasting effects makes it clear too that we should aim to have measures that cover salience and attitude as well as sales, and frequent enough reports to allow us to analyse both immediate and cumulative change.

IMPROVING ADVERTISING DECISIONS

There is nothing very new in research methods, and nothing new in this framework for making marketing and advertising decisions. But if we judge research methods by their effectiveness at helping to answer questions at each stage of the planning cycle, I think a lot of the difficulties of integrating them disappear. For some the principles of integration are clear, even if some of the details are not. And some do not need to be integrated, any more than the ruler and the thermometer need to be.

While we should of course always strive to improve research methods, I think our basic problems remain (as ever) those of recognizing the essential nature of the planning process as one of learning and improvement, not of proof and magic solutions; and of helping and encouraging the users of research to go through the proper planning processes at all.

REFERENCES

AGB: Prices Audit.

Barnes, M. (1971) "The relationship between purchasing patterns and advertising exposure", JWT.

Bloom, D. (1976) "Consumer behaviour and the timing of advertising effects", *Admap*, September.

Bloom, D., Jay, A. and Twyman, T. (1976) "The validity of advertising pre-testing", MRS Conference.

Clarke, D.G. (1975) "Econometric measurement of the duration of the advertising effect on sales", Marketing Science Institute, April.

Ehrenberg, A. (1972) *Repeat-Buying: Theory and Applications*. North Holland Publishing Co.

Ehrenberg, A. (1976) *How Good is Best?* London Business School, May.

Hopkins, C. (1923) *Scientific Advertising*.

King, S. (1975) "Practical progress from a theory of advertisements", *Admap*, October.

Leman, G. (1969) "Sales, saleability and the saleability gap", *Bulletin No. 5*, BBTA.

McDonald, C. (1969) "Relationships between advertising exposure and purchasing behaviour", *Admap*, April.

Parfitt, J. and Collins, B.J.K. (1967) "The use of consumer panels for brand share prediction", MRS Conference.

Peckham, J.O. (1975) *The Wheel of Marketing*, A.C. Nielsen Co.

The Media Planner's Revenge

By Marco Rimini, Head of Communications Planning, Mindshare Worldwide

An introduction to:

6.1   Inter-media Decisions: Implications for Agency Structure

Media and Account Planning: One Job or Two?

Sounds dry, doesn't it? It could be but it isn't. By calmly, slowly and subtly peeling the layers off this question, Stephen King takes a discussion about the making of boring old media decisions and turns it into a treatise on how agencies should be organized. In the process he also lays out the thinking that led him to create account planning.

It was the single thing that Stephen King was most famous for and it is fascinating to see how he got there.

The article was written almost 40 years ago but the issues he discusses are suddenly very topical again. How do you get media researchers and media thinkers involved in the development of advertising to make sure the team produces the most effective advertising possible? In fact so topical is the issue that the era he is writing in peeps through only occasionally.

First, account planning. Whatever it has come to mean, the roots of account planning grow from Stephen's intent, which was to simplify and codify a clear way of team working to produce the most effective form of advertising. By combining the skills found in the marketing function (then housed with the agency, and what we might now call market analysis) , and the media planning function within one discipline and one person, called the account planner, he believed that the team working to create effective advertising would be better balanced and produce better results.

Carts Before Horses

This, he felt would be superior to a system that artificially separated the forms of thinking and put them in a production line process with the market analysis before the creative work and the media plan after it. It is this production line mentality that is still too common. The media thinking becomes the back end of the creative development process. Instead, he makes an effective case for media thinking being at the very start of the process, integrated into the market and consumer analysis.

As he says,

the skills of knowledge, the mental and social skills required for inter-media planning are precisely those needed for the initial development of the campaign itself (the actual advertisements). Setting objectives for inventing and testing campaigns requires the same knowledge of research and marketing, the same social skills of negotiation and cooperation, the same mental skills of analysis theorizing and inventing. *The execution of the campaign may require other skills, just as inter-media decisions do, but up to a certain point, planning of media and advertisements is virtually the same job.* (My italics)

Planning of media and advertisements is virtually the same job! Not two sets of actions, one driven by the creative function and one the buying function. Not two types of people, one guru and one blinded by numbers. No! One process designed to arrive at the best possible plan. I wonder what he would make of account planning today. Or indeed media planning.

Specialist Companies Lead to Fragmented Thinking

Account planning has succeeded but I'm not sure that he would now recognize it as performing the role he intended it for. In a world of creative agencies without media departments, and media companies without creative departments, we have made it structurally much harder to merge the two ways of thinking into one. We have managed to divide everything up into smaller roles, smaller specialisms and smaller mental models just when the world needs greater breadth of thinking.

Pessimistically we could take this as a backward step; I prefer to see it as simply the interim stage before we reunite the two ways of thinking around a new form of creativity for the requirements of brands in a digital age.

Surely the production line was just a consequence of TV actually being the only answer for 30 years. Since that's not always the case nowadays, surely we will go back to a more objective planning approach. Let's hope so.

The Magic of Teamwork

The second piece of thinking I want to discuss is project group rather than production line working. At its best our industry is a world leader at putting together groups of people from different disciplines to work on a common problem, and then disbanding and reforming them on a different project. The fluidity of working, the diversity of the people in the team, the lack of hierarchy, dress code or deference have been important reasons for people entering and staying in the business.

And it works. No one doubts that the best work comes from project groups, not production line processes. More than titles, roles, P&L structures, holding company structures, branding systems or any other of other corporate puffery, the ability to get the right people together, brief them and getting them to enjoy working to a common goal will let us find the solution required for our complex world.

Brief as Stimulus not as an Order Form

Thirdly, and to the point of how to brief a project team, King put the derivation of the correct objectives of the communication at the core of his philosophy and his views on structure. As he says "deriving the advertising objectives from the marketing objectives is the most subtle and difficult of these tasks". It became embedded in the Thompson way of planning advertising and their creative briefs.

The idea was simple, but difficult to do. Identify the response, the result, the objective you want to achieve clearly, and imaginatively formulate it to inspire people, not just direct people, and then organize imaginative people to decide how to achieve it.

This is the principle with which we are struggling most today. The increasing breadth of communications options means that setting marketing and communications objectives for each of the channels, as distinct from the ideas that will bind these channels together, is virtually impossible.

It is also why we need to try again to identify common thinking skills and to work in project teams whose members share these skills. And why we always need to be objective led, not input led.

Media Myths and Media Metaphors

Too often our planning is based on mythology and Stephen lists a common set of myths, where often one myth contradicts another. For example, it's best to be where your competitors are, and it's best to be where your competitors are not. We could all do our own list, and perhaps we should just to clarify our own inconsistencies, as he wittily does here.

In media metaphors, we have the concepts of:

- Media as vehicle
- Media as medium
- Media as message

Not only are we choosing media to carry messages but we should be choosing them to be the best canvas for expressing specific ideas and for the message that the choice of media itself conveys.

We still plan and buy media too often with only the media as vehicle in mind. The messy divorce between creative and media agencies was partly because media people didn't feel as valued as they thought they ought to be, given the power of media as medium, and media as message.

An Inspiration and a Guide to Doing it Better Now

In fact it's now time to get over that divorce and find a new way of working together to achieve the same objective as King did with account planning. I'm trying to do that within a media agency. Others will do it from their own different environments. Who knows where it will end up but it should be fun trying to do something new. King's article reminded me that what we are all trying to do is not impossible and that we can learn from others who faced the same problem in a different generation and different environment.

6.1
Inter-media Decisions: Implications for Agency Structure*

By Stephen King

Is it television, cinema, outdoor, radio, press or other media? How should agencies make inter-media decisions? This simple question is a neat little brick thrown into a calm pond. Quite quickly the ripples cover the whole pond and get involved with counter-ripples. The inter-media question quickly brings up most of the fundamental questions about how advertising works, what is good and what is bad advertising, what to do about it and so on.

Decisions about the right structure in an agency are really the last in a chain of these very fundamental questions. There can be a sort of logical approach, and I have tried to follow it here. The article is in three sections:

- What are the criteria for deciding on any organization and working methods?
- How do these criteria apply to the making of inter-media decisions?
- How my own agency – JWT – has organized as a result.

ORGANIZATION DECISIONS

I think there are probably four main criteria for making any organization decisions, and they interact quite considerably:

1. Job to be Done

First, quite simply we have to analyse what it is that has to be done, both as a total objective and as a sum of many pieces of work. With certain sorts of job the pieces fit together in a fairly tidy flow. Where the task is to make moulded plastic toys, the man buying the raw materials needs very little contact with the man operating the moulding press or the people putting the toys in the boxes.

With other jobs there is still a flow but there are more complex interrelationships. On a car production line the welder's work does not directly affect the electrician's, but the welding cannot always be completely done before the work passes to the electrician; some of it has to be done after the wiring is fitted, and the product therefore has to pass back and forth between skills.

At a more complex level, the product passes back and forth, and also the way in which the job is done by each skill can affect others (in quality, timing and general approach). The house builder is usually faced with this situation, and quite often special finishing teams are brought

*Published in *Admap*, October 1969. Reproduced with permission.

in to deal with the results of unfortunate interactions between plumber, carpenter, electrician and decorator.

So the first task is to define the nature of the end product, the scope of the actions needed to achieve it and the degree to which these will interact. It can be a very complex matter.

2. Skills Needed

Following directly from this is an analysis of the skills needed for these various actions. They have usually been worked out fairly carefully in the world of manufacturing, though demarcation disputes suggest that classifications solidify rather too easily. I suspect that in advertising they may have been worked out rather less carefully, but all the signs of solidity are there, all the same. In advertising there seem to be three categories of skill; *physical skills*, like drawing, typing, designing, etc.; *skills of knowledge*, like research, electronics, etc.; *mental/social skills*, like organizing, creating, planning, analysing, bargaining, comforting, etc.

Again, some of these are interrelated, and a person will often need to have, for instance, a knowledge skill in order to use his physical or social skills properly. But of course the whole reason for organization is that no one person will have all these skills, or even many of them, at a high level of excellence.

Decisions about organization, after this analysis of skills, typically involve compromise. A very large number of people will not be able to cover all the skills at a high enough level. A very small number can encompass all the skills at a supreme level of expertise, but run into problems of complexity, work flow, communication and cost. What is the right number in between? Which skills should be lumped together? Which skills must stay at the highest possible level, and on which can some compromise be accepted?

3. Modes of Work and Working Methods

Working methods will depend a good deal on the answers to the first two questions. Perhaps the basic question here is where the organization should lie on the scale running from production line to integrated project group. Our moulded toymakers can be organized on a production line basis; building workers cannot – if the plasterer and carpenter will not cooperate with each other, the client is going to suffer even more than usual.

There are also questions of physical constraints: different actions take different times to complete, for instance, and there are differences between producing one thing repeatedly and slightly different things each time. There are questions of the depth of interest or involvement needed by different individuals with different skills.

4. Relationships and Job Satisfaction

Finally, following the decisions about what is to be done, what skills are needed and how they are to be deployed in working methods, the question is how to motivate the required people to do it at all, within the allowable cost. Organization and structure have to take into account status needs within project groups, scope for personal development, the needs for enjoyment, feeling of free will, responsibility, involvement and so on.

Though logically these considerations come last, they may well be the ones making the most difference between good work and mediocre work. They are often the hardest problems and may be the ones concerning people most. It may be significant that there are frequent conferences on how to integrate the work of creative people and media men, creative people and researchers, marketing men and media men, and so on. Agencies, which tend to be smallish organizations, are only just beginning to tackle the problems seriously.

What seems to follow from this rapid list of criteria is that the answers to questions of organization are likely to be complex and to vary somewhat according to specific situations. This makes it all the more necessary to tackle organization in a systematic way and emerge with solutions that are variations on a fairly simple theme. Unless the underlying structure is comprehensible, the result will be chaotic and eventually very costly. The next section examines how each of these main criteria apply to advertising agencies in general and to the job of inter-media selection in particular.

HOW DO THESE CRITERIA APPLY?

Despite the immense amount of writing about the selection of main media and a certain amount of research, it seems probable that we simply have not yet made enough progress in this first stage of analysis. We have slipped into a certain form of organization without fully considering the totality and the constituent parts of the job to be done.

It seems significant that this conference sets as one of its questions: Who really makes inter-media decisions? We apparently don't even know yet who does it, let alone whether it is right that he/they should. The Thomson Silver Medal question, six years ago, asked for ways of finding out who makes inter-media decisions, but no one answered well enough to get the prize.

Without claiming to provide a complete picture of the inter-media decision, we can at least provide a short list of the main criteria that affect it. We can say that the job is analysing, evaluating and interrelating these criteria to reach a decision. I have divided them into three groups – mythology, marketing and media.

Mythology

In real life, mythology may be the most powerful factor. Myths are not necessarily untrue, and they are usually related in some way to less mythical factors. I use the word to mean views that are quite generally held, but are not backed by any real evidence and have not been questioned for a long time. We sometimes use them by implication, sometimes overtly. Sometimes they are derived from mythical authority figures (like Sir William Crawford or Claude Hopkins or David Ogilvy). Sometimes they contradict each other. Here are a few:

- Advertising must concentrate on one medium
- Multi-media advertising works because it approaches people from different directions
- Posters work by being near point of sale
- Nobody reads/consumes anything in August
- They are barely civilized in Westward/Anglia/Border/Grampian, etc.
- Television works quicker/has more impact than press
- Cinema gives brands a young image
- You can't go on television nationally on less than £50,000 / £100,000 / £150,000 / £200,000
- We must be in the medium our competitors are in
- We must dominate the media where our competitors aren't
- Posters are a reminder medium
- A full page has the same effect as a 30-second spot
- You can't sell cars (etc., etc.) on television.

The danger is that, as media research and advertising theory become more and more compli-cated, so there will be greater need for simple ideas as a basis for making decisions. It could be that as we progress in understanding media, mythology will tend to play a more important role in decision making. The organizational implication is that people who do understand ad-vertising theory and media research should come into the planning at a stage early enough to challenge the myths before people take up entrenched positions.

Marketing

Marketing considerations play an important part, and can be expected to do so increasingly in the future. Again, as we learn more, we will be more inclined to discard the simple models of "how advertising works". Increasing complexity in advertising theory is likely to lead marketing men to a more pragmatic approach. They will become irritated with the (perfectly true) ideas that nothing is certain; that the future may not be like the past; that the margins of error in the research could be greater than the differences between the alternatives put before them; that they really cannot understand the agency's point without reading the last five issues of *Admap*. They will turn more to assessments of "what happened last time we used television", to market tests of different media, and so on. (An exactly parallel movement is going on in the testing of advertisements.)

Thus a major part of the job of inter-media decision is analysis of market place changes associated with media use; the setting up and analysis of market experiments; analysis of competitors' expenditure (using either the beat them or the join them principle); relating media choice to regional or seasonal marketing tactics.

To make inter-media decisions on these grounds will require considerable skills in interpre-tation, research and experimental design. It will require methods for translating the marketing plan into an advertising plan, which will mean having a clear-cut idea of advertising's precise role in the marketing plan. Exactly how will it work? Exactly who will do what or change in what way as the result of the advertising?

Media

All these are powerful forces operating on inter-media decisions, almost before media consid-erations (or the media man) come in at all.

Then there are the media criteria themselves, which are complex and uncertain, compared with the assurance of myth. They can operate on the decision in three ways

- medium as vehicle
- medium as medium
- medium as message.

MEDIUM AS VEHICLE

There has always been a very heavy concentration on media as vehicles, both in media de-partments and in industry and syndicated research. With the development of single source research we have an almost embarrassing amount of data. But, however valuable in general terms and for inter-media decisions, they cannot help very much in the selection of the right basic medium. We are dealing here essentially with coverage and cost per thousand. Both concepts tend to fall apart in our hands.

Cost per thousand what? The straight answer is opportunities to see, but it is fairly clear that we use this phrase in different senses for different media. On the conventional use of the phrase most appropriations would end up in posters. And we run straight up against the problem of how many seconds a full page is worth. The same is true of course when we consider special deals – we can only compare television summer rates with television winter rates, not with press rates.

Coverage gives us a slightly firmer grip, particularly in a negative sense. (We can at least say of a medium that it is *not* covering X% of our target group at all.) At the positive level, what we are really interested in is effective coverage. Not only do we have to make a judgement of what effective coverage means, entering the well-trodden arena of the response function (Broadbent and Segnit, 1967), but we have to judge the relationship of an opportunity-to-see on television (which cannot last more than the length of the spot) with one in a monthly magazine, which might last several minutes and/or be repeated several times (or of course might not).

The job here therefore certainly requires skills of analysis and knowledge of statistics. But evaluating these **medium-as-vehicle** criteria for inter-media decisions means much more to rely on judgement. And everything of course depends on the correct setting of the target group for advertising, which will derive from decisions about the precise role of advertising in the marketing plan and the precise way in which the advertising is expected to work. All the evidence is that these are much more important decisions than most of those resulting from all our computer runs (Corlett and Richardson, 1969). It remains unfortunately true that much media work is still taking guesses to four places of decimals.

Creative/Medium Relationship

In practice, within agencies, it is probably the criterion of the **medium as medium** – using the word in the same sense as an artist's medium – that most affects the decision. That is, which medium is most suitable for the creative people to achieve their objects? There are many examples of "unsuitable" media being successfully used – like radio to advertise paint colours – but on the whole certain media are simply more effective, as media, for certain types of communication. Considerations here would include availability of colour, movement, sound; quality of reproduction; size; duration of the advertisement; time of day; flexibility for tactical use, and so on.

Inter-media decisions on these grounds are dependent on two sorts of work. First, setting the advertisement objectives (again, translated from marketing plan, role of advertising and how it is expected to work) – which requires analysis and invention. Secondly, creating campaigns to meet the objectives.

It is here that creative people most overtly affect media decisions. Where agencies have become too immersed in rigid categories of skills, this influence has often been seen by media men as sinister or mystical, or both. But of course creative people should no more think of a creative treatment apart from a medium than media men should think of a medium apart from anything that will appear in it. The influence is only sinister if it is not governed by aiming to meet the campaign objectives. In practice, of course, things are not as tidy as this. The medium cannot be decided until the campaign idea emerges, and the campaign idea will not emerge neatly, in logical order and in finished form. There can be a change of medium as the idea develops from its tentative beginnings, either by creative chain reaction or as the result of developmental research. It may not even be possible to agree on final advertising objectives until the idea emerges; there is feedback here too. What this can easily mean is that choice of medium will depend partly on who is chosen as creative director; it may be that some people think immediately, or produce their best work, in television, others in print. This may seem slightly shocking at first; but not when one remembers that the object is to produce the best *treatment-within-medium* that the particular account group can, against the advertising objectives. We are not dealing in absolutes.

The organization implications here are that good inter-media decisions will depend, among other things, on a close dialogue between creative people and those responsible for setting the advertising objectives.

Much the same considerations apply to the choice of **medium as message**. It may or may not be what McLuhan (1964) meant (who knows?), but I think it is worth making this distinction from medium-as-medium. I would put under medium-as-message anything that a medium adds to a brand or its advertising through its own intrinsic values, simply by being associated with the brand. This is not to do with a medium being, say, 120-screen black-and-white newsprint (which has certain characteristics different from colour imitation art paper, as an artist's medium); it is to do with whether it is the *Daily Sketch* or *The Times*.

This is an extraordinarily difficult area, and fertile country for myths. There is perhaps today a tendency to discount such effects, partly because there is no really good evidence that they exist (Broadbent and Segnit, 1968). But think we may have been looking at rather crude hypotheses, expressed in suitably crude terms, like "editorial rub-off" (Clemens, 1962; Thelen, 1954); and at differences likely to be small (like two different newspapers, rather than women's weeklies versus television). In any case, in trying to measure medium-as-message effects we are up against the same problems as in testing advertisements: our research tends to measure single exposures in artificial circumstances, while we feel that advertising works over a long period in natural circumstances.

Devalued in the Eyes of the Customer

What we do know with reasonable assurance is that there is some interaction between the different elements of advertisements. For instance, within commercials, by association, between a brand and, say, a presenter. Over time a young presenter makes an old brand seem a bit younger and the brand makes the presenter seem a bit older. It thus seems to me a fair assumption that certain of the intrinsic values of, say, television (its "message") have some effect, by association, on brands advertised on it. Just as, I believe, a brand featured on bargain basement pages or promoted by a constant series of tawdry on-pack premiums runs a risk of being devalued in the eyes of the consumer. Just as, I think, in the early days of television certain brands gained enormously by association with its excitement and novelty. Just as, I feel, an advertisement in a national newspaper communicates something slightly different from the same ad in a local paper. But it's hard to be sure.

Inter-media decisions on grounds of medium-as-message will be based on characteristics like the believability, integrity, sincerity, atmosphere of a medium; the context in which it is used; its secondary effect (e.g. on the retail trade). Perhaps one of the most important is its privacy or public-ness. If people choose brands to some extent as extensions of themselves, it may matter a lot to them who is presumed to be aware of the values of the brand or to whom the manufacturer is presumed to be selling it.

A dress advertised in *Vogue* is likely to appear more valuable to the reader than the same dress, advertised in the same way, in *Woman's Own*, on the (possibly subconscious) grounds that it would have to be a better dress to appeal to the sort of people who read *Vogue*.

In view of the very subjective nature of these criteria (and virtually complete absence of research), there is even more need than with medium-as-medium to operate through a constant dialogue between creative people and those who set the advertising objectives.

Organizational Implications

Analysis of the job to be done in inter-media decisions leads to some fairly firm conclusions affecting organization:

(i) There can be no question of any one of the traditional departmental skills (Account Executive, Marketing, Media, Creative) alone making inter-media decisions. All are deeply involved.

(ii) Nor is it possible normally (if we want to make a good decision) to fix it at one brief meeting of all four. This is because one of the crucial elements – the creative treatment – does not normally arrive suddenly and complete. The process requires fairly constant interrelations and feedback, involving all the interests.

(iii) The difficult decisions all depend on skill at deriving the advertising objectives from the marketing objectives, and defining the precise role of the advertising.

(iv) There is a slightly paradoxical danger that, if we do not organize ourselves properly, as the media world becomes more "sophisticated," more inter-media decisions will be influenced by simple myth.

SKILLS NEEDED

The sort of skills needed to make inter-media decisions follow fairly directly from this analysis of the job to be done:

Physical Skills

There seems no particular need for physical skills. The creative skills needed for judgement of medium-as-medium and medium-as-message require the ability to visualize the finished form of an advertising idea, but not necessarily to produce it on the spot.

Skills of Knowledge

The recurrent thread running through all the individual actions of the job is that of setting precise advertising objectives from marketing objectives. Thus the main skills of knowledge needed will be of *marketing* in general terms – experiments and experimental design in particular; and *research* (the main source of data for decisions) – its meaning and its reliability. This will become more important with the emergence of more television channels, UHF, colour, commercial radio, single source data.

Perhaps surprisingly, knowledge of media and media owners is needed at a rather more superficial level. It is needed with consideration of medium-as-vehicle (coverage and cost-per-thousand), but as we have seen, these are two rather fragile concepts. And in any case assessment of their importance depends more on knowledge of the reliability and meaning of the research from which we derive them than on intimate knowledge of the media themselves.

Knowledge of media certainly comes in importantly in considerations of medium-as-message – partly because this is an entirely judgemental area. Maybe, one day, there will be some research available, and then considerable knowledge of research and how it is produced will be needed to understand what the results mean.

Social Skills

There are undoubtedly social skills involved in inter-media decisions. Since myth is a powerful force but needs to be looked at dispassionately, skills of negotiation will be needed – particularly when it is the client who holds the myth. More important, since analysis of the job to be done shows that a fairly wide range of interests have to be involved, continuously and with constant feedback, there are considerable social skills involved in keeping these various interests working together harmoniously and productively.

But there are certain social skills available in an agency which are not particularly needed in making inter-media decisions. There seems no need, for instance, for a very high degree of administrative ability. Nor is there for bargaining skills – bargaining really does not affect the decision.

This last is an important point, since similar analysis of media buying and intra-media decisions makes it clear that bargaining skills are absolutely crucial. It is already apparent that for choice of individual medium within the category of, say, women's magazines (that is, once the inter-media decision has been made and once the magazines that are obviously wrong on coverage or cost have been removed from the list) bargaining can achieve far greater differences than evaluating different schedules on the computer at card rates. If, as seems likely, the growth of new media is greater than that of advertising expenditure, bargaining will become even more important. The invasion by American media brokers suggests that others have come to this conclusion.

Mental Skills

However, our analysis makes it fairly clear that it is mental skills that are most called for in inter-media decisions. First, there is the analysis of increasingly complex research data. This draws on knowledge of research and how it is done, but goes much further. The real skill clearly lies in using and interpreting the data in a green-fingered way, relating one finding to another, often from a different source, or relating quantitative and qualitative data. Secondly, there are the vital skills of translating marketing objectives into advertising objectives, strategically and tactically. This will certainly require ability to analyse, but beyond that an ability to theorize – since the job is concerned with very complex relationships. And beyond that, to some degree, an ability to innovate and invent. Thirdly, creative skills by which the advertising objectives are translated into campaigns. For this the ability to invent is supreme, but skills of analysis (possibly through observation and introspection more than research) and at theorizing are very important too.

ORGANIZATIONAL IMPLICATIONS

It is a matter of judgement always how many different people are implied by a given number of skills. But it does seem most unlikely that any one person could have to any marked degree the diverse skills shown to be needed for inter-media decisions.

It also seems a little unlikely that high (social) skill at bargaining would be combined in one person with the main (mental) skills of inter-media planning. They appear to require rather different sorts of personality. We are left with the paradox that the skills that are most vital to media buying will not often contribute very much to inter-media decisions.

One very important point emerges clearly. The skills of knowledge, the mental and social skills required for inter-media planning are precisely those needed for the initial development of the campaign itself (the actual advertisements). Setting objectives for inventing and testing campaigns requires the same knowledge of research and marketing; the same social skills of negotiation and cooperation; the same mental skills of analysis, theorizing and inventing. The execution of the campaign may require other skills, just as inter-media decisions do; but up to a certain point, planning of media and advertisements is virtually the same job (Jones, 1968).

Working Methods

The complexity of the process and diversity of skills shown so far must make it quite clear that, if we are to go beyond a primitive level of skill, working methods for inter-media decisions must be based on:

- project group working, not production line
- a system of feedback, with experiments and tests, followed by adjustments, over a long period of time.

Though inter-media decisions may be made finally (by the client) on the day of the big annual presentation, the process of reaching the point of decision is more or less continuous.

RELATIONSHIPS AND JOB SATISFACTION

Relationships

It is unfortunate that the organizational models most of us have in the back of our minds most of the time are those of a hierarchical line management (1 boss, 2 deputies, 4 assistants, 8 deputy assistants, 16 assistant deputy assistants, and so on) and of a production line (A takes the job to point 5, B from point 6 to point 10, C from point 11 to point 15, etc.). These seem totally inappropriate concepts for the project team work described above, with its complex relationships and need for continuous feedback. (One might add that they also seem wrong for the spirit of today, if what is happening in universities now will be affecting agencies in five years' time.) There is a great deal of evidence that a small group working properly, through the very interaction of people, is more creative than individuals working alone, produces ideas faster and modifies them faster (Klein, 1963; Miller and Rice, 1967; Rice, 1963). There is evidence too that a small group fairly quickly sets its own norms and loyalties and methods. These can be a great source of strength and productivity, provided the group is properly constituted and has sufficient independent existence to develop real involvement.

The departmental, hierarchical, production line way of thinking can lead people to try to avoid overlap of jobs, on the grounds of wastefulness. This can mean rigid job specifications and demarcation disputes. But of course in a project group, working as a group, overlap of interest and understanding is essential. It is the confrontation of different ideas springing from a common understanding of objectives, leading to improved and extended ideas, that makes a group more productive. Productivity comes not through avoiding overlap, but by getting fundamentals right before dealing with details, by having people skilled enough to get most things right the first time and by spending the minimum time in blind alleys. (We should never, for instance, allow ourselves to get into the situation of presenting a detailed media schedule, showing individual insertions in individual women's magazines on certain dates with certain positions, only to get the response "what would it look like in cinema?")

Job Satisfaction

May be a much more important problem than we ever admit. Skill at making inter-media decisions will ultimately depend on getting and keeping good-quality people, and this will depend on the total satisfaction offered by jobs. I think it would be fair to say that there have been some serious problems with the total satisfactions of the job, particularly in terms of status, in agency marketing, media and research departments. The account executives and creative people seem to rank higher. There is always the danger of a vicious spiral in the "technical" departments, with lower satisfactions attracting less ambitious people, leading to lower status, leading to less satisfaction, and so on. This situation can greatly affect the balance of a working group, and balance seems important. The aim must therefore be to achieve among members of the group a reasonable parity in three areas:

1. *Status*: This can be formal status – the man with responsibility. It is usually part of the account executive's status, or the man with a label like the Associate Director. Or, it can be association with the end product, often a large part of the creative man's status. Or recognition as having special skills, either internally (the person whose opinion is sought or one with a carefully leaked high salary), or externally (in the media world, as for many media buyers, or through learned articles). Or through the balance of power in buying/selling relationships for instance, media buyers.
2. *Depth of involvement*: One of the problems of having too many specialists can be that the generalist is much more deeply involved in the project than each specialist; and this prevents balance and smooth working. This would tend to happen, for instance, if an account group contained a marketing man, a media planner and a research man; almost inevitably each would be less involved than the account executive or creative group head. This sort of division of experts may at times have led to some dilution of the skill status of research and media men.
3. *Skills*: Getting the right balance of skills is likely to depend partly on getting parity of age and experience among group members, and this will depend a lot on building the skills of individuals where necessary. That is, turning any vicious circles into virtuous ones.

Organisational Implications

The implications here follow on from the whole of the rest of the analysis. What we seem to need for making inter-media decisions (and, as we saw, for developing campaigns) is a project group:

- that is balanced in status, involvement and skills;
- that will, as a group, cover the necessary social and mental skills and knowledge, in an overlapping way;
- that is small enough to be operational, large enough to interact;
- that operates on a continuous basis, developing its own personality and skills as a group.

What will be helpful to guide the different skills and people in the group – that will hopefully grow as the group develops its own working methods – is a clear generalized philosophy about how to translate marketing objectives into advertising objectives, and how advertising may be expected to work, and so on.

FORMAL STRUCTURE

In this section, I shall be describing briefly the structure that we now have for planning campaigns, advertisements and media selection in JWT. This is not because I think we necessarily have the "right" structure or have solved all problems. There are two particular reasons for looking at JWT experience.

First, we have been through all the analysis and reasoning described above, and have done something about it. It is not just a theoretical exercise. Secondly, it seems that we will all face quite radical changes over the next 10 years (more than in the last 20), and I think that many other large agencies will move in the same direction as JWT – at the very least to reach a more flexible structure.

Formal Structure

First, how we are formally organized for planning. There are of course endless minor variations according to particular needs on accounts – but it all fits into a total pattern. I should make the point, of course, that planning campaigns is only one part of what an agency does. We have laid stress on it because part of JWT's philosophy has always been a belief in the vital importance of proper planning (in the widest sense of the word). Quite clearly, dividing agency work into planning and operations is fairly artificial; the two overlap and interrelate. But to keep within bounds, I am sticking to planning here.

"Structure" is itself a rather misleading word for it, redolent of hierarchical family tree type organization charts. What we have set up is a system whereby *a project group of three skills* is the norm for planning of advertising campaigns. That is, it is not necessarily three people – one of the skills could have two people representing it – and it is not necessarily the same three people dealing with, say, a minor advertisement test as dealt with working out the essentials of the advertising strategy. *The point is that for each piece of planning work each of the three skills should be represented and that they should work together as a group, not as individual contributors*. The three skills are in fact organized into three departments, as in most agencies. They are: Account Representative (Account Executive), Creative, Account Planning.

The project group of three for advertising planning on any account is drawn from a larger account group which will include various operational and organizational skills (such as media buying, promotions buying, package design, progress control). And the level at which it operates can vary. On a major project, at the top level there could be an account director, a creative director and an account planning group head, all overlooked by a management supervisor. On a smaller project, it might be an account representative, a creative supervisor and an account planner, with an account director having overall responsibility.

PLANNING PLUS OPERATIONS

Three important points emerge from this. First, where one man has overall responsibility for an account (the account director for the smaller project quoted above), then he is overlooking the whole of planning plus operations. Though historically most account directors have been drawn from account representatives, the job covers a much wider area. As far as planning is concerned, it is the difference between being responsible for the whole group and having a certain role within the group. Secondly, the planning group of three is set up to give a balance of skills, involvement and status. However, it is the account representative who has the job of coordinating the group and representing the views of the client, and thus his role within the group is one of "first among equals". Thirdly, there is just one person in the group of three, the account planner, to represent the "technical" skills of campaign development, research, advertising testing and media planning, where many agencies have at least two. JWT used to have two – the marketing man and the media planner – and combining the two into one is the main formal change we have made. One immediate result is a rather better balance of involvement within the planning group. Not only that; we are beginning to find that a group of three is much more practical than a group of four. It seems quite large enough to be stimulating and productive of ideas, but small enough to meet frequently and in a properly constituted way. With a group of four, there is always that much more danger of, say, the account representative finding it easier to have three informal meetings of two (himself and each of the others) than a meeting of the whole group.

1. Division of Job and Skills

Although of course each member of the planning group draws largely on traditional, departmental skills (we have to live in the real world), the whole point of working by project group methods is to get away from job demarcations. Unless there is considerable overlap of job and skill, we shall not benefit from the interactions of the group. So the listing here is a very broad one; it indicates the main spheres of interest for each member, without suggesting that the others don't get involved at all. (For instance, the account representative has, as one of his main spheres of interest, contacts with the client; but this is not to suggest in any way that the other two should never meet the client).

Account Representative:
- Coordination of the planning group.
- Contacts with the client and the client's marketing plan.
- Adviser to the client on his marketing plan – especially on roles of advertising and merchandising/promotions in the marketing mix.
- Effect of the marketing plan on advertising objectives, strategical and tactical.
- Effect of marketing plan direct on inter-media decisions.

Creative:
- Contacts with communication skills and techniques.
- Defining precise role of advertising within advertising objectives.
- Creating campaign ideas from advertising objectives.
- Knowledge of capability and meaning of media (i.e. medium-as-medium and medium-as-message).

Account Planning:
- Knowledge of capability and meaning of research.
- Contacts with media buyers, research companies.
- Using research skills, green-fingeredly, to set campaign and media objectives, theorizing on precise role of advertising.

- Devising and managing continuous programme of research (e.g. using it to evaluate advertising against objectives).

One important point in looking at these spheres of interest is that while all three will be involved in operations – putting the plan into effect – the account planner will be much less involved than the other two. Concentrating more on campaign planning, he will tend ideally to take many of the planning initiatives, write documents and so on.

2. Status and Job Satisfactions

It is difficult to legislate for status and job satisfactions. But, again, the group of three should get a better balance. For one thing, there should be considerable pleasure in working *as a group* on a project. It is significant that we tend to fall into the group-of-three approach naturally when there is major planning work to be done under pressure (as, for instance, in preparing initial planning to a brief for a vital new business presentation). In such circumstances, people will happily work at an intensity that would be most offensive to them, if they were not in a close-knit project group. Secondly, there is opportunity for a rise in status for the "technical" side, when represented by one man, the account planner. The account representative and creative man still have their traditional sources of status. The account planner will have status through recognition of his skills of knowledge, especially as they become more complicated, and through his concentration on advertising planning. To a large extent his status will depend a lot on his ability to show that it matters.

3. Working Methods

What is new about all this is essentially a breaking down of the traditional approaches and of the traditional media, marketing and research departmental barriers, and re-examining the scope of the job and people's roles. Where this is done, there needs to be a fairly strong central link in the agency's theories of how to produce advertising and how it works. Otherwise, deprived of traditional structures, people might feel rather lost.

So, in JWT, the whole process has been a continuation of the development of such a "philosophy", which had come increasingly to the conclusion that campaign planning and basic media planning (inter-media decisions) are really the same job. They are linked by the way in which we set advertising objectives. The sequence has, in grossly oversimplified terms, been worked out in this way:

(a) Advertising for mass-consumption brands works, first, in the long run by adding to the total satisfactions of the brand (Leman, 1968); secondly, in the short run, by adding salience or immediacy to the brand (McDonald, 1969).
(b) The total satisfactions of a brand are caused by a unique blend of physical product and communication, and they are a blend of sensual, rational and emotional satisfactions.
(c) Being a unique blend, the brand will not appeal to everyone. The specialization of appeal aimed for will depend on the nature of the market and competition.
(d) Therefore, translation of marketing plan into advertising objectives will mean, first, working out the precise nature of the brand's satisfactions and whom it is to satisfy, in terms of appeals to senses, reason and emotions; then deciding what particular contribution each marketing factor (including advertising) can play. Secondly, relating marketing tactics to the salience values of marketing.

(e) Thus we end with a simple format for setting objectives that will link all aspects of advertising planning, based on:

(i) a *target group* (including its size, whereabouts, attitudes and current behaviour);

(ii) a set of *desired responses* at the sensual, rational and emotional levels;

(iii) *timing*, which deals with the salience values, by way of a theory of how precisely the advertising is expected to work.

(f) So in terms of inter-media decisions, advertising objectives are set in exactly the same way as for creative strategy. The questions to be answered are:

(i) What is the target group? So into analysis of medium-as-vehicle.

(ii) What medium or media can best contribute to the brand's appeal to the senses, reason and emotions? Or, what are the media values – physical, functional, emotional – that will best contribute? So into analysis of medium-as-medium and medium-as-message.

(iii) How to schedule the advertising to maximize salience, while building up long-term added value to the brand?

4. What Next?

All this approach to organization may just be the start. There is obviously a continuum between a totally departmental structure and a totally project group structure, and agencies may well find themselves moving continually on the scale. The advertising business is becoming more complex; clients' organizations and needs are changing; public attitudes to advertising and profits may change; people's needs in their working environment are changing; sheer growth in agencies will bring problems. All this is likely to mean a much more searching and systematic look at the structure of agencies. In the end the only constant thing may be the need for change.

REFERENCES

Broadbent, S.R. and Segnit, S. (1967) *Response Functions in Media Planning*. The Thomson Organisation Ltd.

Broadbent, S.R. and Segnit, S. (1968) *Beyond Cost per Thousand*. The Thomson Organisation Ltd.

Clemens, J. (1962) *The Effect of Media on Advertisement Reception*. The Thomson Organisation Ltd.

Corlett, T. and Richardson, D. (1969) "An examination of some of the tolerances in press media schedule evaluations", *Journal of the Marketing Research Society*.

Jones, R.W. (1968) "Are media departments out of date"? *Admap*, September.

Klein, J. (1963) *Working with Groups*. Hutchinson.

Leman, G. (1968) *Sales, Saleability and the Saleability Gap*. BBTA.

McDonald, C.D.P. (1969) "Relationships between advertising exposure and purchasing behaviour", MRS Conference.

McLuhan, M. (1964) *Understanding Media*. McGraw-Hill.

Miller, F.J. and Rice, A.K. (1967) *Systems of Organisation*. Tavistock.

Rice, A.K. (1963) *The Enterprise and its Environment*. Tavistock.

Thelen, A.J. (1954) *Dynamics of Groups at Work*. Chicago University Press.

Part II
Planning: Craft Skills

Tim Broadbent observes in his piece in this section that "the standard advertising agency functions such as the creative department, for instance, or account management, evolved messily over time from the primordial ooze of Victorian media agencies. But account planning is a *made* thing. It was deliberately designed to meet an agency need that in-house research and marketing departments did not meet."

As a "made" thing, it clearly needed guidelines as to how it should work; or put more accurately, how individuals aspiring to be account planners should approach the various problems and dilemmas the task involves. No one thought harder and more coherently about the intellectual underpinning than Stephen himself and this section details some of the specific features that should live in the planner's mental tool kit.

A Revolutionary Challenge to Conventional Wisdom

By Paul Feldwick, Former Worldwide Brand Planning Director BMP

An introduction to:

7.1 What Can Pre-testing Do?

As all readers of the Tintin books will know, Thomson is not to be confused with Thompson. Neither is J Walter Thompson to be confused with the Thomson Organisation, founded by the Canadian-born Roy Thomson, which during the 1960s was one of the main media proprietors in the UK. Between 1962 and 1971 it was the Thomson Organisation that sponsored a series of annual awards "to stimulate fresh thinking upon advertising research problems which are not adequately dealt with by existing techniques".

It was a worthy intention and it seems a shame that, since 1971, as far as I know, neither media proprietor nor agency has supported anything comparable. Each year, Gold and Silver medals, with substantial cash prizes, were given for the best papers written on set topics. For the first five years, the focus was very much on media planning questions, but in 1967 the Thomson judges broadened the field to include issues of creative research, inviting papers for the Gold Medal on "the pre-testing of press advertisements".

The original request for submissions suggests that, in the judges' view, media planning had already become "analytical and sophisticated". The challenge they saw now was for the development of creative content to be brought up to a similar standard of efficiency, and for press advertising – Thomson's main interest – the state of practice was particularly problematic. In an elaborately worded brief, the winning paper was required to deal with four specific aspects of the topic:

(a) An analytical review of the main techniques currently in use for the pre-testing of press advertisements.
(b) A review of whatever evidence is available to indicate what order of contribution the pre-testing of press advertisements can make to the overall efficiency of campaigns.
(c) A discussion of the parameters that might be regarded as relevant in pre-testing research, and of the means by which they may be assessed.
(d) Consideration of the mechanisms whereby pre-testing procedures may be employed to increase the efficiency of press advertising decisions.

This brief, which manages to be both pedantic and vague (there is also half a page of further explanatory notes which I omit), provides the jumping off point for Stephen's paper "What Can Pre-Testing Do?"

A Fundamental Criticism

His criticism of it, while couched in the most diplomatic language, is fundamental – that the terms in which the problem is being posed have already pre-judged or avoided the really important issues of advertising research. For creative research to make advertising better, it has to generate understanding and guidance, and that involves much more than a simplistic go/no-go decision – even if such a "test" were a credible possibility.

Creative research also needs to be planned and conducted within an appropriate set of assumptions about how advertising works, and how its eventual marketplace performance can be evaluated – both topics that pre-occupied Stephen throughout his life. But the Thomson brief rather implies that the question of "pre-testing" can somehow be addressed as a purely technical issue, without considering this larger context.

Hence Stephen's comment early in the paper that "if I wanted to get anywhere, I wouldn't have started from here."

Understanding, not Formulae

It is clear in his paper, as in much else that Stephen wrote, that he valued research highly as an aid to creative judgement, and as a tool for making advertising better through understanding consumers and their responses. He did not, on the other hand, believe that there could be any research formulae that would predict actual advertising performance, and even less that one single formula could somehow be devised that would work for all campaigns.

This position has been reiterated by many others since 1968, and it seems to me incontestably the most useful attitude to take to creative research: neither rejecting it wholesale as a "rear view mirror", nor imagining that simplistic measures applied uncritically to advertisements will form any reliable substitute for judgement.

For the earlier part of my career I worked in an agency that put this view into constant practice, with a commitment to diagnostic, qualitative research on everything we did (at least, this was true of TV – we never found an entirely satisfactory way to get similarly useful feedback about print material). Quantitative research we hardly used at all. (I do believe it is possible to do worthwhile quantitative creative research, but I think it is very difficult to do well and requires careful thought.)

The campaigns that BMP produced as a result of this way of working during the 1970s and 1980s were generally acknowledged as being both creative and effective – campaigns that influenced brand relationships more through craft, sympathy and charm, than the conventionally respected constructs of message transmission and factual persuasion. The qualitative research we used may not have been "scientific", at least not in the traditional, positivist sense, but I cannot imagine we could have produced the work we did in any other way.

Nor do I believe that greater use of quantitative research would significantly have improved its efficiency. (It remains a matter of fact that there is an inverse correlation between the use of quantitative pre-testing and success in the IPA Advertising Effectiveness Awards.)

The Curse of Standardized Measures

However, my personal experience and convictions seem to be remote from the general trend of the past 40 years. Although Stephen, Stanley Pollitt, Alan Hedges and others all wrote forcefully about the limitations of pre-testing in the 1960s and 1970s, the decades that followed saw the widespread adoption of standardized, quantitative techniques to an unprecedented degree.

When Stephen wrote dismissively about "setting advertising objectives in terms of 'just go on trying until you get a score over 7+'," he may have hoped that this was already an outmoded attitude. Sadly it seems today to be more and more what the market demands. International marketing corporations require standardized measures to be used from Caracas to Kuala Lumpur, and believe that to improve the efficiency of their advertising, they just need to insist on beating certain scores. Meanwhile the techniques in use are essentially little changed from what they were in the 1960s.

It seems that organizational pressures for control, measurement, standardization and rationality, in increasingly risk-averse cultures, make it harder than ever to develop brand communications that create complicity and a positive emotional relationship with their audience. It may not be coincidence that, according to yearly monitoring, the proportion of the British public agreeing that "the ads are often better than the programmes" has steadily declined since peaking in 1991.

In an age when people have more and more power to avoid communications that don't engage with them in the right way, it's high time the old Rosser Reeves model of "getting a selling proposition into people's heads" was finally, belatedly laid to rest; and along with it the antiquated research paraphernalia that pretends to predict "effectiveness" by measuring message recall, attention, comprehension, believability, and other such irrelevancies, in artificial situations that bear no relation to real media exposure. There's little sign, however, 40 years on, that this is about to happen.

The winning Gold Medal paper in 1967 is an intelligent, well written, and thorough review of the topic, but it follows closely the "exam question" as set and thus remains fundamentally unchallenging. The judges commented that the papers entered had revealed "an inadequacy in research techniques for the pre-testing of press advertisements", and while they duly praised the winning paper, they admitted that their overall response had been "frank disappointment . . . because so little emerged to suggest that the situation is likely to undergo any speedy improvement".

In other words, the Thomson Gold Medal for 1967 failed to produce any breakthrough thinking because it had already posed the problem in terms that did not admit a useful solution. If instead of searching for "pre-testing techniques", the judges had asked for ideas on "how research can make advertising more effective", they would I hope have received some better answers. Perhaps Stephen King himself might have offered them something like the article that follows.

7.1
What Can Pre-testing Do?*

By Stephen King

An article specially commissioned on the subject of the Thomson Gold Medal for Advertising Research for 1967.

Most people would agree that the Thomson Awards have made an outstanding contribution to the development of new ideas in advertising research. And in 1967 the scope was broadened to cover problems outside media research; the subject for the Gold Medal was the pre-testing of press advertisements. This is clearly an area of great importance to advertisers, agencies and research companies; a great deal of time and money is spent on pre-testing – several hundred thousand pounds a year. Yet I suspect that, however excellent the winner, there was not a large entry of thoughtful papers for the Gold Medal. This seems a little disappointing, and it is worth asking why.

Inevitably one is led to look at the assumptions that lie behind the questions themselves. It must be as hard to set the questions as it is to answer them, and the Thomson Organisation carefully introduced several notes and qualifications, to avoid restricting entrants. It was clear too that, for this first competition outside media research, they must start from the ideas and language which are current in the area of pre-testing advertisements. Indeed I think they caught the flavour of much of the current talk about pre-testing very accurately. Yet in spite of this, or perhaps because of it, the questions set for the Gold Medal had a slightly dated air. They may well have left the would-be entrant with a feeling of frustration, a disinclination to fight again battles which he thought had already been won. Perhaps above all a feeling of "if I wanted to get anywhere, I wouldn't have started from here".

STRAIGHT ANSWERS

It is quite possible to give straight answers (in a very superficial way) to the four sections of the question set, but the answers do not actually take us very far (except perhaps by relieving the sense of frustration):

(a) An analytical review of pre-testing *techniques* hardly seems the point. People have been studying the techniques for many years, especially since the ARF's Printed Advertising Rating Methods report of 1956. It is not too hard to be destructive about most of the current (often fairly ancient) techniques. It must surely be pretty clear by now that there can be no magic solutions – no all-purpose measure for pre-testing.

(b) We can hardly begin to examine the order of contribution made by pre-testing to the overall efficiency of campaigns. until we have made a little progress towards measuring

---

*Published in *Admap*, March 1968. Reproduced with permission.

the overall efficiency of campaigns. That is, unless we cheat and define the contribution of pre-testing as what is left when the contributions of all the other factors in the efficiency of a campaign have been accounted for. Of course, Thomsons were only asking for a review of the evidence.

(c) A discussion of the parameters relevant to pre-testing seems a reasonable request. But it may be that, in a sense, there are no universally relevant parameters that can usefully be discussed. Many would say that there are different parameters for different advertisements. Even if we accept the existence of universals, we are up against the old problem that we can never find the direct link between the research measure and advertising effectiveness. For instance, I can define "involvement" as a logically necessary parameter in advertising effectiveness – that is, as the relationship between a person and any advertisement that works; but then of course I cannot tell whether standard "involvement measures" are measuring involvement in this sense. Or I can define it as whatever is measured by "involvement measures", in which case I do not know how relevant it is. There has been a great deal of argument that slips quietly from one type of definition to the other, but the gap must remain unbridged.

(d) I am not too sure what would be included as "mechanisms whereby pre-testing procedures may be employed to increase the efficiency of press advertising decisions". But presumably not *interpretation* of research (too imprecise to be called a mechanism) or *organization* (which is referred to specifically later in the statement of problems). There is maybe an implication here that some formula could be found whereby a certain type of pre-testing score could be applied directly to advertising decisions (rather as, for instance, television attention factors might be applied to ratings to help media scheduling decisions). Again, this seems to presuppose a relevant all-purpose measure, or at least a relevant set of parameters.

The trouble may very well lie in the implications of the very word "pre-test". It is normally used to mean a quantified measurement of future performance in real conditions. (This is thought of in much the same way as pre-testing the tensile strength of a new alloy; by using a universally accepted and meaningful measure, it predicts the later performance of the material when made into a finished object.) This type of definition is supported in the Gold Medal questions by the use of words like "mechanism", "parameter" and "validation". The strong inference is that it is possible to predict advertising performance in real conditions by a pre-test, and that the real point at issue is therefore that of the *right techniques*. In fact, I believe that this may be begging the question, and that most of the progress made in recent years has come from treating techniques as the last in a chain of decisions. There are three areas in particular in which developments have been helpful.

Usefulness

First, there has been a more determined move to look at advertising research from the point of view of its *usefulness* and to ask to whom it is useful, for what and when? It is this pragmatic approach that has mainly cast doubt on the very idea of looking for all-purpose techniques.

It has emphasized, for instance, that there are many different uses for research in the different stages involved in the development and evaluation of a campaign. Different people want different sorts of information. Decision making in advertising is a good deal more complex than the accept/reject choice that is implied by the word "pre-testing." In its turn, this emphasis has led to a more systematic examination of the processes of producing advertising, and shown that research has an important contribution to make at the stages of setting strategy, of creative development and of market-place evaluation.[1]

The principle of usefulness and the idea of a cycle of advertising have led to a clearer assessment of the role that research can play in the "pre-test" situation. It has become clear that advertising must have objectives that are meaningful to both researcher and creative man, and that to say "Here's an advertisement: please test it" is unlikely to yield anything of value. To make the link, the objectives are best set in terms of the desired responses to the brand of the target consumer. If this is done, the same strategy and the same criteria for evaluation can be used by product designer, copywriter, art director, pack designer, researcher and everyone involved in marketing planning. Informal research, properly interpreted, can give a reasonably clear indication of whether any piece of communication is getting the desired responses, and if not, what to do about it.

This is, of course, a very different matter from pre-testing in the sense of using research to predict whether an advertisement will work, or which of two will work better. But here, too, looking at the usefulness of research methods (before getting involved in arguments about validity) can solve many problems. A recent example can illustrate this. In one analysis of 86 pre-tests we were able to show, from both theoretical and empirical checks, that the spread of "scores" from testing *different* advertisements for a brand was almost the same as from testing *the same* advertisement a number of times. Whatever the reason for these results, we could certainly say that this pre-test method was not useful for decision making.

Developing Advertising Theory

A second advance in recent years has been the growing recognition of the importance of improving our theories of advertising (Joyce, 1967). Indeed, any detailed consideration of pre-testing techniques leads us straight back to questions of theory. In any pre-test we have "options" in terms of the type of material to use (from rough to finished); the sample of respondents (who can be chosen in demographic terms, by product usage, media use, special needs or psychological characteristics); the method of exposing the material to the sample (from highly artificial to entirely naturalistic); and the type of questions to use. The hardest option perhaps is that of the right questions; there is a basic choice of physiological measures (basal skin response, pulse rate, heart beat, pupil dilation, eye movement, etc.), verbal measures (attention, recall, comprehension, belief, interest, liking, attitudes to brands, attitudes to buying or using, involvement, mood, persuasion, etc.) and behavioural measures (gift choice, coupon response, buying).

Any criteria for choosing among these options go straight back to fundamental questions about how advertising works. What sort of material adequately represents the effect of a finished advertisement? When is a rough too rough? Who are the people on which advertising works? What are the critical terms in which to set target groups? What is the effect on people's responses of an artificial environment? What is the effect of being interviewed on people who have been exposed to advertising naturalistically? Which questions are relevant to effectiveness? How can we be sure that they are measuring what they purport to measure? It seems to me to be impossible to start answering such questions without developing some theory of what elements in advertisements affect which sort of people in what sort of way. In particular, one has to come

---

[1] This and other points raised here have been more fully discussed in King (1967).

to some sort of conclusion about whether advertising is essentially preaching to the converted or converting the ignorant, the apathetic and the hostile; whether it works by changing rational beliefs or intensifying emotional responses or through familiarity, or some combination of them.

Gestalt Theories

Thirdly, the type of theories of advertising which are emerging seem to take us further and further from techniques as a starting point. Underlying most techniques of pre-testing (though rarely stated explicitly) is the idea that a single advertisement converts a non-user into being a user by persuading him of the functional benefits of the brand (King, 1967). It seems to correspond to Pavlov's theories of conditioned reflexes or at any rate the later work of Thorndike and Kohler, who recognized the importance of motivation in the effects of communication (that is, the communications did not have the same effect, if the animals were not hungry).

But most psychologists since then have suggested that the mind is a good deal more complicated than that. The Gestalt psychologists developed the idea of a complex interaction of forces, usually categorized into "cognition, affection and conation"; that is, the believing, feeling and trying of elements. More recent work has emphasized that the reception and effect of a communication depends largely on what is in the mind already and in particular on a drive for consistency of beliefs and feelings.

I believe that we are moving towards a theory of advertising which is a good deal more coherent than those implicit in most pre-testing techniques and whose starting point is the Gestalt theory of perception. That is, the theory that what we perceive is partly determined by the physical objects themselves and partly by a tendency to modify their formal qualities so that they become meaningful: and that the result is a totality, not a collection of bits. The main elements in this advertising theory could be summarized as:

1. Brands are *totalities,* with a blend of appeals to the senses, the reason and the emotions. This totality is created by the physical characteristics of product and pack, and by many different forms of communication (of which advertising is one). To put it in neo-McLuhanistic form, the brand is the advertising.
2. This totality makes a brand in many ways like a person (and not, as some seem to suggest, like an Identikit). Indeed, recent experimental work that we have done suggests that people are quite happy to consider and talk about a brand's personality; that brands are in many ways extensions of their users' personalities, rather as friends are; that the concept of an "ideal brand" makes as little sense as that of an "ideal person"; that market segmentation is most likely to be brand personality segmentation.
3. The differences in the way in which advertising works are likely to depend on where the brand lies on a scale roughly running from *habitual, casual or impulse purchase* at one end to *single or considered purchase* at the other. The position of the brand will depend on its cost, frequency of purchase, importance in scale of values, personal versus social in nature, availability, balance of hidden and open values, degree of difference between brands, consistency within the product type and several other factors.
4. Consumer advertising and advertising research are heavily concentrated on brands at the habitual, casual or impulse end of the scale. For these brands, advertising works mainly by reinforcing the existing attitudes to the brand among people who are already experienced in it – that is, who know its attributes in use from direct experience. The reinforcement

can come either from strengthening favourable attitudes or from reducing unfavourable attitudes to the brand, to make it competitively desirable as a totality.

5. The gaining of new users (those not already directly experienced in the brand) is likely to be rare for established brands and more often caused by "events" than advertising – product development, promotions, sampling, recommendation. For new brands, gaining new users is clearly important, but getting triers to buy repeatedly becomes very quickly much more important (it is a matter of weeks rather than years). Advertising can play a part in getting new users, but it is mainly indirectly, through reinforcing the attitudes of pioneering triers and of retailers, to influence word-of-mouth communication. Here again it is preaching to the converted, not directly converting.

IMPLICATIONS FOR PRE-TESTING

The implications of this theory are not very encouraging for pre-testing in the sense of predicting the effect of an advertisement in normal use.

First, the whole Gestalt theory casts doubt on taking elements of the product-plus-communication out of context. Most researchers nowadays, I think, would accept that pre-testing verbal propositions is downright misleading (King, 1965/66). Most would accept that pack designs can alter people's perceptions of a physical product. Blind versus named product tests show this clearly enough. Table 7.1 gives one example, from a straight question to matched samples on preference for two products after use.

As a result, particularly in new product development work, many people today are moving from the straightforward blind product test towards the product test in which the brand is tried out at home in a pack, with other forms of communication, maybe against a competitor; that is, in a total context nearer to that of real life. But this is not yet being done very much with advertising, and there are probably limits to which it could ever be done in any pre-testing situation. Already there is some evidence that an advertisement's effect depends partly on the medium in which it appears (Winick, 1962).

Secondly, if advertising's main job is to intensify existing total impressions of a brand and maintain the buying of existing buyers, it seems very unlikely indeed that one exposure of one advertisement will produce a relevant change in people that is large enough to measure. It is hard enough to measure the changes in attitudes to a brand after hundreds of exposures to advertising in real life.

Thirdly, the theory outlined here suggests that the "learning" caused by advertising is unconscious or incidental learning – what one picks up rather than what one learns by rote. If this is so, it may be that its effect is destroyed by the very act of interviewing people (Bogart, 1967). The pre-test interview may be forcing people into acts of choice and clear-cut opinions which they might not have had solely as a result of the advertising. It may be that the questioning

Table 7.1   Examples of preferences after use

	Products blind	Products in normal packs
Preferred Brand A	27%	39%
Preferred Brand B	47%	40%
No preference/DK	26%	21%
	100%	100%

involves people more than the stimulus. Certainly some experimental work we have done suggests that in gift-choice research situations respondents have an idea, if perhaps a rather hazy one, of what is really at issue. We are left with a paradoxical belief that "involvement" in the brand is an important objective for advertising, but that the act of pre-testing may so overlay it with a spurious involvement that we cannot really measure this vital element with any confidence (Krijgman, 1965).

WHERE DO WE GO FROM HERE?

What seems to emerge is that it is not now possible, and it is not going to be possible, to go very far in predicting the effect of a campaign in the market place by means of research. Some of the standard measures may on occasion be both valid and relevant, but there seems neither *prima facie* nor experimental evidence for them; I doubt if there ever could be. And since the word "pre-test" carries the strong implication of accurate prediction of performance in real conditions, I think we would all do much better to drop the word altogether. It would join on the black list a growing number of words which used to mean something but now serve mainly as a substitute for genuine thought – like "image", "mood", "proposition" and "quality".

It is perhaps easy to be destructive. But I think that we should not be too worried about saying "it can't be done", because this clears the way for doing a lot of things that can and should be done. Once we accept that there is no quality control mechanism, we have to stop setting advertising objectives in terms of "Just go on trying until you get a score of +7 or more". More work can go into discovering the nature of creative strategy and how to set it. Research can be of immense value for this, and in particular if some of the money currently spent on the more dubious forms of predictive pre-testing were to go into attitude research and brand personality research, I think this would be a tremendous advance.

We can also recognize that at the creative development stage research has a very important function in improving advertisements. This is partly through providing a measurement of responses compared with communication objectives, and thus eliminating crude errors. But it is mainly valuable for providing a basis for interpretation and creativity – it is the interpretation and what is done about it that matter. This leads us to judging research methods at this stage mainly for the depth of information and the insights that they provide. Also to realizing that such research can only be used by the creative people (or whoever else modifies the advertising); and thus to valuable improvements in organization and contacts between researchers and creative people, the development of a language and ideas meaningful to both, and to new ways of presenting research findings – like tape-recordings or videotapes of interviews or sitting in on group discussions.

Realizing the limitations of predictive pre-testing can also emphasize the importance of an experimental approach to advertising. Of course, there are plenty of difficulties in comparing the results of different campaigns in different areas, but if the experiments are bold enough and well enough planned, the results are usually clear enough for judgement and interpretation to reach a reasonable decision. At any rate, it seems a much more sensible approach than changing a campaign nationally on the basis of a predictive pre-test.

I think that the subject set for the 1967 Gold Medal will have stimulated a clearing of the ground for new approaches and new ideas. There are still plenty of massive problems to tackle in the area of evaluating advertising. There is the whole topic of advertising theory from the point of view of patterns of buying and their relationship with patterns of exposure to advertising. There is the problem of the right terms in which to set target groups. The old one of impact versus frequency has hardly been scratched yet (we must clearly look a lot harder at the nature of the data that are being shovelled into the computers). There is the question of brand personality; do brands have them? There is the whole subject of "involvement" in an advertisement and whether research itself introduces a spurious involvement. There are the full implications of a Gestalt theory – for instance, should advertisements always be evaluated with the brand itself? Maybe some of these might even be suitable for future competitions.

REFERENCES

Bogart, L. (1967) "No opinion, don't know and maybe no answer", *Public Opinion Quarterly*.

Joyce, T. (1967) "What do we know about how advertising works?" ESOMAR Seminar.

King, S.H.M. (1965/66) "How useful is proposition testing?" *Advertising Quarterly*, Winter.

King, S.H.M. (1967) "Can research evaluate the creative content of advertising?" *Admap*, June.

Krijgman, H.E. (1965) "The impact of television advertising", *Public Opinion Quarterly*.

Winick, C. (1962) "Three measures of the advertising value of media context", *Journal of Advertising Research*, June.

8

Four of the Wisest Principles
You Will Ever Read

By Simon Clemmow, Partner, Clemmow, Hornby, Inge Ltd

An introduction to:

8.1   Practical Progress from a Theory of Advertisements

The scope of this article is astonishing. In just six pages of *Admap*, it made an important distinction between advertisements and advertising; it dealt with response rather than stimulus in considering how advertising works; it created a simple and practical framework for identifying and defining the role for advertising; and it showed how advertising research could be better used.

If you take "advertising" in 1975 to mean "marketing communications" today, you have four pieces of enduring wisdom that couldn't be more relevant to planning in our current media and business environment. Let's take each piece of wisdom in turn. Throughout, I use the term "advertising" in the spirit of the context in which Stephen King was writing more than 30 years ago. Like him, I mean "marketing communications".

Four Pieces of Wisdom

1. Advertising vs Advertisements

The distinction between advertisements and advertising is the important difference between content and channel. Advertising is an available channel of communication, which allows people to make contact with one or more other people for an almost infinite number of different reasons. Advertisements are the messages that advertising carries in an attempt to achieve those reasons.

A good analogy is the telephone. Like the telephone system, advertising, as such, can do absolutely nothing. It's simply there, waiting to be used. Like telephone conversations, on the other hand, advertisements can do a lot. That's why Stephen talks about "a theory of advertisements", not a theory of advertising. He's interested in the effect of the content, not the use of the channel – a distinction that's even more important for the successful practitioner to understand in today's complex media environment.

---

*This paper is based on a speech given at the Conference of the Market Research Society, March 1975.

2. Stimulus v. Response

It's not what advertising does to people that's important, but rather how people respond to advertising. This idea was the single most significant contribution to advancing our understanding of how advertising works. While not wholly attributable to Stephen King, the "Scale of Immediacy" that he invented and describes in this article brought together many strands of thinking and research from previous years.

"Classic" theories of how advertising works are mainly of the single-model kind: that is, "The way advertising works is this way." These include AIDA (which states that Awareness is necessary before and leads to Interest which is necessary before and leads to Desire which is necessary before and leads to Action); USP (Unique Selling Proposition, which depends on finding a motivating point-of-difference within the product); and Brand Image (which asserts that image is more important in selling a brand than any specific product feature, and that advertising works by adding value to the gestalt).

However, as early as the 1930s it was acknowledged that advertising could work in more than one way, and frameworks began to be constructed. The most enduring from that time is James Webb Young's "Five Ways", which says that advertising works by familiarizing, by reminding, by spreading news, by overcoming inertias, and by adding a value not in the product.

Stephen mentions the USP theory, Brand Image and James Webb Young in his article, but only in his references does he mention the work of a colleague, Timothy Joyce. An article by Joyce called "What do we know about how advertising works?" had appeared as a three-part article in *Advertising Age* in 1967 and had been published separately as a JWT booklet. It perhaps does the most to pave the way for Stephen King's "Scale of Immediacy".

Joyce's article questions in earnest the premise that the consumer is a passive, rational receiver of information, and suggests that advertising works via a complex relationship of interacting variables. Most importantly, Joyce's model inserts "Attitudes" between "Advertising" and "Purchasing", and it is these attitudes – in the form of responses – that Stephen King fleshes out so compellingly.

3. Defining the Role for Advertising

This is the most important part of the planning process, and the one most demanding of the planner's craft skills. The role for advertising is the starting point for all that follows. If it is left ambiguous, inaccurate or unclear, then there are no solid foundations for developing advertising strategy or execution. Neither, as Stephen points out, is there a basis for meaningful research or evaluation.

This is where the "Scale of Immediacy" is so useful. It identifies a number of stages between advertisements intended to motivate direct actions (such as buying something from a website or magazine page) and the most indirect stage of all – reinforcing attitudes.

These in-between stages are defined by the intervening intended responses between advertising and action. For instance, the receiver relating the brand to his own needs, wants, desires or motivations (the "What a good idea" response), recalling satisfactions and making shortlists (the "That reminds me" response) and modifying attitudes (the "I never thought of it that way" response). The great strength of this model is that it recognizes that advertisements can differ in terms of how direct – or "immediate" – the intended action is. That's what brings this scale to life for the planner and makes it workable.

And, as King says:

It does not seem to require all those disclaimers that we all write at the beginning of pieces on advertising theory ("only fast-moving grocery goods need apply"). It does seem to be able to cope with today's changing circumstances, changing consumer attitudes, different product types, and different types of advertising, different media values.

In short, it's future proof.

4. What Sort of Research to Use Depends on Which is the Most Important Role for Advertising

This sounds obvious, but it wasn't fully understood in 1975, and it isn't always practised today.

The year before this article, 1974, had seen the publication of some seminal thinking on the uses and abuses of research in advertising – *Testing to Destruction* by Alan Hedges. This is a book about the ways in which research can help to make advertising expenditure more effective. It is not just about testing advertisements, but about all the ways in which research can (and cannot) make a useful contribution towards improving the effectiveness of advertising.

It draws some fundamental conclusions that were revolutionary at the time, are still true today, and, if agreed as principles between client and agency, would avoid the erosion of time, money, goodwill and quality that so often characterizes day-to-day working relationships.

Alan Hedges says:

> It is not possible to make a realistic test of the effectiveness of a commercial in a laboratory situation in advance of real-life exposure. Until this simple but uncomfortable truth is grasped much advertising research will go on being sterile and unproductive.

He goes on to say that research can't prove whether or not a particular ad will be effective before it is run, and neither can it do much in a direct sense to prove that advertising money has been well spent.

He does, however, then say that there is a great deal that research can do to help get better value for the advertising pound, and spends the rest of the book explaining what and how. It is this kind of thinking on which Stephen King builds. He shows how decisions about what sort of research to use depend on which is the most important role for advertising, and in doing so advances the cause of using research properly as an aid to judgement rather than it being a source of "tensions" and "squabbles" (his words), perhaps because the agency is required to take dictation from the standard focus group, pre-test or tracking study.

Here are Two Things You can do Next

1. Read *Testing to Destruction*. So enduring is Alan Hedges' thinking that his book has been reprinted twice by the IPA, most recently (in 1998) with a short commentary at the end of each chapter.
2. Try experimenting with the "Scale of Immediacy" for yourself. For every single piece of communication you are planning or creating or testing, ask yourself: "What do we want people to think or do, and what role does this have in the overall response we are trying to achieve?"

Perhaps you can improve on it. Stephen King ends his article in typically modest fashion, claiming that his invention is not a great breakthrough, and that the next stage might be to disprove it or invalidate it, and produce something better.

To my knowledge, none of these things has yet happened.

8.1
Practical Progress from a Theory
of Advertisements*

By Stephen King

This article is based on a speech given at the conference of the Market Research Society, March 1975.

Marketing and advertising are changing very fast today. There is a bewildering succession of short-term pressures, as government and government agencies intervene directly – sometimes speeding up long-overdue reforms, sometimes heavy-handedly mistaking effects for causes. There is the destructive force of a long period of high inflation. And perhaps most powerful of all, there are marked changes in people's attitudes to life, their aspirations, their understanding of marketing and their responses to it.

Sometimes it seems that the only things that aren't changing are the arguments about advertising research. This year, for instance, the Thomson Silver Medal question has revived the 10-year-old debate on reinforcement versus conversion in advertising. And no one seems yet to have finally scrapped all the tachistoscopes and psychogalvanometers. Indeed, there are danger signals here and there of marketing people trying to return to simplistic, universal advertising research solutions. They feel, reasonably enough, that over the last 10 years there has been a lot of talk, but little progress; and that, in today's tensions, it may be better to grab something that's simple and solid and comprehensible, rather than face the uncertainties of judgement and qualitative data and interpretation.

It would be both very sad and very time-consuming if we allowed all the arguments to come full circle and became enmeshed again in doctrinal squabbles about research techniques. What we need for these new marketing conditions is not new research, but an improved and more practical approach for setting advertising objectives.

Beliefs about the nature of effective advertising are clearly the basis for research methods, and it's worth looking back to see how we've got to where we are today. The first systematic approaches were based mainly on direct response advertising; most notably by Claude Hopkins (1923).

Results of this sort of advertisement were directly measurable and so rules could be worked out experimentally. Then, in the 1920s and 1930s, as advertising and its effects became more complicated, theories of how it worked were based more on intuition and experience. The best of the theories, by James Webb Young (1963) is certainly as good as anything produced since; but it was not related to any form of consumer research more complex than the split run.

In the next, post-war, stage there were two powerfully expressed intuitive approaches to advertising – Rosser Reeves' USP theory and David Ogilvy's espousal of the Brand Image – which were for the first time "supported" by advertising research. From then on, the arguments

*Published in *Admap*, October 1975. Reproduced with permission.

were as often about the research techniques as about the advertising objectives; so that by the mid-1960s off-the-peg pre-testing systems were looking almost powerful enough to be affecting the very nature of advertisements.

Then there was a change of direction in the UK. People argued that pre-testing systems inevitably made an assumption about how advertising works: that these assumptions were not always valid (hence the reinforcement versus conversion argument); and that unless you knew what an advertisement was trying to do, you could hardly work out the best method of measuring whether it was doing it (King, 1967). This started a long study of "how advertising works", and a great deal of valuable work has been done (Joyce, 1967; Hedges, 1974). Unfortunately, it is such an impossibly broad and complex subject that quite clearly no one will ever master it completely. Meanwhile people became tired of waiting. A healthy scepticism of the more complicated "model-building" approaches grew up, and there have recently been stirring calls for a more pragmatic approach. Colin McDonald (1975) wants more "facts" collected and David Berdy (1974) wants our concentration to move away from fundamental theories about cause and effect towards analysis of persuasion techniques in advertising.

I find myself in sympathy with both the theorists and the pragmatists. I don't think we should try to produce advertisements or evaluate their effect without having *some* theory of how they are meant to work. At the same time, I don't think we will ever solve the "how advertising works" problem. But there is surely a middle course.

What we need (and what I am aiming to put forward here) is not a wholly comprehensive theory of advertising, but a slightly more advanced *theory of advertisements*. A framework for thinking how different sorts of advertisement might work, for different people, in different circumstances, at different stages of time. Within such complexity, the framework should be simple enough to be of practical use to the people who have the job of planning and creating advertisements, and those who have the job of evaluating them.

A SCALE OF IMMEDIACY

The new framework that I am suggesting is based on a very simple, much-used idea. The starting point is the primitive view that advertising affects action (see Figure 8.1).

And this is modified by the idea that it relatively rarely affects action *directly*. There is more often an intervening response in the consumer's mind which leads ultimately to action. Hence the *indirect* effect of advertising or "black box" approach[7] (Joyce, 1965) as shown in Figure 8.2.

I think we should look on advertising effects not simply as being either direct or indirect, but as lying on a continuum between the two. That is, I have found it helpful to think of a *scale of immediacy*. Advertisements can differ in terms of either the speed or the complexity of intervening responses, or both. Figure 8.3 shows a first hypothesis about points on the scale.

So far, I have been encouraged by the way this helps to bring together many of the results of JWT's basic research programme over the last 10 years. It does not seem to require all those disclaimers that we all write at the beginning of pieces on advertising theory ("only

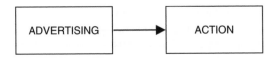

Figure 8.1   Primitive view of how advertising works

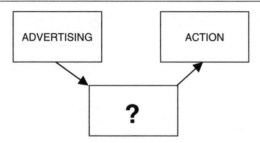

Figure 8.2 'Black box' approach

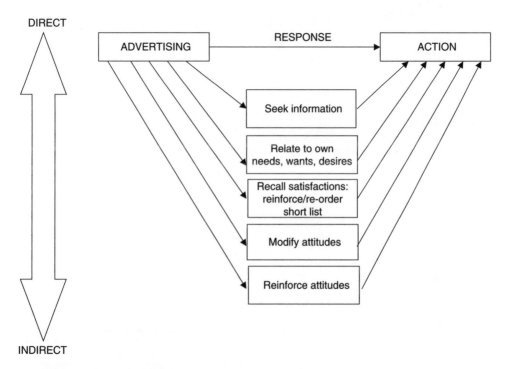

Figure 8.3 Scale of Direct/Indirect Responses to Advertising

fast-moving grocery goods need apply"). It does seem to be able to cope with today's changing circumstances, changing consumer attitudes, different product types, different types of advertising, different media values. The attractive thing about a scale is that it is a nice simple entity, yet it does not suggest that one single mechanism can explain everything.

THE SCALE IN DETAIL

Let us look at the scale now in more detail, relating it to different sorts of advertisements, starting at the direct end.

Figure 8.4   Direct response ad

1. Direct

There is a great deal of advertising that we have come to call direct response, as shown in Figure 8.4. In a sense that is a misnomer, in that there is some sort of mental process between reception of the advertisements and the desired action. (Maybe "watch this space" is the only example of truly direct response.) But the action required – usually filling in a coupon, an envelope and a cheque – happens fairly immediately. Normally, the more immediate the response, the more likely that the advertisement will be successful.

Direct response advertising, for the most part, will be aiming to convert rather than reinforce.

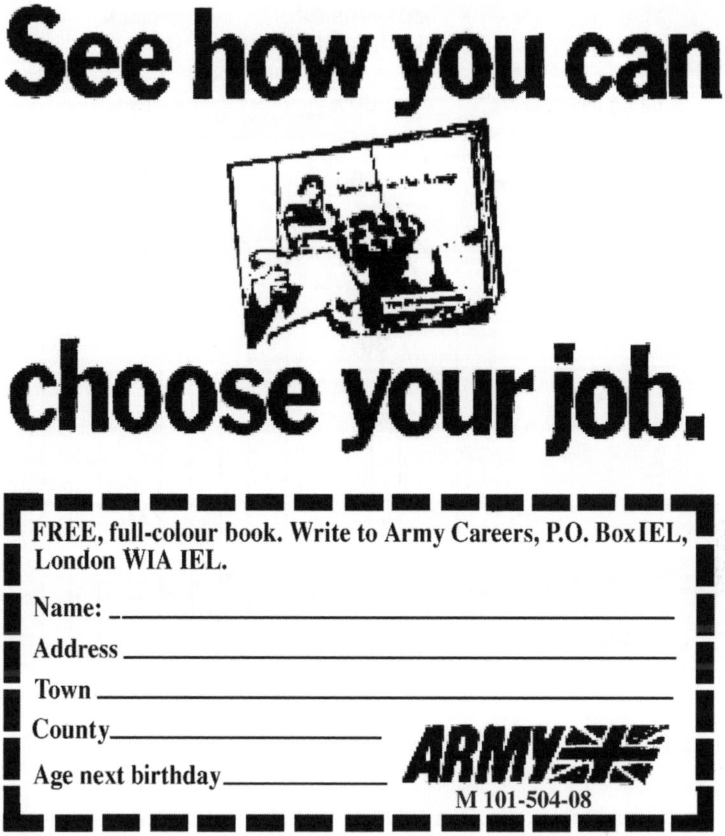

See how you can

choose your job.

FREE, full-colour book. Write to Army Careers, P.O. Box IEL, London WIA IEL.

Name: _____

Address _____

Town _____

County _____

Age next birthday _____   **ARMY**

M 101-504-08

Figure 8.5   Tell me more

2. Seek Information

The next point on the scale calls for an action rather like the first – filling in a coupon. But it is less direct, in that it is only a step towards the ultimate desired action. The advertising response is a *tell me more response*. In Figure 8.5 the ultimate end is not filling a coupon, but joining the Army.

This is often the role for part of an advertisement – such as the coupon offering the furniture catalogue or the list of car dealers. Part of London Transport's commercials aims to get people to ring up about jobs as drivers. The headlines of many government advertisements aim to get people to seek information in the copy (the Save It campaign, for instance).

This *tell me more* response is usually the objective of classified advertising, which has grown so rapidly in recent years. I believe this growth is very closely related to the huge growth in people's aspirations for individualism (which was the main finding of JWT's Social Change research). If that is so, the *tell me more* response may be a much more important one than it has appeared to be for mass market brands.

We have found too that defining the different roles of advertisements in this way helps us to make use of our research into the qualitative aspects of media – the values beyond coverage and

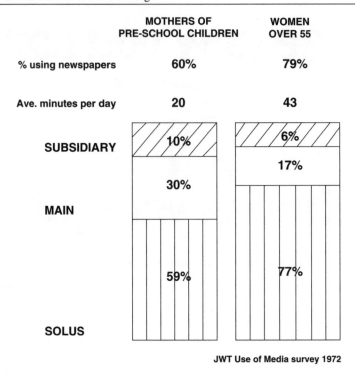

Figure 8.6   How Different Groups of Women Use Newspapers

cost per thousand. There are certain physical and psychological aspects of different media types and different media within a type (say, daily versus Sunday papers, or The *Mirror* versus The *Express)* which make them more suitable or less suitable for a *tell me more* response. Equally, different groups of people use media in different ways (see Figure 8.6), which shows that, in NRS terms, daily newspapers give a lower coverage of mothers of pre-school children than of women over 55. But the real differences are qualitative. The older women spend more than twice as long per day with their papers, and they're far more likely to be treating them as a main activity. Which of the two groups is the more likely to respond to the "semi-immediate" appeal to seek more information?

3. Relate to Own Needs, Wants, Desires

The next response along the scale is one in which the receiver relates the brand to his own needs, wants, desires or motivations. It is less direct than *tell me more*. The receiver is not actively seeking more information, but rather finding information new to him or interpreting old information in a new way. It is the *what a good idea* response. It happens particularly when there is something new, either at the sending or the receiving end; a new brand or new formula or new price or when an individual's needs change.

For instance, Figure 8.7 shows a classic form of advertising; it shines forth if you've got the problem. If you haven't, it is probably invisible.

Some of the most effective and long-lasting advertising has worked by finding a need or an occasion to which a brand can be firmly linked. Horlicks owes its success to becoming a

Figure 8.7   Answer to a problem

bedtime drink; Black Magic to being a romantic gift; Babycham to solving the what-does-a-nice-girl-drink problem.

In a rather less dramatic way, a recent commercial for Fiesta paper towels shows their use in limiting the chaos caused by a baby eating a soft-boiled egg. One of the aims was to get the *what a good idea* response, to encourage a fairly immediate revision of attitudes to the uses of Fiesta rather than to Fiesta itself.

It seems fairly clear that at a time of rapid economic and social change, there will be many changes in people's needs, wants and desires; and increasing opportunities for this particular role for advertising. To borrow from Martin Fishbein's insights (not, happily, his maths), it seems likely that advertising will be aiming rather more often at changing attitudes to an act (buying or using) and rather less often at changing attitudes to the thing acted upon.

4. Recall Satisfactions: Reinforce/Re-Order Short List

The next position on the scale is half way between direct and indirect, and covers part of the effect of most advertisements for repeat-purchase goods. It is the *that reminds me* response.

It is quite clear – and commonsense notions here have been amply supported by analysis of buying patterns (Barnes, 1971) – that most people in most repeat-purchase markets have a short list of brands which they buy in complex patterns and cycles. One of the major tasks of a great deal of advertising is to ensure that a brand stays on this short list, creeps onto it or climbs up within it.

The response to advertising in this role is fairly short term and fairly small. It does not entail any very deep or dramatic or even conscious rethinking of life's priorities or the fundamentals of the weekly wash. It does not require the receiver to re-evaluate a brand's attributes or to weigh up importance factors on the back of an envelope. It is not expecting housewives to pause before the supermarket shelves to whip through a quick brand-switching matrix or cost–benefit analysis.

It works more through the receiver's mind being jogged to recall past satisfactions – the delicious meal, for instance, as in Figure 8.8. This ideally keeps our brand on the top of the short list or helps it to move up within the list.

That of course begs the question of how the brand gets onto the short list in the first place. Advertising can only help people to *recall* satisfactions if they were previously satisfied. It seems to me that advertising's undoubted role in *giving* satisfaction belongs at the indirect end of the scale (see later). Many of the most painful and fruitless arguments about advertisements are really arguments about what is the right balance, in the circumstances, between recalling satisfactions – which might require maximum frequency and stimulus – and giving satisfactions – which might require maximum space/length, "quality" and relevance.

Only when the direct and indirect roles are sorted out can we judge advertisements sensibly. For instance, Kodak runs commercials whose prime objective is to reinforce the association of Kodak film with the pleasures of watching a family grow up; they are helping to give satisfaction. At the same time, there are simple black and white newspaper advertisements jogging the minds of those who would otherwise have left the camera behind this weekend. The roles for these two types of advertisement, and so the ways they are judged and researched, are necessarily quite different.

One of JWT's basic research projects has been particularly valuable in demonstrating the *that reminds me* role for advertising. This was a diary study (McDonald, 1970) in which housewives kept 13-week records of their buying and their media use, from which could be derived their opportunities to see specific advertisements.

One of the innovations was to look at purchase intervals – that is, for any individual the period between two consecutive purchases in any product field. All these purchase intervals could then be added up, and analysed for a composite Brand X.

Figures 8.9 and 8.10 show the two ways in which advertising appeared to be working in the short run.

Figure 8.9 shows people who started a purchase interval by buying a brand other than the composite Brand X. The column on the left shows that where such people had 0 or 1 opportunity to see advertising for Brand X in the last four days of the purchase interval, 18% bought the brand at the end of the interval. Where they had 2 or more OTS, 26% bought Brand X at the end of the interval. There was clearly a short-term effect *attracting* people to Brand X, within their short lists (see Figure 8.10).

In exactly the same way, we can look at those who started the interval by buying Brand X, and see that where they had 2 or more OTS for the brand, they were markedly more inclined to stick with it. In other words, a short-term *retentive* effect.

Figure 8.8   Recalling past satisfactions

This sort of finding makes much of the writing about "brand-switching" seem very naive, and it poses the advertising research problem of measuring the effect of something which often works by maintaining the status quo.

5. Modify Attitudes

At the next stage, we are getting much closer to the indirect end of the scale. The role of advertising is more concerned with *changing* the satisfactions given by the brand than with bringing them to mind; maybe a *really?* response. Unlike the *what a good idea* response, the

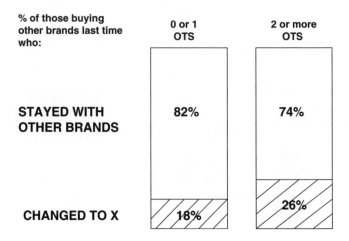

Figure 8.9   Short-term Effect of Advertising

advertising is aiming to modify people's attitudes without giving them a new product or new ingredient or new occasion or new use. Everything we have all learned about attitudes suggests that modifying them is a slow and difficult business. And the pay-off in terms of consumer action is far from certain; there are many brands which have a high reputation but are not much bought.

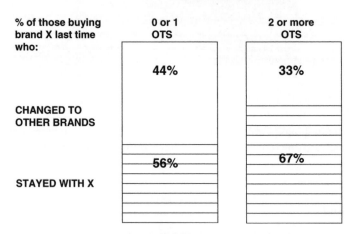

JWT/BMRB Diary study (9 product fields)

Figure 8.10   Short-term Effect of Advertising

Figure 8.11 Modifying prejudices

The Guinness ad, shown in Figure 8.11 – "Every girl should have a little black drink" – is clearly aiming to modify a fairly old-established prejudice. No one would expect that a single insertion of this would lead to lightning changes in people's views about Guinness. The gap between reception and action could be a very long one indeed.

But this sort of modification of attitudes or changing of competitive brand position *is* possible, and the rewards can be enormous. Think of gas before it went High Speed. Or Oxo Cubes: one cannot doubt the long-term effect of advertising in what has been a massive change in the association of the brand with good cooking.

6. Reinforce Attitudes

Reinforcing existing attitudes is the most indirect of roles, because it is aimed at *protecting* a brand from the inroads of competitors. It aims for the *I always knew I was right* response. This is one of the most common and fundamental roles for advertising; yet because it is mainly defensive and is dealing with the stability and intensity of attitude, it is always going to be very hard to measure. The main effect of such advertising may be on profits rather than sales, through making consumers disinclined to try lesser brands for the sake of 2p off.

This sort of response, not surprisingly, works well for brand leaders. Think of the advertising for Heinz soup, Persil, Kelloggs Corn Flakes, Embassy cigarettes, Polo. Or the Black Magic advertisement shown in Figure 8.12; this is not very much attempting to give new information, modify attitudes or lead to direct action. It is (like most ads) partly acting as a mind-jogger; but mainly it is reinforcing the total appeal of the brand. It is acting as an integral part of the satisfactions given by Black Magic.

JWT's diary study suggested great value in this role for advertising (see Figure 8.13). This chart shows that of all the buyers of our composite Brand X, 33% used it as a very minor brand. It made up less than 20% of their purchases in the product field. Equally, at the other end of

Figure 8.12   Reinforcing attitudes

**% of buyers for whom composite Brand X
is major or minor brand**

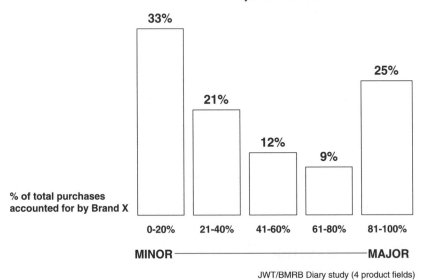

% of total purchases
accounted for by Brand X

JWT/BMRB Diary study (4 product fields)

Figure 8.13   Brand Loyalty?

	ONE EXAMPLE	
	PERCENT BUYING OVER 12 WEEKS	**BRAND'S SHARE OF ITS BUYERS TOTAL PURCHASES**
BRAND A	29%	44%
BRAND B	11%	29%
BRAND C	5%	20%

Figure 8.14   In What Ways do Large and Small Brands Differ?

the scale, 25% of its buyers used Brand X as a major brand – it made up over 80% of their purchases. Not so very many people fell in the middle.

Of course, the 25% of buyers who were "loyalists" were a very great deal more valuable to the brand than the 33% who were disloyalists – nearly 10 times more valuable in terms of volume and even more so in profit terms if it is accepted that they need less coaxing with money-off.

One theory suggested by our diary study was that advertising works in the long run by reinforcing the depth of loyalty at the loyalist end of the scale; and in the short run by acting (as we saw above) in both an attractive and retentive way at the disloyalist end.

It seemed fairly clear that the slow reinforcement effect *could* be the more powerful of the two, though the less easily measurable. It would be more concerned with whether the brand were on the short list at all, rather than whether it came to the top that week. Though there is surprisingly little direct evidence of how brands do grow, there are hints to support this theory. We can look, for instance, at how big brands differ from little brands (Corlett, 1974).

Figure 8.14 shows two mechanisms at work. First, in any time period the big brand has greater penetration. More people buy big Brand A than middling Brand B and small Brand C in 12 weeks. Secondly, Brand A has a higher share of its own buyers' purchases than the other two. In terms of Figure 8.13, Brand A would have a higher proportion of loyalists, and the larger the time period the more important this difference would become.

In other words, if advertising is to help a brand become big, then maybe it will do its best by promoting loyalism – a greater *intensity* of affection. That is, working at the indirect end of our scale.

THE REALITIES OF LIFE

In real life, it is clear enough that many advertisements work at several points on the scale. It may be that this is itself a criterion of effectiveness.

£5,995 FHLD ! Broken-down Battersea Bargain. Erected at end of long reign of increasingly warped moral & aesthetic values it's what you expect—hideous; redeemed only by the integrity of the plebs who built it—well. Originally a one skiv Victorian lower-middle class fmly res, it'll probably be snapped up by one of the new Communications Elite, who'll tart it up & flog it for 15 thou. 3 normal-sized bedrms & a 4th for an undemanding dwarf lodger. Bathrm. Big dble drawing rm. B'fast rm & kit. Nature has fought back in the gdn—& won. Call Sun 3-5 at 21 Surrey Lane, S.W.11. then Brooks.

Figure 8.15   Long term response

For instance, the Katie and Philip campaign has brought Oxo Cubes to the top of a short list of gravy makers; it has modified prejudices; it has congratulated and reinforced existing users; and it has (for instance, by showing how to cook chops with Oxo in foil) promoted the *what a good idea* response.

Mr Kipling advertising has most obviously worked at the indirect end of the scale, reinforcing the values and personality of the brand. But when a commercial has gone on the air, there has also been a direct and short-term response in sales of the line featured.

The Jimmy Saville seat belt campaign has aimed to modify people's attitudes. It also set out, in a more direct way, to relate the desired action to people's lives by appropriating an occasion and a noise.

Or, to look at the other end of the scale, most house advertising is aiming at the *tell me more* response. But what about Roy Brooks? He was clearly expecting a long-term response too, which might lead to action years later when the reader had a house for sale (Figure 8.15).

If it's all as complex as this, why have the scale at all? It seems to me that this sort of framework does not *solve* anything, and is not intended to. What it can do is help one through the complexities a little, make the arguments and discussions about real issues rather than superficialities, and help one to set priorities. For instance, think of a buyer of tyres and his propensity to respond to advertising at different points of his buying cycle – when he has just bought a set, the long period in between when he would rather not think of tyres and the ominous period when he knows he needs new ones. And then try to answer the question: What is the role for advertising for tyres?

Or let us neatly finish by looking at advertising research again.

BACK TO ADVERTISING RESEARCH

It seems distinctly easier to discuss which advertising research measures are best, if one can work out which is the most important role for advertising. To look at it very simply indeed:

- *Direct:* Post-exposure, the old familiar direct response measures of keyed advertisements. Pre-exposure, small-scale simulations, in time working out weighting (or aiming-off) factors.
- *Seek information:* Same as Direct.
- *Relate to own needs, etc:* We need some way of measuring "impact" here, to get a hint of whether there is a *what a good idea* or an *I must try that* response. I think it might have to be qualitative research, but it could be more purposively directed than usual.
- *Recall satisfactions:* We know that diary studies work here but they could be impossibly expensive. There is some evidence (Axelrod, 1968) that first brand coming to mind or brand choice from constant sum scales *may* be measuring the mind-jogging effect.
- *Modify attitudes:* The changes here are likely to be so sensitive that it is hard to see anything other than qualitative, diagnostic research helping pre-exposure decisions. Post-exposure, continuous attitude research.
- *Reinforce attitudes:* At this level, I think the most one could hope to do pre-exposure is eliminate elements from advertising that are dissonant with the existing brand personality, through sensitive qualitative research. Post-exposure, it seems unlikely that any research will ever positively link individual advertisements with reinforcing attitudes. It can only be done, with great leaps in interpretation, for whole campaigns over long periods. And the measures will have to be of the intrinsic worth of a brand as a totality – maybe through blind versus named product tests.

I hope this brief look at advertising research puts the scale of immediacy into perspective. It is not a great breakthrough, but it might be a modest aid to coherent thought.

The next stage is to try to experiment with the scale, disprove it or invalidate it, and produce something better. Whatever comes next I just hope it makes it a little bit harder to get back to the old simplistic theories of advertising and research.

REFERENCES

Axelrod, J. (1968) "Attitude measures that predict purchase". *Journal of Advertising Research*, March.
Barnes, M. (1971) *The Relationship between Purchasing Patterns and Advertising Exposure*. JWT.
Berdy, D. (1974) "Towards an alternative advertising theory". *Admap*, January–March.
Corlett, T. (1974) "Consumer purchasing patterns: a different perspective", *Admap*, June.
Hedges, A. (1974) *Testing to destruction*. IPA.
Hopkins, C. (1923) *Scientific Advertising*.
Joyce, T. (1965) "Model-building and advertising research", MRS Seminar.
Joyce, T. (1967) "What do we know about how advertising works?" and other papers in ESOMAR Seminar. Noordwijk
King, S. (1967) "Can research evaluate the creative content of advertising?" *Admap*, June.
McDonald, C. (1970) "What is the short-term effect of advertising?", *ESOMAR* and *Admap*, November.
McDonald, C. (1975) "The hunting of advertising effectiveness". MRS Seminar and *Admap*, February.
Young, J.W. (1963) *How to Become an Advertising Man* (based on lectures given at Chicago University, 1930s).

JWT's Debt to Stephen King

By Guy Murphy

It should come as no surprise that Stephen King's work remains relevant to us today. Stephen described his original construction of the account planner as "the combination of the Media man and the Marketing man". In a stroke he mirrors two of the keenest problems that face brands in the noughties: how can brands truly help build a business and how should the money be spent to support them?

As this book demonstrates, Stephen wrote prolifically throughout his career. But, perhaps his most valuable contribution is the *JWT Manual of Tools of the Trade for Advertising Planners* or *Toolkit* for short. He worked on the *Toolkit* for a number of years and the papers in this collection could be thought of as "works in progresses towards this end". The full *Toolkit* was actually published as a manual in 1987, distributed throughout the network and formed the basis of JWT seminars and training around the world. Many offices produced their own versions with their own local examples.

The book contained 12 chapters, each devoted to a particular aspect of the entire brand planning process from start to finish:

- Planning Cycle
- Consumer Buying System
- Brand Objectives
- Unique Brand Personality
- Advertising Expenditure
- Role for Advertising
- Target Group
- Target Responses
- Choice of Media
- Creative Brief as Stimulus
- Advertising Idea
- Tailor-made Research

So the JWT *Toolkit*, published some 20 years ago, still represents a very valuable resource for the media and marketing ambitions in all of us.

But it is not just the subject matter that continues to impress. It is also the fact that it is represented in a toolkit – a practical, self-help format. We are in an era where the "known unknowns" abound. While many fashionable books are published on the back of our growing knowledge gap, there is nothing to compete with a profound set of "guidelines, aids and checklists" that offer genuine, timeless direction and not headline-grabbing rhetoric.

Just recently I conducted a survey among the planning community of JWT across the world. I asked the planners for their top three most pressing needs. More than half asked for "more training" and "more access to planning tools'. I'm sure that, today, this would be true of every agency in the world.

The editors and I wanted to publish an extract from the *Toolkit* to give a flavour of how it is written and an insight into its usefulness. Which to choose? It was a difficult choice but we felt that because the challenge of how to manage ideas in the increasingly complex media environment is the major concern today, we chose one whole chapter: "The Advertising Idea." This is introduced by Rosemarie Ryan and Ty Montague from JWT New York in Chapter 9.1. In Chapter 9.2, and still on the subject of managing creativity, we publish a contribution from JWT China by Tom Doctoroff . This piece demonstrates the value of the Consumer Buying System: how the ways people make buying decisions is critical to understanding how to use media to engage people at each stage in the process.

One of Stephen's most attractive characteristics was that he saw knowledge as constantly evolving to meet new needs. Although the sub-title to this book is "the timeless works" they are only timeless as principles, not rules. He was never prescriptive, and was delighted when people supplied fresh thinking and new examples. In 2008 the original *Toolkit* needs just that.

In Pursuit of an Intense Response

By Rosemarie Ryan and Ty Montague

An introduction to:

9.2 Advertising Idea

Much has changed in the 20 years since Stephen published his thinking on the advertising idea. The fragmentation of the media landscape, the advent of the digital era and sweeping advances in technology have significantly changed how and where we consume advertising. The arrival of Tivo, iPods, Blackberrys and the like have greatly influenced what form our advertisements take. Digital programming such as YouTube and Second Life create opportunities for audiences to interact with advertisements in ways that Stephen never imagined.

Some would suggest that our business has changed more in the past 10 years than in the 40 years that preceded them. Yet one can find little to argue with or debate when you read Stephen's work, largely because, while advertising has clearly morphed, what constitutes a good advertising idea has not.

What Stephen would characterize as constituting a good advertising idea – original, relevant communication that generates an intense response – is as true today as it was then. Technology may change how we interact with advertisements, but it won't change what people respond to.

People respond to ideas that are fresh yet familiar; ideas that they can relate to, aspire to, share with others; ideas where there is clear understanding of what's in it for them; and ideas that help them to make sense of the world (or in our case a brand, product or service). Sometimes those ideas take the form of an advertisement, sometimes books, films, or blogs. People have responded to those kinds of ideas for decades, centuries even, and will continue to do so for the foreseeable future.

So What has Changed?

Well, the answer to that, surprisingly, is foretold by Stephen himself. Like many visionaries, his writings are not just enduring but often prophetic.

Stephen writes that "if advertising is to succeed, it has to involve the receiver and entice him into *participating actively* in whatever is being communicated about the brand. It has to stretch his imagination and make him an accomplice." Here Stephen comes very close to predicting recent US marketing sensations like "Subservient Chicken", "Lonleygirl 15" and "Beta 7". He is outlining the principles that will lead to the rise of consumer generated content, both in advertising, but even more importantly in the entertainment world and in the broader consumer culture.

We would wholeheartedly agree with Stephen that the key to advertising's success . . . in fact, to its very survival, is predicated on our ability to entice audiences to participate actively with our advertisements. The "death of advertising" as predicted in the mainstream press in the past five years is based on the assumption that the advent of technology has put all the power in the hands of the audience. They surmise that the audience will use that power to eradicate all "marketing messaging" from their homes and lives forever. Hogwash, is what we would say to that.

We acknowledge (as he virtually predicts in this essay) that power is now firmly in the hands of the audience. However, we believe that audiences will not just choose to opt out of marketing, but choose to OPT IN, in ways that will make big advertising ideas and brands more valuable and potent than ever . . . as long as we stop interrupting what people are interested in and *be* what they are interested in.

The idea that audiences are very selective about what they choose to "let in" is not new. Stephen tells us, "All of us spend our lives subconsciously zapping what we have decided almost instantaneously, not to be interested in." What is new is our ability as marketers to feel that rejection instantaneously.

The good news is that today when we invite participation, our ability to dialogue, play, interact with our audiences has never been greater and creating work that builds ACTIVE PARTICIPATION into its DNA is where planning plays a crucial role. When developing work or evaluating its worth, the question too often posed is: What will the advertising do to the audience? We believe the more pertinent question is: *What will the audience do with the advertising?* This question acknowledges that the audience is in control and must actively engage with the idea if it is to have any chance of working on behalf of our clients. In fact, the higher the audience is on the engagement scale – first internalizing, then sharing and contributing – the better our chances of success.

Turning Your Audience into Accomplices

Stephen's notion of making the audience an accomplice is a marvellous way of describing the nature of this engagement. It is not news that good brands have loyal followers, and nothing is more powerful than their advocacy. However, today more than ever technology and digitalization enable them to share their passions. The more we can unlock and activate those passions and put them to work on our brands' behalf, the more successful we will be. We need to do more than understand them; we need to collaborate with them.

Advertising ideas, good ones, are not static, they are dynamic. Producing an advertisement, regardless of its form, is the beginning of something and needs to be treated as a living breathing entity. It means that we and our clients have to give up control (or the pretence of it) and be more fluid and open to where our ideas take us. That is, after all, the true nature of a dialogue. Facilitating that dialogue is in large part where planning can help.

Where do Ideas Come From?

Stephen reminds us again and again that getting to an advertising idea is more art than science and can best be described as "messy'. That has never been truer than it is today. In fact, today, big ideas are no longer the sole domain of ad agencies. From a client perspective in the modern world, a big idea can come from just about anywhere. From an ad agency, from a media agency, from a TV network, from a Hollywood agent, from a gaming company, from an interactive agency, *et al.*

The job of a truly integrated modern advertising agency is often to play ringmaster to all of these potential resources on behalf of our clients. To have the ability and the will to collaborate closely with many outside entities in the creation of ideas. And to know a big idea when we see one, regardless of the source. The ability to recognize a big idea and to activate it powerfully in different cultures is what we do better than any other creative entity in the world.

So what does a big idea look like today? *How do you know you've got one*? They are all different, but we believe that big ideas share certain immutable characteristics.

- Big Ideas don't fit neatly into any individual medium. In fact, they want to burst out of any single medium you try to jam them into. Big ideas sprawl.
- Big Ideas appeal to the things that we all share as human beings – to universal truths. If you look around the globe, and you seek to identify differences between people and cultures, you will find them. But if you look for the things that make us all the same, you will find those as well. Big ideas travel well.
- Big Ideas are the kinds of ideas that people truly want to participate with. You see people finding ways to quickly make a big idea their own and ultimately to share the idea with all of their friends. Big ideas spread quickly.
- Big Ideas don't just compete with other advertising or marketing ideas. Big ideas compete head to head with books, movies, music, etc. Big Ideas compete for the attention and time of the audience on the broader pop culture stage. Big Ideas generate fame for their brand.

We cannot imagine a more exciting time to be in the business of Big Ideas. And because of the crucial role that planning must play in their creation, we can't imagine a more exciting time to be a planner.

If we have one criticism of this article, it is that Stephen left out the most important part: how to ensure that you are always going to have a really big idea, on time, executed perfectly and delivered on budget. Alas, for whatever reason, this is a secret he chose not to reveal.

Planners. Selfish to the end.

Advertising Idea*

By Stephen King

So far, we have set our creative objectives in terms of target responses – what it is that we want the target group most of all to notice or believe or feel or do. But advertising has to do more than simply to get the right *structure* of responses. It needs to stimulate the maximum *intensity* of response.

This means that the creative treatment should not only use the "best" craft skills of writing, art direction, film production, etc., but also be based on a genuine advertising idea. It should not be either a mere description of the brand, a dull shopping list of product attributes, or, on the other hand, a mere dazzling executional technique with no centre to it. It should not be a standard family smiling at the brand while the voice-over reads out the strategy. Nor should it be simply tacking a pack-shot onto a frog singing "Hello Dolly".

Creating strong advertising ideas, however, is not something that can be systematized. The whole point of originality is that it cannot emerge directly from a logical and deductive process. Trying to make how-to-do-it rules for creative people would be wholly counter-productive.

Nevertheless, there is a good deal the planner can do to contribute to the process. For instance:

- Help to produce creative briefs more likely to stimulate good advertising ideas.
- Recognize the potential of ideas in their early vulnerable form; and contribute constructively to improving them.
- Help to produce the arguments that will persuade clients to back what at first sight may look risky.

WHY ADVERTISING IDEAS MATTER

What is an Advertising Idea?

There have been many attempts to define "ideas". James Webb Young wrote: "An idea is nothing more nor less than a *new combination* of old elements." It is one of those words which we're all comfortable about using, but which slips through the fingers when we try to define it; and it may be better not to try too hard to do so. All definitions suggest, in one way or another, that an idea is something that is original, novel, fresh, unexpected or surprising.

An *advertising idea* goes further than that. A good advertising idea has to be original enough to stimulate people and draw an intense response from them; it also has to be directly related to its commercial purpose. It must uniquely and single-mindedly epitomize *our brand*. It is

*From the JWT *Toolkit*, originally in published in 1986. Reproduced with permission.

the link between these two purposes that has to be both powerful and unexpected – an original way of restating the values of the brand.

The call for original advertising ideas is not just because we want to give creative people full and interesting lives. There are two sound commercial reasons for it:

Intense Response

First, any advertisement is competing for attention not only with other advertisements but also with editorial, programmes, people, events and life itself. It's easy to ignore advertisements; most of us, in fact, ignore most of those to which we are in theory exposed. There is much discussion nowadays of "advertising clutter" and "zapping". In fact, they are no more than the latest physical versions of much older and more powerful phenomena – all the stimuli that bombard our senses all the time and the selective perception with which we deal with them. All of us spend our lives subconsciously zapping what we have decided, almost instantaneously, not to be interested in.

If advertising is to succeed, it has to *involve* the receiver and entice him into *participating actively* in whatever is being communicated about the brand. It has to stretch his imagination and make him an accomplice. It has to suggest that there will be an answer to "What's in it for me?" – self-interest being the most powerful motive for involvement. The idea has to be fresh enough to tempt the receiver into the advertisement, so that the brand has a chance to present its appeal to self-interest. If his immediate response is "Same old story again", he will mentally switch off straight away.

Sophisticated Consumers

Secondly, consumers nowadays are extremely expert in advertising; they see a great deal of it and they have quite precise – and usually accurate – ideas about what it's for. Again and again research has shown them analysing advertisements much as agency people or brand managers do, often using the same jargon. They show skills in decoding visual imagery, working out the strategy, picking up clues, seeing the company behind the brand, accepting quick cuts, recognizing the actors in voice-overs, and so on.

What has changed most in recent years is that today they are more inclined to believe that not just the brand but advertising itself should give them some sort of reward – aesthetic, emotional or intellectual. They see advertisements not only as a medium through which a company talks to them but also as part of the style, skills and personality of the company itself. To them, the style of the advertising is as much a part of a brand as the pack is. There is a fairly direct and recognized link in their minds between rewarding advertisements and therefore a good company and therefore good brands. "Rewarding" can mean well-made, beautiful pictures, newsy, enjoyable, funny, moving, a good tune, subtle acting and any of the other criteria that they apply to films. TV, books, papers, etc. – anything that makes an advertisement worth attending to or seeing again.

In effect, this means that most good advertising ideas will ultimately be derived from the ways used by people outside advertising – writers, artists or filmmakers – to get an intense response. For instance:

- Appeals to basic emotions: love, fear, anger, patriotism, nostalgia, peace, etc.
- Suspense: horror movies, detective stories, some comic strips, etc.
- Humour: slapstick, parody, hyperbole, understatement, etc.

- Fantasy, wish-fulfilment: cartoons, romantic novels, sexy stories, etc.
- News.
- Shock: the initial reactions to, for example, the impressionists, Picasso, Stravinsky.

By contrast, research shows that people are very aware of the more hackneyed themes of advertising itself, especially television: the musical wallpaper, the side-by-side comparisons, the talking heads, the "new" computer graphics, the miracle-everything-slashed-unique-opportunity sales, etc. They deride with relish the old enemies, like:

- "Mrs Smith has just washed . . . ."
- "We offered Mrs Jones . . . ."
- The boys in the Bar
- Slow motion through the cornfields
- "Coming back to . . . ."
- "In 1864, Mr . . . ."
- "Mummy, Mummy, Mummy . . . ."
- "America's favourite . . . ."
- "Mmm. Tastes delicious . . . ."

In competitive markets, brands will not succeed unless they are unique. It is quite clear that unique advertising – based on original ideas – is more than ever essential to make them so.

HOW ADVERTISING IDEAS ARE CREATED

Exactly how ideas get created – how the "eureka" moment happens – is fairly mysterious. But the general process of invention has been much discussed, and there is a sort of consensus. It is very relevant to what the advertising planner can contribute.

The process starts with background knowledge. You have to understand the issues, the subject, the people and their motivations and lives very thoroughly. Very often invention starts with a dissatisfaction with existing theories and the status quo. This stage ends with working out what is the right problem to solve.

Then there has to be an idea – the first vision of a solution. This is a non-logical process, subconscious and often very messy. It is spurred on by an obsession with the whole issue, but does not derive vertically or logically from the problem itself – much more from a free-flow association with something completely different. The point is that when we're obsessed with any issue, almost everything is subconsciously related to it. Any attempt to work at it in a strictly logical way is actually inhibiting these random associations.

There are various devices used to help generate ideas – brainstorming, synectics, de Bono's lateral games, discussions in smoke-filled rooms, corridor conversations, liquor or simply leaving the issue alone to allow the subconscious to take over. James Webb Young suggested in *A Technique for Producing Ideas* that, at this stage, you should drop the subject altogether and then, out of nowhere, the idea will come; it will come to you when you're least expecting it.

Next, the idea has to be patted into shape, nurtured and worked into some sort of practical form. Then there is some sort of experiment, in which the results are tried out – on colleagues, consumers or clients.

Finally, there is a feedback stage in which the results of the experiment are used to develop or modify the idea (or indeed restate the problem). The point of the feedback is *not* to accept or reject, but to help improve. It is very rarely indeed that an idea emerges fully formed and perfectly adjusted first time round. Equally, it is very rarely that an idea has no merit at all lurking in it. So this cycle of theory/experiment/feedback is repeated until everything makes sense.

If we apply this general process to advertising, we can see more closely the interdependence but difference in roles for creative people and advertising planners. And we can see more clearly what contribution the planner can make. But first we have to consider what it is that makes an advertising idea a good one.

WHAT MAKES A GOOD ADVERTISING IDEA?

Just as it is a contradiction in terms to have a book of rules for constructing original ideas, so there cannot really be any rules for what they are when they emerge.

There are very many ways of being original and it is a great deal easier to recognize originality than it is to define it. We're all familiar with the feelings of being stopped in our tracks by something new, savouring it and wishing we'd said/written/drawn it ourselves. Equally, we've all experienced somebody proving that what we thought was original isn't new at all.

In general, we don't find it difficult to agree whether the ending of a serial is a dramatic cliff-hanger or a trite and constantly repeated situation. Whether a news item is a genuine shock or a bit of media hype. Whether a joke is brilliantly original or a new twist on an old joke or a rotten stale joke. Whether a film or book is a new interpretation or a tired repetition. Whether prose is original – for instance, being strikingly simple (as with Orwell) or rich with diverse imagery (as with Shakespeare) or vividly idiosyncratic (as with Damon Runyon). Whether phrases are original or tired: Churchill talked not of a fundamental breakdown in communications but of an "iron curtain". He said, "Never before . . . was so much owed by so many to so few" not "We owe a great deal to the Royal Air Force". We are constantly making judgements of this sort in daily life, in effect asking ourselves: "Does this create an intense response in me?"

We make the same judgements about advertising. For instance, relaunches of detergents, with new ingredients, are familiar enough, and are usually treated with a sort of synthetic rational excitement which seems stale to viewers. Equally, show biz spectaculars are featured regularly on television. But we can all recognize that Persil's "Showstopper" commercial is highly original through linking the two. It is equally easy to show that most detergent advertising is not. ("But three other brands tear shirts in half in their commercials.")

There is, however, a difference between a good idea and a good *advertising idea.* Originality for its own sake is not enough. Advertisements have a commercial purpose. Having worked out the brand objectives and the contribution that advertising can make to them so carefully, we clearly have to make sure that our campaigns do actually make it, by being *both original and relevant.*

The nature of originality means that there cannot be universal rules about what good advertising ideas are. There are, however, some brand principles that can help the planner to recognize and contribute to them. They spring from the decisions made about The Role for Advertising – broadly, whether it aims to get a fairly direct response or a fairly indirect response.

Vivid Demonstration

Direct Responses

At the more direct end of the scale ("I'll do/get/buy that right now", "I must find out more about it" and "What a good idea! Just the thing for me"), advertising is aiming directly to answer the receiver's question "What's in it for me?" It is trying to put forward our brand as the answer to the question, most of the time *before it has been asked.* That is why it has to be done with originality.

In very broad terms, most good advertising ideas at this end of the scale are based on *vivid demonstrations* of what's in it for you. Not just any old demonstration, but an original way of restating an old truth – just as "Showstopper" was an original way for a detergent to announce an improvement.

These vivid demonstrations are usually picking out some specific *attribute or feature* of a brand; they are about what it does better than the competition. They are *not* expressing the total brand personality.

Some of these demonstrations represent a real-life setting of how the brand performs; some involve unusual torture tests; some involve hyperbole; some are using external props for their demonstrations. But they are all essentially showing people how the brand works, in an original way. For instance:

- *Vision Saucepans TV: "Fire"* – a conventional pan catches fire and burns inside an unharmed Vision pan.
- *Tower Saucepans TV: "Hats off"* – the non-stick surface demonstrated via classic pan-stuck-on-child's-head.
- *Lego TV: "Tommy Cooper"* – the variety and scope for imagination in Lego via an illustrated fairy story.
- *National Batteries TV: "Fireman"* – the battery goes on and on and on working.
- *Volkswagen TV: "Snowplow"* – the only way the man who drives the snowplow can get to it is in a VW.
- *Band-Aid TV: "Egg"* – adhesive plaster that sticks on even under water.
- *St Ivel Gold TV: "Karate"* – half the fat of butter and margarine "demonstrated" by karate-chopping a plank in half.
- *British Rail TV: "French Connection"* – quoting the famous film to demonstrate the competitive advantages of rail travel.
- *Pepsi: "Challenge"* – better taste "demonstrated" by the invention of a blend taste test.
- *US Sprint TV: "Pin Drop"* – the quality of the telephone line is so clear that you can hear a pin drop thousands of miles away.
- *Araldite Poster* – car stuck to a poster with Araldite.
- *ICL Press: "A doctor explains"* – the values of computer records, by means of "typically" illegible doctor's handwriting.

Vivid Metaphor

Indirect Responses

At the indirect end of the scale of roles for advertising ("I never thought of it like that" or "I was righter than I thought to buy X"), advertising is aiming to modify or reinforce people's attitudes towards a brand. It is trying to change or build the brand personality, in an original way. And because its personality is a lasting element of a brand and changes very slowly, advertising aims to do it in a way that is consistent over time.

Almost invariably, good advertising ideas that do this are based on a *vivid metaphor* for the brand's personality. That is, they are borrowing something from outside the brand itself which:

- has personality characteristics that are similar to the ones we want our brand to have;
- can be associated *uniquely* with our brand (in a way that physical characteristics almost certainly can't);
- can be reasonably long-lasting;
- in some way illuminates and enhances the brand itself.

For instance:

- *Marlboro: the cowboy* – The loner, rugged, individualistic, facing the elements of the great outside – but still a mythical creature, not a testimonial.
- *Andrex: the puppy* – Soft, durable, utterly wholesome; a wonderful metaphor for a brand whose physical characteristics can't easily be demonstrated.
- *After Eight: the smart dinner party* – A metaphor for smooth, subtle, delicate chocolates.
- *Black Magic: love letters, romance, secret passion* – Metaphors for a gift which is (like all gifts) intended to say something, and happens to come in the form of chocolates.
- *Volkswagen: the beetle* – Small endearing animal, ugly enough but it works. A metaphor for everything that the VW stood for then – a rebellion against the vast, gas-guzzling, flashy monsters associated with its competitors.
- *Esso: the tiger* – A beetle would hardly have done for Esso. The tiger is fast, graceful, powerful and aggressive.
- *Hathaway: Baron Wrangel* – Mysterious, distinctive, chic, rich, with suggestions of mid-European romance. (Note how more recent Hathaway advertising – "In ten minutes your daughter will give her first recital. And that's why you're wearing a Hathaway" – seems not to understand the importance of man and eyepatch as *metaphor*.)
- *Mr Kipling: the voice* – A tone of voice and use of words as a metaphor for obsessive craftsmanship.
- *Persil: mother love* – A metaphor for a detergent that, above all, takes care of clothes. Mother love is a lasting association, but, of course, the way it is expressed has to change as social attitudes change.
- *Oxo: the rewards of family life* – A metaphor for adding richness and "goodness" to cooking. Again, the nature of families has changed, but this metaphor has been successfully used for 25 years.

Demonstration versus Metaphor

We should be careful not to get too concerned with whether a new advertising idea is a vivid demonstration of a vivid metaphor. (But we should think very hard when it appears to be neither; asking ourselves both whether it's really original and how it is intended to work. Sometimes the answers will satisfy us, sometimes not.)

The whole point of the scale of responses is not to say that advertising can work at only one level. It is to help us to set priorities between direct and indirect responses. We usually find that the best advertisements work at more than one level, but one type of response is more important than any of the others.

Equally, many good advertising ideas *both* demonstrate a functional quality in the brand *and* add to the brand personality by a vivid metaphor.

* *Lux Toilet Soap: "Film stars"* – A vivid demonstration of mildness and purity; but film stars are also a vivid metaphor for a luxurious self-indulgent brand personality.
* *Volkswagen TV: "Snowplow"* – A demonstration of ruggedness; but the small ugly car up against the massive snowplow was also a metaphor for VW's Jack the Giant-killer personality. True also of much of DDB's press work at the time.
* *Rolex: "Famous characters"* – Not only a demonstration of meticulous construction, but also a metaphor for the aspirational exclusiveness of Rolex's personality.

THE ADVERTISING PLANNER'S ROLE

It is the creative people who have to invent the advertising ideas. It's the hardest job in advertising. They deserve all the help they can get, but (as discussed above) any attempt to lay step-by-step logic on them is actually a hindrance.

Nevertheless, our look at the creative process and the nature of good advertising ideas does show where the planner can help.

Setting the Brief

First, of course, by setting the brief concisely and accurately, and by making it stimulating:

* Working out the right problem to solve.
* Being precise about The Role for Advertising. If it is one of the more direct roles and requires a vivid demonstration, working out *exactly what* has to be demonstrated; finding out all the facts about the feature to be demonstrated; putting together the evidence that supports the demonstration. If it is one of the indirect roles, expressing the brand personality clearly and inventively enough to inspire a vivid metaphor.
* Setting the target group and key response in a stimulating way.

Getting Ideas

Secondly, by (tactfully) contributing to the creative person's task of actually getting ideas.

* Discussing and clarifying the brief (not just handing over a piece of paper), talking through the background.
* Setting up and reporting on qualitative research that will bring the issues and people's responses to life.
* Analysing the advertising conventions in the market, to show in advance what would *not* be an original advertising idea.
* Knowing when to keep out of the creative people's hair.

Developing Ideas

Thirdly, by making the experiment and feedback process constructive.

* Recognizing a latent demonstration or metaphor, even if it's not quite right yet; encouraging its development and protecting it from predators.

* Using research that aims to pick out the elements that do get an intense response (not just yes/no research) and that explains why people respond as they do.
* Giving creative people the confidence to submit their work to research. Encouraging them to see the improvements/feedback cycle as part of the creative process rather than as a hideous obstacle imposed on them by Authority.
* Convincing clients that the experiment/feedback process is the proper one and is entirely to their advantage. Encouraging them, too, to think in terms of vivid demonstrations and vivid metaphors, and to look on the unexpected with optimism.

9.3
JWT Engagement Planning in China:
The Art of Idea Management

By Tom Doctoroff

A Brave New World?

As the twenty-first century unfolds, Stephen King's truths about the importance of ideas have taken on an urgency, but for reasons even he may not have anticipated. Technology has liberated consumers to accept or reject both advertising and entertainment as they, rather than manufacturers or network executives, see fit. From YouTube and MySpace to iPods, DirecTV and Netflix.com, the new generation is in the driver's seat. Even celebrity creation has been taken out the Boardroom and put into the texting thumbs of American Idol or China Supergirl viewers.

We no longer assume "threshold weight" is enough to stimulate sales. Rupert Murdoch licks his lips. He sees opportunity in chaos:

> The internet is a creative, destructive technology that is still in its infancy, yet breaking and remaking everything in its path. We are all on a journey, not just the privileged few, and technology will take us to destination that is defined by the limits of our creativity, our confidence and our courage.

Good heavens.

A digital big bang has yielded a new horizon. The sky has opened and we have been deluged by bits and bytes. In order for order to emerge, *ideas* – ones with the gravitational pull to unify communications – are more crucial than ever. As attention spans shorten and choices multiply, big, populist, unified ideas can harness the tsunami of consumer empowerment to increase brand relevance. Ideas must also be extended across the entire media landscape, both traditional and new. From a client's perspective, they can:

- increase media budget efficiency because fewer messages need to be seeded;
- maximize profits by strengthening consumer loyalty and price elasticity;
- provide a clear mandate, one rooted in a vivid definition of a brand's relationship with consumers, for both CEOs and department heads;
- elevate management of intellectual capital and equity resources to the Boardroom level, where it belongs;
- centralize accountability with the advertising agency, the steward of idea management. (If not us, then who?)

Engagement Planning: Three Interlinked Components

To realize these benefits, however, our thinking has to be sharper, more penetrating, than ever. Those of us who master the art of idea management will thrive. That's why, at JWT Asia, we have introduced "Engagement Planning", a conceptual framework that builds on Stephen King's thinking while bringing it into alignment with the new reality of blogs and podcasts. Traditional execution-driven agencies will become dinosaurs, fossils from an era that no longer exists.

Insight

Uncovering a consumer insight will always be the first step in developing big ideas. Insights are not observations. They are fundamental motivators to behaviour and preference.

They answer the question "why"? Why are Chinese men willing to spend a year's income on a new car? Why are most Chinese women unwilling to buy premium underwear? Why do insubstantial boy bands such as F4 intoxicate new-generation youth as equally well as Faye Wong's rebellious lyricism? Why are Shanghai men so willing to buck against traditional definitions of masculinity by assuming kitchen duty?

Compelling insights touch the heart by identifying struggle, enabling marketers – commercial cultural anthropologists – to boost brand relevance and invite interaction with the brand. At JWT, we believe that *all* insights spring from tension between or within "human truths" (i.e. Maslovian needs that transcend cultural or geographic boundaries) and "cultural truths" (i.e. motivations that differentiate). Chinese men, for example, crave glory but fear losing control. Chinese women want to be tough without sacrificing feminine gentility. (One memorable focus group quote: "I want to be strong as steel inside but soft as Hello Kitty outside.") From Memphis to Mumbai, everyone loves delicious food but no one wants to get fat. Omo/Persil know all parents want their kids to explore the world but hate stains.

Some powerful insights, both functional and emotional, are shown in Table 9.3.1.

Table 9.3.1   Powerful insights

Human vs Human truths	Zazoo Condoms	Sex is great but I don't want to worry about the consequences
	JetBlue Airways	I want to travel in style but I don't have the money
	DTC Diamonds (engagement)	I want to be in love for a lifetime but I don't want it to become mundane
Human vs Cultural truths	Nike Soccer	I want to be a hero (human truth) but showing off is not cool (Confucian truth)
	DTC Diamonds (self-purchase)	I want to shine (human truth) but, as a modern Chinese woman, I still need to be gentle and feminine
	Hazeline Shampoo	I want to be beautiful (human truth) but anything unnatural concerns me (mass-market Chinese truth)
	PPP Health Insurance	When I'm sick, I want to be protected (human) but I want to stay independent (Western truth)
	Safeguard Soap (germ kill)	My kids should explore the world (human truth) but danger lurks everywhere (Asian truth)
(Chinese) Cultural vs Cultural truths	Rejoice & Lux Shampoos	I want to move forward in society without sacrificing graceful femininity
	Mont Blanc	I want to project my accomplishments but, even for men, understatement counts

Table 9.3.2   Brand visions

Brand	Consumer insight	Unique brand offer	Brand vision
Anta (sports shoes, China)	I want to be the greatest but life isn't fair	Shoes that withstand the toughest test	"Forge Yourself"
Philadelphia (cheese, global)	Food is delicious but I don't like fat	$\frac{1}{2}$ the calories of butter	"Guilt-free Indulgence"
Sofy (sanitary napkins, Asia)	I don't want to stop, even during those days	Side-gatherers for leakage protection	"Freedom's Wings"
Smartone/Vodafone (Hong Kong)	It's an exciting world . . . out there	Cutting-edge 3G	"Move closer!"
Oscar Mayer (meat, USA)	There's a kid inside even the biggest boy	Pure American taste	"Through the eyes of a child"
Siemens (mobile phones, PRC)	To move forward, you gotta have smarts	Phones with innovative features	"Intelligent phones for intelligent people"

The Brand Vision: DNA

The brand vision is a strategic concept. It is the brand's long-term identity and basis of all consumer engagement, not to mention corporate decisions regarding resource allocation.

In order for the brand vision to take hold, it must be advocated by the CEO. It defines the relationship between a human being and a mass-produced product. It is a *fusion* of the consumer insight and unique brand offer, the latter a physical "product truth" that must be "dug out" or a pre-existing equity-based "brand truth" or a combination of the two. A great brand vision – Omo's (Persil in the UK) "Dirt is Good", Ford USA's "Bold Moves" or Ford China's "Make Every Day Exciting" – boasts an *unexpected* combination of insight and offer, a paradoxical juxtaposition that liberates desire.

Some compelling brand visions are shown in Table 9.3.2.

The Engagement Idea

To underline the need for the consumer's involvement, we have relabelled the "advertising idea" an "engagement idea," a concept that is "bigger" than any single execution but still "creative".

The engagement idea can be tactical or thematic, short or long-term but it must be, first, inextricably rooted in the brand vision and, secondly, capable of being "woven" into daily life. In Japan, for example, Kit Kat (brand vision: "stress breaker") transformed itself from a candy, transcending the category by redefining chocolate as a pre-exam "lucky charm". In the UK, Knorr, a meal enhancer, depicted peas and potatoes as "charity cases", pleading with mums to "rescue vegetables". Recipes were disseminated on radio, television, in-store sampling, websites (at fooddeservesbetter.com) and blogs. The DTC (Diamond Trading Company) USA invited the public to help a stranded traveller intent on proposing to his girlfriend on Christmas Eve by "proving that absolutely nothing will come in the way of love". Each of these engagement ideas enhances consumers' involvement by integrating the brand into actual lives.

A few more successful engagement ideas are shown in Table 9.3.3.

Table 9.3.3   Successful engagement ideas

Brand	Engagement idea definition	From less to more active by . . .
Ford Escape (Taiwan)	Drive **over** the barrier between ordinary city life and a boundless horizon!	Bringing a sensation to life
Nike Beijing Marathon	It's time for the little guy to stop following. Have some fun by taking the lead.	Jolting the audience into action
JetBlue Airways	Satisfied JetBlue fliers: from their lips to your ears. It's amazing the stories they'll tell.	Enabling consumers to experience superior service first-hand
Schick razors	Liberate yourself by saying "No!" to the dictatorship of shaving convention!	Facilitating identity expression to elevate a challenger brand

Importantly, unless engagement ideas are properly articulated, we cannot extend them across relevant media, both traditional (television, radio, print, promotion, direct) and new (websites, micro-sites, blogs, mobiles, etc.). However, if well defined, they become sticky, bouncy, unstoppable forces helping to embed the brand in popular culture. Engagement ideas also tame the potential of viral marketing by enabling marketers to mould the brand experience on their own terms.

Evolving the Consumer Buying System to Suit Today's Media Market Place

The Consumer Buying System is a fundamental component of the JWT *Account Planner's Toolkit* (see Guy Murphy's description, page 139). Essentially this is a framework that helps to show how a market works by identifying the *process* by which people buy and use a product or service and how it fits into their lives.

As Stephen King himself observes:

> The Consumer Buying System is the name we use to cover this total process of buying and using a brand – from the very first ideas about it, to the actual purchase, to using it and beginning the process of buying again. Since all marketing activities are aiming to reinforce or modify people's sequences of ideas and actions, the buying system is really the starting point for all marketing and advertising planning. (This is true even where we're dealing with people "buying" an idea.)

And this is what it looks like (in brief):

- Trigger   "Something starts us off, consciously or subconsciously"
- Consider   "We consider the options, if we feel we need to"
- Search   "We look for more information, if we feel we need to"
- Choose   "We choose from among our options"
- Buy   "We actually buy, though not necessarily the brand we thought we'd chosen"
- Experience "We use, give or otherwise experience what we've bought. That affects us as we go into the next cycle of buying"

As media opportunities have exploded and diversified, it is even more important that the creative idea (or engagement idea) is appropriately executed to elicit the desired response, at each stage of the process.

Connection planning is what happens next to ensure that the appropriate media are deployed at each distinct point. "Media"in this sense, of course, refers not only to traditional print and television but the vast array of new media – indeed anything that touches the consumer and is capable of carrying an idea.

The Connection Plan

Connection planning is not media planning in the conventional sense (e.g. analysing cost efficiency based on exposure), it is a marriage between the creative idea and possible media vehicles. The Connection Plan is a creative process whereby the engagement idea drives the choice of media and ensures that the creative idea is a coherent totality that is reinforced at every touch point. (The origins of this idea are described in Stephen King's article in Chapter 6, written in 1969 and underlined in Marco Rimini's introduction on page 87).

Connection planning involves three "Golden Rules".

Use the right tool for the right business objective

We have christened this process the Consumer Engagement System to reinforce the role of: (a) traditional mass media in shaping preference; (b) newer (e.g. digital, CRM, mobile) media that has to have a more direct effect on sales or encouraging repeat purchase; and (c) the engagement idea itself in coalescing an endless stream of messages into one coherent idea that can, again, transform passive exposure into active involvement. Thus defining the specific role for each media vehicle is crucial.

Use the engagement idea in traditional media in unexpected ways

Philadelphia cream cheese's global engagement idea is "a little taste of heaven". Ordinary women become fallen angels, submitting to temptation in the clouds, so ads are placed high up in airports and on blimps. Nike Air Hong Kong's "run on nothing" campaign was brought to life on billboards with shoes floating on real air bubbles.

Use the engagement idea to stimulate use of completely new media

For example, the Economist's engagement idea revolves around: (a) bold use of red as a branding device and (b) copy using puns present the magazine as, literally, the *key* to success. So it uses electronic hotel door cards as a medium. In China, Bayer's Saridon dramatizes headache pain with skulls literally split open; with this idea, outdoor posters can be simple silhouette die cuts placed over cement fissures. Wall cracks become a new medium! In Taiwan, Ford Escape's engagement idea – "driving **over** barriers between ordinary city life and a boundless horizon" – led to Taipei City Hall morphing into a giant billboard. An actual vehicle, with tyre tracks streaked across the façade, was suspended on the side of the building.

The Art of Idea Management: A Quick Recap

Engagement ideas must be "managed". Great engagement ideas do not grow on trees. They are born of consumer insight, fundamental motivations for behaviour and preference. All insights should be expressed as tensions; if a brand can resolve an internal conflict, its relevance will, *de facto*, be strengthened. The brand vision, its long-term identity, springs from the consumer insight. It is a seamless, evocative *fusion* – one idea, not two – of insight and unique product offering. Engagement ideas, short or long term, thematic or tactical, breathe life into brands by transforming them into real world experience. Finally, the connection plan is more than a communications schedule. It is a synergy between engagement idea and media, a marriage in which the former increases the latter's cut through and vice versa.

Engagement planning is not complicated. But it requires disciplined thinking, articulation of the abstract and the courage to persuade. Tomorrow's industry leaders will embody these qualities, just as Stephen King, a role model for all times, did decades ago.

10

Short-Term Effects may be Easier to Measure but Long-Term Effects are More Important

By Tim Broadbent, Regional Planning Director, Ogilvy & Mather Asia Pacific

An introduction to:

10.1   Setting Advertising Budgets for Lasting Effects

The standard advertising agency functions such as the creative department, for instance, or account management, evolved messily over time from the primordial ooze of Victorian media agencies. But account planning is a *made* thing. It was deliberately designed to meet an agency need that in-house research and marketing departments did not meet.

King put effectiveness at the heart of account planning. His *Account Planners Toolkit* is the manual J Walter Thompson circulated to all its offices in the 1980s when it adopted account planning globally. Its first sentence reads, *"This manual contains J. Walter Thompson's views on how to plan the most effective advertising."* That is what account planning is for: to get "the most effective advertising".

How can we tell whether a particular campaign is effective? What do we mean by "effective"? – do we mean a short-term increase in volume sales, or a long-term increase in the strength of the brand? Questions such as these come under the general heading of "evaluation", and make evaluation central to account planning.

Evaluation is a Dynamic Activity

Evaluation is often seen as dry and backward looking, a bit like doing last year's accounts. However, Stephen saw evaluation as a *dynamic* activity. He took evaluation out of the backroom and thrust it into the hurly-burly of creative development. The *Account Planners Toolkit* introduces the "planning cycle", the process by which creative briefs are developed. It comprises five questions, with the fifth question feeding back to the first:

1. Where are we?
2. Why are we there?
3. Where could we be?
4. How could we get there?
5. Are we getting there?

Evaluation is how we answer questions 1, 2, 4 and 5, and informs the answer to question 3.

The idea behind the cycle is straightforward. We need to find out what worked last time in order to do better next time; King wrote that planning is "*based on understanding what it is that we've done well when we've been particularly successful*". Without that understanding we might change a part of the campaign that made it successful, or keep a part that was ineffective. Planning without evaluation is like firing a shotgun in the dark, hoping that some pellets might strike the target. Evaluation turns the lights on.

This view of evaluation was shared by Stanley Pollitt of BMP, planning's second father. In *How I Started Account Planning in Agencies* (1979), Pollitt wrote that the planner has three roles: the development of advertising strategy and creative ideas, and 'campaign appraisal'. Appraisal was continuous. When I was a BMP planner in the 1970s, we researched the strategy, then we researched rough versions of the creative execution, and then we researched the finished work after it appeared in the market. Pollitt was committed "to getting the advertising content right at all costs" by listening to consumers; getting it right was "more important than maximizing agency profits, more important than keeping clients happy, or building an agency shop window for distinctive-looking advertising".

Despite the central importance of evaluation to account planning, King did not see himself as an expert analyst. This is an important point. Evaluation is not just a job for specialists with two degrees in statistics. It is a job that all planners can do, indeed it is what they *must* do if they are to be what King or Pollitt would have regarded as true planners.

The Two Most Difficult Problems

Stephen published little on the subject, but he tackled two of the most difficult problems in evaluation: (1) how do we evaluate the success or otherwise of advertising for new products? and (2) how do we evaluate advertising's lasting effects? It seems logical to review his approach to the new product problem first as it leads towards his article on budget setting.

He was one of the judges of the the the first IPA Advertising Effectiveness Awards, the competition that was created by my father, Simon Broadbent. Broadbent's Introduction to *Advertising Works* (1981) quoted King's note on principles of evaluation in full. As the book has long been out of print, I am happy to quote from it:

> *Advertising's contribution to launching new brands*
> One problem with this category of entry is that, by definition, new brands start off with no sales, no usage, no awareness, and no attitudes. Thus a presentation that simply shows increases in all these does not seem to me to *demonstrate* advertising effectiveness, except in a totally trivial way. Of course all the measures go up (there's no other direction) and of course most manufacturers would not contemplate a launch without advertising.
>
> In my view, to qualify for an award the entry has to demonstrate that launch advertising has caused sales, usage, etc., to go up *more than might have been expected*. That is, there has to be some form of *comparison* – with previous experience of new brands, the "norms" of existing brands, different regions, different time periods, the same money spend in another way, "econometrics", etc.
>
> In other words, I think there needs to be a demonstration of a *particularly successful* launch; not an assertion that one cannot launch a new brand without advertising.

Isolating Advertising From Everything Else

The evaluative challenge is to isolate advertising effects from among the other factors that influence consumer demand. This is very hard for new products. For instance, consider one of the most successful new products of recent years, Apple's iPod. People have always wanted music on the move. First there were musical boxes, then portable wind-up gramophones, then battery-powered record players, then the cassette-based Walkman, all ways of meeting the same consumer want. The iPod is the best product so far – it carries more songs more conveniently than the old technologies. One might therefore have expected the iPod to be a great success even without its launch campaign. How can we isolate the effects of that campaign?

King suggests the answer: we need "some form of *comparison*". We might compare the iPod's sales curve against the sales curve of similarly revolutionary products, for instance digital cameras or mobile phones. Or we might look more closely within iPod sales to find regions with higher or lower levels of adspend and compare sales in those regions, or to find times of higher or lower adspend.

He continued:

Advertising's contribution to the successful establishment of a new brand
The post-launch situation seems rather different. The evidence is that the key to success in a new brand is its repeat-purchase rate, and that this depends on the response of triers of it as a totality. The brand has to be "better and different". If triers like its *blend of physical and psychological values*, they'll go on buying it and paying a reasonable price for it.

Our rules mention the difficulty of disentangling the effect of advertising from that of other marketing activities. For new brands, it seems to me not simply difficult to do, but actually wrong to try. In a sense, for a new brand, the advertising *is* the brand. Maybe its most important objective is to contribute a *distinct personality* to the new brand as the basis for the brand's saleability – that is, its long-term ability to sustain sales at a price premium or a profitable price.

To some extent, therefore, if a brand becomes established as a successful business proposition, the advertising *must* have succeeded. But it is very hard to see how this can be *demonstrated*. Maybe blind versus named product tests, in demonstrating brand values, could be said to measure advertising's contribution. Maybe demonstrations of price premium are evidence.

King's *Setting Advertising Budgets for Lasting Effects* (1984) is effectively a working out of these demonstrations applied to the issue to budget setting. His technique is worth examining. He needs to get from A to C, where A is adspend and C is long-term sales and profitability. He does this by means of an intermediate variable, brand strength (the article calls it "asset strength"). Call brand strength B.

Using a kind of proof that is familiar to mathematicians, he first shows that A = B. That is to say, he shows that adspend builds brand strength. It is shown here by the extent to which consumers who bought the brand go on to buy it again. Next he shows that B = C. That is, he shows that brand strength contributes to lasting sales and profits. He has two demonstrations: that brands are preferred to apparently superior products in blind versus named tests, and that brands command premium prices. Thus, by a simple syllogism, A = C; that is, adspend contributes to lasting sales and profits.

Not all Proofs of Effectiveness are Equal

The big message in this article is that short-term advertising effects may be easier to measure than long-term effects but that does not mean they are more valuable to the advertiser. On the contrary, he argues that one of the key competitive strengths a company can enjoy is a "unique hold on the hearts and minds of consumers", which is seldom if ever created overnight. Stephen was writing in 1984, six years before the IPA Effectiveness Awards under Paul Feldwick purposefully encouraged the search for "longer and broader" advertising effect. Stephen saw sooner than many that not all proofs of effectiveness are equal.

The Main Points to Take from this Article

- King introduced account planning in order to get "the most effective advertising".
- Telling whether a campaign is effective or not, and deciding what we mean by "effective" in the first place, are questions that come under the general heading of "evaluation". For King, evaluation was at the heart of account planning.
- King (and Stanley Pollitt of BMP) took evaluation out of the backroom and thrust it into the hurly-burly of creative development. We need to find out what worked last time in order to increase our chances of doing better next time.
- King did not see himself as an expert analyst yet he tackled some of the most challenging evaluation problems. Evaluation is something every planner can do – it is something they *must* do if they are to be true planers.
- Long-term effects can be harder to evaluate but may be more valuable to the advertiser than short-term effects, and so must not be overlooked when setting the ad budget.

10.1
Setting Advertising Budgets
for Lasting Effects*

By Stephen King

One of the long-term effects of *Admap* has been a lasting discussion about the long-term effects of advertising (Bloom, 1976; Clarke, 1975; Corlett, 1978; Cowan, 1977; King, 1977). There have been arguments about what we mean by "long-term", whether such effects exist at all, whether they are different in kind from short-term effects, maybe requiring different creative treatments, and how we should measure them if they do exist (or, indeed, if they do not). It is clearly an important topic, so abstract and so difficult that on the whole the arguments have not greatly impinged on the daily decisions of practical marketing people.

By contrast, the recent one-day workshop, "Cut the Advertising – or Spend More?", had a very practical point of view: it covered "how to set the advertising budget in 1984/5". I had drawn the shortest of some not very long straws, and was essentially asked to give views about taking the long term into account, when setting appropriations *in the next few months*. This article is more or less what I said at the workshop. Accordingly, it does not pretend to be a deep analysis of the nature of the problem, but an attempt to say what, in the present state of knowledge, it might be both reasonable and practical to do now. It covers, first, some preliminaries about the nature of lasting effects; next, why it seems important to bother about them; then how we might set about measuring them; and finally, what we might actually do in the current budget-setting season.

LASTING EFFECTS

A belief in the lasting effect of advertising is fairly deeply embedded in most advertising agency people (Cowan, 1977), and it is why they think that consistency of creative treatment really matters. Equally, the use by marketing people of the term "brand loyalty" suggests that, whatever short-term responses they need to make to the market place, they feel the need for a degree of permanence too. The general feeling is that probably advertising has both long-term and short-term effects. Grahame Leman (1969) expressed this broad view in writing that the long-term task of advertising is to build and sustain the "saleability" of a brand, and the short-term task is to exploit it.

But, however general this view might be, one of the practical problems has been that, while there has been a steadily increasing precision about measuring short-term effects, rather less attention has been paid to long-term effects. The IPA's Advertising Effectiveness Awards (Broadbent, 1981/1983) have done a great deal to stimulate short-term measurement, and the use of market modelling (or econometric methods) has grown. Meanwhile, most

---

*Published in *Admap*, July 1984. Reproduced with permission.

arguments about long-term effects have had to rely on a few, rather selectively presented, case histories.

This has led some people to doubt the existence of long-term effects or to believe that they are so weak in relation to immediate effects that advertising decision makers should ignore them (Bloom, 1976). Part of their argument has depended on the implausibility of a "time-bomb" mechanism (in which nothing happens for a long time, and then suddenly the advertisement works). But the most common interpretation has in fact been of a "lasting" or cumulative model: that is, the immediate effect of an advertisement decays, but a small amount remains and is lasting – Alan Hedges (1974) called it a "sedimentary" effect. (I have used the word "lasting" in this article to make it clear that it is this model that I am using.) The effect of each piece of sediment from each advertisement could be tiny, but *cumulatively* the total sediment could be the most important effect of advertising over the years.

This model of advertising suggests that one of the questions the budget-setter has to ask is what legacy he wants to leave to his successors in, say, five years' time. Does he want them to start with the brand in a more favourable competitive situation than himself, or the same or further behind? The amount to be put into advertising in 1984/5, and possibly the creative approach, will to some extent depend on his answer.

WHY BOTHER WITH LASTING EFFECTS?

In some cases, the marketing manager's answer will be quite straightforward: a fair number of advertisements are not intended to have any lasting effect. This is usually because they are dealing with a unique offer or circumstances that will not be repeated in the future; for instance, most classified and much direct response advertising, most advertising for events and some for special promotions. In such cases, the question about the legacy for successors does not arise.

But the question will always arise in markets where the norm is repeat-purchase. That applies most obviously to cheap packaged goods, but also to more durable goods in markets where consumers may not repeatedly buy the same model (it may well have been discontinued), but do have the opportunity to buy from the same company.

I believe that, even though more emphasis has been put on the measurement of short-term effects, it is becoming relatively more important to measure the lasting effects of advertising. In these repeat-purchase markets the rules have changed. Since 1964 there has been a fundamental shift in the balance of power between manufacturers, retailers and consumers. Competition, in-cluding import penetration, has increased considerably, and many of the traditional approaches to marketing no longer work very well.

As a result, the only route to success for most manufacturing companies in the 1980s is going to be *marketing from strength* (or asset marketing, as Hugh Davidson (1983) has called it). Adequacy in all departments is unlikely to be enough. In other words, the starting point will have to be a thoroughly realistic analysis of the company's assets and strengths in relation to competitors and retailers; then a ruthless concentration on points of strength. Of course, weak areas will have to be brought up to par, but unless there is a determined marketing from strength it will be difficult to avoid being an also-ran.

The crunch will come when companies do their realistic analysis. Some will be lucky enough to have clear-cut competitive advantages in functional areas like product quality or performance, costs, distribution, price, service or access to raw materials. But most compa-nies will not; they will be no worse than competitors in these aspects, but they will not be permanently and demonstrably better. They will certainly find it hard to beat the retailers on their own ground of distribution and price.

Many companies will conclude that one of the few competitive strengths that they either do have or could have is a *unique hold on the hearts and minds of consumers*. They could have an adequate set of functional attributes (maybe with some marginal or temporary strengths) linked by a continuous and strong brand personality. Or, to put it another way, they could market from the strength of their brand's added values. Increasingly, with today's growing retailer power and more rapid technological change and more rapid product copying, this is going to be the norm for both repeat-purchase brands and repeat-purchase companies.

If advertising, by its lasting or sedimentary effects, can contribute to building or sustaining these added values – in addition to its short-term stimulative effect – then that could be its most important role in today's conditions.

MEASURING ADDED VALUE

Before considering what part advertising might play in building this unique hold on the hearts and minds of consumers, it is worth trying to get an idea of the nature and importance of these added values. It is quite easy to get the impression from the precision of much market modelling work that after the short-term effect is measured there is very little left to "explain".

In fact, I think that we do know quite a lot about how advertising works in the short run. Some 15 years ago the JWT/BMRB diary study had indicated that it does it by reordering the priorities within a buyer's repertoire of brands (Barnes, 1971; King, 1975; McDonald, 1969). It can *retain* someone as buyer of our brand when she might otherwise, in the normal ebb and flow of life or shop pricing, have shifted to another; or it can *attract* her to our brand when she might have stayed with a competitor. What this research did not show (or set out to show) was how brands got into repertoires in the first place and why they stayed there over many years.

Equally, market modelling has a pretty good record over the past 20 years (it is not as new as some seem to imply) for raising testable hypotheses about the causal factors in a market and their relative importance. But we have to be clear as to how much it is that the models are explaining, as Figure 10.1 indicates.

In this recent market modelling exercise the fit between the actual and model lines is quite good; and had the scale been indexed on the "25" line it would have been easy to conclude that the formula gave a more or less complete explanation of the market. However, it is clear from looking at Figure 10.1 that we are at best explaining variations from a base, and that the variations are mostly quite small (10% or less of total sales). It may well be that the most important questions are: How did the base (the constant in the modelling equation) get there? Is it moving, and if so, in what direction? If it is not moving, is something keeping it still, and if so, what?

I am a firm advocate of market modelling as a basis for setting short-term advertising budgets, but we have to recognize that it leaves the question of long-term effects completely open. (One of the few attempts that I know to estimate long-term effects took 17 years of data on detergents in Australia (Metwally, 1976). The result of considering the long run in the models, in addition to the short run, was to put up the "optimal" advertising/sales ratio by a factor of 4. While this is a pleasing thought to an agency man, I have to say that I take the findings with a pinch of salt.)

How then can we measure added values in a brand and see whether they are changing? Let me put forward three simple methods, all of which would be available to most marketing companies and the data for which probably already exist for many. They do not represent

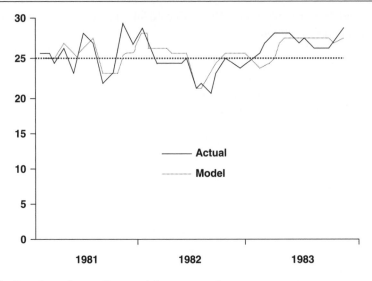

Figure 10.1   Brand p: volume sales – model versus actual

a great breakthrough in sophisticated technique, but it seems to me more important that we should make a start in this crucial area. (More complex methods have long been advocated, which might well be adopted when we have gained experience and courage (Corlett, 1976).)

First, blind *versus* named product tests. Table 10.1 gives the headline results of the test of two brands. In one sample of users of this particular type of household product the brands were tried blind, and in a matched sample of users the brands were in their normal marketplace packs. Brand J was market leader and Brand K had recently had a significant product improvement.

The implication is strong that the name of Brand J, with all its associations, added competitive values that were not in the naked product. A series of such tests carried out over time would give a measure of changes in such added values.

This approach need not be confined to packaged goods. In one piece of experimental work, we showed to two matched samples of people photographs of two brands of television set, with their specifications printed below them. In one sample the sets were named, in the other they were blind. In the blind test the Philips set had a 22% lead in overall preference over its British competitor, and in the named test a 52% lead. Other questions asked people their views on likely price. In the blind test 23% reckoned the Philips set would cost over £10 more than the competitor, and in the named test 34% did so. Again, this sort of research could be repeated

Table 10.1   Blind versus named product test – overall preference

% of users who said:	Brands blind	Brands named
Prefer Brand K	47%	38%
Prefer Brand J	28%	41%
NO preference	25%	21%
	100%	100%

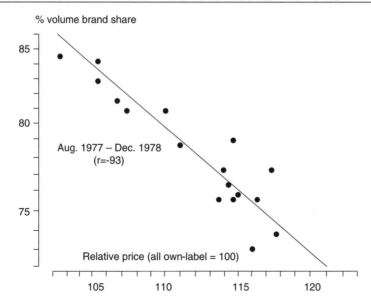

Figure 10.2   Kellogg's versus own-label corn flakes

to indicate movement in the added value of the company reputation, maybe supplemented by some form of continuous attitude measure.

The second approach to measuring added values is to look at demand curves. Since 1964, when resale price maintenance was abolished, the price that people pay for a brand has varied widely, and in most markets there is some sort of trade-off between volume brand share and competitive prices. The brand with a high added value will be able to sustain a higher brand share at a certain price than one with lower added value (or be able to sustain a higher price at a set share).

Tom Corlett, who first advocated this approach, has written at length on it (Corlett, 1978). Figure 10.2 gives a simple example, taken from one of Jeremy Elliott's entries for the 1980 IPA Advertising Effectiveness Awards (Broadbent, 1981/1983).

Figure 10.2 shows the added value of Kellogg's Corn Flakes compared with private label. Volume brand share is plotted against relative price, and each bullet represents consumer purchases over a four-week period. Over these 16 months, for instance, Kellogg's can be seen to get a share of about 82% with a 7% price premium and about 77% with a 14% premium. The bullets lie pretty close to the demand curve line, and this suggests that the trade-off or Kellogg's competitive added value was stable during this time. These sorts of data should be readily available in many markets, so that it should be possible to track changes in added value by repeating the analysis over time – remembering, of course, that it is a measure of competitiveness and that the other brands in the market may be moving too.

The third approach to measuring added value is really a simplified version of the second. In many markets, despite all our sound and fury, brand shares are fairly stable on any basis longer than the traditional four-weekly or two-monthly reporting periods. If that is so, then we can get an idea of long-run movements in added value simply by plotting relative price, smoothed out over, say, quarterly or six-monthly periods. If a brand can retain its share of market volume, while the price people that will pay for it increases relative to the rest of the market, clearly it has been adding value. It does this normally by not needing all the special offers and discounts that its weaker competitors need in order to survive. (In other words, a brand can increase its relative price without necessarily going up faster than the general rate of inflation.)

Andrex toilet tissue is the long-term brand leader in a market which, in many countries, is overwhelmed with private label, generics, cheap lines and special offers. It has been marketed in the UK by a company with a firm belief in added values; and it shows. Its volume brand share for the past 20 years, on a quarterly basis, has hardly ever varied by more than two and a half percentage points from its average. But its price premium over all other brands has risen fairly consistently throughout the period. In 1964 it was about 10%, and by 1984 it was about 35%. In other words, the brand has built up lasting added values. It seems most unlikely that it could have jumped from a 10% to a 35% price premium in, say, a couple of years. The gradual improvement over 20 years means that each year built on a slightly higher base than the year before. The current management must be pleased that their predecessors were not concerned with the short term only.

THE CONTRIBUTION OF ADVERTISING

So far, I have been putting forward the rather unrevolutionary idea that some brands do build increasingly profitable added values and that, if the will is there, some fairly simple research methods and analyses can chart progress. The problem is to relate this to advertising. How can we tell what part, if any, advertising has played in this? I think that the short answer is: we cannot, unless we are prepared to mount some form of experiment. (The same is true for evaluating the long-term effect of product quality, new plant and equipment, better ingredients, R&D, labour relations, management training, and so on.) The thought of setting up meticulously designed long-term experiments is usually too appalling to contemplate, but it need not be an all-or-nothing thing. In fact, in each of the instances I have quoted so far there was an element of experiment involved. If we are prepared simply to think experimentally, I am sure we could make some progress and get some hints of advertising's contribution.

For instance, in the blind *versus* named product test, each of the matched samples was broken down by the brand "normally used". Figure 10.3 shows the results.

In the blind test, preferences were virtually the same, whether people normally used Brand J or Brand K or neither. This suggests that differences in added values lay in the associations of the brands rather than in some sort of habituation to the different physical products. In the named test, clearly people (and particularly Brand J users) were inclined to support their normal brand – no doubt from a combination of advertising, recall of past satisfactions and desire for internal consistency. But the views of the neutrals, those who normally used neither brand, also reflected greater added values for Brand J than Brand K; and their views would have been much less likely to reflect past satisfactions and desire for consistency. This does not, of course, *prove* that advertising was responsible for a lasting effect; but repeating the test with this and other sorts of breakdown would get one nearer to a coherent view of advertising's contribution.

In the case of Kellogg's Corn Flakes, in early 1979 there was a new campaign based on the addition of vitamins to the brand. The evidence was that, after this advertising, the demand curve moved to the right (Broadbent, 1981/1983).

Even in the short term, the combination of product improvement and new advertising based on it can be shown by this method of analysis to add values that might become lasting – in the sense of moving the brand to a new base, improving its saleability. Bearing in mind the fact that the added vitamins cannot be tasted or seen, it seems fair to conclude that the advertising played

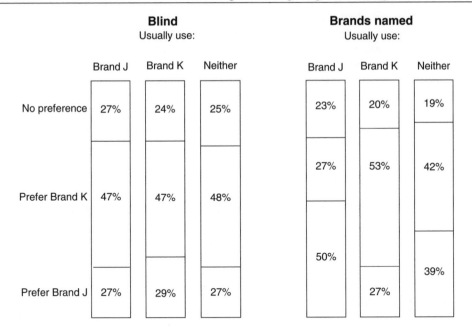

Figure 10.3   Blind versus named product test – household product

a major part in the shift. A simple before-and-after experiment as a small window on known long-term changes in added value can at least give an indication of the order of importance of advertising's contribution.

The experiment for Andrex was of much the same type. It happened that for one lengthy period, due to supply problems, Andrex was forced to drop all advertising. During this period and after advertising was resumed there was very little change in volume brand share; it had the same pattern of relatively small fluctuations referred to earlier. However during the time without advertising relative price stabilized; and when advertising resumed, gradually relative price started going up again. Again, there was enough in the data to build a reasonable hypothesis about how advertising was building a cumulative added value.

IMPLICATIONS FOR SETTING ADVERTISING BUDGETS IN 1984/5

The Andrex story seems to me to highlight the dilemma for budget-setters. There can be very little doubt that one of Bowater-Scott's most valuable sources of continuous profit is the competitive added value of Andrex as a brand. That value has grown cumulatively over time, with each year starting from a rather higher base than the year before. It seems highly likely that advertising has contributed. If it has, it has been a lasting effect: where Andrex is today in terms of added value depends as much on what was contributed in year 1 as in year 25.

Yet, even if advertising alone had been responsible, it would surely have been impossible to measure the effect of each piece of added value sediment at the time; relative price improved on average by only 0.2 percentage points per bi-monthly period. The paradox is that while market modelling is very successfully indicating the effect of advertising expenditure on the size of the short-term fluctuations from the base, the arguably more important role of building lasting added value into the base required something of an act of faith.

It seems to me that the only way out of this sort of dilemma is to examine a fairly long period of the past, using some of the methods outlined above, to get a *broad feeling* of the order of contribution that advertising, at its various levels of expenditure, may have made to added value. (We may be surprised how much of the necessary data are already there, gathering dust in the archives.) Then use this broad view to *modify* the more precise calculations that we make about the short term. This may seem impossibly vague and disappointing to those looking for a firm technique for measuring long-term effects, but I do not think it is any worse than methods in most other business decisions; we must not fall into the error of believing that there is any real precision about return on investment calculations in production, R&D or personnel.

As a result, I suggest that there should be five fairly distinct stages of budget setting:

1. The most important stage is at the corporate management level. When the rule is marketing from strength, top management has to make the strategic decision: what is our strength? Are we going to build it, change it, replace it? How are we going to exploit it? It is not enough to do corporate planning as a financial exercise: it has to deal with the company's whole *raison d'être*.

   Unless such questions are answered, no one can start to set advertising budgets. They cannot be set by some formula in the marketing department.

2. On the basis of these strategic decisions, the next stage is considering the role of advertising: exactly how is it supposed to work (King, 1975)? Again, without a clear judgment here, it is not feasible to plan budgets, media selection or creative approach. Specifically, we have to consider whether (in addition to short-term stimulus) advertising does have or should have a role in building lasting added values. Should it be aiming for more, less or the same added values as in the past?

3. Next, we can set the base cases or "no-change" advertising budget. Ideally, this is done by market modelling. If that is not possible, at least it should be done by thinking in the same mode as market modelling. That is, by *judging* what are the main factors, in what proportions, that "normally" affect sales and profits. It will then be necessary to modify this no-change figure, if the strategic decision is to build the brand or to milk it.

4. Then there is the stage of adjusting the budget to deal with the lasting effects of advertising, depending on decisions at stage 2. This will not, in my view, ever be a matter of applying a formula, but it can be a matter of reasoned argument from looking at the growth or stability or decline of added value in the past. Typically it will be necessary to ask whether the advertisements planned will do more than the necessary short-term job of mind-jogging. It may be, for instance, that 10-second spots work well in the short run in bringing our brand to the top of the buyers' short-list: but they may not be doing enough to build the values that will ensure that it stays on or gets on future short-lists at all. Clearly there is a strong budget implication in judgements about the right mix of spot lengths or advertisement sizes or quality of production. This is where qualitative research can be particularly valuable, if properly briefed; as can continuous measures of attitudes to brands – provided that they are done at a less superficial level than is currently the fashion.

5. The final stage is to write into the marketing budget sufficient funds to do the research properly, if it was not in the past. At the very least, we should try to do some of the simple

research and analyses that I have suggested above, and try to develop better methods too. Above all, I think we would do well to develop a much more experimental approach in budgeting. Unless we are prepared to be a little more adventurous, we will never put ourselves at risk of learning something useful.

I think it is *relatively* easy to set advertising budgets on a short-term basis; but it is certainly very difficult to do it for lasting effects. We need all the research and thinking help that we can get. The fact is that in the marketing conditions that are likely to prevail in the 1980s and beyond, it could make all the difference between success and failure.

REFERENCES

Barnes, M. (1971) *The Relationship Between Purchasing Patterns and Advertising Exposure.* JWT.

Bloom, D. (1976) "Consumer behaviour and the timing of advertising effects", *Admap*, 12(9), September.

Broadbent, S. (1981/1983) *Advertising Works*, vols. 1 & 2, Holt, Rinehart & Winston, London.

Clarke, D.G. (1975) *Econometric Measurement of the Duration of the Advertising Effect on Sales*, Marketing Science Institute.

Corlett, T. (1976) "How we should measure the longer-term effects of advertising on purchasing", *Admap*, 12(9), September.

Corlett, T. (1978) "Anyone for econometrics?", *Admap*, 14(8), August.

Cowan, D. (1977) "Long-term advertising effects: an agency view", *Admap*, 13(4), April.

Davidson, H. (1983) "Putting assets first", *Marketing*, 17 November; "Building on a winner," *Marketing*, 24 November; and "Making an entrance", *Marketing*, 1 December.

Hedges, A. (1974) *Testing to Destruction.* IPA.

King, S. (1975) "Practical progress from a theory of advertisements", *Admap*, 11(10), October.

King, S. (1977) "Improving advertising decisions", *Admap*, 13(4), April.

Leman, G. (1969) "Sales, saleability and the saleability gap", *Bulletin No. 5, BBTA.*

McDonald, C. (1969) "Relationships between advertising exposure and purchasing behaviour", *Admap*, 5(4), April.

Metwally, M.M. (1976) "Profitability of advertising in Australia: A case study", *Journal of Industrial Economics*, March.

The author is particularly grateful to Bowater-Scott and Kellogg for permission to quote their data.

Part III
Market Research

Stephen never had specific market research training. But he worked very closely with the J. Walter Thompson owned company, the British Market Research Bureau, in developing different research tools that this new discipline of account planning required.

His articles on market research stand as excellent examples of how research should be used. He was deeply sceptical of most of advertising research techniques, questioning their promises of certainty; he looked at opinion research with a somewhat jaundiced eye, wondering in an increasingly fragmented social order, what "public" opinion could possibly mean; and his views about research "for decision making" are genuinely radical and important for decision makers to grasp.

Throughout these writings is the constant search for the right balance between what is measurable and what is not and the need to balance good data with judgement.

Part II

Methodologies

11

A Theory that Built a Company

By Mike Hall, Founder, Hall & Partners, Specialist Research Agency

An introduction to:

11.1   Can Research Evaluate the Creative Content of Advertising?

In a mere seven pages in *Admap*, where it was published in 1967, Stephen addresses a crucial question with simple analysis, lucid reasoning and a certain conclusion. This analysis is what originally inspired my company.

I first read it in 1977, 10 years after it was written and two years into my own career. I had two aims in mind: I wanted to understand how advertising worked and, far more important to me then, I wanted to get to the annual Market Research Society Conference the following March, which, as a junior researcher, I could achieve only by presenting an article of my own. Of that effort, the less said the better, but it had the singular benefit of forcing me to discover what had already been written on the subject.

With the rigours of the Oxford tutorial still freshly impressed on my psyche, I devoured the critical literature – and felt intellectually nauseous. I've never been able to read that American *Journal of Advertising Research* since, and frankly I doubt I've missed much. Stephen's writings, by contrast, were like thunderbolts, flashes of light and manna all rolled into one – a multitude of effects, all emanating from heaven.

When, 14 years later, I delivered my second MRS conference article, unveiling the four models of how advertising works, the philosophy on which Hall & Partners' work is based, I re-read this article. And now, coincidentally another 14 years on, I am asked to read it again.

How has it aged?

Here's my verdict: it's a classic, for all that it shows its age; drink deeply thereof and be stimulated. It will make you thirsty for later developments of comparable stature, and will enhance your appreciation of them.

It's impossible to read this article without detecting signs of its age, and rather like a movie-goer watching Hitchcock's *The Birds* gets a little disenchanted nowadays by its unimpressive special effects, it's possible that modern readers might miss its undoubted impact if they were to focus on the *passé* rather than the eternal truths that it contains.

Many of the Same Problems Still Exist, Despite Progress on Several Fronts

And yet there is much to be gained by identifying the concerns that exercised Stephen then but no longer strike us as major issues. They show us how far we've come since those days, as a prelude to the shock of realizing that the remaining concerns are still present 40 years after they were presented as a burning issue.

Take Stephen's second summary point of four: his identification of the need for three stages of creative evaluation research. It's a given now that we need to separate creative development from pre-testing from campaign evaluation (or "exposure" as he called it), and difficult to appreciate that it was radical then. But we cannot say the same of his other summary points, which remain still true but not always observed in practice, so bear continued repeating:

- Can most communications agencies, let alone marketing people, honestly claim that they set creative strategy in terms of people's desired responses? When I developed the models of how advertising works 14 years ago, it was still revolutionary thinking, and though many have now taken this on board, many others still argue in terms of measuring what we put into the advertising, rather than what people take out of it.
- Stephen's exhortation to "be bolder in our experimentation" was all the encouragement I needed at the time, but his cautionary words might still be heeded by most qualitative researchers I've come across: ". . . (we should) not try to measure the effect of minor differences in advertisements before we know how to measure major ones."
- His request of research that it concentrate on "measures of 'involvement' and of the intensity and structure of attitudes" is again astonishingly far-sighted. We first did it fully 23 years later and that second part of the clause exercises us – and can provide a challenge for other researchers – still.
- His final point (that more basic research needs to be done) is one that provokes some sense of pride myself, for he describes it as "so massive a problem" that I sat down in 1991 determined to do it for the simple reason that it still needed to be done. So Hall & Partners emerged from the article because this subject was the only thing I was really interested in when I looked back on my advertising career.

But in reading an article like this it's important to realize the progress that's been made in thinking, and for people not to trot out the old platitudes any more. I scream when I read some lazy journalist – or worse still a dumb agency person – repeat the dull Leverhulme quote about not knowing which half of his advertising isn't working. Any client who says that should be fired the next day. We can tell which bits are working and aren't working, and if they're satisfied with 70% let alone 50%, their CFO should be clawing back their annual bonuses.

Theories of How Advertising Works

What I personally love about this article is, of course, its analysis of theories of how advertising works. The point I've always argued is that a model of advertising is simply a set of assumptions about desired responses, and this principle stems directly from Stephen's own thinking. In fact it's right here: "it becomes clear that all discussion about what material to expose, in what way, to whom, in order to ask what questions, depends ultimately on our theory of how advertising works". And it's worth reminding every researcher about that as they propose the latest methodological gimmick.

The theories analysed here are those extant at the time: the "standard theory" is what I've called the Sales Response Model. Stephen says himself that the Brand/need and Penetration theories are similar, and they represent what I call the Persuasion model. Starch and Reeves merely use different terms, although Reeves has much to answer for in terms of poor communications thinking and research methodology over the last 50 years in emphasizing the objective as being Creative Response (and recall in particular) rather than Brand Response.

What Stephen calls "the succession of mental states theory" is not a model in itself but a theory of the process by which the different variants of the Persuasion model work. Latterly there has been a bit of a backlash against the idea of models, suggesting that they make communications seem too mechanistic. But here is evidence that although all of advertising follows a process, only *some* processes are mechanistic. And here Stephen is putting the intellectual and research case for what I've termed the Involvement model: the notion that advertising can work successfully by reinforcing existing predispositions.

The case made for Involvement advertising reflects JWT's culture and philosophy. Now we might place it equally among three other models – and of the Salience model there is here not a whisper. It came into the foreground later and dominates today's thinking in the same way that means of involving the target audience did then.

Involvement Theory: Most Important Now

But perhaps we should give the Involvement model the status of *primus inter pares*, for it is now part of almost every piece of communication however badly conceived and executed.

So, overall I find it's aged very well indeed, and it's still radical in the sense that the roots of thinking about how advertising works are visible here. Just as today we can listen to Beethoven's Fifth and still appreciate how radical it is without feeling the shockwaves of its first performance, so we can read this article again and still utter involuntary cries of "Oh yes!"

The mark of Stephen's stature is that he not only set the agenda for research years before it showed itself capable of responding, but he also showed us the way forward. It's quite simple for anyone interested in communications research nowadays: start here. (But do not end here.)

11.1
Can Research Evaluate the Creative Content of Advertising?*

By Stephen King

Based on the award winning paper presented by Stephen King, head of advertising research, J. Walter Thompson Ltd, at the 1967 conference of the Market Research Society

The marketing manager who deals with mass-consumer goods usually finds nowadays that advertising expenditure is by some way the largest part of his annual budget. Thus if research is to help him to make major marketing-mix decisions, it must be capable of dealing with the results of varying the advertising expenditure. Various marketing models have been invented, but though they have tended to suggest a general relationship between advertising expenditure and sales, the margin of error has often been so large that the marketing manager's decisions continue to be based on well-established (though not necessarily completely valid) rules of common sense.

One of the major snags has been the problem of assessing the *quality* of the advertising. Since advertising is so important an element in consumer goods marketing, it may well be that marketing models will make no further progress until the effectiveness of the creative content can be evaluated.

This article aims to examine where we stand today in advertising research, and in particular to ask three questions:

1. What sort of evaluation is both valid and useful?
2. On what areas of advertising research should the inevitably limited budgets be concentrated?
3. What should advertisers, agencies and researchers be doing next to improve methods and approaches?

THE CURRENT SITUATION

I stressed as the first question the need for research that is both valid and useful. This is hardly a new requirement, but I think that we see the extremes of failure more often in advertising research than, say, market research. On the one hand, there have been furious arguments between researchers about research techniques, with the baffled user on the sidelines waiting for someone to give him some results that he can use. Great edifices of analysis and jargon have tempted us to forget at times that it is all based on one human being asking another some questions. On the other hand, many users of research are playing the plain blunt man who doesn't want any of these fancy theoretical arguments about methods – he just wants something that will help him to make decisions. Any research, he says, is better than none.

---

*Published in *Admap*, June 1967. Reproduced with permission.

I think that American experience suggests that, in the long run, the second danger could be the greater – that of users picking their favourite measure, sticking to it through thick and thin, making decisions on it and closing their minds to doubts or progress.

These two dangers can be considerably lessened by improvements in working methods. Two areas in particular are important, both to do with setting objectives.

Defining the Objectives of Research

The first improvement in working methods involves defining more clearly (and being seen to define) the objectives of each piece of advertising research. The research can only be integrated properly into the advertising *process* by having a model of the stages by which advertising actually gets made, and looking at its practical usefulness in terms of:

- Useful for what?
- Useful to whom?
- Useful when?

It then becomes clear that different sorts of research are needed by different people for different purposes at different stages of the advertising process rather than one all purpose system.

Figure 11.1 shows a simple version of the model of the advertising process that we use at JWT. It is obviously a cyclical or feedback process. And here is a summary of the research job, main users and the end result of using the research at each stage.

Stage 1: Planning

Research job: Provide current data to help to set strategy.
Main user: Client, marketing man, creative man.
End result: Agreed creative strategy.

Stage 2: Creative development

Research job: Stimulate new ideas
                         Assess rough campaigns
                         Improve advertisements
                         Eliminate errors
Main user: Creative man
End result: Improved rough campaigns.

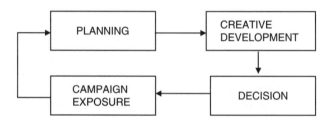

Figure 11.1   Model of advertising planning process

Stage 3: Decision

Research job: Help final choice between alternative campaigns
Main user: Client, account executive
End result: Decision on which campaign to run.

Stage 4: Campaign exposure

Research job: Measure changes in consumer's attitudes and behaviour, linking them to
                   marketing actions
Main user: Client, marketing man, creative man
End result: Assessment of campaign: refinement of strategy

So we essentially have a planning stage, and three separate and different evaluation stages.

Defining the Objectives of Advertising

The second improvement in working methods follows from looking at the advertising process in this way as a cycle. If we accept that evaluation is a matter of setting objectives and then assessing performance against those objectives, then clearly the same terms and criteria ought to be used for both the planning and evaluation stages.

And yet I think it is still the rule, rather than the exception, that creative people are asked to achieve one objective, and then their work is turned down because it hasn't achieved something completely different. This is particularly true when the creative strategy is set as a consumer proposition, which the researcher doesn't know what to do with (King, 1965/6); or with some of the measures regularly used at the decision-making stage, which do not mean much to the creative man.

The link between creative man and researcher is clearly the consumer's responses to a brand. The creative man is trying to get certain responses to the brand; and responses are basically what the researcher measures.

At JWT, therefore, we set creative strategy by setting out the answers to this question:

- What do we want the target group:
  – to notice about the brand (with the senses)
  – to believe about the brand (with the reason)
  – to feel towards the brand (with the emotions)
  as a result of advertising, packaging, merchandising, and other marketing activities?

This format supplies a clear brief to researchers throughout the cycle of advertising: Does *this* advertising get *these* responses from *these* people?

It makes much clearer than usual what sort of research is needed to set strategy in the first place – buying pattern research for setting target groups, and measures of sensual reactions, rational beliefs and emotional feelings for setting the desired responses.

It doesn't destroy creativity by telling creative people what to *put into* the advertising; thus it improves their relationships with researchers – and thereby increases the likelihood of the research actually being used.

What About Sales?

These two simple improvements in working methods can certainly lead to a more carefully considered approach to evaluating advertising. But so far we have been dealing with communication only (in the very wide sense of the effect of advertising on mental processes), just as DAGMAR does. And this raises again the old question of whether advertising should be evaluated in terms of communication or sales.

This problem is a very simple one. The creative strategy for a campaign *must* be set in terms of communication (in this wide sense), if it is to have any value or meaning to creative people. Yet the final measure *must* be of sales, if it is to have any operational value to the manufacturer.

At least if we have a programme of research, we do not have to look on the two as alternatives; we can have both. But in practice there must be some stage at which communication and buying measures are linked. The question is: at which of our three stages of evaluation should it come?

In theory, it should come at the decision-making stage. By that time alternative campaigns will have been developed, improved and roughly checked back against the communication objectives. Now it is up to the agency and manufacturer to choose between the alternatives, and the only sensible basis for choice is to take the advertisement that will cause more sales. What the main user at the decision-making, or last pre-test, stage wants is a measure that looks forward and predicts relative sales effectiveness.

With this background, let us examine the success of current research methods at each of these three stages of evaluation.

CREATIVE DEVELOPMENT STAGE

At this stage the demand is for means of improving advertisements and assessing whether they actually do get a fairly complex set of responses, at the sensual, rational and emotional levels rather than crude stop/go indications. Thus the results need to go into detail on the nature and quality of responses, and there must inevitably be a good deal of interpretation. In addition, to be useful and used, this sort of research needs to be quick, flexible and fairly cheap.

Many companies, particularly agencies, are using small-scale qualitative research here. It aims to give an idea of whether the target group responds and understands the advertisement as intended; the sort of mood and involvement aroused; language used; points ignored or rejected; and it aims to answer some of the specific questions that arise over any advertisement. The problem of small sample sizes is perhaps lessened if the sample is carefully selected as a homogeneous target group related to the market and its motivations. In any case, at this stage it may be more important to deal with majorities and minorities, rather than figures to the nearest 5 %.

Sometimes larger-scale structured research is valuable for quantifying the responses to the brand and for measuring interest or involvement. However, there is one important reservation about its use. It is far from clear to what extent structured research can be regarded as of the same nature as unstructured; it may well be measuring something completely different.

There is clearly scope for improving methods of measuring the *degree* of responses to stimuli – possibly through use of physiological measures, such as of pupil dilation; indirect methods of questioning, such as use of analogies and projective material; or adjective check-lists. But as a measure of the *nature* of responses this sort of small-scale research does seem reasonably valid. And it is certainly useful. Our own creative workshop has now done some 300 checks of this sort, and roughly one-third of them have led to creative changes.

What Sort of Measures?

As we have seen, the demand at the next stage of evaluation is for a very different sort of research – one that predicts later sales effectiveness. It is obviously impossible to simulate the full complexity of the market place in a pre-test; so it clearly must be a predictive measure.

Despite some work by Schwerin, nobody has made much progress in showing any correlation between a pre-test measure and later buying behaviour as a result of the campaign. Until this is done, use of any measures as predictors must of course be fairly speculative.

Indeed it is somewhat doubtful whether we ever will see such correlations. The problems are formidable. There are problems of matching areas or samples; problems of the variations in competitive activity which swamp many controlled experiments; there is the virtual impossibility of controlling word of mouth. There is the problem of deciding whether the merchandising should be the same for campaign A and campaign B, or whether each needs, for instance, its own showcards in order to be fully exploited as a campaign. There is the problem of persuading the manufacturer to run campaign B in the market place at all, when some form of pre-testing has shown A to be "better". And even if these problems are solved, there must be a big programme of pre- and post-testing before we can be sure that any relationships are not pure chance. From time to time, plans for such validation experiments have been discussed – particularly in ITV overlap areas – but they have tended to be engulfed by the practical problems.

WE LIVE IN A REAL WORLD

However, we have to live in the real world, and the real question we are asking is perhaps less demanding. Granted that we cannot have certainty, we are looking for a measure whose *surface validity* is such that using it as a predictor gives a high probability of being more accurate than naked judgement.

And when we talk about surface validity, this must mean a measure that appears, from a commonsense point of view, to represent the way in which advertising works. The more nearly we can simulate in a pre-test the real advertising situation, the more likely the measures are to be meaningful.

It becomes clear, in fact, that all discussion about what material to expose, in what way, to whom, in order to ask what questions, depends ultimately on our theory of how advertising works. This is not to say that all advertising works in the same way, or that a campaign or an advertisement work in one way only. But there is clearly a *single theory* of advertising assumed in each research measure, and if we are to accept any as being predictive of sales effectiveness, it must surely represent the *main* way in which advertising works. In the area with which we are dealing in this article, it must represent the main way in which display advertising works for highly-advertised consumer goods.

In practice, there are great similarities in the advertising theories implied by practically all the measures in regular use:

Standard Theory of How Advertising Works

This is hardly a theory at all, but it is still very pervasive, and it seems to be the origin of many others. In this, each single advertisement "converts" the recipient (in the narrow Billy Graham or evangelical sense) and causes a non-buyer to turn into a buyer, once.

The roots of this theory lie in mail-order advertising – one of the earliest types of advertising, the analysis of which by Hopkins lies behind many theories. Another thought lurking behind this theory is that advertising is a special variety of personal selling; this is above all the salesman's theory. We have all too often thought that what can be learned from using one medium of communication must automatically apply to another.

While this seems a fairly crude model, I think there are elements of it in gift choice techniques or any other in which a single advertisement is said to make a "sale in the mind".

Brand/Need Association Theory

This old-established theory comes, I think, from Starch (1925), who said: "The purpose of advertising is to associate a brand with a need." It is a development on the direct theory, in that it has implications about motivation and the states of mind required. The measurement of success with this theory is the brand awareness check – in effect, what brands do you associate with the need met by washing powders, etc.?

This, too, is essentially a conversion model – advertising associates the need with Brand A, and this then converts a non-buyer of Brand A into a buyer. It is also the origin of other theories which have placed emphasis on the idea of just one rational or functional claim ("need" is in the singular, and clearly cannot be peripheral to the purpose of the brand) as the basis of successful advertising.

Penetration Theory

This is an extension of the last theory, designed to deal with its essential non-competitiveness. Instead of a "need," advertising is said to associate the brand with a selling proposition unique to it. "Proposition" again is in the singular, and while it is unique to the brand, it clearly cannot be too marginal. The USP then penetrates the consumer and switches him to the brand advertised.

This too is a conversion theory. Rosser Reeves (1961) says: "The proposition must be so strong that it can pull over customers to your product." Penetration is the means of conversion, and is measured by the "number of people who remember your current advertising".

In line with this theory, recall of advertising and "sales points" is perhaps the most frequently used advertisement testing measure.

Succession of Mental States Theories

These are theories that suggest a stage by stage succession of mental states leading from ignorance to buying; these particular ones include mental states in relation both to advertisements and to the brand advertised. The Starch theory (Starch, 1925) is most closely linked to the advertisements. He says that to be successful an advertisement must be:

1. Seen
2. Read
3. Believed
4. Remembered
5. Acted upon.

The old AIDA model is more concerned with the product:

1. Attention (to the advertisement)
2. Interest (probably, in both advertisement and product)
3. Desire (for the product)
4. Action.

The DAGMAR (Colley, 1961) model still more:

1. Ignorance (of product)
2. Awareness (of product)
3. Comprehension (of some claim about the product in the advertising)
4. Conviction (about this claim)
5. Action.

These succession of mental states theories implies that advertising works by taking people from one point in the sequence and moving them along the chain; and that they must pass through each point. There is an implication too that people stop for a finite period at each point, so that it would, *in theory*, be possible by research to trace each person's journey through the stages. As it is put in DAGMAR: "Advertising accomplishment should be measured in terms of the extent to which it moves people up the ladder from one level to another." In the same way, it is said that if there is no advertising people slip back from conviction to comprehension and comprehension to awareness.

These theories too imply that advertising converts people from non-buying to buying by changing their mental states, and that it is done through memory or conviction about claims. They have resulted in the use of measures of recall, interest, attention value and belief in claims as indications of successful advertising.

Mental States to Brand Theory

The final theory goes rather further, in that it is a theory about campaigns, not single advertisements and that it deals exclusively with mental states in relation to the brand, not the advertising.

The Advertising Planning Index theory (Joyce, 1964) suggests this succession:

1. Ignorance of brand
2. Recognition of brand
3. Spontaneous awareness of brand
4. Image: Beliefs about and associations with brand
5. Intention to buy brand
6. Buying brand.

This theory too has implications that non-buyers are converted into buyers by advertising shifting them up the scale. But it does not require specific attitudes to or recall of the advertising itself. And in that the image stage is a complex one (there can be differences in degree or structure of associations), there is no need to suggest that people have to pass through *exactly* the same stages on each occasion that they travel towards buying.

In some ways the David Ogilvy "brand image" theory is like the latter stages of the API theory. He says "Every advertisement is part of the long-term investment in the image of the brand" (of course, Ogilvy backs most of the other theories too).

Summary of Standard Theories of How Advertising Works

To sum up, these theories are uneven, and difficult to compare. Some deal with the effect of single advertisements, some with complete campaigns. But they do seem to have some things in common:

1. They all seem to imply that advertising has a converse function. The non-user is converted into a user. The Brand A user is switched into being a Brand B user. People are persuaded not to use Brand A, but Brand B instead. The empty mind is filled.
2. They tend to look on the effect of advertising as causing people to make rational decisions, choose between brands, solve problems. They contain words like "belief" and "conviction". They rely on memory of factual messages.
3. They are based on *a priori* arguments, not experimental evidence.

Evidence about How Advertising Works

If we are to accept as predictors the well-known research measures implied by these theories, we have to accept that advertising works in the main by converting people to a brand, through implanting the brand's factual advantages in their minds.

There is certainly no proof of how advertising does work, but there is an increasing weight of circumstantial evidence available. It all seems to me to suggest that advertising does *not* work in this way.

Commonsense Ideas

There are two points of common sense which suggest that, in certain circumstances, at least part of the advertising should be aimed at retaining existing buyers. First, for many packaged food products, for instance, the unit lasts for more than one meal, and each particular food product nearly always has substitutes available in the home; hence an important job for advertising is to stimulate the users to use what they have already bought.

Secondly, if we have a multi-brand market in which each brand is trying to gain new users from the others, then it may be that advertising can be doing a worthwhile job in preserving the brand's existing users.

Blind Versus Named Product – Tests

The evidence of blind versus named product tests may well be demonstrating the effect of past advertising. They suggest that it works over a long period of time by giving a brand a total personality or gestalt. Frequently Brand A wins comfortably over Brand B, in a blind product test; but when brand names are attached, the results are reversed. The implication is that brand names are a clue to sets of associations, based on past experience and communication that can completely outweigh the present experience and perceptions of the test.

This sort of result is achieved without overt persuasion and is much more dramatic among users than non-users.

Communication Researchers

Psychologists and communication researchers provide more circumstantial evidence about how advertising works.

The most important new theory in communication psychology in recent years is the recognition that one very powerful motivating force is the desire for consistency of beliefs and feelings – or "cognitive balance" (Hovland *et al.*, 1953; Festinger, 1957; Cohen, 1964). Many experiments have been done, and there is overwhelming evidence of people's ability to pay attention to things selectively, and to bend communications so as to fit in with their existing system of beliefs, feelings and desires. This has several important implications for advertising theory:

1. Any theory based on crude conversion seems a little dubious (Klapper, 1960; Cox, 1961).
2. People are likely to eliminate the tensions and "dissonance" that researchers have found to exist in the making of choices, by forming habits and buying routines.
3. In order to achieve and maintain this cognitive consistency, people are likely to find rationalizations for *having bought* a brand. They are likely to be more favourable to a brand after buying it than before. Practically all the psychological theory implies very strongly that rationalization has an important part to play in confirming and strengthening behaviour, but it does not promote the original desire for a product, and cannot work without this desire.

Gestalt Theory

The other important psychological work that seems to have a very direct relevance is that of the Gestalt psychologists (Koffka, 1935) on perception. Their basic theory was that we do not attempt – even if we could – to perceive accurately every detail of the physical structure of objects viewed or to listen to every word of a verbal communication. We take the trouble to perceive only as much as is necessary to help us to classify the object or the message; the rest is ignored as redundant. In other words, we perceive things as a whole, using only the minimum of clues or symbols to help us.

And virtually all psychologists have noted that perception is selective, and depends on motives and desires.

Learning

A third area of communication research that is relevant is that of learning. What seems to have been shown by a number of experiments is the irrelevance of learning by rote to other forms of learning – especially the incidental learning of advertising and buying habits (Hovland *et al.*, 1953; Festinger, 1957; Cohen, 1964). Hence the irrelevance to behaviour and attitude change of learned slogans (Haskins, 1964; Maloney, 1962, 1963). My favourite case history is one in which Brand A was clearly associated most with the advertising slogan "Costs least to buy"; but Brand B was thought to be lower in price.

Krugman (1965) goes further and suggests that since the learning process in advertising is really one of non-involvement, any signs in advertising research interviews of the sort of learning that exists in a high-involvement situation are the result of the interviews themselves.

Systematic Studies of Buying Behaviour

Andrew Ehrenberg has shown that, in some 25 heavily advertised consumer product markets, buying behaviour is extremely systematic (Chatfield *et al.*, 1966). It is systematic enough to make it possible to predict accurately how buyers of a brand will accumulate over fixed periods of time. It allows us to say that frequent buyers of a brand will go on buying the brand frequently, less frequent buyers will continue to buy it less frequently.

This sort of stability is perhaps not too surprising in markets which are defined as "stationary". (What is perhaps more surprising is the number of markets which can be defined in this way.) However, we do know that within these markets there are big differences in the way in which advertising for different brands is scheduled. In some months Brand A is advertising heavily and Brand B has stopped; in others the situation is reversed. If advertising worked in the short-term by converting users of Brand A to Brand B, we ought in this situation to see fluctuations in the accumulation of buyers. But in practice, we do not.

Analysis of Advertising Planning Index

Analyses of the results of several hundred surveys over some 20 product fields for the Advertising Planning Index (Bird and Ehrenberg, 1965) have confirmed these systematic patterns of usership. (Though these are always reported users, there is some evidence of consistency with consumer panel data.) For instance, in any market the number of people saying they are "likely to buy" a brand is mathematically related to the number saying that they use it. The formula linking the two is the same for every market – only the size of a product field constantly varying, probably because of different usage questions. Another consistent pattern is that the number saying they intend to buy a brand is roughly two-thirds of those who have ever tried it.

The evidence is that those who are "likely to buy" but are not "users" are in fact the less frequent users; and the picture emerges of a continuum of "users" running from very frequent to practically never. The interesting thing is that the shape of the distribution of frequency of use appears to be a very consistent one – and again this implies gradual movements in usership, not sudden conversions.

This appears to be the case. In most markets measured by the API, changes in the number of people "using" a brand are very small – perhaps 1% of households a year – and the number becoming new triers rarely goes above 3% per year for established products. Even for the sort of product normally classified as "new" changes in the number of users are often relatively small.

Bearing in mind the part played by all the other marketing and communication activities to encourage new trial – sampling, savings schemes, coupons, price cuts, promotions, mother to daughter learning and other word of mouth recommendations (note the psychologist's theory of the two-step flow of communication) – one can say that if advertising's job were indeed *solely* to convert new buyers to a brand, then it would appear to be a rather ineffective and expensive operation. Indeed some small-scale work done on levels of usership suggests that much of the limited amount of switching from one brand to another that does occur is the result either of deliberate experimentation on the part of housewives or of some external event – not advertising at all.

All this implies that the elements of rational persuasion and conversion, conviction and deliberate learning, do not play the most important part in advertising's effectiveness for this sort of brand. Indeed the API analysis clearly shows that changes in brand awareness *follow* changes in brand use, and that there is no close relationship at all between brand use and advertising recall. (There is, on the other hand, between brand use and long-term advertising expenditure.)

Case Histories

These analyses of consumer buyer behaviour and of the Advertising Planning Index are to some extent saying that when total market shares are relatively stable, their substructures are stable too. Another approach is to examine markets where there have been large changes in sales or share of market, and to ask how the sales have gone up; who has changed her buying habits in what way? And from this: If advertising has been responsible, how must it have worked?

After analysis of five heavily advertised markets, we reached these conclusions:

(a) Buying is very complex, and over quite small periods of time, large proportions of people buying any one brand also bought other brands. To talk of a Brand A Buyer as if she bought nothing else ever can be very misleading.

(b) Sales of established brands tend to go up without marked changes in the number ever trying, buying in the short term or spontaneously aware of the brand. When Brand A's sales went up, it was normally because those people buying Brand A and other brands bought rather more of Brand A and rather less of the others. In other words, if advertising were responsible for the sales increase, it was not through converting people from Brand B to Brand A, but intensifying usage of Brand A by those already using it.

Conclusions about How Advertising Works

At the very least, all this evidence makes a very strong *prima facie* case for the view that advertising's *main* effect, for most brands of cheap consumer goods, most of the time, is not to convert non-user to user. Rather it intensifies the frequency of buying by existing users, through intensifying existing attitudes and predispositions towards the brand and over the long term strengthening the total impression of the brand. It works through being perceived selectively by these people, not so much because of attention-getting devices as because of links with these existing attitudes, desires and motives.

If advertising does work primarily on existing users, then the old problem of whether attitude change occurs before or after buying (or simultaneously as Krugman ingeniously suggests) becomes one of the relative priority of the chicken and the egg.

With new products a different theory must apply, because by definition they start with no users. However, even here, it may well be that quite quickly it is more important that advertising should intensify repeat-buying than get new buyers (Parfitt and Collins, 1967). And even with new products it could still be true that other marketing activities play a major part in getting new triers. In fact, new products may fairly rapidly follow the pattern of established ones.

This is not to say that for established brands advertising does not ever cause *changes* in behaviour or *changes in* attitude. There is overwhelming evidence (Joyce, 1967) that over time it can "work" in the sense of changing the direction of some people's behaviour and attitude (not, one suspects, in the sense of reversing them). But such changes are likely to be very gradual indeed.

IMPLICATIONS FOR PREDICTIVE PRE-TESTING

All this evidence has some disturbing implications for the validity of the standard methods of predictive pre-testing, used at the second stage of evaluation.

First, it suggests by direct experiment that none of the measures, popularly used, of brand awareness, advertising recall or sales point recall is universally connected with sales effectiveness. And it is not much use falling back on the "other things being equal" fallacy. This is the comforting line of argument which says: "Other things being equal, I'd rather have a high preference shift than a low one." Or high recall, rather than low. Or high liking, rather than low. Or high apparent conviction, rather than low. And so on. The fact is that other things are not equal. There is a great deal of evidence that on many occasions these measures move in different directions. One has to balance them, and this can only be done through a theory of how an advertisement is intended to work.

And this is where the evidence casts more serious doubts on the standard predictive measures. They all seem to be based on a theory of advertising – the rational conversion theory – that represents at best only a small part of advertising's effect. In particular, the use of measures that simulate brand switching might easily do more harm than good. It is at least arguable that the best way of appealing to existing buyers of a brand would not necessarily be to use the advertising that is best for appealing to non-buyers.

Secondly, if advertising does, either in general or in a majority of particular cases, work mainly by intensifying long-term attitudes among existing buyers, then it seems questionable whether just one exposure of a new advertisement will produce *any relevant effect that is large enough to be measurable*. If we are to measure it, then we will almost certainly have to improve our methods of measuring the intensity, rather than just the existence, of attitudes. I think there is some scope too for improved measures of interest or "involvement" in the brand as a result of advertising, on the grounds that both attention and perception have been shown to be highly selective; thus there may be a fairly close correlation between "involvement" in a brand and intensification of existing attitudes towards it.

However, I think we have a very long way to go in improving methods before we can say with any conviction that pre-testing research can evaluate the creative content of advertising in the sense of predicting sales effectiveness.

CAMPAIGN EXPOSURE

The theory of evaluating the creative content of advertising at the campaign exposure stage is by contrast simple enough. Campaign A is run in a control area and campaign B in a test area, all other marketing activities being held constant; then the differences in sales between the two areas are measured.

In real life, of course, there are endless and well-known practical difficulties. There are theoretical difficulties too; for instance, what is constant advertising expenditure – is it constant £ per capita of the population or of the target group? And there is the impossibility of getting competitors to hold their own activities constant.

Nevertheless, I think that it can be done well enough to allow us to evaluate the creative content of campaigns in broad terms. The campaign exposure type of evaluation cannot ever be as well controlled as a pre-test, but it has two massive advantages. First, it is real life and thus can be made more easily to represent how advertising works. Secondly, it can take place over time, and thus there is not the problem of trying to measure the effect of only one exposure.

Table 11.1   Changes over one year

	Test area	Control area
Consumer sales	+9%	+14%
Housewives "using" brand	+1%	+4%
Housewives "likely" to buy brand	−7%	+2%
Brand awareness	−18%	+3%
Housewives believing about Brand:		
Attribute A	+ 26%	−1%
Attribute B	+25%	+4%
Attribute C	−10%	−1%

If at the campaign exposure stage there are adequate continuous measures both of attitude change and of changes in buying pattern, then I believe that in many cases the creative content of advertising can be evaluated. The pattern of such tests can be shown by a brief case history.

One frequently bought, heavily advertised branded food product had its main campaign running nationally and a radically different campaign running in a large test area, each backed by the same weight of expenditure.

At the end of the year, consumer sales in the test area had risen rather less than in the control area as a whole, but more than in some regions within the control area. In other words, the test was inconclusive in purely sales terms (perhaps like the majority of area sales tests?).

However when changes in attitude and usage were also measured, it became much easier to conclude that the test campaign was less successful than the control campaign (see Table 11.1).

Not only was the creative content of the test campaign thus evaluated, but guidance was given for refining creative strategy at the next stage in the cycle, the planning stage. It was clear that gains in beliefs about attributes A and B would not be worth while, if gained at the expense of losses in beliefs about attribute C.

Experience with the Advertising Planning Index (continuous measures of attitudes in about 20 product fields over several years) show a number of instances of changes in the structure of attitudes towards brands, which can be associated in common sense terms with changes in campaigns (Joyce, 1967). However, the trouble is that rather more often, by the time that they reach the market place, the more daring changes in campaigns have been whittled down to minor differences. Often the API has shown very small changes in attitudes over time, and frequently it seems that this is because there is no good reason for expecting anything else.

There are two ways of approaching this problem. First, we should aim to be bolder in our experimentation; and if it is a question of an area campaign, rather than a national one, there is far less reason for playing safe. Secondly, we can try to improve our methods of measuring changes in the intensity of attitudes; and, perhaps as important, our methods of reporting such changes to the people who want to use the findings – marketing and creative people. I think researchers here can go much further than they have done in themselves helping to evaluate the creative content of campaigns and refine creative strategy as a result.

These improvements in research methods might include:

1. Giving interviewees more opportunity to make non-verbal responses – like associating brands with photographs of people, houses, styles of life.
2. Trying out new sorts of indirect question, perhaps making more use of analogies – questions like: "If this brand came to life, what sort of person would it be ?"

3. Devising new methods of questioning or coding to differentiate between "yes" = "maybe", "yes" = "yes but ... " and "yes" = "yes, definitely".

4. More interpretation by analysis – which may mean more expensive research and more intellectual doodling by researchers (Channon and Joyce, 1966). More meaningful measures of frequency of use of a brand.

5. Devising new ways of bringing the users of research into closer contact with the interviews. This could mean new methods of presentation, such as the use of film or portable videotape equipment. It could mean more *subjective* interpretation by interviewers. It is of course important that research should be done as accurately and objectively as possible. But if research has to be interpreted by someone before it can be used, why should it not be done by the interviewers, who will often be in the best position to do so? In addition, some current methods of presenting results may in fact be giving a far more distorted picture than the Interviewer's impressions – for instance, straight counts of verbal responses. After all, the tone of voice in which something is said is just as much a "fact" as the words used, and frequently much more significant.

But the greatest drawback, in my experience, to the campaign exposure type of evaluation of creative content is simply that very few advertisers are doing this sort of area test. Sometimes it is through unwillingness to run in an area what may be a worse campaign. (No account is taken of the possibility of its being a better campaign.) Sometimes it is unwillingness to incur the extra advertising production costs. Sometimes it is the cost of the extra research needed that puts them off. Most often, I suspect, the reason is that controlled (or semi-controlled) experimentation is not the sort of method that they are accustomed to use for solving marketing problems.

So it is not uncommon to find the situation of advertisers changing directly from Campaign A nationally to Campaign B nationally (spurred on sometimes by little more than the dawning of a new financial year). They make the change without even a chance of discovering whether B performs better or worse than A in the market place, relying often on predictive pre-test methods which may be little more than a means of bolstering the courage.

I am sure that provided we can get over these last difficulties, be bold in experimenting and spend the necessary money, research certainly can evaluate the creative content of advertising in the market place.

HOW FAR CAN RESEARCH EVALUATE THE CREATIVE?

To sum up:

1. A preliminary to evaluating the creative content of advertising is to improve working methods, so that creative strategy is set in terms of people's desired responses and so that we distinguish between the separate stages of a programme of evaluation – not look for all-purpose measures.

2. From this programme, three stages emerge – creative development research; decision-aiding or predictive pre-test research; and campaign exposure research.

   In our present state of knowledge, expenditure should be concentrated on the first and third stages – creative development research, to assess advertising against its communication objectives; and campaign exposure research to compare a control area and a test area in terms of both attitude and buying changes. And of course setting strategy accurately and comprehensively in the first place is crucial.

We must be bolder in our experimentation, and not try to measure the effect of minor differences in advertisements before we know how to measure major ones.

3. Development of improved research methods should concentrate on measures of "involvement" and of the intensity and structure of attitudes; and on ways of lessening the gap between interviews and the user of the research.

4. We are unlikely to make major progress in this difficult area until more basic research is done into how advertising works. This is so massive a problem that it may require some form of cooperative action.

REFERENCES

Bird, M. and Ehrenberg, A.S.C. (1965) "Intentions to buy and claimed brand usage", ESOMAR Congress.

Channon, C. and Joyce, T. (1966) "Classifying survey respondents", *Applied Statistics*.

Chatfield, C., Ehrenberg, A.S.C. and Goodhardt, G.I. (1966) "Progress on a simplified model of stationary purchasing behaviour", *Journal of the Royal Statistical Society*.

Cohen, A.R. (1964) *Attitude Change and Social Influence*.

Colley, R. (1961) *Defining Advertising Goals for Measured Advertising Results*.

Cox, D.F. (1961) "Clues for advertising strategists", *Harvard Business Review*, November/December.

Festinger, L. (1957) *A Theory of Cognitive Dissonance*.

Haskins, J.B. (1964) "Factual recall as a measure of advertising effectiveness", *Journal of Advertising Research*.

Hovland, C.I., Janis, I.L. and Kelley, H.H. (1953) *Communication and Persuasion*.

Joyce, T. (1964) "Setting targets in advertising research", ESOMAR Congress.

Joyce, T. (1967) "What do we know about how advertising works?" ESOMAR Seminar.

King, S. (1965/6) "How useful is proposition testing?" *Advertising Quarterly*, Winter.

Klapper, J.T. (1960) *The Effects of Mass Communication*.

Koffka, K. (1935) *Principles of Gestalt Psychology*.

Krugman, H.E. (1965) "The impact of Television Advertising", *Public Opinion Quarterly*.

Maloney, J.C. (1962) "Curiosity versus disbelief in advertising," *Journal of Advertising Research*.

Maloney, J.C. (1963) "Is advertising believability really important?", *Journal of Marketing*, October.

Parfitt, J.H. and Collins, B.J.K. (1967) "The Use of consumer panels for brand share prediction", MRS Conference.

Reeves, R. (1961) *Reality in Advertising*.

Starch, D. (1925) *Principles of Advertising*.

The Great Bridge Builder: Searching
for Order out of Chaos

By Creenagh Lodge, Chairman, Corporate Edge

An introduction to:

12.1   Advertising Research for New Brands

Although this article was written nearly 40 years ago, it remains a relevant and important way of looking at research on new products and their communication. It is also a model of how such an article should be written: lucid and beautifully argued, allowing the readers to draw their own conclusions.

The implicit premise is that research can constitute a valuable, probably essential, contribution to a new product's success, by understanding how the intended target market approaches and adopts a new idea; and by discriminating between researching the intention behind the thinking, rather than solely judging the execution.

A Holistic Rather than Atomistic Approach

The core thought that influences the argument is that consumers think holistically, not atomistically. For them a new brand, in Stephen's words, "is a totality . . . one thing, not an aggregate of bits". They don't separate the emotional from the rational, or the sensual from the functionality. Therefore, research which scalpels out each of these elements for isolated scrutiny is, by definition, unsatisfactory, because of the mutuality of influence exerted by all the elements.

The argument for a holistic approach is laid out so gently and clearly that the unbiased reader might be forgiven for wondering why this philosophy is not universally adopted.

The fact is that it is not.

Then, as now, there are those who consider that research on new products exists to prevent marketplace failure, and therefore must remorselessly identify faults. So it is not surprising that many innovators and creative people dislike what they see as the dead hand of research, which functions to kill ideas not help to readjust them. (Or, as E.B. White said of analysing humour, "it's like dissecting a frog – few people are interested and the frog dies").

Bridging the Gap Between Research and the Creative Process

Stephen King really was the consummate planner, the builder of bridges between research and the creative process; and his article shows how this is to be achieved in the matter of new products. Not only does he advocate sensitive, early exploratory research as a vital means of understanding the consumer's holistic perception and choice process, he also allows for – and encourages – the inclusion of judgement on the part of those involved.

He believed that research exists to help to develop sound judgement, not act as a substitute for it. But, sadly, there still exists a sizeable market for research which acts as a cop-out for people too frightened to exercise their judgement.

As part of this bridge-building process, he advocates the development of "a language meaningful to both creative people and researchers". Observation shows that when this is achieved, the barriers between the two disciplines dissolve. Sadly, all too often, the researcher either (generally qualitative) struggles to ape the creative language, or (generally quantitative) abandons the attempt and baffles the creative people.

More importantly, without this language, research cannot satisfactorily distinguish between response to the creative person's intention and the particularity of the execution. The result can often be either the loss of a good concept or, almost worse, the progression of a poor idea with an attractive presentation.

But this holistic approach is taken further still, and to even greater effect. The final diagram in the article shows the broadening of the holistic philosophy to include company policy at the outset and pilot marketing at the end. Yet again he makes a critically important point that all factors and influences must be acknowledged and included, however awkward. He says: "... as in all states of uncertainty and complexity, we must devise models and systems to organize the chaos into some manageable pattern".

His premise is that models must precede systems, yet again identifying a key role of the planner, but this time as a bridge builder between research and corporate thinking.

The Importance of the Corporate Context

Much research on innovation is less than satisfactory because researchers are not informed about corporate thinking. It has been said elsewhere that the first, and most important, target market is the manufacturer, or otherwise producer, of the intended new product. If a new product concept does not match the particular financial targets, or the production capability or even the corporate culture, then no amount of market research, however much it demonstrates strong consumer demand, is going to make it a success. Nor will apposite and brilliant advertising.

Stephen's inclusion of company policy, as an important influence on the generation of new product concepts, clearly implies that this, like early research and market data, should continue as a reference point throughout the development and evaluation process.

More obviously but equally importantly, his inclusion of pilot marketing at the end of the process expands the scope of the process still further and, by implication, should be taken as an influence on the preceding research studies. Here, yet again, is another bridge to be built by the planner, this time between research and the client's marketing people who, at this advanced stage of the programme, will be focused on sales and repeat purchase data, and likely to want a research design content that bears little or no resemblance to the preceding research.

If this final evaluation is not positioned as part of a continuum of learning, then it will fail to provide sufficiently sensitive diagnostic data to help to remedy problems of expectation versus delivery. If it is seen as part of the learning continuum, then the early research is encouraged to characterize those in the target market who are merely experimenters (and thus an eventual and predictable loss) versus those who are predisposed to adopt the new brand for the duration (and thus whose numbers must be significant).

A Series of Linked Stages to Produce a "Manageable Pattern"

Early in the article, Stephen emphasizes the need to see the various research stages – and indeed all the stages in the whole development process – as *linked*. The link he describes specifically is that of the consumer's response, but the theme of linkage is developed throughout the article, and is extended to include many further elements, all logically accounted for and equally logically incorporated. The impression gained is of a highly efficient, inclusive and richly productive learning continuum.

If his purpose was to answer his own challenge "... as in all states of uncertainty and complexity, we must devise models and systems to organize the chaos into some manageable pattern", the article shows that he succeeded. The "manageable pattern" is achieved through recognizing that only a holistic approach can organize an essentially holistic process, and thereby accommodate the apparently unmanageable (the creative and inventive processes).

It allows for and encourages experimentation in the early stages of the programme, particularly in the development of the model and in research design. And it can do this because the thinking is arrived at and justified on a *causal* basis – one of the reasons that this article is so readable and so persuasive is that the innate logic is so clear.

Stephen shows us the way to manage the chaos of new product development without losing the inspiration; to blend several different disciplines and approaches into fruitful partnership; and thereby to launch successful new brands.

12.1

Advertising Research for New Brands*

By Stephen King

It would be rash to suggest that there is general agreement on an approach to advertising research for existing brands. But we have to start somewhere, and any theoretical approach must be able to cope with both new and old brands. So this article starts by summarizing a point of view about advertising research in general, and then examines what modifications have to be made for new brands.

The user of advertising research is faced today with a baffling number of options in terms of what material to submit to research; to whom to expose it; how to expose it; and, most difficult, what questions to ask. The researcher's problem is one of designing research in a situation of both complexity and uncertainty, in which the specific purposes of the advertising are not often clearly stated.

In this sort of situation, there seem to be three particularly important principles that should affect an approach to the problem.

First, we must accept the idea of limited objectives for research. If we cannot, with any confidence, provide a single method to measure the total effectiveness of advertising, we must neither give up in despair nor shut our eyes and nominate one magic solution.

The best approach will be one in which there is a blend of judgement (where we are not very confident of the meaning of the research) and research (but only where we are confident about its meaning). There is clearly an acceptable middle course between hunch and complete reliance on a single figure or research method.

Secondly, we must examine research methods from the point of view of their usefulness, before we get fully embroiled in the inevitably more elaborate arguments about validity. As soon as we examine the principle of usefulness, we can see opportunities of reducing the complexity. It becomes clear that different research results will be useful to different people, for different purposes, at different stages of the advertising process

Thirdly, as in all states of uncertainty and complexity, we must devise models and systems to organize the chaos into some manageable pattern. These can be models both of the processes of producing advertising and of the effects of running it. They may be very simple models at first and we may have to adapt or abandon them as we learn more from the basic research. But the important thing is to make a start.

*Published in the *Journal of the Market Research Society,* 10(3), 1968. Reproduced with permission.

A PLANNED PROGRAMME OF RESEARCH

The first step for JWT was to set out a simple model of advertising process, as shown in Figure 12.1.

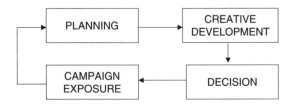

Figure 12.1   The advertising process

The various elements are:

1. *Planning*, which ends with an agreed creative strategy.
2. *Creative development*, in which creative people are looking for ideas, developing them, rejecting, adopting, improving. It ends with a number of creative proposals and rough advertisements being put forward and assessed.
3. *Decision*, at which the agency has finally to decide which of several campaigns to recommend; the client which to run, and what backing where.
4. *Campaign exposure*, in which the campaign runs and people respond, both in terms of attitude and behaviour. Ideally an experimental campaign runs in test areas, so that changes in attitude and behaviour can be measured both as trends over time and as a comparison with control areas. This stage produces the information for the next cycle of planning, which may end with revisions to the creative strategy.

It is clearly a cyclical process, and there can be feedback from each stage to the previous one. For instance, creative strategy can be modified in the light of what is creatively possible, and there is an opportunity, cumulatively, to build knowledge and improve advertising. It is quite unnecessary to regard any single piece of advertising research as independent of the totality of information built up during the cycle.

LINK BETWEEN THE STAGES

The next step was to examine the links between the stages. Clearly advertising objectives must be set in the same terms as the criteria for their assessment. There must be a terminology to make possible the blend between judgement and research. There must be a language meaningful to both creative people and researchers. The link must be capable of being related to both a theory of advertising and to other marketing activities.

The crucial link is the consumer's responses to the brand. The advertising is aiming to get certain responses from certain people; research aims to measure people's responses to stimuli.

This can be taken further by categorizing responses to the brand in terms of responses from the senses, the reason and the emotions: and of course, by specifying the people (the target group) in detail, according to their potential value to the adviser.

In simple terms, at the planning stage we have to decide (by research and judgement) exactly which people should notice what about the brand (with their senses), should believe what about the brand (with the reason) and should feel what towards the brand (with the emotions). At the creative development stage, we have to ask "Does the target group respond in this way to the brand as the result of the advertising?" At the stage of the decision making, judgement and research must decide "Are the people who respond in this way to the brand likely to buy more?" and at the campaign exposure stage "Have they bought more?"

RESEARCH METHODS TO FIT THE SYSTEM

When we put together all of these elements – a cycle of events, a link running through them and the principles of usefulness and limited ends – it becomes clearer what sort of research is needed. We can plot a pattern of research functions and objective, users, stages of the cycle and hence methods (see Table 12.1).

1. *Planning:* Retail audits, consumer panels, ad hoc surveys, etc. show who is consuming how much of which. Product tests measure people's sensual reaction to brands. Continuous structured attitude research can measure people's *rational* beliefs about brands. Unstructured attitude and motivation research can get some ideas of *feelings* towards brands.

Analysis of this data will help basic marketing policy, plus area sales experiments, plus experience and judgement, to set the desired target group and the *desired* responses. The whole model makes it clear that this strategy-setting stage is of crucial importance; and is partly analytical, partly inventive.

2. *Creative development:* Informal "research" can be a very useful stimulus to creative people – for instance, group discussions among members of the target group, with the creative man present. This is aiming, not so much to measure attitudes as to set up hypotheses, and put flesh on the bare bones of statistical tables.

Table 12.1   Cycle of advertising and research

	Stage 1: Planning	*Stage 2:* Creative development	*Stage 3:* Decision	*Stage 4:* Campaign exposure
Research job	Provide current data to help set strategy	Stimulate ideas; assess rough campaigns; eliminate errors; improve advertisements	Help final judgement between alternative campaigns	Measure changes in behaviour and attitude; link them to marketing activities
Main users	Advertiser Marketing Creative	Creative	Advertiser Account Executive	Advertiser Marketing Creative
End result	Agreed creative strategy	Improved rough/final campaigns	Decision which campaign to run	Assessment of campaign; refinement of strategy
Methods	Retail audit; consumer panel; ad hoc surveys; product tests; attitude research	Small-scale informal	Quantitative advertisement testing methods	Continuous consumer buying/using measures linked with attitude measure

When rough advertisements have been developed there is a need for a preliminary assessment of them against the creative strategy set at the first stage. We have found that small-scale informal research is the best, with deep probing with the report containing a lot of verbatim comment. It must be quick, flexible and reasonably cheap. The aim is to *improve* advertisements, not just accept/reject. This sort of research can examine understanding, involvement, mood, language; and it can show up mistakes.

There is sometimes scope for quantitative research (such as that provided by ASL) at his stage, for general diagnostic purposes and in order to check that the advertisement is eliciting the desired responses to the brand, on a larger sample. However, this usually means a much more structured form of research, which inevitably reduces the depth of information generated.

The ideal would be to have single informal interviews of a large sample of people from the target group, who had been exposed to the advertising in a reasonably naturalistic way. Unfortunately this would be extremely expensive and probably take too long.

Our own view is that the best compromise is to have the maximum depth of information from 20 people, who have been meticulously selected as belonging to the target group, out of perhaps 60–70 initial contacts.

3. *Decision:* The ideal at this stage – with the advertising improved until it is getting the desired responses from the target group – is research that will *predict* the effect of this in the market place. A frequent situation is one in which two different campaigns both seem to convey adequately the desired ideas about the brand; but a decision has to be made between them, and the only valid basis for decision seems to be a prediction of sales effectiveness in the market conditions. (Predictions of "impact" or "interest" or "recall", though of value as background information, cannot be finally satisfying for decision-makers.) Many of the standard methods of advertisement test (e.g. folder tests, Schwerin and ASL theatre tests, Gallup Impact tests, etc.) are used for this purpose.

However, this sort of research has presented many problems. An analysis we have done of nearly 200 theatre tests of commercials and many quantitative press tests, plus special experiments, has shown up two in particular. First, the differences between two advertisements in their "scores" have often been no higher than both statistical theory and practical experiments have shown between two tests of the same advertisement. It is not too surprising that research finds it difficult to discriminate between the effects of two advertisements, each exposed once only, when we often find it hard to tell how much a whole campaign, backed by hundreds of thousands of pounds, is affecting people.

Secondly, we have frequently found that measures move in different directions. That is, if Advertisement A is superior to Advertisement B on one measure, it will as often as not be inferior on others. This leads either to an indecisive result or to the nomination of one measure only as a tie-breaker – a nomination normally made with little firm idea of what the measure is really measuring and no experimental evidence of its relevance to sales. Neither alternative seems at all satisfactory.

We are continuing, like others, to look for research methods to suit this stage of the advertising process. But in the meanwhile we feel that decisions are better made on the basis of the research results of the previous (creative development) stage. The implicit problem of linking communication effects with buying effects is in any case much better dealt with experimentally at the campaign exposure stage.

4. *Campaign exposure:* The ideal here is to have integrated measures of buying and attitude running continuously; with one campaign in control areas and another in properly planned test areas.

There are many well-known problems involved in area testing. But considerable progress has been made with research into attitude change and the basic patterns of consumer buying; *provided that the experiment is bold enough,* we have found that it is usually possible with campaign exposure research to say not only which is the better campaign, but also why. This information is then fed into the next, planning, stage; strategy is revised as necessary, and a new cycle begins.

THEORY OF ADVERTISING

Implicit in this, as in any systematic approach to advertising and research, is a generalized theory of how advertising works.

This is not to say that it always works in the same way. We believe that the main differences are according to where the brand lies on a scale running roughly from *habitual, casual or impulse purchase* at one end to *single or considered purchase* at the other end. The position of the brand will depend on:

- Its cost
- Its importance in the buyer's scale of values
- Its frequency of buying
- Social v. personal in nature
- Availability
- Balance of hidden and open values
- Degree of difference between brands
- Consistency within the product type.

Consumer advertising and advertising research are concentrated overwhelmingly on products at the habitual, casual or impulse end of the scale, and it seems reasonsable to base the system on a theory of advertising for this type of product – recognizing that there will be exceptions.

Our system outlined above is based on three main assumptions (supported by a good deal of circumstantial evidence (e.g. Joyce, 1967; King, 1967):

1. Advertising works by affecting people's attitudes to brands, both in structure and salience.
2. What people receive from any new communication is governed mainly by their existing ideas and predispositions.
3. For most heavily advertised established brands, advertising works mainly by reinforcing existing attitudes to a brand among people who are already experienced in it (i.e. who know its attributes in use from direct experience). The reinforcement can come from strengthening favourable attitudes or reducing unfavourable attitudes to the brand in relation to competitors.

The gaining of completely new users, by conversion from a competitor, is likely to be rare and more often caused by "events" than by advertising – product development, promotions, sampling, recommendations.

HOW DO NEW BRANDS DIFFER?

Users v. Non-users

On the face of it, there must be a different advertising theory for new brands. New brands start with no users, by definition. So advertising's job cannot be to reinforce the existing attitudes of users of the brand; the first job must be to get new users.

But, if this is so, for how long does it go on? What is the shape of the curve of penetration? How long is the *marketing* job to get penetration or awareness of the new brand; how soon should it concentrate on getting repeat-buying? What part does *advertising* play in each of these jobs, and what part do other marketing activities place, and how do they fit together in the marketing mix? We must obviously answer these questions in each case before we can decide criteria for the measurement or judgement of the advertising.

In fact, we know a lot already about the buying patterns for new brands.

The work of John Davis (1964) and of Parfitt and Collins (1967) suggests two important conclusions.

First, a new brand tends to set its own pattern. The quickly reached stable level of consumer sales depends mainly on the reactions of it of those who have experienced it.

Secondly, the marketing job is very quickly to concentrate on repeat buying more than (not of course instead of) increasing awareness or penetration. To quote Parfitt and Collins (1967):

> Failure usually takes the form of exceptionally low repeat-purchasing rates; i.e. the brand makes a reasonable penetration into the market but very few people feel disposed to continue to purchase it.

It seems sensible, therefore, to take the common view that for a new brand there is a fairly brief launch period, followed by a long period of promoting gradual growth. The evidence here suggests that advertising's main job in the second, "going-concern", period is much the same as for an established brand – that is, to reinforce the favourable and reduce the unfavourable attitudes of people who already have direct experience of the brand.

The question still arises of the part that should be played by advertising in the launch stage – the first few months of the new brand's life. Many surveys have suggested that shop displays and recommendations are more important than advertising in getting initial penetration for a new brand.

Though one cannot necessarily take the low mention of advertising at face value, this does emphasize the importance of other marketing actions and *indirect* influences on first trial of a new brand. The advertising could be working most in getting penetration by helping to get displays and recommendations – that is, working on people (retailers and pioneer triers) who are already experienced in the new brand.

There is clearly some job of *conversion* from existing brands or from existing habits that the advertising can do. But it seems to emerge that the job of reinforcement of favourable attitudes among people experienced in the new brand starts almost from the very beginning – and grows rapidly more important.

Another factor comes in here: the future competitive situation. Nowadays competitors, and private label products, are quick to copy. It cannot be very long before the new brand, however revolutionary, is in a standard established-brand situation. There is much to be said for producing advertising that looks forward to this time right from the beginning.

WHAT IS A NEW BRAND?

It seems then that we should judge the advertising of a new brand according to its contribution to the repeat-purchasing rate. Or, on the view that the brand sets its own pattern, the *contribution of the advertising to the brand as a total object.*

Thus to examine the role of advertising and research in developing a new brand, we should analyse a little more deeply what a new brand really is. There seem to be four particular elements that are relevant.

The first is that a new brand is a new means of satisfying people's wants, desires or needs. Levitt (1960) warns very powerfully against confusing means (which are of great interest to the manufacturer) with ends, which are really all that interest the consumer deeply. The consequent requirement for advertising research for new products is to get back to basic motivations and human activities; not be too concerned with existing means of meeting the needs.

The second element of what a new brand is concerns *the way* in which it meets a need. In other words, how does any brand appeal to people?

The appeal can be roughly divided into three areas:

1. *Appeal to the senses:* Soup – taste, texture, smell, colour etc. Toilet soap – perfume, shape, lather, colour, etc. Floor polish – consistency, colour, perfume, etc.
2. *Appeal to the reason* (functional appeal): Soup – convenience, quality or amount of ingredients, contains protein, etc. Toilet soap – contains germicide, deodorant, cold cream, purer ingredients, lasts longer, etc. Floor polish – easy to dispense, use or apply, deeper shine, longer lasting finish, cleans/disinfects as well as polishes, etc.
3. *Appeal to the emotions* (brand personality): Soup – plain English, farm house, continental, sophisticated, etc. Toilet soap – medical/cosmetic, down to earth/luxurious, masculine/feminine, etc. Floor polish – tough/delicate, synthetic/natural, quick and superficial/ hard work and satisfying, etc.

Every brand is an interrelated complex of appeals, and every brand has some appeal in each of these areas. There is a different balance in each. The soup's appeal to the senses is maybe its strongest; the floor polish's appeal to the reason; the toilet soap's appeal to the emotions.

Not only are there different blends of the three types of appeal, but different people have different balances of requirement in each type. For instance, one person requires decay-free teeth that are quite shiny, another, shiny teeth that are quite decay-free.

A new brand can succeed through improvement in appeal to the senses, or the reason or the emotions; or a combination of all three. It can come through meeting, directly, the specific balance of requirements of an identified sub-group of people – and this is usually the pattern of markets that fragment (e.g. the soap market).

So research needs to analyse the appeal of existing products and the basic needs in terms of appeals:

- To the senses
- To the reason
- To the emotions

and to pick out target groups not by standard demographics, but by their different blends of requirements in these three areas.

It can be seen, of course, that these are just the areas covered in the use of research for developing advertising for existing brands.

The third element of what a new brand is follows on from this. To a consumer it is a combination of a *physical thing* and *communication*. On the whole, sensual appeals are conveyed mainly by the physical thing; appeals to the reason partly by the physical thing, partly by communication; appeals to the emotions mainly by communication – name, styling, pack, advertising, merchandising, word-of-mouth and other associations.

The balance between the physical thing and the communication varies according to the product field. For instance, a new physical product may be especially important for a successful new soup, perhaps a little less for a floor polish, still less for a toilet soap, and hardly at all for a cosmetic.

There have almost certainly been more success for new branded consumer products based on radically new communications than on radically new physical entities. Usually it has been a matter of an entirely new communication and minor changes in formulation – for example, Camay, Babycham, After Eight, Horlicks as a night-time drink, Swoop.

With some new brands the balance has been perhaps the other way – for example, Bird's Eye frozen foods, Vesta, ScotTowels, Wilkinson Stainless razor blades, the Instamatic camera, Dual floor-cleaner. *But* even when there is almost an entirely new physical product, it is frequently not long before competitors can copy it; thus the first brand in with the new formula does not get the full advantages *unless there is new communication that goes well beyond mere functional description.*

In fact, it would be nearer the truth to say that inventing successful new consumer products is inventing new communications and then getting physical products to fit them, than the other way round (the traditional way). Both these extreme views are wrong, of course; the two sorts of invention should be done together and integrated.

One advantage of looking on a product in this way is, of course, that new communications can be produced and roughly evaluated much more quickly than new physical products.

The fourth element of a new brand is quite simply that it is a totality. It may be made up of a blend of different effects and appeals, but to a housewife a brand is one thing, not an aggregate of bits. Housewives buy things, not concepts or naked physical products or propositions or attributes.

This suggests that all the elements of a new brand must be developed cooperatively as a totality. The advertising and the pack are not mere useful additions – they are part of the essence of the brand.

One cannot test the bits separately either – we all know that a physical product in one pack tastes different or works differently from the same physical product in another pack. It also means that one cannot satisfactorily test abstractions and verbal descriptions. The difference between examining the pieces separately and examining the whole brand is the same as the difference between an Identikit and a person.

ADVERTISING RESEARCH FOR NEW BRANDS

A systematic approach to advertising research for new brands emerges when we link this analysis of what a new brand is with the general approach to advertising research. There is not very much difference in principle between old and new. What is different is that there is an opportunity to mould the new brand as a *totality*, whereas for an existing brand the most that can normally be expected is a slow change of direction.

As a result, there appears to be three main changes in emphasis. First, setting the creative strategy, for the design of both physical product and communications, assumes an even more

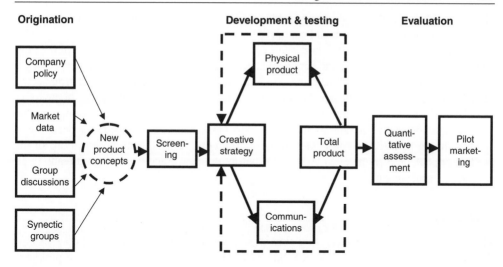

Figure 12.2   Developing a new brand

crucial importance. Secondly, the new product and the new communication must be developed and tested together. Thirdly, there must be far more experiment and feedback in the early stages.

Figure 12.2 sets out the usual flow of development work for a new brand.

Origination

The end results of this stage are screened product concepts – or loose theories of products that might work. Each concept would be a proposed synthesis of appeals to the senses, reason and emotions. From this we can work out a product-plus-communication strategy in exactly the same terms as the advertising strategy for an established brand.

The research methods used to help in setting new brand strategy would be much the same as for established brands – analysis of the current behaviour and consumption patterns within the chosen area of human activity; analysis of desires and needs; analysis of the appeals of existing means of meeting these needs, in terms of appeals to the senses, the reason and the emotions. There is clearly scope for using some of the more elaborate methods of analysis of attitude research to show up opportunities – like factor analysis and gap analysis. But in the end working out the creative strategy is a matter of invention. Sheer analysis can never complete the job; we want to design a car, not a new improved horse.

Development and Testing

Here, as with an advertising campaign, research has to stimulate as well as measure. Thus group discussions, followed by small-scale informal research, can be used in exactly the same way as for existing brands. Again, there are two important differences. First, there usually has to be a far greater element of experiment, feedback and repetition of research. It is much rarer to get a total new brand positioned right first time than it is to achieve the right new response to an old brand. Secondly, we have found it important to test the new communication and new physical product together as soon as possible; any test of product and creative work separately can give little more than a crude indication.

Usually a dummy pack is the best summary of the total communication of a new brand and the best way of expressing the new brands personality. Thus the most frequent type of the small-scale research we have done is that in which members of the proposed target group come in to discuss the context of the new brand and their reactions to dummy packs; go home to try samples of the physical product, packed to resemble the dummy packs, often accompanied by a leaflet; and return a week later to discuss the new brand and how it related to expectations.

There might be three or four cycles of these group discussions, with modifications of the product or pack or even the creative strategy, before the new brand is considered ready to go on to larger scale testing.

Evaluation

The final stage before pilot marketing aims to validate hypotheses and tentative conclusions, or to choose between the possible new brands so far emerging Many of the same problems arise here as with the quantitative pre-testing of advertising – those of predicting response in the market place on the basis of a single exposure of a new brand, introduced in artificial conditions. Maybe the most that one can hope for from standard replacement or product-in-use tests is a rough indication and an insurance against gross error.

Again, this absence of reliable predictive research seems to make it all the more important that thorough and imaginative qualitative research is done in the early stages, and that everything is aimed at producing a new brand with a distinctive personality as well as physical attributes that compare well with competitors.

REFERENCES

Davis, E.J. (1964) "The sales curves of new products", Market Research Society Conference, March.
Joyce, T. (1967) "What do we know about how advertising works?" ESOMAR Conference, May.
King, S.H.M. (1967) "Can research evaluate the creative content of advertising?" Market Research Society Conference, April.
Levitt, T. (1960) "Marketing myopia", *Harvard Business Review*, July–August.
Parfitt, J.H. and Collins, B.J.K. (1967) "The use of consumer panels for brand share prediction", Market Research Society Conference, March.

You Can't Make Sense of Facts until you've Had an Idea

By Kevin McLean, Co-founder, Wardle McLean

An introduction to:

13.1 Applying Research to Decision Making

I met Stephen King once at a Christmas party a long time ago. I remember someone tall, head held slightly back, an amused expression. He seemed rather shy, very intelligent but very nice, in a slightly mischievous way. Maybe it was those glasses, part Oxford don, part Ronnie Barker.

Stephen King presented the article at the Market Research Society Conference in 1983 and asked: What kind of research should we be celebrating, 30 years on from the incorporation of the MRS? Should we be doing *action-oriented* research, or should we do research that *stimulates innovation*? This extraordinary article should be read by anyone who thinks about marketing or research, as it has probably become more and more *relevant* over the last decade or so.

A Surprising Conclusion

The extraordinary thing is the radical conclusion. In a paper entitled "Applying research to decision making", he concludes that applying research directly to decision making is not only *wrong* but has probably had economically disastrous consequences for the UK! Whoops. Research should be about *ideas,* understanding and innovation, not about measurements or trade-off analysis. We should *educate* ourselves, *experiment* and then *evangelize*. We should use good research within differently structured organizations to stimulate innovation and generate economic value.

He argues so engagingly in order to soften the effect of the bombshell. Listen, we're really good at what we do and everything, but actually, we're doing the wrong thing! We should change the *fundamentals* of research and marketing; we should apply Popperian new science (observation as interpretation), not Baconian "playing safe science". (See "Advertising: Art and Science" (Chapter 3.1) for further explanation.)

To put it another way, making rational "decisions" (the word meaning literally, to kill the alternative) is about avoiding risk and responsibility, rather than choosing or creating. No creativity, no connection; no connection, no progress. It's not about the decisions of "clients" or "consumers", it's about people, how we react, talk, dream, choose, behave.

As the MRS Conference celebrates its Golden Jubilee (2007), embracing the *next* 50 years, what better time to re-examine his radical plea: forget research as decision making, do more research that stimulates innovation. Was he right, and have we taken this on board? I think the answers are yes and no. In that order.

Research should Provide Ideas Rather than Data and Distinctions

He says you can't make sense of the facts until you've had an idea. Ideas and innovation are messy, subconscious, of the moment. Research has to *provide* something from these ideas, rather than merely *produce* endless data and distinctions. Research has a key role in the cycle of innovation, connecting ideas, knowledge and experience. Theory can only be invented, so help the invention! And try to make sure that the good ideas make it through the various barriers and vested interests within the organizations involved with the research.

The three roles for research he prescribes are:

- Exploring, building background knowledge, illuminating the problem
- Stimulating and developing ideas
- Experimenting, testing.

Research should help to stimulate ideas, where innovation is viewed as a constant stream of minor improvements. Ideas would be fed through to a multi-disciplinary project team, made up of management, marketing and manufacturing. Project team leaders would be closely involved in the idea generation process, not removed from it.

The Recommendations

His six recommendations were:

- Sell research in at a higher level (get into the Boardroom).
- Do more research within the innovation process, "preaching the values of occasional beautiful research".
- Have longer-term relationships between clients and researchers.
- Involve those in the project team more directly with "original data and respondents" (ideas and people).
- Researchers, clarify your "black boxes".
- MRS must advocate more and better experiments and more and better education.

So, how have we done?

I think that research *has* moved in some of the directions King advocates, but his recommendations still apply – there is still work to be done. I have done a quick reckoning:

- Research in the Boardroom is a perennial conference platform issue. Some progress, but much more is needed. (I say we score 48%)
- Insight and innovation *are* on the agenda and in the job titles, although I am not convinced that having more insight departments has produced much more insight. I am not hearing many people "preaching the values of occasional beautiful research", not even researchers. Maybe we're too busy with our black boxes. (34%)
- Longer-term client relationships? In some cases, but with so many *more* researchers than clients now, I'm not sure relationships are generally better. (61%)

- Clients getting more closely involved with "real people"? Research methods such as "ethnography" or participant observation are increasingly popular. But the opposite is also happening, discussion guides are getting longer, viewing facilities are thriving; the divisions and barriers in the research and marketing process ("the problem of the long tail") are still with us. (64%)
- More and better education and experiments? Professional evangelizing? The MRS has progressed on training, education and standards of accreditation, but there are no "sponsored experiments" and precious little evangelizing, outside two windy days in March on the Brighton beachfront. (So that's 26%)
- Nor am I sure that there has been the organizational change in client companies leading to the emergence of the multi-disciplinary project team with the focus on innovation for which King argued (29%)

The temptation to use research to make decisions is still with us. We are still doing mechanistic research although we are using more up-to-date mechanisms. On-line makes everything faster and cheaper but still promises "action-oriented" results, now deliverable next day not next week.

Sad to say, I fear that we are still doing the wrong kind of research for the wrong kind of reasons all too often – and falling into the same traps of measurement for measurement's sake, over-prescription and short-termism.

So, I'd make that 43.66667% overall. Could do better, indeed.

Refresher Course Needed

It seems, therefore, that we need a refresher course in Stephen King's ideas. Not only are the ideas still relevant, they are so well written. For example:

- *Beware gap analysis that goes, just because people like iced tea and a lot of people like boiling tea, there's immense potential for tepid tea.*
- *Avoid spurious trade-off analyses: "would you rather have a house with a roof, heating and a front door OR a house with walls, windows and a conservatory?"*
- *Don't measure what advertising does to people, start at the other end and ask what people do with ads.*

The last lines in the article form one of the best descriptions of research I have ever read:

> The researcher must be seen as an expert on what is, not on what to do about it ... we should insist that his real role is to interpret and bring to life what goes on in the world ... not advising marketing people what to do ... but to stimulate innovation.

It has been a privilege to write this short introduction to one of Stephen King's articles and this collection of his work is a huge asset to our industry. We need people like Stephen King, we should celebrate him and we shall miss him.

What to Think and Do

1. THINK: Stephen King uses the phrase "occasionally beautiful research" to describe the kind of research he admired. What is beautiful research, how do you do it and why does it matter?
2. DO: Read the other papers and articles in this collection.

13.1

Applying Research to Decision Making*

By Stephen King

INTRODUCTION

We don't seem to have any celebrations yet, but this is the 30th anniversary of the incorporation of the MRS. The Articles of Association were signed on 16 April 1953. During those 30 years the membership has climbed steadily from about 150 to 4000 – a demonstration that market research and marketing have been two of the great post-war growth industries. An amazing success.

The *achievement* of marketing and market research over the period has been a touch less impressive. Figure 13.1 shows the UK's share of world trade and import penetration in manufactured goods. You can see that in the 30 years our share of world trade declined from 26% to 9.5%, while import penetration grew from 5% to 26%. Whatever the precise balance of the many underlying causes, there can be no doubt that this is the *mechanism* of relative economic decline – a substantial loss of market share, both at home and abroad.

So this satisfying growth of marketing and market research has come at the time of the fastest decline in the UK share of market since the Industrial Revolution. What I want to suggest today is that this may not be entirely coincidental.

Of course, there has been a very great deal of excellent market research in the UK – it is probably better than in any other country. But I don't want to bother you too much with praise today. I'm a great deal less happy about the way in which a lot of research is *used*.

In fact, I think there has been some use of research which has actually contributed to the unhappy direction of the lines on Figure 13.1. If I'm right, we'd better see what, as the MRS, we can do about it.

So what does lie behind this mechanism of relative decline? Let's take just one specific example: textile machinery. This was a market that the UK dominated in the late nineteenth century, with some 80% of the world trade and virtually no import penetration. By 1955, the world market had greatly expanded, but we still had 30% of it. However, in the next 20 years, the UK share dropped to 11%. Germany took up most of it, becoming world leader, with Switzerland and Japan getting the rest.

At the same time as our exports weakened, the UK started importing textile machinery. Between 1970 and 1975, 89% of textile manufacturers bought foreign machines, and the average price of those machines was about 20% higher than the machines we exported. A survey was mounted to see why they'd done so (Rothwell, 1980). Of the reasons given, 45% were that the foreign machines worked better, were more advanced designs; 38% were that there simply wasn't a suitable UK machine available (and that tended to be suitability in terms

*Published in *Marketing Intelligence and Planning*, 11(3), 1983. Reproduced with permission.

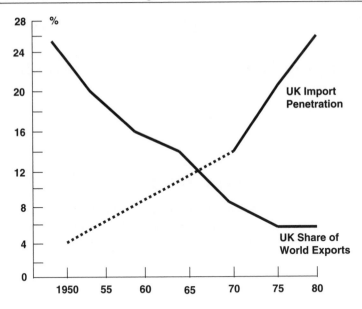

Figure 13.1   UK trade in manufactured goods
Source: Department of Trade

of quality, modernity and standards); 9% were that the foreign firm seemed to understand the user better and gave better service. Only 4% were on the grounds of price.

It seemed very clear, with all the other findings in the survey, that the basic UK problem was a *lack of innovation*. By innovation I do not mean the grand, one-off, fundamental, breakthrough invention. I do not mean a process like the discovery of the structure of DNA or the invention of the jet engine. When I talk about innovation here, I mean a constant stream of minor improvements, modifications, regular small advances in design, in quality, in service or in utility.

It seems to me that behind the decline over the last 30 years in British textile machinery lies a failure to develop this sort of stream of improvement. As NEDO put it: "The long-term fall in the UK export share appears to be associated with a fall in the relative quality or sophistication of UK exports, i.e. their non-price competitiveness rather than a decline in their price competitiveness." And there are many UK markets where imports seem to have led in innovation – for instance, cars, motorbikes, tyres, electronic goods and some domestic durables.

Or take packaged grocery brands. An excellent analysis by John Madell (1980) of BMP looked at the fate of new brands. Of 585 new food brands he identified as being launched and advertised between 1969 and 1976, 53% were dead, off the market, by 1978; and 43% were still alive, but selling at under £4 million at retail selling price. Only 4%, 21 brands from the original 585, were selling more than £4 million a year.

In many ways, I think the 43% walking wounded will often have been more destructive to their companies than the outright failures, because over a long period they will have been taking up time, resources and commitment which would have given a far better return if it had been applied to innovation and improvement of the old-established brands at the centre of the company's business.

Now the fundamental reasons why new brands so often fail are really quite clear. There have been many analyses and they all come essentially to the same conclusion. One of the most vivid was that by Hugh Davidson (1976). He took 50 successful, new brands and 50 failures and looked at various aspects of them to work out why. Briefly, he showed that price was not critical; the failures tended to be more expensive than competitors, but so were the successes. But performance, as measured by blind product tests, was crucial; three-quarters of the brands with a better performance than the competition succeeded, three-quarters of those with the same performance or worse failed. Exactly the same with distinctiveness; 70% of those that were not very different from competitors failed; 70% of those that were very different succeeded.

In other words, all the analyses suggest that to succeed in packaged goods, the new brand has to be "better and different". So innovation is absolutely critical here too. What is disturbing is that, from the very terms in which Hugh Davidson did his analysis, the 50 failures had their blind product tests just as the successes did. Presumably many of the results were in some way misused.

FLAGSHIP BRANDS

If new brands all too often fail for lack of innovation, what about the old-established brands? A few years ago I did an analysis of 67 "flagship" brands (King, 1980). These were food brands, and they were all the food brands that were on the market from 1964 to 1978 and also spent at least £250,000 on press and TV advertising in 1977 – that is, the old-established brands central to their companies' success. What was most fascinating was their pricing history. Over the 14-year period 1964–1978, the retail price index for food went up 308%, but the flagship brands went up in price by only 211%. To put it another way, if their prices had kept up with those for food in general, they would have been selling in 1978 at 30% more than they actually were.

That is a huge gap, and I am fairly sure that it can only be explained by concluding that, in the face of huge pressure from retailers, intense competition from other manufacturers and high inflation in raw materials, on the whole these manufacturers took the negative approach. They underestimated the consumers' growing desire for quality and they cut back on everything to do with future progress – research and development, process improvement, product improvement, packaging, advertising and market research. Meanwhile, private label brands tended to improve in quality. In the end, many manufacturer brands didn't get higher prices because they didn't deserve them (Bennett and Cooper, 1981). Manufacturing companies got into a vicious spiral – the "crisis in branding" which has been a topic of such anguish for marketing men for the last decade or so (King, 1978).

Again, the crisis in branding seems to me, in essence, a problem of innovation at the product level – a failure to introduce a constant stream of improvements in order to keep ahead of competitors and private label and to satisfy social change. Yet all of these flagship brands must surely have had market research available. Did they have the wrong sort of research? Or did they use it wrongly? Or did they ignore it?

Clearly one can't generalize, but I do think there is some evidence that a lot of market research is wrongly used; and I believe that the misuse is very much related to the theme of this conference: "The application of market research to decision making."

I came across two pieces of evidence recently put to the MRS about what marketing men are looking for in market research. First, Michael Leach, a real live marketing man, speaking at the 1980 conference (Leach, 1980) said:

> Marketing men do not have the time, probably not the willingness and maybe not even the expertise to decipher the important (in research) from the unimportant. So the requirement for the researchers to lead the marketing man by the hand is crucial.

I think that what he was really saying was: "Look, fellows, cut out the fancy stuff. Give me market research results that I can apply *directly* to my day-to-day concerns, especially the guerrilla war against the retailers." In Professor Dahrendorf's terms, he was interested in questions rather than problems (Dahrendorf, 1983).

Rather more explicit evidence came from the survey presented by Martin Simmons (1982) at last year's conference. It showed that marketing managers thought market research agencies to be fairly reliable, with quite good standards and a good understanding of the marketing process. But there was an appreciable desire among marketing managers for market researchers to "get off the fence and recommend courses of action". They were saying in effect: "It's not enough to tell me what's going on; tell me what to do about it. Let's have some research that is *action-orientated*." They wanted research that could be *directly applied* to decision making (I suppose rather as you apply paint to a wall). What I'd like to do now is consider some of the implications of this sort of approach, and what it's done for the use of market research.

Let's start with the most action-orientated, decision-making-orientated research – the retail audit. Maybe some of you don't sit in on retail audit presentations, so let me explain how they go. There's a meeting of the top people in the company, all neatly sorted out into hierarchies. The Managing Director sits in the front row. Not only can he see the figures on the chart, he can see the presenter's crib of pencilled comments on them. Suddenly he turns round to the Deputy Sales Manager, North East, and says: "Carruthers 20% out of stock in Tyne Tees." Carruthers, who sits a long way back and can't read the figures but knew that something like this was going to come up one day, says the first thing that comes into his head, which is: "Sir, we've got a 15 for 12 discount coming up and a tailor-made over rider and a new consignment of shelf-wobblers." The Managing Director, who doesn't know what any of that means, says: "Well, make sure that you do," and puts a tick in his Action This Day Noddy pocket book and feels that the whole thing has been worth while.

Actually, what the research says is that on the day of the audit, and that day only, some six weeks ago, if you're lucky, about 20% of shops were out of stock, give or take a few either way. The action called for could be something completely different. For instance, if the brand involved was a seasonal alcoholic drink, the proper action might be to organize a really good 24-hour emergency delivery service next Christmas – not "get moving on it, Carruthers, today". I think that the greatest value in retail audit research lies in the understanding it can give of long-term cause and effect. But it tends to be treated as a here-and-now, action-orientated description of what happened yesterday, because the terms in which it is reported are those of the daily preoccupations of marketing men – retailers, prices, stocks, deliveries and out-of-stock.

Let's take another of the big spenders – the TV ratings from the well-loved BARB. This research again is concerned with questions in the Dahrendorfian sense – the marketing man's question: "What am I getting for my TV spending then?" Let's say the company has been fortunate enough to get a 20-rating spot among housewives in the London area. In reporting this, the agency media man should say something along the lines of:

> Well, bearing in mind the panel size, at the 95% confidence level you had a cost per thousand housewives of somewhere between about £8 and about £12.

He would then go on to add:

> I am, of course, ignoring the very considerable problem of attention values, the current difficulties of measuring the use of videotape recorders and watching on second sets. I'm assuming, as we always do, that people are perfectly able accurately to assess that they have watched at least 8 minutes out of 15 and that zapping between channels is randomly distributed. We must, of course, remind ourselves too that we won't ever get this precise pattern of competitive programmes again, to guide us about future ratings for a similar spot.

He could drone on for several more minutes on the limitations of the data and the uncertainty of their meaning.

He doesn't, of course, say any of this. He presents, without comment, a densely packed page of computer print-out. A vast entrail-gazing industry has sprung up, in TV companies and advertising agencies and marketing companies and research companies, dedicated to taking informed guesses to four places of decimals – in the name of action-orientation.

Let's take another important problem that has been turned into a question: "What motivates people to buy brands?" For centuries philosophers, psychologists, biologists and all sorts of academics have puzzled about what goes on in the human mind. They have reached no sort of common conclusion. Rather little of this academic work has filtered through to the world of marketing, probably because it's not sufficiently action-orientated. Perhaps the best bridge comes from anthropologists. Mary Douglas (1982) in particular, has written about why people buy goods, saying, "goods are for thinking with". In a splendid piece called "Beans Means Thinks," she wrote: "Consumption decisions are a vital source of the *culture* of the time ... the individual uses consumption to *say something* about himself and his family and his locality" (Douglas, 1977).

Despite this sort of insight and the complexity of academics' views about what goes on in the mind, marketing men are looking for simple answers about the motivations for buying their brands, because they want market research to tell them what to do. They're hoping for a nice, neat, rank-ordered list of motivations so that the top half-dozen can be stuffed directly into products and advertising. There are various sorts of research that have pandered to this demand, and I think that all of them tend to treat the mind as if it were some sort of mixed box of Lego waiting to be put together.

For instance, put yourself into the frame of mind of a real consumer, a respondent, a person. I tried to think of something for which everyone in this audience is sometimes in the market, and picked on houses. So, imagine you're thinking of buying a house and this nice lady interviewer comes along. She asks: "Which of these features of a house is most important to you – walls, doors, windows, heating, roof, being 345 yards from a tube station open until 11.43pm, green front door, mock half timbers, attractive garden, no dry rot ... ?" And it goes on for another three pages, because of course today the computer can cope with the answers; indeed, to be economic, it needs to be regularly and fully fed.

TRADE-OFF

Maybe there is less of this particular type of action-orientated research going on today than there used to be, but there's a sort of Son of Primitive Compartmentalism, coming along in some of today's refinements. Take trade-off research, for instance. That can give us questions like: "Q.346. Would you rather have a house with a roof, heating and a green front door *or* a house with walls, windows and a lean-to conservatory? Q.346a. Would you rather have a house

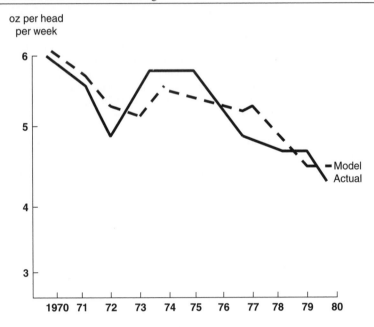

oz per head
per week

Figure 13.2 Butter consumption: Actual vs model
Source: NFS, CSO, IBM, stat pack.

with two recep, an attractive garden and one of those bells that go 'ding-dong' *or* a house with
a roof, a wealth of oak beams and a lock-up garage?" Plus 108 more combinations, because
the computer wants to show it can deal with them.

Or can we move on to the Fisbein version of the Lego of the mind, with questions like:
"On the whole would you say that your mother would approve or disapprove of you buying a
house with leaded lights?" – all on a lovely 7-point scale. And the answers can be carefully
multiplied by other data to be fed directly into decision making.

Another rich area for the mechanistic application of research is econometrics. Let me give
you a quick example. Figure 13.2 represents what an organization called the Yellow Fats
Marketing Council might be looking at to try to explain the rather unfavourable trends in
butter consumption. They ask why butter sales are down and set out to model the market. The
figures shown here are all quite genuine, but for the sake of simplicity I've used only two
independent variables in the model.

You can see that the model gives a fairly good fit. In fact, I know it was a good fit because the
computer used for the regression analysis told me that the multiple correlation was 0.90338.
(It must be accurate because there are five places of decimals.) The R-squared adjusted is
0.77013, which isn't bad, and the F value is a massive 17.51.

In other words, this simple model with just two variables can clearly be applied directly to
decision making. Because all this is published data, and you can do the exercise for yourselves,
I can reveal what the equation was. It was:

$$B = 8.59225 - 0.00089V - 0.00080M,$$

where B = butter consumption (ounces per head per week), V = business visits abroad ('000
per year) and M = consumer spending on motor vehicles (£ million at 1975 prices).

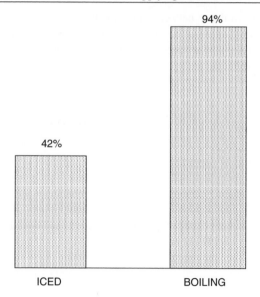

94%

42%

ICED   BOILING

Figure 13.3   Gap Analysis: % who like tea

This is clearly action-orientated. The government must be the prime target group and the YFMC must clearly be pressing them to bring back exchange controls on businessmen and bring back HP controls on cars or put up the car tax. I think you can see from this year's Budget that part of this strategy seems already to have worked.

Of course, every one of us here has piously pointed out at times that correlation isn't causation; but I'm not sure we always take it into account in our hidden assumptions. I don't think anybody should ever use the term "best fit" without a blush and without re-reading Andrew Ehrenberg's elegant piece "How Good is Best?" (Ehrenberg, 1982).

Another very fertile field for mechanistic decision making via research is new product development. Many of the systems are designed as filters or ways of preventing things happening, but there are some which purport to be directly applicable to inventing new products (Holmes and Keegan, 1983). Figure 13.3 symbolizes the use of gap analysis, for instance.

ICED V. BOILING

These simple figures would be used to demonstrate that since a lot of people like iced tea and a lot like boiling tea, there is an immense potential market for warm tea. The reason for this is that between the two columns, though sadly it can't be picked out by the naked eye, is a very large amount of *n*-dimensional concept space. And within that *n*-dimensional concept space there are masses of new products just waiting to be analysed into the open. This is just one of many infallible systems based on the idea that you can invent by deduction. Somehow an invention can be produced by a step-by-step method, untouched by human mind.

This deductive approach is by no means confined to quantitative research. All over the London suburbs are little collections of eight housewives who are expected to tell manufacturers what the strategies and brand positioning for new brands should be. They are there to pass judgement and discriminate between things called Concepts – a sort of Platonic Idea of a brand from which all emotion has been drained. Once these modern Delphic oracles have chosen the idea concept, the manufacturer can of course hype it up with the optional extras like naming, advertising and packaging, and sprinkle a little brand image over the whole dish.

ADVERTISING RESEARCH

Perhaps the most overt attempt to apply research directly to decision making has been in off-the-peg advertising research. Advertising research is an unusual type in that as often as not the research method is chosen first and the problem to be solved is only sorted out afterwards, if indeed at all. This happens because it's terribly hard to know how advertising works. So people say: "At least let's pick a measure that we know how to use." It's as if an art critic said, "I don't know how to measure artistic merit, but I do understand how this tape measure works, so we'll use that."

The trouble is that any measure used implies some model of how advertising works; there is no way of evading the problem. Lurking behind most off-the-peg advertising research systems are some very questionable ideas – for instance, that the mind is some sort of inert and passive receptacle for messages, an intellectual sponge, or that all advertising works by converting people *in toto* from Brand A to Brand B. Or that it always works by rational persuasion. What nearly all the off-the-peg systems have in common is that their underlying models are opposed to more or less every other theory there has ever been about how the mind works or how markets behave. They're based on our trying to measure what ads do to people rather than starting at the other end and asking what people do with ads, how they use them and how they respond to them. Once again, I think, the desire for action-orientation tends to push us into misuse of research.

There's a marked contrast to this in the case histories put forward for the IPA's Advertising Effectiveness Awards. The winners presented in *Advertising Works* and now *Advertising Works 2* (Broadbent, 1981, 1983) show how market research is used at its best. I don't think a single entry relied on just one measure of how advertising worked. What the judges were looking for and what they found was a *convincing argument* based on the interpretation of many different forms of research.

I think that these case histories symbolize how we should use all these forms of research that I have been commenting on. Just to make it absolutely clear, I am very much in favour of most of them *as research methods*. I couldn't live happily without retail audits and consumer panels. I do find valuable insights in the concept of tracking people's motivations. I am a great believer in, and advocate of, the use of econometrics and marketing modelling. I'm greatly stimulated by both quantitative and qualitative research. But I also think that each of these can be, and quite often has been, destructive to innovation, and that, where this happens, it tends to be because of a desire to apply them *directly* to decision making.

In other words, I believe that part of our national failure to innovate has come through trying to use market research not as an *aid* to innovators, but as a *system* that ideally reduces all personal judgement to a decision as to which of two numbers is the larger. In my view, there are two main reasons for this. First, I believe that too many marketing people have clung to the wrong model of the process of innovation, and, secondly, I think that all too often we have the wrong sort of organization for innovation. Let me take each of these in turn.

Innovation

Choosing the right model of the innovation process seems to me to relate to a choice between two schools of science. (This is obviously very simple analysis, since there are clearly many variants in schools of science, but I still think the distinctions made here are valid.) The old science, Baconian science, was essentially a four-stage process. You start off with controlled observation. Secondly, you accumulate data. Thirdly, some sort of general laws emerge. Fourthly, you verify these general laws with more observations and that becomes new knowledge – a sort of brick-by-brick progress. Then you can apply the new knowledge to specific instances. It's a sort of playing-safe science, with no shots in the dark. It seems to me that this is the sort of science that lies behind what I've been describing as misuse of market research – that is, the attempt to discover general laws which can be applied directly to decision making.

What I think of as the new science evolved gradually, following challenges to Newton's theories, and has been described most vividly by Karl Popper (1959) and his disciples. (I hesitate to mention Popper, because I think there has been great competition in the MRS to be more Popperer than thou and argue on matters of textual criticism (Alt and Brighton, 1981; Lawrence, 1982). What I will be referring to here is much more concerned with what I believe to be the spirit rather than the letter of Popper.) The key difference in the new science, I believe, was put by Popper as: "Observations are always interpretations of the facts observed. They are interpretations in the light of theories." Or, as Einstein put it: "Theory cannot be fabricated out of the results of observation. It can only be invented."

In other words, you can't make any sense out of the facts until you've had an idea. Whereas in the old science there's a step-by-step, risk-free build-up of knowledge which can then be directly applied, the new science involves inventing a trial solution right from the very beginning.

Very loosely based on these ideas, I'd like to put forward what seems to me the proper process of innovation – a five-stage process, as it applies to marketing (Figure 13.4).

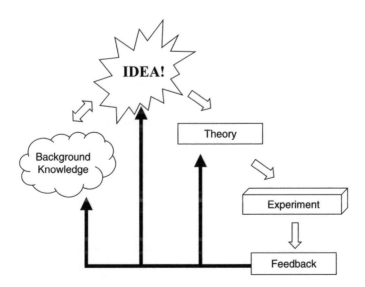

Figure 13.4   How innovation happens

BACKGROUND KNOWLEDGE

Idea/Theory/Experiment/Feedback

First, we have to have some background knowledge, an *understanding* of the people and issues and the motivations in the market. That includes some understanding of what is the right problem to solve, what is the situation we want to improve.

Secondly, we have to have an idea. In Popper's language, we could call it the vision of a trial solution, often to a trial problem. The idea clearly relates to the background knowledge, but it doesn't emerge directly, deductively and logically from it. Everyone who has written about having ideas has made the point that it is a non-logical process; it is essentially subconscious and is often extremely messy. All the devices that are available to stimulate having ideas – like brainstorming and synectics and Edward de Bono's lateral thinking – are in essence deliberate interruptions to the normal logical flow. Or as James Webb Young (1972) wrote: "At this stage what you have to do is drop the subject. Out of nowhere the idea will come; it will come to you when you are least expecting it."

Thirdly, the idea has to be patted into shape; a sort of coherent theory has to be put forward – a hypothesis, a sentence which starts with "I wonder if . . . " The implications of this theory have to be put into some form that is testable: in our case, usually something physical. This is a stage in which marketing tends to differ from "real science". Very often in scientific tests there are just two alternatives to be tested against each other. In marketing there is an enormous amount of judgement involved in putting the theory into physical form, since there is a huge variety of forms into which it might be put.

Fourthly, there is an experiment. I use the word in its popular sense – not a scientifically controlled experiment, but a "let's give it a whirl and see what happens" type of experiment. I doubt if there could ever be such a thing as a true scientifically controlled experiment in marketing. Our competitors, like fish, simply won't sit still to be counted. At our nearest approach to real science, there tend to be irreducible placebo effects. I think the real contribution that Popper made at this stage was, in effect, to say that what we should attempt to do is not verify, but try to disprove. In the terms of our own less rigorous experiments, what one has to do is challenge the theory, and that can be a constructive and exciting process. As Popper put it:

> It is part of the greatness and beauty of science that we can learn, through our own critical investigations, that the world is utterly different from what we ever imagined.

The fifth stage is of course feedback of the results of the experiment. This can help at three different stages of the next cycle. It adds to our background knowledge, and indeed can modify our statement of the problem. (We often don't really understand a problem fully until we've tried to solve it.) It can directly stimulate a new idea. And it can modify or improve our theory.

This is all clearly a continuous cyclical process. In marketing we are constantly trying to learn to improve, not to discover some final solution. What this five-stage theory of the process of innovation does is make much clearer what the roles for market research are. There seem to me to be three main roles.

First, research can help at Stage One in giving people understanding, building up the background knowledge, illuminating the problem to be solved or the situation to be improved and interpreting the flow of past solutions. And I think there is a strong case in marketing, as elsewhere, for doing a certain amount of "beautiful research" – research into an area which might, or might not, turn out to be interesting, even if no one can think in advance of how they might want to use the results. We will never be in a position to exploit the unexpected, if we insist on measuring only the near certain.

The second role for research is at Stage Two – to stimulate ideas directly. This is typically what much small-scale qualitative research has been used for. It seems to me that if we don't make it clear that this is a specific and important role, we will go on having those dreary arguments in which one lot of people say "qualitative research isn't really respectable" and another lot say "we find qualitative research particularly valuable". At the same time, I can't, for the life of me, understand why advocates of quantitative research don't make more of the stimulus to ideas which it can undoubtedly offer.

The third role is, of course, at Stage Five – measuring what's happened when you've tried out an experiment.

Where I think there isn't really a role for research within this innovation process is in decision making. That is, I cannot see any scope for its *direct* application to decision making. Its values are enormous throughout the process, but they are essentially indirect. Even where we are at the challenging experiments stage – let's say a product test – we are still only discriminating between a few testable forms of our theory. We can say from research whether, in the terms of the test dimensions, A, B or C performs better. But we can't say whether there may, or may not, be many other testable forms of this or another theory that would perform massively better.

So what I am saying is that the first important reason for misuse of research is a tendency to cling to the old, wrong model of the innovation process, and so to the wrong roles for research. And the second lies, I think, in the way in which some companies organize themselves.

If you consider the sort of organization that is best for real invention, you'll usually conclude that it's essentially a purposive project group. It will need a fair amount of institutionalized "straddling". If, for instance, you are trying to develop a radically new brand, there will be constant trial and feedback; all the elements of the new brand will interact – the formula interacts with the taste and the taste interacts with the colour and the colour interacts with the packaging and the packaging interacts with the advertising and the advertising interacts with the formula. The production line approach of A doing his bit and handing it to B who does his bit and hands it over to C, etc., simply won't work. There has to be a project group and a group leader and an interacting team of specialists.

If we are dealing with innovation as I've defined it – the constant stream of minor improvement is rather less demanding than real invention. But it seems to me that we still need most of the same elements of organization, for the same reasons.

But what we find in most marketing companies is something very different from project groups. We find a full-scale traditional family-tree type of organization with clearly defined hierarchies, functionally separate departments and strongly entrenched department barriers. Now that might be fine for building up and improving efficient routines (which is of course very necessary in companies) but it's pretty hopeless for innovation. All too often any sort of communication between departments is difficult and formalized, let alone that sort of informal iconoclastic project work that I've been describing and the essential messiness of idea generation. It's all too easy to see why, in the hierarchical sort of organization, there is a call for the direct application of research to decision making.

At last year's conference, Martin Christopher and Gordon Wills (1982) said: "The key participants in the marketing decision-making arena are the accountant and the manufacturing director." I think that's a rather stark way of putting it, but I see what they mean. I think I would put it more like this: If we want real brand management, proper decision making about marketing, we have to have a project group working at the top – say, a group consisting of managing director, manufacturing director and marketing director. Only if such an authoritative group works on a regular and interactive basis will a company have much chance of being good at innovation.

Even if this happens, there's another block to the sensible use of research. Think of the line of communication between the respondents and this top project group. First, you have real people out there answering questions. Then a market research agency, normally split between interviewer and analyst, who may sometimes talk to each other, but usually not much. Then there is often some form of black box – manipulation of the raw figures in which the assumptions behind the maths may or may not be clear. Then there is a report, in which the reworked figures are, very properly, selected and interpreted. Then, very often, you have the Market Research Department in the company which has commissioned the research; and to justify its existence it may need some further research to reselect and reinterpret and summarize the report. (Sometimes it can do this inventively and practically; sometimes it acts as a form of heavy-handed bureaucratic Purchasing Officer.) The Market Research Department may itself be regarded as a bunch of raving intellectuals who have little to do with real decision making. Either way, that's another barrier. There can be other filters too – such as brand managers and advertising agencies.

Finally, what the people said in answer to the questions will reach our top project group, the people who really manage innovation in the company. But after so long and hazardous a journey it would be surprising if the information were wholly fresh and ungarbled and if it were never misapplied.

There clearly is a great deal of skilled and helpful market research in this country, and a great deal of successful marketing. But I think there is also evidence of weakness in innovation, and that this is fundamental to our relative economic decline. Part of the weakness, in my view, is a failure to understand the proper process of innovation, which leads to misuse of research. Market research is inevitably pulled into this by demand, and I think it is reasonable for us to consider, as members of the MRS, what we ought to be doing about it.

Clearly it is hard for individual researchers, as part of a service industry (and a cottage industry at that) to change the nature of the demand. But I do think we might consider where the MRS itself might concentrate its marketing strategy, its education and its evangelism.

Here is a short list from me of areas for consideration:

1. *Marketing*
    (a) Concentrate the MRS's own marketing activities much more on higher level management. Seek to influence not just the market research managers and marketing departments, but also managing directors, finance directors and manufacturing directors.
    (b) Concentrate more on the roles for research and the uses for research, particularly within this innovation process – not just research techniques. That would include preaching the values of occasional beautiful research.
2. *Organization*
    (a) Make people aware of the values of the project group type of organizations in the innovative process.
    (b) Advocate more firmly the values of long-term relationships between research companies and their clients, especially in the growth of understanding that this brings, with the benefit of effectively shortening that communication chain.

(c) Bring out the problem of the long chain, and try to develop and market techniques that will bring the final users much closer to the original data or original respondents.

(d) Urge members to clarify some of their black boxes.

3. *Experiments*

Marketing men have no right to criticize market researchers for being too academic, if they themselves steadfastly refuse to mount marketing experiments. The MRS must press harder on this, perhaps sponsoring more education in the running and measurement of marketing experiments.

4. *Role of the researcher*

I think the MRS may have to take on the job of making it clearer what the role of the researcher is, since the individual may be in no position to do so.

It seems to me that the researcher must be seen as an expert on *What is*, not on *what to do about it.* Despite the demand for him to produce results that in effect take decisions, we should insist that his real role is to interpret and bring to life what goes on in the world. He cannot possibly know enough about all the other factors that lie behind decisions to be justified in advising marketing people what to do.

In fact, I think we should question very hard the whole idea of applying research directly to decision making. I hope that the next time the MRS has a conference on this sort of topic it will be called "Research to stimulate innovation".

REFERENCES

Alt, M. and Brighton, M. (1981) "Analysing data or telling stories?", *JMRS*, 23(4).

Bennett, R.C. and Cooper, R.G. (1981) "The misuse of marketing", *Business Horizons,* November/December.

Broadbent, S. (ed.) (1981) *Advertising Works*. London: Holt, Rinehart & Winston.

Broadbent, S. (ed.) (1983) *Advertising Works 2*. London: Holt, Rinehart & Winston.

Christopher, M. and Wills, G. (1982) "Marketing research as action research", MRS Conference.

Dahrendorf, R. (1983) "Research and decision making", *MRS Newsletter*, June.

Davidson, J.H. (1976) "Why most new consumer brands fail", *Harvard Business Review*, 54(2).

Douglas, M. (1977) "Beans means thinks", *The Listener*, 8 September.

Douglas, M. (1982) *In the Active Voice*. London: Routledge & Kegan Paul.

Ehrenberg, A.S.C. (1982) "How good is best?", *Journal of the Royal Statistical Society, Series A*, 145, Part 3, pp. 364–366.

Holmes, C. and Keegan, S. (1983) "Current and developing creative research methods in new product development", MRS Conference.

King, S.H.M. (1978) *Crisis in Branding*. London: J. Walter Thompson Co. Ltd.

King, S.H.M, (1980) *Advertising as a Barrier to Market Entry*. London: Advertising Association.

Lawrence, R.J. (1982) "To hypothesise or not to hypothesise?", *JMRS*, 24(4).

Leach, M.L. (1980) "Marketing in the 80s – The challenge for research", MRS Conference.

Madell, J. (1980) "New products: How to succeed when the odds are against you", *Marketing Week*, 22 February.

Popper, K.R. (1959) *The Logic of Scientific Discovery*. London: Hutchinson.

Rothwell, R. (1980) "Innovation in textile machinery", in Pavitt, K (ed.), *Technical Innovation and British Economic Performance*. London: Macmillan.

Simmons, M. (1982) "The image of the British Market Research Industry in the business world", MRS Conference.

Young, J.W. (1972) *A Technique for Producing Ideas*. Chicago: Crain Communications Inc.

14
Measuring Public Opinion in an Individualistic World

By Chris Forrest, Partner, The Nursery

An introduction to:

14.1   Conflicts in Democracy: The Need for More Opinion Research

The broad argument here is the challenge that a more individualistic society presents to the proper workings of representative democracy. Media events staged to put a particular case were becoming more common, and these media events had research at their core. Stephen argued that opinion research will become more important and, therefore, researchers should be alert to the dangers inherent in trying to measure "public opinion".

There are now plenty of suspect polls doing the rounds, and the "research events" that Stephen predicted are now rampant. Producing a poll to generate a story is elementary PR and "slow news day" journalism.

Polls as research events are now understood. Joe Public has become much smarter at spotting probable bias and not taking the results too seriously. The polls themselves often encourage this by seeking to entertain more than inform. In the mid-1990s Michael Moore's TV show pioneered a post-modern playfulness with dumb research event polls ("46% of Americans said they would rather be killed by a serial killer than by a mass murderer").

There is now awareness that there are proper polls and dodgy "research event" polls. It's easy to identify the extremes, but in the dangerous middle ground between preferences for trivial personal tastes and voting intentions there are still plenty of horror stories.

There is no simple way to spot the rogue poll but the name of the research company producing the poll has become a roughly understood yardstick of whether this should be treated as real research or just a bit of journalistic licence. A YouGov, NOP, ICM or MORI poll carries more heft than an unattributed poll or reader survey.

The Classic Wrong Call

Even these big-name pollsters are not perfect. Their biggest wake-up call for a generation came on the morning of 10 April 1992 when the pollsters were stunned to find John Major back in Downing Street. They'd all called it for Neil Kinnock because they had overestimated the Labour vote by, on average, 9%.

Interestingly the research industry's 1992 post-mortem analysis agreed to implement changes that Stephen had suggested in this article 13 years earlier. It was recognized that, as he argued, factors such as home and car ownership were more important predictors of how people voted than the creaky old classifications of social class.

Famously it was found that Conservative voters thought their opinion was an unpopular minority view and were reticent about expressing it. Clashes between public and private opinions were found to have been elements that polls should try to unearth – just as Stephen had predicted. If only more pollsters had read the article years earlier.

What Exactly is Public Opinion?

This issue, Stephen calls it "the basic issue", of public or private opinion is one to which we still haven't paid enough attention. Even the definition of it remains unclear. As he says: is public opinion *"the complete opinion of the public"* or just *"people's outer thoughts"*?

Stephen's five suggested guidelines for trying to ascertain the right mix of public and private opinion are still a good starting point.[1] So why aren't they "basic" research practice?

1. *Salience: a meaningful opinion is one which the respondent was previously aware of holding. Not a reflex response to a question.* I'm not sure that today's researchers would agree with this. It's probably worth identifying a sub-sample of people who have a spontaneous opinion but the views of the "consciously opinionless" shouldn't be discounted. Neuroscience has shown how many of our attitudes and opinions are inaccessible to our conscious minds. We don't always know what we think until presented with a situation. That shouldn't dismiss our reflexes as invalid.
2. *Asking the questions from different positions* remains ideal but cost means that it is not often used. Moreover, most of the time the sponsoring client knows that the other side will react with a poll of their own so "the market" will achieve the desired balance.
3. *Personal and concrete versus general and abstract*: *"Advertising often misleads people"* will still get strong agreement. *"I am frequently misled by the ads I see"* will still produce strong disagreement.

   This seems to be an issue that the research industry is aware of but likes to keep as its own trick of the trade to produce polls phrased in the right place on the public/private spectrum to keep its clients happy. Until there is agreement on whether the public or private view should take precedence (see below), this is likely to continue.
4. *Views on what others think.* People who think their own views will not prevail remain less willing to admit publicly to their opinions. Today, in 2007, pollsters have identified a pro Labour bias across all polls as a continuing issue they need to try to correct for.
5. *Actions speak louder than opinions* is something the research industry has taken to heart. Electoral polls invariably look at actual voting behaviour, not just claimed intentions, and have educated the media as to the importance of this distinction.

What Next?

Unfortunately there is not much hunger for the debate Stephen tried to start. Opinion polls are the research industry's flagship and no researcher is in a hurry to undermine them. It takes disasters like 1992 to provoke reappraisal.

---

[1] These points are expanded upon in the longer version.

Oddly the industry is still very vulnerable to all of the dangers Stephen outlined. Regulation is almost non-existent. The Market Research Society relies on membership contributions from exactly the organizations it seeks to sanction. Hence it has never been comfortable in its role as regulator. Beside which, MRS membership is voluntary. Anyone with a telephone and a laptop can set up as a researcher and there is nothing to stop them producing opinion polls that are as biased as the market wants to commission.

In 2004 there were Parliamentary calls for better regulation of opinion polls, perhaps kitemarks, combined with a simultaneous recognition that the real problem is in the nature of the selective reporting. The big poll companies had become increasingly fed up with the hesitant attempts of the MRS to regulate them and took this mini debate as their cue to set up the British Polling Council with its own guidelines, commitment to making all details of polls open to scrutiny, and a laudable focus on trying to ensure accurate reporting of the polls.

Educating journalists to investigate the question wording is probably the most realistic focus of researchers' efforts. Finding the ideal way to ask questions, and attacking the issue from all directions – pro, anti, private, public – would make for more expensive polls and the industry senses that its clients would prefer a poll that is fairly right to one costing twice as much that is a couple of points more "right" – especially given that both will be subject to the same secondary reporting biases. The truth will not necessarily out.

How to Define "Truth"

And the bigger question, the one the industry ought to be debating, is how to define "the truth". For example, during the foxhunting debate polls showed that "73% think hunting should be banned" and "59% want to keep hunting". Both results were "true". They reflected emotional distaste on the one hand and libertarian beliefs on the other. Head versus heart.

In my focus groups the same person would agree with both perspectives and then laugh at their apparent muddle. Which figure is "the right answer"? It's hard for an individual to know. It's hard for research to know because it becomes a philosophical, not a technical, question. It depends how you believe we function as humans and how we should organize our society. Which should prevail, the head or the heart?

We live in an increasingly emotionalized society and neuroscience is showing that this is "truer" to our underlying nature, but we still govern ourselves by rational, enlightenment principles.

Curiously it is at this micro level, the daily designing of question wordings, that the integrity of opinion polls is preserved. Reconciling what the client wants to "prove" with the research company's own ethics and guidelines, the collective understanding of "the way we do things here," is what thrashes out best practice. In effect, the research company's internal and external brand image, their fear of peer disapproval, and pride in a job done to the best of their professional abilities is what holds back the floodgates of "horror story" polls.

It's a thin, defensive line but it seems to be holding.

So market research companies' concern for their reputation and their brand image, may not be ideal, but it is probably better than government regulation and a situation that would have made the great man smile.

14.1
Conflicts in Democracy: The Need for More Opinion Research*

By Stephen King

This article is a very much abbreviated version of a powerfully argued ESOMAR paper, presented in Brussels 1989, entitled: Public vs Private Opinion, available via WARC. Although the highlights are presented in this article, market researchers, in particular, should search out the longer version.

We are likely to see a marked increase in opinion research in the 1980s. It will be a period of increasingly difficult search for new forms of democracy in an era of new technology, new international relations and new problems over resources. There will be plenty of clashes between groups in society and opinion research will be needed to mediate. What we have to ask is whether today's methods are good enough for such an important role.

Two powerful trends in society have emerged in the 1970s. First, the growth of the *producer bureaucracy*. Organizations have been getting bigger. The proportion of UK manufacturing output coming from our 100 biggest firms has doubled in 20 years. Just five retail chains now control half of all grocery sales. Six public corporations have over 150 000 employees each, and 11 trade unions each have over three-quarters of a million members. Research shows considerable public disquiet at the size and unresponsiveness of large companies, public corporations, schools, hospitals and local authorities.

Producer bureaucracy means more than size alone. It is the tendency of all organizations – and particularly large ones – to put themselves before their customers. It has been a major cause of UK industrial decline – the tendency to make what our organizations want to make, rather than what people want to buy. Governments have been forced into supporting, for social and humanitarian reasons, companies that are in trouble for failing to recognize and respond to customers' wants. They have thereby reinforced the tendency.

The producer bureaucracy is by no means confined to the private sector. All around us are examples of public organizations which seem to believe that their primary purpose is to exist. As Keith Waterhouse put it: "Nowadays airports, like prisons and hospitals, are run entirely for the people that operate them." We are in danger of becoming a producer-led, not a consumer-led, society.

The producer bureaucracy would have been a problem in any circumstances, but it is especially so in the context of the second major trend – *the new individualism*. There is considerable evidence that people, particularly younger people, have been moving from fixed and inherited values to individual and discovered values. They have wider horizons in every way. Their aspirations and expectations are more expansive; they have a greater desire for self-expression and self-determination. They are more aware of what is going on around them. There has been a boom in education, both formal and informal: television, specialist magazines, art

---

*Published in *Advertising*, Autumn 1980. Reproduced with permission.

galleries, museums, travel. Two of the most potent symbols of change – owning a house and driving a car – both involve the *ownership of private space*. All in all, most of the social change in recent years can be related to the growth of individualism.

The trouble is that these two powerful forces – the producer bureaucracy and the new individualism – are bound to clash. Sometimes the clash is intense enough to lead to violence. Almost always, when there is violence, behind it is frustration on the part of some special-interest group that is has been unable to get through to the authorities. It does not seem to be able to communicate its ideas, to persuade others of what it feels is self-evident and obvious. Individuals and small groups feel they cannot apply enough pressure, while bureaucracies develop great skills in burying inconvenient ideas.

Happily, violence is rare in this country. That is at least partly because, in the end, minorities have found a means both of communicating and applying pressure: *the media event*.

A media event is an event staged mainly or wholly to get sympathetic coverage by the press, television and radio. Publicity is essential. It is not enough to make a protest; the protest must be seen to be made. The "women's movement", from Mrs Pankhurst to Ms Greer, is perhaps the best example of relatively small groups of people achieving at least some of their aims by the ingenious use of media events, from railing-chaining to bra-burning.

Media events have proliferated, as the new individualists and special-interest groups see them as an essential means of fighting against the producer bureaucracies. It goes further. There are media counter-events. Special-interest groups are using them to fight each other: those for and those against blood sports; those who want economic benefits and those who want rustic peace; those who want a decent wage for school caretakers and those who want the authorities to cross picket lines to provide education for children.

Clearly, one of the challenges for society in the 1980s is to get a just and democratic balance between the conflicting demands of these different groups of people. The problems will be all the harder, as it is perfectly clear that the views of many "representatives" often diverge wildly from those of the people they represent. There is, for instance, evidence that trade union leaders and TUC delegates have diametrically opposed views from trade union members on matters like nationalization, representation on company Boards and trade union reform. Labour Party voters do not share many of the views of the National Executive Committee and there is the same "dealignment" in the Conservative Party. Research has shown clearly and often that "activists", however valuable they may be, are very unrepresentative of the general population.

All this points to the opportunities and need for more opinion research in the 1980s. People will increasingly see through the mythologies of "the mandate", "democratic procedures" and "representation". Government and all forms of organization will need, even more than today, to find out and respond to what the public *really* thinks and wants. If "representatives" cannot be relied on to speak accurately for their members, then research must be used more often to supplement their views. It will be necessary, simply to make society work.

However, an increase in the amount of opinion research will not by itself solve all the problems. It is not just a matter of using it to mediate between different groups and viewpoints. *It must be seen to be used*. The results must be publicized, if they are to satisfy the public. The snag lies in how that is done.

It will be rare for any survey to be widely published in full. Nearly always, results will appear as news items on radio and television and in the newspapers. This means that the way in which opinion research is presented will depend most on the way that the media put together their news. Normally, editors want their journalists to provide entertainment, scoops and drama. It must all be in the smallest feasible space, topped by a snappy headline from a sub-editor.

As a result, research often seems to be publicized in the form of a superficial, arbitrary and unbalanced summary.

For instance, one recent survey on the opinions of young people covered a very wide range of subjects – parents, leisure, work, marriage, equal pay, saving, education, world events, and many other topics. The main findings suggested that young people's opinions were not very different from anyone else's, and this was accurately reflected in *The Times* headline: "Survey finds old heads on younger shoulders." However, the other media hardly gave this impression: headlines included "Teenagers look on marriage as a short-term contract"; "So young and sexy"; and "Young love shock".

If the only result of publishing opinion research was this sort of dramatic trivializing, it would hardly matter. Put together this tendency with the growing clashes in society and their accompanying media events, however, and a disturbing new phenomenon emerges. It is *the research event.*

A research event is research designed mainly to have its more dramatic results published and thereby put the pressure of "public opinion" on opponents. Nowadays the public can usually see media events for what they are: a dramatic way of presenting the arguments of a self-interested group, in the hope of establishing those arguments as the majority view. A research event is much more convincing and harder to ignore. It is saying *directly* that a certain opinion is the majority view.

There is a growing tendency for special-interest groups to fight their social and political battles via research events. Here are a few recent examples.

In October 1978, when it was widely believed that a general election would be called, opinion research was commissioned in five marginal constituencies by a group of companies. One newspaper reported the results to show that "76% thought that further nationalization would not be in the public interest . . . the survey also records a strong current opinion in favour of moderate policies".

At a critical stage of a new round of incomes policy, newspapers reported research to have shown that "nearly two-thirds of the public believe that the Ford Motor Company should stand firm in limiting the pay rise to its manual workers to 10%".

Newspapers reported that at the Windscale Inquiry one protesting group had tabled a public opinion survey which suggested that "19 out of 20 people would prefer the development of alternative energy schemes to the continuation of a nuclear power programme".

In a period during which the Government was cutting down the number of private beds in public hospitals and trade union spokesmen were active in calling for the abolition of private medicine, research was reported in the papers showing that "73% of all trade unionists supported or were prepared to accept its existence, while only 11% were definitely opposed".

Both the Committee of London Clearing Bankers and the Campaign Against Building Industry Nationalization selectively quoted the results of opinion research in their advertising to justify their resistance to the nationalization proposals of the National Executive Committee of the Labour Party.

There are two things which all these research events have in common. First, they greatly oversimplify what are usually very complex issues. They are making use of the media's demand for the dramatic. Secondly, they rely for their effect on numbers rather than depth. There is no room in research events for open-ended questions or qualitative research. In other words, as reported, they are not the sort of research that most opinion researchers would regard as adequate.

There are two particular dangers arising from research events. First, some very dubious opinion research is being done. For instance, the survey presented to the Windscale Inquiry: one look at its questionnaire shows that its results, as reported, were wholly misleading.

The second could, in the long run, be more destructive. Research events are becoming more competitive, like media events. Conflicting research results are being published. For instance, just four months before the Windscale survey, in which apparently 96% opposed nuclear power, *New Society* published research (properly conducted) to show that 49% were in favour of more nuclear power stations to produce electricity.

The danger is, of course, that people will become wholly cynical and dismissive of all opinion research. The precedent is there with political opinion polls, whose usually minor divergences arouse a quite disproportionate scepticism and hostility (especially from those who don't care for their findings).

If the pressures to produce research events leads to bad research and conflicting results, the whole process of opinion research could be discredited. We could revert to a situation in which unrepresentative "representatives" decide what the public thinks and in which politicians believe that "being in touch with people" is the same as talking to their own activists. That is not what I would call democratic.

After the 1970 election, most of the political opinion polls were criticized for "getting it wrong". The Market Research Society set up a committee of enquiry, and the leading companies set about producing a code of practice and a programme of education about the realities of political opinion polling. A reasonable amount of progress was made and there were signs of considerable improvement by the time of the 1979 election.

I believe that the same approach now has to be made to the more serious issue of research events and the practice and publicizing of general opinion research. It is a much harder and more complex problem. It will be more a matter of long-term education than a simple technical code of practice. All the more reason to begin now.

As a starting-point for discussion, I would like to put forward five guidelines for opinion research. They are not new. The basic issue is simple enough. The media will tend to present – or be given to present – on each topic one or two superficial opinions. But the reality is that on most topics we have very complex sets of ideas and feelings.

I think it is helpful to view people's opinions as lying on a scale, one end of which can be called *private opinion*, the other *public opinion*.

At the extreme end of private opinion are inner thoughts and feelings, ideas that are not verbalized and are not really accessible to conventional opinion research. At the extreme end of public opinion are outer thoughts, thoughtless reactions, thoughts that can be expressed in public without unease, repetitions of the conventional wisdom, ideas that are accessible to standard interviewers in public places in instant response to predigested statements.

In between is a wide range of the half-formed opinions that we all use in daily life, accessible to a variety of research methods.

Research events clearly operate near the public end of the scale. We have to make it clear that the scale exists, that opinions go all along it and that all of them are valid. Here are my suggestions for guidelines:

- *Salience*: Opinion research should try to establish how interested people are in a topic or how much they know about it, before asking for their views on it.
- *Variety of questions*: A variety of questions and techniques will be needed to give a full picture of people's opinions, both private and public, on most topics.

- *Personal and concrete v. general and abstract*: Personal and concrete questions are likely to be necessary to get people's private opinions, while general and abstract questions will elicit public opinions. Both sorts may be necessary.
- *Views on what others think*: People's views on what other people think can be an important influence on their own opinions. Research must take this into account.
- *Opinions and actions*: What people do may be a better guide to their private opinions than what they say. Opinion research should aim to relate opinions to actual or likely behaviour.

I have had absolutely no difficulty in finding examples of research that observes these guidelines. We must now try to control the black sheep among its users, and to prevent research events becoming the threat to the democratic process that they might be.

15

The Perfect Role Model for
Researchers Today

By David Smith, Chairman and Chief Executive, DVL Smith Group

An introduction to:

15.1   Tomorrow's Research

Stephen King linked together two evolutionary changes that were taking place in the early 1990s when he wrote this article. The first was the emergence of the concept of the company brand, and the second was the way new ever more complex service offerings were becoming available. Putting these observations together, Stephen went on to alert us to the way that, in the future, market researchers would need to be more adept at understanding the complexity of brands.

Looking Around the Corner at the Era to Come

Today, we are familiar with the complexity surrounding the way you research service-intensive company brands, such as Google and Amazon. But when Stephen wrote his article, marketing professionals and market researchers were still operating around the "classic" fmcg paradigm of the benefits of a top brand. We were then an industry tooled up to cope with traditional brands, such as Nescafé, masterminded by central command and control style marketing departments that were supported by market researchers thinking in a fairly orthodox way.

Today, we have to operate with less rigid marketing structures and employ more flexible and creative approaches to market research. How else could we deal with the concept of consumer-to-consumer marketing and get to grips with brands, such as, ebay? But, when Stephen wrote his article "post-modern" marketing and market research had not really left the starting blocks.

Describing the Next "Little Box"

Stephen's skill, however, was not just in being able to paint a general impression of how the world was changing. He was able to provide us with the concepts to make sense of the next marketing "paradigm" – the next model, or framework, that explains how we will operate as market researchers.

We need to be able to trace the journey from "controlled" consumers caught up in the class system, through to the marketing appeal of "individualism", and on to today's cult of "instant celebrity".

So a key lesson from Stephen's article is to remind market researchers of the importance of stepping back and looking "outside in" at the emerging concepts that help us to understand the changing world, as Stephen did with such clarity.

Challenging Shibboleths

Another lesson from the article is not to be afraid to speak out and challenge cherished shibboleths. We should not – as the dormouse did in *Alice in Wonderland* – "hide in the teapot". But instead, we should stand up and be counted, and identify those techniques, approaches and methodologies that are clearly no longer appropriate in an ever-changing and more complex environment.

Stephen was never afraid to do this. He always remained deliciously dangerous in commenting on different methods and approaches. In the article he describes as "ridiculous" such concepts as the *ideal* brand, and also attacks the "futility" of putting people into rigid watertight customer segments. The point Stephen was making was that segmentation may be the bedrock of marketing, but we must be adult in the way we interpret the output of such studies.

So, today, how would you describe someone's flying habits? It could be EasyJet flights for long weekends in Nice, Premium Economy to New York, but a flat bed to Sydney. Into which segment are you going to put this person? In short, we need segments that reflect this complexity.

Platitude Busting

Building on the above, the article is also valuable in reminding market researchers to avoid "superficial" surface measurements of attitudes. Stephen stresses the importance of working hard to assess "true" attitudes and not to fall into the trap of simply playing back what could be referred to as 'platitudes'.

By a platitude, we mean a generalized, clichéd, easy to access, off-the-shelf view of an issue learned from others (usually journalists) that can be repeated back, parrot fashion, by respondents keen to extricate themselves from a loosely worded, ill-constructed or ambiguous survey question. It is true that sometimes obtaining a view at a more shallow or superficial level is all that is required.

We need to work harder to appreciate some of the complexities of "attitude measurement". For instance, asking a question about what people think about "marriage today" is totally different from pinning the question down to ask how person X feels about getting married to person Y next Saturday at 3 o'clock! These are two different questions. The former approach would provide us with some lightweight clichés, whereas the latter takes us to the heart of the matter.

And we have to remember that when Stephen wrote this article and was commenting on the need to avoid naïve assessments of what people really think, he would not have had the benefit of the latest findings from neuroscience. These – if we were to briefly condense them here – tell us that in a straight choice between rationality and emotion, emotion usually wins!

Connecting the Old with the New

Stephen's writing also reminds us to embrace new ideas and change, but to constantly and critically evaluate the latest ideas to ensure that they do not become accepted without challenge. Stephen's article addresses the importance of not simply slavishly going with the next 'fad', believing it will work as a universal, one-size-fits-all panacea for all situations.

So, by way of illustration, today we need to be realistic about some of the hype that surrounds the emergence of ethnography as a research tool. It is, of course, a powerful technique. After all, observation studies were a key plank of the market research craft when it first got under way in the 1930s. But, what is the point of just watching people do something if, through various types of intelligent, sensible and sympathetic questioning you can *also* find out what they are thinking of while they are carrying out this behaviour.

So, reeling from the attack on market research as being about 'asking stupid questions of unreliable witnesses and then believing what they have to say', it is then easy to reject the inevitably coarse art of solving problems by asking questions and listening to the answers by then placing an over-reliance on observation. Whereas, surely the solution is: improve the quality of the interviewing *and* also undertake observation research. It is true, then, that watching a disabled person struggle with his wheelchair to gain access to a public place is powerful. But, so too is an intelligent dialogue aimed at assessing whether this particular wheelchair user has been broken by his disability, or has he retained that fighting spirit?

Bridging the Gap Between Business Practice and Academia

Another major lesson that emerges from reading Stephen's article is the importance of building on what we know – making sure that change is grounded in what others have written. Glancing at the references in this article, you can see that he never made the mistake of failing to build on what has gone before. This is important because, unlike the USA, market research practitioners and academics in the UK, seem to hold each other in mutually low regard. This is a very unhelpful state of affairs. And in reading Stephen's work we can see how he enjoyed fashioning various academic theories and ideas into actionable suggestions for practitioners.

The Forerunner of Evidence-Based Business Consultancy

Inevitably, when one reads an article there will be an element of selective perception to the messages received. So, for me – with my interest in stretching market researchers' skill set to embrace "business consultancy" – I took much encouragement from Stephen's comments about developing market researchers' consultative skills.

In this 1989 article, he seemed to be laying down the foundations for what is emerging as a "new category" in market research, namely "evidence-based business consultancy". Stephen wrote:

> I think what I have outlined suggests that there is still enormous scope for invention, ideas and leadership from the market research craftsman. The whole development of service intensive company brands will need – at the "consulting end" of the spectrum – the market research skills of thinking about complex notions" and will entail researchers getting more deeply involved in people and their curious ways.

The Perfect Role Model

In short, Stephen is for me, the perfect role model for newcomers coming into marketing intelligence research and consultancy. From Stephen they can learn the value of combining clarity of thinking and methodological soundness with creativity and a keenness to always change with the times. Stephen would have been a perfect coach for today's newcomers. He would have been able to stress the value of mastering the market research basics, while at the same time engendering in youngsters the confidence, creativity and credibility needed to go beyond the data if one is to succeed in understanding today's more complex environment.

15.1

Tomorrow's Research*

By Stephen King

Market research has fresh fields to conquer, as pressures on marketing companies alter the nature of brands. Two key evolutionary changes are the "company brand", and the complex new service dimensions. But this is unfamiliar research territory, with pitfalls.

Market researchers will know better than most that, despite the abrupt slip into a new decade, life goes on more or less seamlessly. However, I think there are two major evolutionary changes in the nature of marketing that will in the end greatly affect market research in the 1990s.

In this article I want to cover:

- The special pressures affecting brand building
- The two evolutionary changes
- The implications for market research methods.

The early parts of the article are in effect a summary, as I have written about the same area at length elsewhere. Equally, I will not be dealing directly with the development of research company brands, which has been well covered recently (e.g. in the specialist literature – Bowles, 1991 and Whitten, 1991).

SIX PRESSURES ON MARKETING COMPANIES

There are six particular pressures affecting the brand building by marketing companies. All these have grown steadily through the 1980s and are likely to intensify:

1. *More confident consumers* – People are more confident, readier to experiment and to trust their own judgement. There is more individualism and tribalism, more know-how, more understanding of all aspects of marketing. There will be a cooler analysis of the values given by brands, products and services; and maybe a more critical approach to some forms of research.
2. *New concepts of "quality"* – Consumers will continue to look for quality, but their interpretation of it is changing. It is increasingly based on what they feel are real values not superficial styling. They will be more interested in values such as responsiveness, service and greenism; and will be willing to pay a little extra for a clear conscience. That is, demand will become more complex, and so will the measurement of it.

---

*Published in *Admap*, September 1991. The full title of the article is: "Tomorrow's Research: Brand Building, Pressures on Marketing, and the Implications for Future Market Research Methods". Reproduced with permission.

3. *Shortage of skills* – Demographic changes and educational weaknesses may mean a shortage of the skills needed to invent and produce these high quality goods and services, to manage all aspects of their marketing and to plan their research.
4. *Increased competition* – Competition is intensifying in almost all fields and is becoming more international. It is clear that there will soon be considerable overcapacity in many markets – for instance, cars, retailing and financial services.
5. *The side-effects of new technology* – However much we have all talked about new technology, progress on using it in marketing has been a bit slow. But that will surely change in the 1990s. There will be more rapid copying of goods, more flexible manufacturing systems, more automation of services, faster technological leapfrogging, shorter life cycles. The database revolution will at last actually happen. Retailers will make use of their scanning data not just for stock control and arm-wrestling with their suppliers, but also for building a closer relationship with their customers.
6. *Restructuring* – The wave of mergers, takeovers, LBOs, MBOs, corporate alliances, bundling, unbundling and barbarians at the gates shows little sign of slowing down. Many organizations and employees will be wondering who they are, to whom they owe loyalty and what their corporate culture is. Customers will be wondering just how committed to their brands some of the suppliers really are.

All these changes will make life difficult for companies. How will they keep up their margins in face of stronger international competition? How will they make the most of economies of scale when national mass markets are being broken up into transnational tribes? How will they attract the skills to keep ahead on quality? If they are being constantly restructured, how will they build an enduring link with their customers?

Most people in marketing (e.g. Doyle, 1989) would agree that building and maintaining powerful brands will be critical to success. Indeed, brand building may be the only way in these circumstances to get stability of demand, to add the values and variations that people want, to provide a base for expansion, to protect the company against the power of intermediaries and to attract the right staff.

This is hardly a new idea. Building brands is at the centre of all marketing. The trouble is that we tend to equate the word "brand" with the classic brand leaders in packaged grocery products (such as Coke, Pepsi, Marlboro, Ivory, Persil, Lux Toilet Soap, Oxo, Bovril, Kit Kat, Mars, Andrex). Yet one effect of the pressures of the 1990s will be that, though the old-established classic brands should themselves prosper, this sort of brand will become steadily rarer and a smaller part of consumers' expenditure. *We are going to have to get out of the habit of using the old classic brands as the "true" model for marketing.*

I believe, in fact, that brand building is entering a new mode. This is partly because of the speed and scale of today's pressures. But it is also because the long-promised "service economy" seems genuinely to have arrived at last. White-collar work is now the employment mode of the majority in developed economies, and people are increasingly getting their rewards from the non-functional aspects of brands.

THE EVOLUTIONARY CHANGES

There are two interlocking elements to this new mode – the two major evolutionary changes to marketing in the 1990s:

- The company brand itself will increasingly become the discriminator in consumers' choice, rather than the functional attributes of objects made by the company.
- Almost everything we buy is a combination of "product" and "service". The service element will steadily become the more important part, and the principles of service marketing will become the core of all brand building.

THE COMPANY BRAND

Successful new single-line brands have gradually become something of a rarity (Madell, 1980; Tauber, 1988). Most successful "new products" are range extensions or line extensions; that is, they are variants of an existing brand. Each variant is rapidly matched or trumped by a competitor or a retailer; and still the new individualists demand more variety.

The result is a tendency to stretch a successful product brand to cover fields some way from its original (product) values. When this happens, consumers will often "invent" a parent company to own both the new variant and the original brand – the variant is seen as a new product from "the Nescafé people" or "the Timotei people" – and they will assume certain company values for both.

So it seems that the company brand (whether technically it is a company, like Heinz, or a presumed company, like "the Timotei people") will cover an increasingly wider range of product types and will not credibly be able to maintain that all of them are permanently "better" than their competitors.

This implies that increasingly the company brand itself will act as the main discriminator. That is, consumers' choice will depend less on an evaluation of the functional benefits to them of a product or service, and more on an assessment of the people behind it – their skills, attitudes, integrity, behaviour, style, responsiveness, greenism, language: the whole company culture, in fact.

Company brands have of course been around a very long time, even in the world of packaged groceries. But it seems to me that most of the emphasis in the literature and teaching and conferences is still on the single-line classic brand. The change has in fact been quite rapid. For instance, as recently as 1969, of the 25 brands spending most on press and television in the UK (MEAL data), 19 were repeat purchase packaged goods; by 1989 it was just one, and in 1990 two.

THE BIG DIFFERENCES

I wonder if we have quite come to grips yet with this change. The differences between company brands and the classic (product) brands, though fairly obvious, have some important implications for both marketing and research. To pick out four such differences:

- *The consumers have changed* – Most of the classic brands were launched when authority was respected and so mass marketing was possible. The brand became the authority in its own small world. Now everything is questioned, and people want to be treated as individuals, the company brand's views are not necessarily fully accepted; market research has to take this ambivalence into account.
- *Copying the product element is easier* – Most of the classic brands had a good run before copies came onto the market. This is simply not so for today's company brands. Their discriminators will depend on more subtle, non-functional values that are much harder to measure.

- *Relationships are more diverse* – For the classic brands, the main points of contact are retailers and consumers. For the company brand it is a much wider range of overlapping groups. This means that an individual can have several different relationships with the brand (e.g. consumer, employee, shareholder, pressure group member). It also means that the brand will use a much wider range of communication methods. In particular, the staff (from the CEO to the telephonist) will probably be the most important medium.
- *The core of the brand is people, not things* – Unlike the classic brand, a company brand is not a standard article. It is a changing collection of people, values, styles and behaviour. What binds them together is very intangible – a complex set of norms, conventions, methods, examples, organizational patterns, rules and leaders. It is of course extremely difficult to measure the personality of this sort of brand.

There are some broader implications from the move to company brands. For instance, if the staff become the crucial brand – builders and communicators, there may have to be some changes in staff policies in many companies. They may have to give more attention to clarifying company strategies; to the role of the personnel director in marketing; to training, motivation and leadership; to identifying and establishing a corporate culture; to improving internal networks; to internal communications in general. Where such complexities need to be improved, they will also need to be measured.

Again, the typical hierarchical family-tree type structure that works (more or less) for classic brands is likely to be unsuitable for managing and communicating a company brand. That may need a more interactive group management. It may also need a "brand designer", a new type of animal, whose passion is for the totality of a brand (Lorenz, 1986). Such a person may need to use measurement methods that straddle the gap between the traditions of market research (as used in the marketing department) and those of human resources research (as used in the personnel department).

The increased complexities of target groups and media used for a company brand mean that there is a special need for clarity in setting communication objectives, and a language that is shared between several departments with several budgets and often large numbers of (competing) outside agencies and suppliers. This is a far harder task than for the classic brands (Booms and Bitner, 1981); yet in my experience it is rarely tackled as systematically. This obviously presents considerable problems for planning research to measure the effectiveness of company brand communications.

ADDING SERVICES

The second evolutionary change is more directly related to the coming of the "service economy", but is maybe a little more subtle than is often assumed. It is not merely that more of people's money will be spent on "services" rather than on "products". It is more that virtually everything we buy is a combination of product and service (Foxall, 1985) and that the service element will be increasingly vital to success in all brands (Christopher, 1985). It will provide most of the scope for the innovation and differentiation that all good brands need (Quinn *et al.*, 1990; Vandermerwe and Rada, 1988).

For instance, the archetypal manufacturer, General Motors, is said to be making more money now from financing cars than from constructing them. The computer companies in particular have changed their balance. Apple is now really a management service company which concentrates on designing its basic concepts and appearance and certain key software; its chips, microprocessors, video monitors, printers and power supplies are all bought-in components. IBM now offer a "systems-integration service"; it will make the whole set-up work, whatever brands of hardware the customer buys.

There clearly are many very successful branded services, and a good deal has been written on the subject. Nevertheless, the marketing of services is relatively new. Most of the academic work has come in the 1970s and 1980s, and not very much of it is specifically about brand building. Some of the services that prospered in the boom are finding that their brands are not quite strong enough to stand up well to hard times. Most conferences and articles by practitioners seem to treat service marketing as a specialism rather than as a central aspect of all marketing. I think it is fair to suggest that the principles have not percolated very far yet. There seem to me to be six basic principles that feature in most of the literature, and all of them have implications for market research methods:

1. Services can be Added to Almost any Brand

The horrid word "servitization" has been coined to cover the broader area to of goods + services + knowledge + support + self-service (Vandermerwe and Rada, 1988). The opportunities seem endless. For instance:

- *Adding new links in the buying system* – Most things we buy are part of a long process that runs from a first trigger to the final satisfaction after use; and there are often gaps in the stages. For instance, SAS moved from being just another airline to being a businessmen's "total travel package", with initial enquiry services, hotels with their own check-in counters, tours, catering, "sleep class" and "work class" tickets, limousine service, etc.
- *Adding to the assumed lifetime* – of products with guarantees, insurance, updates, etc.
- *Providing extra information* – on how to use products and with what, health, environmental effects, and so on.
- *Improving customers' and consumers' skills* – from running cookery or driving schools to training retailers' staffs.
- *Defining and publicizing quality standards* – telling consumers and staff what to expect; then accepting and responding to the pressure that this puts on the brand.
- *Setting up extra or better contacts* – hot lines, ombudsmen, named contacts, 24-hour answer phones, newsletters, properly designed and maintained databases.
- *Friendly delivery systems* – For instance, many heating companies just used to deliver fuel to order; now they have automatic refuelling systems, boiler maintenance, spare parts, insurance, etc.
- *Contributing to the local community* – It's not too hard to have ideas for added services.

The problem is to work out which would have sufficient appeal to differentiate the brand and to justify their extra cost. To do that will require having much more knowledge about customers' and consumers' experience, attitudes and behaviour in a much wider context than is usually necessary for a classic product brand. There seems to be a good opportunity for market researchers of the consultant rather than the "standardized" sort and for great ingenuity in controlling the costs of such research.

Table 15.1 Service/quality dimensions

Customers in 4 service sectors	% rating most important
Reliability	52
Responsiveness	18
Empathy	15
Assurance	14
Tangibles	1

2. The Intangible Elements of Services are more Valued than the Tangible

There are many problems in measuring the quality of a service; yet it is critical if the service element of a company brand is its main discriminator. Many writers have made the point that any service is made up of tangibles and intangibles, and that generally the intangibles are the more important to customers (Lovelock, 1983; Thompson *et al.*, 1985). For instance, research among customers for credit cards, repairs, long-distance telephones and banks (Berry *et al.*, 1988), showed the results shown in Table 15.1.

It appeared that the physical facilities, equipment and appearance of staff mattered a lot less than reliable performance and various aspects of the relationship with customers. Many readers of this report might quarrel with the research method used, but all would admit that there are considerable problems of definition and measurement of intangibles in assessing the quality of service.

3. Services are the Key to Customer Retention

For years the rhetoric of marketing has been that of warfare (targets, campaigns and offensives); the macho approach is to beat the enemy and win new customers. Now at last more attention is being paid to retaining customers, the lifetime value of a customer and "zero defections". Bain & Company have put figures on the increasing profits from each year of retention of a customer in over 100 companies, and they all show the same trends. Table 15.2 gives one example (Reichheld and Sasser, 1990).

Most authorities and practitioners say that added services and quality of service are the key to retaining customers (Berry, 1986). BA's famous turnaround, and its "Putting People First" programme of improved service, were aimed at retention. So are the various frequent flier schemes. Volvo has introduced the concept of lifetime care, a commitment to support the car irrespective of age or mileage.

The implications for research are fairly clear. To be effective at retention, marketing a company brand has to have a really good database of present and past customers, with details of the nature of the relationship. It then has to know about the attitudes, in this difficult area of

Table 15.2 Profit from a credit card customer ($)

Year 0	Year 1	Year 2	Year 3	Year 4	Year 5
(51)	30	42	44	49	55

tangible and intangible service quality, of these known individuals; if they have defected, and why they have.

4. Internal Marketing is Essential

"Total Quality Management" is a contemporary buzzphrase. Most people, even in manufacturing companies, are doing jobs with a high service content and everyone in the company should be involved in total quality management. In many ways the essence of an effective service is that the employee and the customer should become accomplices in providing it (Lovelock, 1984; Takeuchi and Quelch, 1983).

So a key idea in all service marketing is the need to treat the staff also as customers. That implies paying a lot of attention to internal communication, motivation, reward and recognition systems. Success will depend on having just as good information on the staff as on the external market, but clearly the relationships are much more complex and sensitive. Research into staff attitudes tends to be specialized, and is on the whole done by human resources people, not market researchers. So there can be problems in linking external and internal attitudes.

5. The Real Test is Problem Resolution

A few things are bound to go wrong. The real test of the calibre of any service company is how well and how quickly it puts them right. It is actually possible to improve a reputation and the relationship with a customer by having problems, and then putting them right promptly, generously and stylishly.

This clearly requires having the right culture, the right systems and the right sort of organization, usually one which has enough people to deal with the non-routine and which gives a fair amount of authority and discretion to those in direct contact with the customer (Berry, 1986). The companies best at this make much use of "brand gestures" – such as Marks & Spencer's no quibble exchange of goods, John Lewis's refunds of cash if found to be undersold, Mercedes' offer of technicians outside the dealers' working hours, Wachovia's "sundown rule" (all customer complaints to be responded to before the sun goes down). The brand gesture is a most effective symbol of the brand's attitudes, both for staff and for customers.

To make this work well the company has to have a very sensitive monitoring system. Most people do not complain directly to suppliers; but they do them far more harm by removing their custom and by talking about them to others. There is a need for research methods which concentrate on the exceptions (not the 99% of cases where all goes well) and on winkling out the hidden dissatisfactions and problems.

6. In Services, what Gets Measured Gets Done

Or, to be more sceptical about it, service quality doesn't improve unless it's measured. Speeches and exhortations do not achieve very much in their own right. Bain & Company found in a survey of chief executives that three-quarters had set up major customer quality programmes; but less than one-fifth reckoned that they'd achieved tangible results from them. The reason became clear when middle managements were asked about their priorities: they rated the measurable aims (such as "hitting plan") far higher than those hard to measure.

Standards need to be set in terms as specific as possible for the performance of services, retention of customers and the attitudes of customers. The results then have to be measured against them, and rewards and incentives related to the measures. This is clearly a difficult job, and since customer attitudes are crucial to it, I would have thought that there is a great opportunity for market research skills. But I rather doubt if a great many research companies have yet got involved in this area.

IMPLICATIONS FOR MARKET RESEARCH

In general then, it seems to me that these two evolutionary changes will bring a lot of opportunities for market research. Some of them are in areas which may be relatively unfamiliar to many market research companies. In almost all of them dealing with company brands and service intensive brands makes the job a great deal more complex than dealing with the classic product brands. Most will involve getting at attitudes, opinions and relationships that are both sensitive and quite individual. Nearly all will involve the measurement and monitoring of intangibles.

To take up the points made in Tim Bowles's excellent review of the issues facing the industry (Bowles, 1991), I think that the proper approach in such a difficult area would be to start with top-quality tailor-made research; from that gradually to develop branded but fairly flexible services; and finally maybe set up some standardized research and monitoring systems.

I have to say, however, that I'm not wholly confident that it will all work out in that logical way. There's a danger of competition pushing us into starting with standardized research that is inevitably superficial. I think much vigilance will be called for.

It's hard to be wholly satisfied with our progress in measuring people's attitudes to and feelings about brands in the very much easier area of product brands. Some of the more awful research ideas still seem to be lingering on. For instance:

- *The ideal brand* – The ideal car would be very powerful and very economical, large for comfort and small for parking, with complex but simple specifications, full of luxury and very cheap, and so on. It is quite clear that consumers compare actual brands, and trade-off research should have killed off the ideal brand altogether. But it still rears its head in research. The ideal company seems to me an even more awful concept.
- *VALSism* – This is the notion that it is useful for marketing purposes to put people into watertight boxes according to their generic attitudes to life. The only sensible sort of segmentation of attitudes is mode or mood segmentation.

  For instance, in shopping, cooking and eating it is clear that there is an increasing polarization between the fast/functional and the involved/enjoyable. But of course this is not a polarization between different people: it's the same people in different moods or circumstances. Yet still naïve people segmentation goes on; in my view, it will be even more dangerous in the era of service intensive company brands.
- *Surface measurement* – For instance, the belief that attitudes are whatever it is that is measured by what we choose to call "attitude research". For years we have conspired to accept that superficial "attitude batteries" are measuring something as complex as an attitude, and that tracking brands on "kind to the hands/not so kind to the hands" is telling us something special – despite the research that suggests that such responses are highly predictable and related to brand usage (Castleberry and Ehrenberg, 1990). I hope we are not going to be content with tracking company brands on "kind to employees/not so kind to employees" or "has friendly staff/not so friendly staff".
- *Rank-ordering attributes* – I think we are still asking respondents to rank-order the importance to them of attributes in a brand, even though it has been clear for years that they find

this a very abstract task, little related to real life, and that the results tend greatly to over-value functional attributes. If it is true that the intangibles in service are the most effective elements, this sort of research is going to be even more dangerous.

It seems to me that, in planning the sensitive tailor-made research that I'd envisage into people's responses to company brands, we may have to remind ourselves of some of the basic principles – such as those laid out in Mollie Tarrant's fine booklet (Tarrant, 1978). Or, to repeat a *cri de coeur* of my own some 12 years ago (King, 1979):

- Find out salience before asking opinions
- Ask a wide variety of question types
- Try to be personal and concrete rather than general and abstract
- Find out what respondents feel other people think
- Use people's actions as a guide to their opinions.

SOME SPECIFIC QUESTIONS

There are a lot of implications for market research methods dotted throughout this article, but let me try to pull them together by setting out some of the issues that are raised in my mind. I leave it of course to skilled practitioners to provide the answers.

1. **Issues of respondents**
   - *Complexity of roles and relationships* – With company brands people are likely to have much more varied relationships than with a single-line product brand. Will this mean more difficult/more expensive sampling; or will we have to accept the risk that unknown to us one relationship is being affected by another? How are we going economically to measure usage of a company brand over time, if that brand covers many product/service fields?
   - *Sensitivity of staff customer research* – Much of the research will involve specific named people who have relationships with each other. There's a danger of the research itself affecting them. Will that mean having special interviewers, with special training? Should they have a background in human resources or anthropology?
   - *Databases and direct communications* – Increasingly the company will have the names of customers and lapsed customers on a database, and be used to communicating directly with them. If so, will it want to use market research agencies at all? How can researchers develop the special skills to get themselves seen as essential consultants?

2. **Issues of research design**
   - *The intangible elements of service* – How can they be made personal and concrete enough to measure sensibly? How can the consumer language be winkled out? How can that be done while doing justice to the irreducibly intangible?
   - *The complexity of communications for a company brand* – The company brand is going to be using almost all formal media for communications, plus a huge variety of speech and non-verbal signals from staff. The communications mix will have many different roles and time scales, and its objectives may not always be crystal clear. How can research be designed to evaluate so complex a mix?
   - *Corporate culture* – No one doubts its importance in the circumstances of the 1990s. But how do we define it and establish the influences on it; hence what exactly to measure, from whom and how?

3. **Issues of analysis**
   - *Complexity versus simplicity* – Much of this article is about trying to measure increasingly complex phenomena, plus a few attacks on our occasional use of very superficial questions. Yet the results of our "new" research have got to be comprehensible to and actionable by people who are not experts in mathematical analysis. Some of them will have found out the hard way that there are sometimes some very questionable assumptions hidden below a certain degree of blinding with science (for instance, in some of the regression analysis used in some market modelling). How can we find the right way of presenting complex data simply?
   - *Analysis of open-ended conversations* – Many of the topics raised here require sensitive, conversational interviewing; with samples large enough to cover the variety of interests and relationships; and later monitoring of the results over time. How are we going to get the quantities without destroying the sensitivity? Will there have to be new forms of qualitative research or semi-structured research? Can new technology help over this?

4. **General issues**
   - *Market research tradition versus human resources tradition* – It seems to me that there's quite a gap between the traditions, methods and gurus of the marketing department and those of the personnel department in the matter of finding things out by asking people questions. Yet a key element of the new company brands is the seamless link between the staff and the customers. How can the two traditions get together, learn from each other and avoid infighting? At the same time, how can market research agencies grab the new opportunities inside companies?
   - *Cost* – It's easy enough to suggest improvements and changes that are likely to cost a lot of money, and I've done so. How are companies going to pay for all these extra complexities in research? How can we design research that meets the challenges without being ridiculously expensive? And how can we make the case persuasively that the necessary extra costs will be essential to the success of company brands?

Others have pointed out the changes likely in the structure and working methods of market research agencies in the 1990s. It is hard to argue with the view that more of the output will be structured and standardized, that there will be a greater emphasis on providing "value for money" services and that the profitability of research businesses may be of more interest to distant owners than the professional skills. That might make gloomy reading for those who value craftsmanship and self-determination above all.

I am a lot less gloomy myself. I think that what I've outlined suggests that there is still enormous scope for invention, ideas and leadership from the craftsmen. The whole development of service intensive company brands will need the classical market research skills of thinking and eliciting complex notions and interpretation and creating measurement packages, at the "consulting" end of the spectrum. And as the changes will entail getting more deeply involved in people and their curious ways, it could be an even more rewarding job than today's.

REFERENCES

Berry, L.L. (1986) "Big ideas in services marketing", *Journal of Consumer Marketing* 3(2), 47–51.
Berry, L.L., Parasuraman, A. and Zeithaml V.A. (1988) "The service-quality puzzle", *Business Horizons*, September/October, 35–43.

Booms, B.H. and Bitner, M.J. (1981) "Marketing strategies and organisation structures for service firms", in Donnelly, J. and George, W.R. (eds), *Marketing of Services*, Chicago: AMA.

Bowles, T. (1991) "Issues facing the UK research industry", *Journal of the Market Research Society*, 33(2), 71–81.

Castleberry, S.B. and Ehrenberg, A.S.C. (1990) "Brand usage: a factor in consumer beliefs", *Marketing Research*, 1 (June), 14–20.

Christopher, M. (1985) "The strategy of customer service", *Marketing in the Service Industries*. London: Frank Cass.

Doyle, P. (1989) "Building successful brands: The strategic options", *Journal of Marketing Management*, 5(1), 77–95.

Foxall, G. (1985) "Marketing is service marketing", *Marketing in the Service Industries*. London: Frank Cass.

King, S. (1979) "Public versus private opinion", 32nd ESOMAR Congress, Brussels.

Lorenz, C. (1986) *The Design Dimension*. Oxford: Blackwell.

Lovelock, C. (1983) "Classifying services to gain strategic marketing insights", *Journal of Marketing*, 47(2), 9–20.

Lovelock, C. (1984) *Services Marketing*. Englewood Cliffs: Prentice-Hall.

Madell, J. (1980). New products: how to succeed when the odds are against you. *Marketing Week*, 22 February.

Quinn, J.B., Doorley, T.L. and Paquette, P.C. (1990) "Beyond products: Services-based strategy", *Harvard Business Review*, March/April, 58–67.

Reichheld, F.F. and Sasser, W.E. (1990) "Zero defections: Quality comes to services", *Harvard Business Review*, September/October, 105–111.

Takeuchi, H. and Quelch, J.A. (1983) "Quality is more than making a good product", *Harvard Business Review*, July/August, 139–145.

Tarrant, M. (1978) *Interpreting Public Attitudes*. London: J. Walter Thompson Co. Ltd.

Tauber, E.M. (1988) "Brand leverage: Strategy for growth in a cost-control world", *Journal of Advertising Research*, August/September, 26–30.

Thompson, P.O., DeSouza, G. and Gale, B.T. (1985, 1988) "*The Strategic Management of Service Quality*", Cambridge: Strategic Planning Institute.

Vandermerwe, S. and Rada, J. (1988) "Servitization of business: Adding value by adding services", *European Management Journal*, 6(4), 314–324.

Whitten, P. (1991) "Using IT to enhance the role of marketing research", *Journal of the Market Research Society*, 33(2), 113–125.

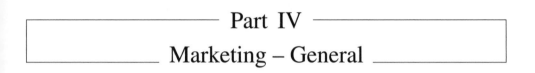

Part IV
Marketing – General

The sheer breadth of Stephen's intellect and interests are present in this selection of articles that touch on various aspects of the wider business world. His book on what makes brands successful is as relevant today as it was when he wrote it. His criticisms of marketing will look familiar to many today but as Hugh Burkitt points out, winning companies show how it should be done.

Perhaps the most relevant of all of this selection is the last article which develops the theme of the rise of the corporate brand. In many ways most of Stephen's thinking comes together in this piece: the importance of brand building; the way companies should be structured to make that happen intelligently; and the ways in which the corporate brand should communicate itself to the wider world. It is a fitting final article.

16
Old Brands Never Die. They Just get Sold for a Huge Profit

By Martin Deboo, Consumer Goods Analyst, Investec Securities

An introduction to:

16.1   What Makes New Brands Succeed?

About 1985 I was handed a copy of *Developing New Brands* (Chapter 1 of which is "What Makes New Brands Succeed?"). I was a planner at BMP at the time and was engaged on a new product development project with my then client, Quaker Oats. Somebody suggested that I might want to read Stephen's book on the subject and I did so, with enthusiasm. The book was already 12 years old by then, but was still considered to be definitive on the subject.

The book had quite a profound impact on me at the time and I was moved to read more of Stephen's writings, not least his article "Has marketing failed . . . or was it never really tried", which is introduced by Hugh Burkitt on page 307.

We have all travelled a long way since 1985, let alone 1973. I moved on from BMP into strategic consulting and now into the City, but have always been involved in consumer goods. In the meantime, the world has changed quite a bit. Retailer power has increased, eliminating many weak brands and raising the barriers to entry for new ones. The right stuff of brand development has moved away from packaged goods in favour of financial services and communications. Marketing has evolved to embrace the intensity of the promotional environment and the possibilities afforded by customer databases and relationship management.

Principles as Relevant to New Categories of Brands as to Old Categories of FMCG

I therefore wondered to what extent the ideas in the book would still resonate within this altered and more chaotic world. To my pleasant surprise, the ideas not only still resonate, but also resonate powerfully.

Two brands that are central to the book are Oxo Cubes and Mr Kipling Cakes. The former have been in existence for nearly 100 years and were given new life by the advent of commercial television and JWT's Katie in the 1950s, followed by the Oxo family in the 1980s and 1990s. The latter was an entirely new brand, developed organically by JWT and Stephen in the 1960s and perhaps the one that most clearly encapsulates the *leitmotif* of what Stephen and the book are all about.

Both these brands are still very much alive and well, and have a monetary value that has been crystallized in the white heat of the capital markets only recently. Oxo, for most of its life a property of Unilever, was divested by them in 2001 to the Campbell Soup Company, and

$800 million of goodwill was recognized in the transaction.[1] In 2006 Oxo was among brands that were resold by Campbell's to Premier Foods for £460 million.[2] At the time of writing, Mr Kipling is also due to be acquired by Premier Foods as part of its acquisition of its owner RHM. RHM's cakes business, the main intangible asset of which is Mr Kipling, records the value of these assets as nearly £100 million in 2006.

I think Stephen would have been pleased to see that these brands still possess such demonstrable value so long after their inception. They perfectly illustrate his point that strong, well-developed brands need never wither or die – and that enormous value can be realized from the longevity and durability of what are ultimately mundane, habitually purchased items.

Getting it Right in the First Place

A brand can endure providing, of course, that one gets it right in the first place. The focus of *Developing New Brands* is on how to engineer (a word Stephen would probably have hated) the brand proposition to maximize consumer appeal and loyalty.

The book's starting point is what makes a successful brand per se – essentially a restatement of the ideas expressed in Stephen's article "What is a brand?" (see page 27). In a really lovely passage, Stephen essays the notion of a good brand as a good friend: "*a compendium of virtues and vices*". Stephen's view was that relationships with brands are characterized by all the fickleness, promiscuity and shifting loyalties that characterize real friendships, and that ultimately these friendships will tend to endure if there is an attraction rooted in personalities.

These important ideas are expressed in Stephen's distinctive style, which is simultaneously down to earth and modest in tone, but also incisive and waspish when it needs to be. Stephen liked nothing more than to puncture the pomposity and rhetoric of marketing, its preoccupation with pat concepts and frameworks and its preference for a sort of perpetual sense of urgency over considered strategic thinking.

I have never forgotten in 20 years things like the packshot of the humble Oxo cube captioned with the words "a challenge to life cycle theory".

This collection of Stephen's articles will emerge into a climate where there is considered to be a "crisis in marketing" and something of a loss of confidence among the traditional fmcg players featured in *Developing New Brands*. Have the ideas encapsulated within *Developing New Brands* in some way sowed the seeds of this crisis ... or has the root of the problem been a failure to follow them?

I favour the latter. Viewed from the perspective of more than 30 years, there seems so much more that is right and true about *Developing New Brands* than what is wrong and outmoded.

Finally Even P&G Comes Round to Brand Personality

The current winners in global fmcg are those who continue to follow Stephen's credo of patient evolution of strong brands, based on superior consumer insight and, above all, a culture of never taking life cycle theory at face value. The consumer goods industry's current growth champion, P&G, manages to grow its sales at more or less twice the rate of its underlying markets by continuing to put its faith in it's portfolio of "billion dollar brands", including Tide, Ariel, Crest and Pampers, most of which have been around for decades.

---

[1] The transaction also included Batchelor's and other minor brands, as well as Oxo.
[2] The transaction again also included Batchelor's.

Perhaps the biggest compliment that can be paid to Stephen is that P&G, who for decades eschewed the cult of the (brand) personality, have evolved their model to combine more of a personality-based approach to their strong heritage in developing performance-based propositions.

Relevance to Marketing Services as well as Marketing

In my view it is the marketing services industry that has most to gain from a careful re-reading of Stephen's ideas. The book conveys a strong sense of a man and an agency who were strategic in their outlook, evidence-based and commercially focused on behalf of their clients.

For all the current talk of strategic partnerships and media-neutral solutions. It seems almost unthinkable today that an agency would be capable of designing a new brand from the ground up, like Mr Kipling. This responsibility has shifted to clients themselves or the growing band of brand and identity consultants of various hues. But along with diversity and specialization has come a lot of dilution and corruption of the elegant simplicity of Stephen's approach.

Evidence from consumer behaviour frequently gets ignored; the client's commercial agenda is often misunderstood and plain language becomes supplanted by psychobabble. If there is a way back to the high table for marketing service providers, then *Developing New Brands* maps the route with clarity and eloquence.

16.1

What Makes New Brands Succeed?*

By Stephen King

It is by no means always clear why companies need new brands at all; or if they do, how many they need. Many companies are fairly ambivalent about it. On the one hand, the Chairman and others are fond of saying "New products are the life-blood of this company", and they wonder uneasily how long the profits from existing brands will keep up. On the other hand, their experience of new product development has often been unhappy; it upsets the routine of the company and the shareholders resent the money wasted on failures. So development work is allowed to drift on, but the funds voted to it are kept under strict control; nobody *acts* as if new products were the life-blood of the company. What usually emerges from this is a fairly large number of not terribly expensive new projects, most of which fail and the best of which are only moderate profit-earners. This middle course is the worst of all possible worlds.

There is little doubt that most new brands or products do fail. An A.C. Nielsen Company Limited (1966b) analysis over 14 years showed that 54% of new products were withdrawn after test marketing; and presumably some of those that reached national distribution were later withdrawn too. The 1971 study by Kraushar, Andrews & Eassie, based on Shaw's *Guide*, notes that 410 new food products (including range extensions, but excluding private label and four food categories) were introduced into the UK grocery trade in 1965; five years later 60% of them had disappeared. A National Industrial Conference Board survey (Hopkins and Bailey, 1971), though apparently weighted in favour of major companies and more generally optimistic, still showed that in US consumer goods the failure rate for the median company was 40%.

What is rather more significant is the extent to which *companies* fail in new markets. A 1965 J. Walter Thompson study (Dunbar, 1965) of 29 grocery and household product markets in the UK, also based on Shaw's *Guide*, showed that of the 294 company names entering these markets between 1954 and 1960, 49 per cent had already withdrawn by 1964. It is not as if the companies involved in these failures were inexperienced; most were marketing their established brands successfully enough. The same seems to be true of the US. In one list (Angelus, 1969) of 75 new product failures in 1968, the companies responsible included Menley and James, Heinz, Campbell, DelMonte, American Home, Revlon, General Foods, Procter and Gamble, Colgate. (Of course, a lot of the successes also come from this sort of company.) Nor were most of the failures glorious bold attempts to introduce radical innovations, which failed because they were before their time. On the whole, the products were very similar to those already on the market.

Diagnoses of the reasons tend to be interesting (A.C. Nielsen Company Limited, 1970a; Napier, 1965; National Industrial Conference Board, 1964), but not very helpful. Certainly

---

*Chapter 1 of Stephen King, *Developing New Brands*, Second Edition, J. Walter Thompson, London, 1983. Reproduced with permission.

some of the causes of failure are basic incompetence in a specific skill; for instance, NICB surveys have stressed inadequate market investigations and shown that a particular problem in industrial machinery in the US was that of the new machine turning out to be less durable than the one it was designed to replace. But on the whole the analyses simply show that to be successful a new brand or product has to be "better" than existing ones.

If it is as hard as this for the most experienced marketing companies to develop new brands successfully, why develop them at all? Do all companies need them? If they do, how many do they need? How often do they need them?

WHY NEW BRANDS AT ALL?

The starting point for a new brand policy must be some consideration of what new brands are for and whether they really are necessary. Until a company has worked this out, it will have no idea of the right scale of operations.

Three sorts of reason for trying to develop new brands have been put forward: the product life cycle, the demands of technological change and the need to grow.

The first is very largely bogus. It comes from a misreading of the product life-cycle theory. In simple terms, the theory says that any product's life is in four stages – introduction, growth, maturity and decline. In its original form, this is a respectable enough theory, and it has been shown (Polli and Cook, 1969) to be a fairly good description of what happens in a number of US markets. In a sense, it is bound to be valid, if taken to mean that every product introduced will reach a peak at some time and eventually disappear. The timing will differ, from sets of 1970 World Cup souvenirs, whose cycle might be complete in a year, to bread, which will take many centuries. The trouble has come when this innocent theory has been used operationally. People have said in effect: "Life cycles are getting shorter. Our brand's sales this year are lower than last year; it must be over the top, on the way to decline. We must introduce a great many new brands."

This way of thinking, which is very common, is really fallacious. The theory is descriptive and general; not predictive and rigid. *Above all it applies to products rather than brands.* It says that a product's sales will grow until the needs it meets are satisfied, after which it is likely to grow only as fast as the population with the needs grows; or until some other product emerges that will fill the needs better. Nearly all new products are new means of meeting existing needs. But there is absolutely no reason why a *brand* should not have its product changed or improved to meet its needs better. Only if the brand is rigidly unchanging will it be overtaken and suffer the decline suggested by life-cycle theory.

The astonishing thing is that in many companies whose growing profits over the years have depended almost entirely on one or two steadily growing brands, there are marketing men who can ignore the evidence before them, in favour of their reading of the life-cycle theory. One result can be a self-fulfilling prophecy. The company's major brand has a bad year; so it is said to be in its late maturity stage; funds are withdrawn from it, both to make the most profit out of it while it lasts and to finance new brands; so the next year it does even worse; this confirms the original diagnosis and panic increases; new brands are hustled along faster and faster, and most fail; the company has talked itself into a decline.

Oxo cubes are a good example of the dangers of the life-cycle theory (Figure 16.1). Sales had reached a peak in 1948 and had tended to decline for the next 10 years, despite the fact that until 1957 the price was held steady at one penny per cube – the same as in 1910. It would have been easy to argue that Oxo was at the beginning of the decline stage of its life

Figure 16.1   A challenge to life-cycle theory

cycle. It was old fashioned and had had a good 50-year run; its sales had notably reached a peak during both world wars, when meat was of poor quality and in short supply – hardly the situation in the new affluent UK. The company took the opposite point of view; it invested in Oxo in 1958–59. There was a new marketing management and a strengthened sales force; the cubes were completely repacked; a new unit size was introduced; rather more was spent on advertising and a new agency was appointed, with a new campaign and media plan. Five years later volume sales were up 35% and the brand had become strong enough to stand two price increases. And six years after that, with the aid of a line extension, sales and profits reached new peaks. Against this, any major diversion of resources, through a naïve reading of life-cycle theory, could have ruined the company.

The second quoted reason for developing new brands is related to life-cycle theory, but it is rather more reasonable. It is that technological change is getting so fast that no single brand can keep up with it. Technological change means new products and eventually new products mean new brands. In other words, the number of new brands a company has to produce depends on its product innovation policy. There is a lot in this argument. In most industries, the rate of technological change has accelerated and nowadays few companies could survive for long without some product innovation. Every time a new constructional material or new fibre or new chemical process or new method of food preservation or new control system is developed it will have repercussions over a huge range of companies.

At the same time, there is a long continuum of product innovation. At one end of the scale, there is the policy of a DuPont or an ICI which, backed by huge resources, sets out to create entirely new materials and product types – replacement for steel, replacements for natural fibres, new forms of energy source, new forms of medicine, synthetic protein and so on. At the other end of the scale, there is the sort of product innovation involved in adding a new green flavour to a range of jellies or changing from a bottle to a plastic squeeze-pack.

It is only a few of the largest companies that could afford to innovate in the DuPont way. The research investment is enormous and most of the really striking technical advances – frozen foods, xerography, transistors, penicillin, television – have taken a very long time to emerge as commercial propositions (Adler, 1966). Any company following a product innovation policy towards this end of the scale must inevitably launch many new brands; the sheer number of technical developments dictates it. Not only directly but also as a by-product of the major research projects. For instance, it was DuPont's research into refrigerants that produced, almost incidentally, the polytetrafluoroethylene used to coat non-stick frying pans.

However, most companies are much nearer the other end of the scale, and a policy of merely keeping up to date with technological change does not *necessarily* mean introducing new brands. The rate of change is often grossly exaggerated, and in practice most new products emerge gradually from modification of existing ideas and technology, from putting together familiar things in a slightly different way. All that most companies need in their existing markets is to make sure that their going brands join in the game of technological leapfrog.

In fact, the successful development of new brands does not necessarily require a higher degree of *technical* innovation than is needed for maintaining old brands. Many of the most successful new brands represent only minor advances over the products already on the market. Professor Levitt (1969) has pointed out that the greatest flow of newness in products is not innovation at all, but imitation. He quotes IBM as imitators in computers; Holiday Inns in motels; RCA in television; Lytton in savings and loans. It is almost inevitable that most commercial ventures are based on product imitation and adaptation; there are a great many profitable brands and relatively few inventors and inventions.

The third reason for developing new brands is, for most companies, the only really valid one. Despite the costs and problems and risks, they need them in order to grow at the rate they have set themselves. This is true even where companies have grown by merger or acquisition. However successful their old brands are, there is usually a limit to the rate at which they can be expanded economically and there may even be a finite ceiling to the profits they can generate. Although very often in the short run, investment in existing brands is a better return than the same amount spent on new brands (Van Camp, 1968), the new brands are needed to give a broader base for profits in the long run.

HOW MANY NEW BRANDS?

This analysis has important implications for development policies. If the primary reason for new brands is to build *long-term* sales and profits, then most companies need occasionally to develop a significant new brand. But only occasionally. Most of the time their technical innovation skills will be better used in keeping existing brands up to date, improving or replacing the physical products that are part of those brands.

Most companies find that a huge proportion of their profits comes from one or two well-established brands. If they want to build their profits for the future, then logically they should be trying to develop something similar – another important brand which, maybe from a modest start, gradually emerges as a sustained profit-earner. And yet so often they appear to be looking for something completely different in their new brands – a large number of instant successes. They seem to ignore what it is that has made them successful so far.

The real object of a development programme is to develop a *successful new business*, not to put a lot of new brands on the market. That does not require, and it is not helped by, a state of constant panic. It is not helped by keeping hundreds of projects going, in the hope that by the law of averages one of them will hit the jackpot.

Looking on the object of the exercise as building a new business can transform the company's whole approach. The mystiques of new product development become less frightening. It becomes a more straightforward matter of sensible analysis, proper planning and the application of the right resources. Concentration on developing only a very small number of new brands can dramatically cut down the failure rate. The whole of this book is really about building a new business, by inventing one good brand.

THE PRODUCT AND THE BRAND

Running through all these arguments is the critical distinction between the product and the brand.

This is hardly a new idea; the importance of branding was generally realized nearly a century ago. Gardner and Levy's classic paper "The product and the brand" appeared in 1955. And, although there are fuzzy areas, the distinction is a fairly obvious one. Yet the whole emphasis both in the literature and in practice, has been on developing *new physical products*. Manufacturers of industrial goods especially seem to feel that brands are relevant only to consumer goods and are maybe a reflection of the illogical world of women; in the honest, tough world of heavy industry what are bought and sold are products. This is of course entirely false. The number of pure commodity markets is tiny. Every other market is one in which manufacturers are competing with brands – unique, named articles – whether they are brands of cosmetics or brands of refrigerator or brands of packaged travel or brands of machine tool.

Brands and branding are going to become more and more important (King, 1970); failure to distinguish between product and brand in development work is going to get increasingly expensive. Of course, brands always have been important, and in the UK they were the means for manufacturers of breaking away from domination by the wholesalers at the end of the nineteenth century. But the long period of manufacturer domination, roughly up to the middle of the 1960s in the UK, is showing signs of ending and it will only be by success at branding that manufacturers will continue to show growth in profits. Conditions in the 1970s and beyond are going to be much tougher. There is far less scope today for concentration in numbers of manufacturers – most markets are already dominated by less than five – or for increased profits through economies of scale. The seller's markets of the immediate post-war era have come to an end. Retailers have gained enormously in power, especially where – as in the UK – resale price maintenance is banned. International competition is growing. And buyers show every sign of becoming much more discerning.

These trends have been particularly clear in the grocery trade. A.C. Nielsen Company Limited (1963, 1970b) have shown that, on the whole, where brands have been strongly established (that is, mainly brand leaders), they have tended to gain market share and can command a substantial price premium. Equally, it is clear that cheap private-label brands have grown rapidly over the past five years. What this has clearly meant is a very severe squeeze on both the sales and the price level, hence profitability, of the weaker manufacturers' brands.

The same thing is happening in consumer durables and in industrial markets. Buying power is being concentrated, perhaps a little more slowly, over the whole retail trade. In the most technically advanced industries, Government contracts are becoming more important and

Government buying methods tougher. And of course the buyers of most industrial goods are themselves manufacturers; as they grow and merge they will develop greater buying power.

Manufacturers in fact are likely to face increasing pressures – through increasing competition, pressure from their buyers and the rapid copying of their physical products (as happens with private-label brands). In this situation their profits will depend critically on the difference between the product and the brand. For their *products* they will get the commodity price, giving them a fairly low margin, and then only if they are efficient. For their *brands* they will get the commodity price plus whatever the brand is worth beyond the product. That is, the level of profits will depend on the values added by the brand (Mayer, 1958/1961; Young, 1963).

Hard as it may be for established brands, it is likely to be even harder for the new brand. Unless it can have added values built into it from the start, it is unlikely to be successful in building a long-term business. Just what these added values are and how to get them is central to what makes a new brand successful.

WHAT ADDED VALUES?

In fact, what makes a new brand successful is becoming like an old one. We should stop worrying so much about how to launch new brands (the launching is really not very difficult), and concentrate on how to invent an established brand. Our models should be brands like Persil, Kellogg's Corn Flakes, Weetabix, Guinness, Bird's Eye, Oxo, Kit-E-Kat, Heinz soups and baked beans in the UK, Campbells soups in the USA, Lifebuoy, Nescafé, Maxwell House, Kodak, Polo mints, Parker pens, the Cortina, Xerox, IBM. They may have had their ups and downs, but all these have established themselves strongly enough to bring in good profits over many years. They were all new brands once.

What do they have that lesser brands do not? Clearly they have had a high standard of production efficiency, control and day-to-day marketing. But that is true of many brands which, though fairly successful, are nowadays increasingly having their profit margins reduced. What is it that the really successful brands have that is extra? What are their added values?

We can get some insights by examining one particular post-war brand, which was first marketed on a large scale in the mid-1950s, became brand leader in 1961, and has remained leader ever since.

The brand is Andrex (Figure 16.2), the first nationally branded soft toilet paper in the UK. Papermaking itself is complex and highly capital intensive; but the finishing production process – paper converting – is not terribly difficult and can be started up on a very small scale. And this is a market in which, for obvious reasons, the marketing man is limited in all sorts of ways.

It might easily have become a near-commodity market, *had the major manufacturer let it.* There are many less obvious markets which have become virtually commodity markets through the main manufacturers failing to realize the values of branding – the UK concentrated soft drink market, for instance.

Andrex was on the market in the 1940s, but its real growth started after Bowater-Scott was formed in 1956 and took over the originating company, St Andrew's Mills. Its main direct competitor was Kimberly Clark's Delsey.

The introduction of soft toilet paper had greatly increased the total market (previously made up of the traditional "hard" paper), and by 1961 the prospects looked good enough to tempt in other manufacturers, both large and small. Private label and price-cutting started earlier here than in most markets; and as both Andrex and Delsey had started off with chemists' retail margins (grocery shops only started selling toilet paper in a big way in the UK in the

Figure 16.2 A triumph for added values

early 1960s), there was plenty of scope for price-cutting. In fact, the retail price of toilet paper declined during the second half of the 1960s.

By 1963, the two new brands had made good progress. Andrex had a 22% share of the market volume, and that was enough to make it clear brand leader. Delsey was not far behind, with 16%. But they were coming under increasing pressure from the retail trade, particularly the rapidly growing multiples. And from that time on the two manufacturers diverged in their response.

One effect of the retailer pressure was that most manufacturers switched their marketing funds from media advertising into trade discounts and promotions. That is, increasingly they were cutting their prices, selectively, to certain retailers; they were accepting lower margins. The net sales value per case of their brands decreased, and they were making up for it by cutting their marketing budgets and their links with the consumer. But there was a great difference between Andrex and Delsey here. By the end of 1965, Delsey had virtually stopped advertising and was concentrating almost entirely on discounting. Andrex kept a balance between the two, even though its advertising expenditure remained at a relatively low level.

The results of these policies were quite dramatic. The cheaper brands of soft paper gained share rapidly. Andrex continued to grow steadily. Delsey slipped back to its share of 1960.

By 1969 Andrex had reached a dominating 31% share of market value and was strong enough to hold a retail selling price well above the market average. Throughout the period it contributed a high proportion of Bowater-Scott's profits. It did this in the face of considerable pressure from retailers, at the time when retail price maintenance was abandoned, when the retail selling price of toilet paper was declining and when multiples were growing very rapidly. The reason was that retailers needed Andrex, because it had been made in this relatively short period into a brand that *consumers valued highly*.

Percentage of housewives attributing to each brand:

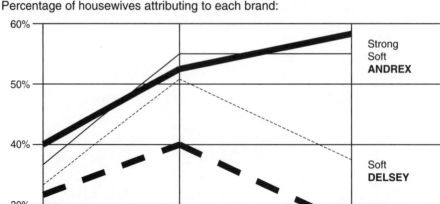

Figure 16.3   Changes in attitude to Andrex and Delsey: Delsey's reputation for softness and strength declined after stopping advertising in 1965

Continuous attitude research showed just how consumers' ideas of the relative values of Andrex and Delsey changed (Figure 16.3). Up to 1966 the two brands were advancing at much the same rate; indeed Delsey's reputation kept up much longer that its market share.

But after that time Andrex continued to advance, while Delsey's reputation for qualities like softness and strength declined. In fact, there was no evidence that objectively the standards of the two physical products diverged in any significant way. Nor is it likely that people suddenly felt that Delsey was not as soft or as strong as it used to be, or that Andrex had got stronger or softer. What seems to have happened is that people simply valued Delsey, as a brand, a little less highly than they used to, Andrex a little more highly.

If Andrex developed more added values – values beyond the physical, functional ones of the product – where did these values come from? It seems clear that there were many sources, all blended into an overall impression of greater value. First, Andrex's early leadership in soft toilet paper and in innovations such as a colour range. The pioneer can clearly get a considerable advantage, if marketed properly. For instance, one Nielsen analysis (1962, 1966a, 1966b) of 27 grocery fields showed that, after a minimum of three years on the market for any brand, the pioneer brand was selling on average more than twice as much as the first "me-too" brand and nearly four times as much as the second "me-too" brand. But that was not the whole answer, because the pioneering advantage wears off in time. Andrex did sell roughly twice as much as Delsey in 1958, but only 40% more in 1963 when their promotional policies diverged. By 1969 it was about three times as much. Secondly, consistently high quality in product and packaging material. Thus good value for money. Again, while this could explain Andrex's success, it could hardly explain the pattern of brand shares after 1963. Delsey was strong there too, and indeed pioneered the polythene pack. Thirdly, Andrex's direct relationship with the final consumer, the housewife. It is not only the fact that Andrex continued to advertise, while Delsey did not. It is the way in which Bowater-Scott used advertising and packaging and merchandising; the way in which Andrex talked to the consumer. Or, to broaden it a little, the consistent way in which Andrex and its values were presented to the public *as a brand*. This was clearly a crucial element in the success.

We can get an idea of the values and strengths of Andrex as a brand by looking at its advertising over the years. There have been many different campaigns, no doubt of differing efficiency, created by different people, adapted by different people, judged and accepted by different people. Different media have been used. Some have concentrated on the softness of the product; some on the strength; some on both; some on neither. Superficially they vary a lot, and yet through them there is a great consistency. *They were dominated by the personality of Andrex itself.* What runs through them is not any unique product claim or unique feature or functional description. It is an attitude of mind and a tone of voice and a set of values that belong to Andrex. Andrex emerges as having a clear personality. She is reliable, dainty, clean-living, domesticated, family-centred; she radiates niceness and confidence in her ability to manage. It is this that makes Andrex, as it were, a nice person to have about the house.

It seems clear, in fact, that Andrex has succeeded as a new brand and a profit-earner because it has added values beyond the physical and functional ones. These added values have contributed to a clear and likeable personality for the brand.

The same is true of many of the more successful new brands in the UK since the war; an element of pioneering, good-quality product (but not necessarily outstanding) and added values through communication. Bird's Eye pioneered frozen foods, with product quality higher than people were used to in processed food and with a personality combining efficiency, hygiene, confidence and completeness; the three elements together have given it a massive share of market for 15 years. Lucozade, a fairly simple glucose mixture with the sort of personality that some people like in a sickroom. Ribena, a blackcurrant cordial, with the personality of a young mother hopeful for the success of her children. Babycham, a fairly conventional perry, given a totally new personality by its advertising and packaging. After Eight mints, the combination of a new sort of peppermint cream, a high-quality product and a highly distinctive personality, expressed in every contact with its public. It is easy enough to add to this list: Camay, Vesta, Ariel, Embassy, Fairy toilet soap, G-Plan, the Mini, Moulton bicycles, Instamatic cameras, Angel Delight. The balance between the elements of product innovation, product quality and brand personality varies; but in every case the successful result has been a blend of the three.

It is easy to assume that this only applies to consumer goods, maybe even only to fast-moving grocery goods. Certainly there are differences of degree, but the principle applies to industrial goods too. An industrial brand will not work as well if it relies solely on product innovation or product quality; to be successful it must have added values and a brand personality. Even patents are not normally a great protection against rapid copying; most patents are highly specific and it is difficult to close all loopholes which might allow in a competitor with a copy plus minor adaptation. It is an illusion that the makers of industrial goods do not need added values. Any mechanical or electronic product needs to be backed with the values of reliability and efficient after-sales service. And as industrial products become more complex, the added values will become more important; just as for the housewife today after-sales service may become the most important feature of the washing machine. IBM has dominated the computer business, not necessarily because its products are more innovative or functionally better than those of other computer manufacturers, but because an IBM computer represents advice and aid on uses for computers, programming services, advice on information systems, training programmes and a whole mass of instructional material. More than that, IBM has a personality which reflects zeal and self-regard so powerfully that it is hard to believe that it would allow itself to be seen to be inefficient. The IBM personality has deeply affected its employees; and as a result it is very rarely seen as inefficient. It has pursued added values harder than the others, and has reaped the reward.

The fact is that practically all goods are bought on the basis of repeat purchase or reordering. Obviously most consumer goods are, but it is true of industrial goods too. Thus the values of the new brand will nearly always depend to some extent on previous experience. The reputation of the manufacturer of a new industrial product is not just a factor affecting it; it is part of the new product – an added value. Levitt (1969) talks of the "augmented-product concept" and sums it up neatly:

> Whether the product is cold-rolled steel or hot cross buns, whether accountancy or delicacies, competitive effectiveness increasingly demands that the successful seller offer his prospect and his customer more than the generic product itself. He must surround his generic product with a cluster of value satisfactions that differentiates his total offering from his competitors'. He must provide a total proposition, the content of which exceeds what comes out at the end of the assembly line.

Brand personality is perhaps a less abstract term than "cluster of value satisfactions", but it expresses the same notion of a range of attributes fused together. The Andrex case history suggests that people do choose their brands in the same way that they choose their friends. There are degrees of friendship, and people very rarely stick exclusively to just one friend; in the same way there are degrees of brand loyalty, very rarely loyalty to one brand alone. Friendships come and go, according sometimes to what the friends say and do. Not everyone will like the same person, though some are more popular than others. People do not usually choose their friends solely because of specific skills or physical attributes, although such things can be very important. They usually choose them because, in addition to the skills and physical characteristics (or maybe in spite of them), they simply like them as people. It is the total person that is chosen as a friend, not a compendium of virtues and vices. The choice and use of brands is just the same.

To some people the whole concept of brand personality might seem a rather fanciful way of describing why one brand is valued more than another. But there is overwhelming evidence (King, 1970) that non-functional values sway people's choices – evidence from blind *v.* named product tests, pack testing, the placebo effect, the Hawthorn experiments (Brown, 1954), as well as most experimental psychology. Just as it is a fact that in industry the contract does not by any means always go to the company that meets the strict specification at the lowest cost.

There is also some direct evidence on brand personalities. Pilot research by J. Walter Thompson has made it quite clear that brands do have personalities and that people can talk fluently about them. Indeed talking about brands as people rather than things usually brings out a much richer vocabulary. These brand personalities tend to be consistent, though what is one person's praise is another's condemnation. For instance, Persil was seen by some as happy and contented; by others as dull and lacking in ambition – two facets of the same personality.

As people become richer, added values and brand personalities are likely to become more important to them. They will get more and more of their rewards in life from the non-functional. One man will get them from listening to a string quartet; another from polishing the "unnecessary" trim on his new car. Clothes are an example of the trend. They are no longer mainly for protection; they are more a demonstration of one's personality and values or of how one wants to be perceived. It was always true of high fashion; now it is true of mass-market clothes. The added values here have become more important than the functional, and this will become increasingly true of other product types. People will require style as well as performance. They will increasingly value brands for *who they are* as much as for *what they do*.

This theory of added values is critically important for new brands. It suggests that no new brand can hope to succeed if it does not have values beyond the functional. But is goes rather further than that. The added values are not simply something lumped onto the brand once the functional features have been settled. They are an integral part of its personality, its essence, its *raison d' etre. The new brand must be conceived as this totality of functional and non-functional values from the very beginning*.

The idea of added values certainly comes mainly from looking at old-established brands. But applying it to the development of new brands is more than just a theoretical leap in the dark. In fact, it illuminates all that we know about how new brands actually do behave. The importance of these added values emerges clearly from analysis of hard factual data.

HOW DO NEW BRANDS BEHAVE?

Today there is enough general information, from retail audits and consumer panels, to show fairly clearly how new grocery products behave. The evidence is that, despite great diversity of product type, there are some typical patterns of sales of new brands which show what is important to success and what is less important.

Retail Audit Data

An analysis by E.J. Davis (1965) of 44 test market operations for consumer goods in the Southern, Tyne-Tees and South Wales television areas, using BMRB Retail Audit data, showed how distribution gradually builds up for new brands. There was a fairly smooth curve in cumulative distribution, with the "shoulders" of the curve reached on average in about three months. In these particular 44 cases the mean distribution at this shoulder was 35% of grocers' shops handling. A Nielsen analysis of 29 new brands (1969, 1970a) showed the same pattern, with a mean sterling distribution of about 38% in grocers at the shoulder, after six months. (The small discrepancy between the Nielsen and the BMRB figures can be largely accounted for by interpretation of what is the shoulder.) After this point, distribution increased at a much slower rate, reaching an average of 43% in the Nielsen sample after 12 months. There were quite wide differences between brands judged by Nielsen to be successes and those judged to be failures; at the shoulder, the distribution of the successes was about 20 percentage points higher than that of the failures, and after that the gap got wider. In other words, the success or failure of the brand was apparent after only a few months (see Figure 16.4).

There are two important implications from these findings. The first is that reasonably good distribution is correlated with success. But this is not to say that it is the *cause* of success; it seems rather more likely that it is the *result* of success. In the Nielsen analysis the gap between successes and failures was less in multiples and co-ops than in independents – indeed some failures achieved better initial distribution than some successes. This and the fact that the gap

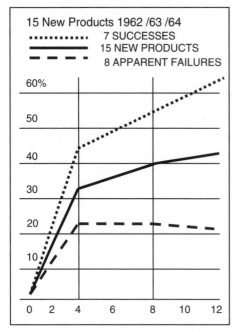
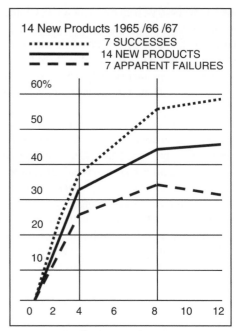

Figure 16.4 £ Distribution of new products: Shops weighted for turnover importance. Nielsen show a link between distribution levels and success or failure for new brands

only really opened mainly according to how well or badly the brand performs. The second implication is that any new brand will have to make its mark in the first month or two when it is not very widely distributed.

These distribution figures are a background to the findings of the Davis study on consumer purchases of new brands (Figure 16.5). There was a typical pattern here too. Consumer purchases rose fairly quickly to a peak, then declined to a relatively stable volume, from which growth (where it came at all) tended to be gradual. In half of the 44 cases the peak level of consumer purchases was reached in the third four-weekly audit period, and it was usually (but not always) in the same period as the brand reached the shoulder of its distribution curve. Virtually all the new brands had reached their peak of consumer sales by the fourth audit period – that is, around 14 weeks after they were launched.

The decline from the peak to the stable level took rather longer, but three-quarters of the brands had stablilized six months after introduction and the rest within eight months. A key finding from the analysis was that the "drop" factor – the percentage decline from the peak to the stable level – appeared to be the same for a brand in all its test marketing areas, even though the levels of peak consumer sales differed widely.

In other words, the amount of drop is related to the brand itself rather than to external factors like regional differences, competitors or differing sales skills.

The only really credible interpretation of these characteristic patterns shown by retail audit data is that a lot of initial buyers of the new brand come in during the first three months or so, as distribution climbs to its shoulder. As JWT's *New Housewife* survey (Tarrant, 1967) showed, the most frequent source of learning about new brands is through shop display or retailers'

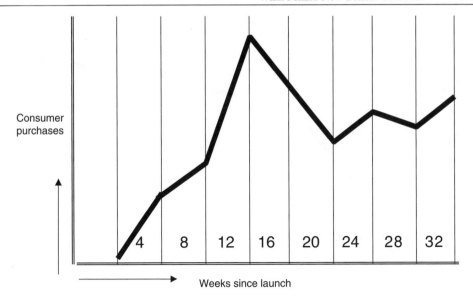

Figure 16.5 Consumer purchases of new brands. Typical pattern of consumer purchases for new brands (Davis, 1964, 1965)
Source: BMRB Retail Audit

recommendations. But some of these new buyers continue to buy very infrequently, and some do not buy again at all. During the next three months or so the drop in consumer sales, caused basically by the lack of repeat-buying by disappointed triers, is offset to some extent by some more people becoming buyers for the first time; this is one reason why the decline from peak to stable is more gradual than the climb from nothing to peak. But by six months or so after the launch, new first-time buyers have ceased to be a *major* factor.

The brand has settled down and consumer sales depend on the established repeat-buying rate. Growth from now on, in distribution, consumer sales, new buyers and the repeat-buying rate will be gradual. That is, unless the manufacturer takes action so dramatic as to alter all the patterns.

Consumer Panel Data

There has been a great deal of analysis of household buying data for new brands, from the MRCA consumer panel in the USA and the Attwood panel in the UK (Ahl, 1970; Fourt and Woodlock, 1960; Parfitt and Collins, 1968; Woodlock, 1964). On the whole, the findings support this interpretation of retail audit data. There is a characteristic curve of cumulative penetration for a new brand; that is, of households ever buying it. This penetration curve reaches its shoulder relatively quickly – in the case of 24 new grocery brands studied by Attwood it was within six months of introduction. One US analysis suggests that the shoulder is related to the number of new buyers attracted during the fourth average buying cycle; that is, at the point of time from launching that is three to four times the average interval between purchases of the product type. (The interval will, of course, vary from product to product – it might be two weeks for tea and two months for canned peaches.) After that growth is much slower, but the evidence is that there will be a fairly regular small gain for years, from new triers and new households. Thus after a brand has been on the market for five years or so it is quite common for

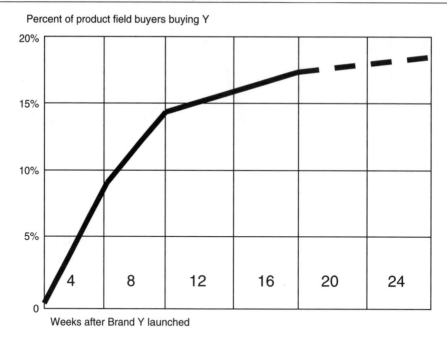

Figure 16.6   Cumulative penetration of Brand Y

the number of households buying it during, say, three months to be a relatively small proportion of those who have ever bought it. But the vast majority of buyers within the first year or two will have bought it during the three or four months after its introduction (Figure 16.6).

The curve of the repeat-purchasing rate is the converse of this (Figure 16.7). Parfitt and Collins' analyses of Attwood data for 24 new brands showed that it tends to start off high and reaches a lower stable level after about three or four months. These two curves, of penetration and repeat purchasing, had reached sufficiently stable levels after six months to allow extremely accurate forecasts of brand share 12 to 18 months later.

The implication of this is that, in the brand's first few months, there is a rapid influx of the most interested buyers, who continue to buy fairly frequently. The less interested are also coming in, but more gradually; they buy less frequently, and thus dilute the total repeat-buying rate. The uninterested – those who do not become buyers in the first six months or so – may not try the new brand for several years, if ever. This interpretation is directly confirmed by case-history studies on the Attwood panel, which showed that on average the sooner the buyer enters the market for a particular brand, the higher will be that buyer's repeat-purchasing rate. The early buyers have a disproportionate influence on the brand's ultimate market share. Thus, although dramatic marketing activities, such as massive promotions or price cutting, can sometimes improve the cumulative penetration of the new brand, the extra buyers gained tend to have a relatively low repeat-purchasing rate. Parfitt and Collins's general impression was that "it is comparatively easy, within limits, to influence cumulative penetration, but it is extremely difficult to create or influence repeat-purchasing for any length of time". Their conclusions about the reasons for failure of a new brand made much the same point: "Failure generally takes the form of exceptionally low repeat-purchasing rates; that is, the brand makes a reasonable penetration into the market but very few people continue to buy it."

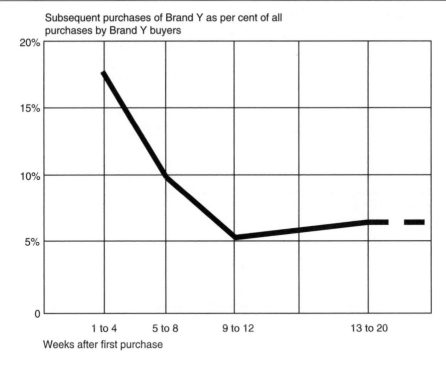

Subsequent purchases of Brand Y as per cent of all purchases by Brand Y buyers

Figure 16.7   Repeat purchasing of Brand Y. Typical pattern of growth in number of households trying a new brand; and typical decline in repeat-purchasing rate (Parfitt and Collins, 1968)

In time, it should be possible to compare the behaviour of new brands with the "norms" of consumer buying established by Ehrenberg (e.g. Ehrenberg, 1969, 1970; Ehrenberg and Goodhardt, 1968). The two case histories published so far by him suggest that it can take a long time for a new brand to settle into the buying pattern of its market. A tentative conclusion from the data is that the difference in pattern for new brands is due to irregularity of buying as much as to infrequency.

Survey Data

Continuous attitude information shows the same sort of picture. Data from the Advertising Planning Index on the introduction of Golden Oxo showed that penetration of households reached a first shoulder at 17% after about six months. It was then sharply increased to 37% by sampling and coupon distribution. However, the number of housewives saying they had bought more than once followed the characteristic penetration curve, only reaching 17% some 18 months after introduction. In other words, the majority of those brought in by sampling or coupon were once-only buyers.

The Total Appeal

One clear conclusion emerges from all these analyses; the new brand tends to set its own pattern. The quickly reached stable level of consumer sales depends mainly on how many people are interested enough to try it in the early months and how the first triers react to it. The regularity of the drop factor, the crucial importance of the repeat-purchasing rate and the tendency of the important buyers to come in first all point to one thing. What makes for success is the *nature of the brand*. No amount of marketing skills or forced distribution or massive promotions can do much for a brand whose total appeal is not quite right.

At first sight, it may not seem very startling to conclude that success or failure depends on how satisfied the consumer is with the brand in use. But in fact it shows us where to concentrate. The actual business of launching and distributing the brand can, if it is done badly enough, make the brand fail; but, however well it is done, it cannot by itself make the brand succeed. And bearing in mind that it is very rare indeed for a brand to be launched when its physical product is noticeably *worse* than existing competitors', it seems that product parity or minor product improvement is not enough to ensure success. What really seems to matter in the marketplace is the *total range of satisfactions* that the new brand offers its early and most interested triers.

ANATOMY OF THE SUCCESSFUL NEW BRAND

Working out why the old-established brand leaders continue to bring in the profits, and analysing the ways in which successful new brands actually start to build up their sales, make it clear that there are certain essential ingredients for success. They seem straightforward enough, but their implications can have a dramatic effect on the way in which companies set their new brand objectives, the sort of organizations they need, their whole approach to development problems and the working methods they use.

There are three elements to the successful new brand, and they run as a constant theme through the whole development programme:

1. It must be salient and relevant to people's needs, wants or desires.
2. It must be a coherent totality.
3. It must be a unique blend of appeals.

It Must be Salient and Relevant to People's Needs, Wants or Desires

That is, the new brand must stand out from the crowd and it must satisfy the whole range of people's wants in a product type, not merely the functional needs. Consumer appeal is today a fairly standard part of the marketing orthodoxy. Levitt (1960), in his famous article "Marketing myopia", warns very powerfully against confusing means, which are what most concern manufacturers, and ends, which are really all that interest the consumer deeply. What we need for planning new brands is to get back to basic motivations and human activities; not to be too concerned with the existing means of meeting the needs. And this affects both the way in which objectives are set and all the methods by which the new brand is created and evaluated.

It is by no means an easy principle to put into practice. If the objectives are set too broadly then nothing practical seems to follow. On the other hand, failure to understand that a new brand must satisfy the *full range* of needs and desires can be very expensive. DuPont's Corfam is an example. Corfam was a substitute material for leather, launched by DuPont in 1963 after about 30 years of discussion, research and development. Leather is chemically a very complex material, the structure of whole fibres varies through the thickness of the hide, allowing it to absorb and evaporate moisture. In shoes this gives it qualities of softness, durability and resilience, while it allows the feet to breathe. After a long and troublesome period of bridging the gap between laboratory and production line, DuPont reckoned they had perfected their material. They launched it with the thoroughness to be expected of them – it is said that the brand name was adopted from an original list of 153,000. By all accounts they appear to have marketed it very skilfully. They did not make the mistake of launching a revolutionary *product*. They anticipated competition and launched a revolutionary *brand*. After about four years the competition began to materialize, and even the leather industry was shaken out of its myopia. But Corfam was well established then and seemed set for a huge success (Gerlach and Wainwright, 1970).

By 1970, the situation looked rather different. DuPont had not managed to reduce production costs of Corfam a great deal, and thus one of its advantages – smaller wastage in shoemaking – had not been fully exploited. Sales were building up, but simply not fast enough. When DuPont decided in March 1971 to stop production, its cumulative losses were said to be over $80 million – no doubt a world record for a new brand.

The basic cause of failure was probably that it is not yet possible to imitate leather synthetically at an economic cost. But in many ways the real problem with Corfam was that it was not relevant to people's total needs. In most respects Corfam was no better than leather, and it did not take a shine quite as well or adapt itself to the shape of the foot quite as well. In one respect however it was markedly superior: it wore much longer. The question is whether a material that is more expensive than leather but longer lasting represents the real desires of buyers of shoes. What has happened in shoes is that cheaper synthetic materials have been used in increasing quantities, particularly PVC. They have been acceptable partly because women's shoes tend to be more ventilated than men's and do not need the same porous material. But the question of relevance to needs goes much deeper than that, to the very nature of the rewards of shoes. It looks as if DuPont, with all their experience, had concentrated too much on the function of shoes – protection of the feet and comfort for walking. At the non-functional level shoes are clearly much more than this – an intrinsic part of fashion, an expression of one's mood or an extension of one's personality, a status symbol, an accessory, a demonstration of style. Durability is irrelevant to all this. What some people want is traditional style, and Corfam could not challenge leather for them. What others want is cheap, up-to-date, throwaway style. If the product lasts indefinitely and costs a lot, it is a positive embarrassment.

The moral for the new brand is clear. It must come not only from the consumer's needs and wants, but from the *totality* of his needs and wants, functional and non-functional.

It Must be a Coherent Totality

All the evidence makes it clear that a successful new brand must be a totality, not a collection of little bits – however good the individual bits may be. The implications of the retail audit and consumer panel data, those of blind versus named product tests, brand personality research, as well as plain common sense, all suggest strongly that the difference between success and failure lies in the totality of the new brand. People buy brands in shops, not concepts or naked physical products or propositions or attributes or special features.

It is clear too that all the elements of the brand are interrelated. The way a food product tastes depends on the style of the pack, and the way the pack is perceived and appreciated and remembered depends on the taste. If the style of pack of a new brand is changed radically, then the people attracted to it will differ and so will their tastes and price expectations. A change to a higher price is likely to require a more refined physical product and more expensive pack; and so on. It is fairly obvious that all the aspects of a new brand are interrelated; yet all too often we find marketing men trying to test them in isolation or predict the results of varying one element in isolation. Concepts are tested as forms of words; tastes are tested apart from names or packs; packs are tested apart from physical products or prices; names are tested on their own.

Looking at the new brand as a whole certainly presents problems of design, planning and evaluation. But if we do not, we shall end up with something that is an Identikit, not a person.

It Must be a Unique Blend of Appeals

The need for uniqueness hardly needs further stress; it is the difference between the brand and the product. Only if the brand has no adequate substitute, only if it can create a sort of monopoly in the mind of the consumer, will it be able to sustain profits against competition over the years.

The elements to be blended are essentially of two different kinds: physical things and communications – on the one hand, the product and on the other, the name, reputation of manufacturer, pack, styling, advertising, merchandising, word-of-mouth and other associations. The balance differs in different industries. In cosmetics a new brand's communications are of crucial importance and can succeed despite a completely standard set of physical products; in machine tools a good new physical product can overcome mediocre communications. But in any market there must be a blend. It was always a myth about the world beating a path to the door of the man who invents an improved mousetrap.

The way these appeals are blended is less simple and, as Corfam showed, it is easy to miss out some elements. For any new brand the appeals lie in three areas: the senses, the reason and the emotions.

Appeal to the Senses

How the brand appeals to the senses of smell, taste, touch, sight or hearing. For instance:

A soup: its taste; smell; colour, etc.
A floor polish: its consistency; colour; smell, etc.
A power drill: its colour; general or surface design; weight and feel in the hand; size;
                noise when running; ease of use and adjustment; length of cable, etc.

Appeal to the Reason

The appeal of what the brand contains or what it does, the basic functional appeal – is *raison dêtre*. For instance:

A soup: its convenience; quality or amount of ingredients; protein content;
                suitability for, say, old people; low calorie content, etc.
A floor polish: its value for money; ease in dispensing or using; speed; durability; depth
                of finish; double action, cleaning and polishing; germicide content, etc.
A power drill: its speed of drilling; power; adjustability; safety features; range of
                accessories; guarantee; after-sales service; durability, etc.

Appeal to the Emotions

The appeal of the style and nature and associations of the brand. Appeals to the emotions make up a very large part of the total brand personality, just as they do with people. Our total judgement of people is certainly governed by their looks and by what they do (their appeals to our senses and reason), but perhaps rather more by their style and manner, their house and clothes and friends. For instance:

A soup: its style of cooking – experimental or plain English; real meal or quick snack; farm house or continental; simple or complex, etc.

A floor polish: its approach to polishing – hard work that is rewarding in itself or a chore made easy; synthetic or natural; tough or delicate; a powerful workman or an understanding friend, etc.

A power drill: its approach to work – industrial competence or understanding of the do-it-yourselfers' problems; simple or complicated; rewarding in itself or through its results; stylish or rugged; male or female, etc.

Clearly the appeals in each of these areas affects those in the other two. For instance, the colour of the drill will affect it on the stylish/rugged scale and it may affect people's beliefs about its power. (Levitt (1969) quotes the case of a coloured front panel on a $600 piece of electronic equipment that substantially improved the interest shown in it by expert equipment buyers.) It is skill in blending these appeals as much as skill in making individual improvements that leads to success.

There are some solid advantages in analysing the appeals of a new brand in this way. First, it means inevitably looking at the brand from the consumer's point of view; we are less likely to run into problems of irrelevance to people's real wants. Secondly, it helps us to be comprehensive. Thirdly, as will become clear, it is a division of appeals which can help to blend the physical product and the communication elements. Fourthly, it relates specifically to different types of consumer research throughout the whole development process.

THE NEED FOR THEORY

These pages spent on analysis of what makes new brands succeed may seem rather over-theoretical to the manufacturer who simply wants to get on with the job. But in many ways understanding the nature of new brands is the most important part of the whole operation. These three apparently simple requirements for a new brand – its salience and relevance to needs; its totality; its unique blend of appeals to the senses, the reason and the emotions – dominate every decision about organization and every part of the development programme suggested in the rest of this book.

REFERENCES

A.C. Nielsen Company Limited (1962) "Seven keys to a strong consumer franchise", *Nielsen Researcher*, May/June.

A.C. Nielsen Company Limited (1963) "Cost of leadership – today and tomorrow", *Nielsen Researcher*, January/February.

A.C. Nielsen Company Limited (1966a) "Some new guidelines for developing the product line", *Nielsen Researcher*, January/February.

A.C. Nielsen Company Limited (1966b) *How to Strengthen Your Product Plan.*

A.C. Nielsen Company Limited (1969) "New product distribution levels", *Nielsen Researcher*, January/February.

A.C. Nielsen Company Limited (1970a) "The realities of new product marketing", *Nielsen Researcher*, January/February.

A.C. Nielsen Company Limited (1970b) "Manufacturers' advertised brands", *Nielsen Researcher,* July/August.

Adler, L. (1966) "Time lag in new product development", *Journal of Marketing*, January.

Ahl, D.H. (1970) "New product forecasting using consumer panels", *Journal of Marketing Research*, May.

Angelus, T.L. (1969) "Why do most new products fail?" *Advertising Age*, 24 March.

Brown, J.A.C. (1954) *The Social Psychology of Industry*, pp. 69ff. London: Penguin.

Davis, E.J. (1964/1965) *The Sales Curves of New Products*. Market Research Society Conference and J. Walter Thompson Company Limited.

Dunbar, D.S. (1965) "New lamps for old", *The Grocer*, 3 April.

Ehrenberg, A.S.C. (1969) "Towards an integrated theory of consumer behaviour", *Journal of the Market Research Society*, October.

Ehrenberg, A.S.C. (1970) "Predicting the behaviour of new brands", Paper read at American Marketing Association Conference, September.

Ehrenberg, A.S.C. and Goodhardt, G.J. (1968) "Repeat buying of a new brand", *British Journal of Marketing*, autumn.

Fourt, L.A. and Woodlock, J.W. (1960) "Early prediction of market success for new grocery products", *Journal of Marketing*, October.

Gardner, B.B. and Levy, S.J. (1955) "The product and the brand", *Harvard Business Review*, March/April.

Gerlach, J.T. and Wainwright, C.A. (1970) *Successful Management of New Products*, p. 153. London: Pitman Publishing.

Hopkins, D.S. and Bailey, E.L. (1971) "New-product pressures", *The Conference Board Record*, June.

King, S.H.M. (1970) *What is a Brand?* London: J. Walter Thompson Company Limited.

Kraushar, Andrews & Eassie Limited (1971) *New Products in the Grocery Trade.*

Levitt, T. (1960) "Marketing myopia", *Harvard Business Review*, July/August.

Levitt, T. (1969) *The Marketing Mode*, p. 54. New York: McGraw-Hill Book Company.

Mayer, M. (1958/1961) *Madison Avenue, U.S.A.*, p. 320, London: Penguin Books and p. 309, New York: Harper & Row.

Napier, J.P. (1965) "What percentage of new products fail, and why?", *Advertiser's Weekly*, 5 November.

National Industrial Conference Board (1964) "Why new products fail", *The Conference Board Record*, October.

Parfitt, J.H. and Collins, B.J.K. (1968) "The use of consumer panels for brand-share prediction", *Journal of Marketing Research*, May .

Polli, R. and Cook, V.J. (1969) "Validity of the product life cycle", *Journal of Business*, October.

Tarrant, M. (1967) *The New Housewife*, p. 94. London: J. Walter Thompson Company Limited.

Van Camp, R.W. (1968) "Essential elements for new product success", p. 7 in *New Product Development*. American Marketing Association.

Woodlock, J.W. (1964) "A model for early prediction of a new product's future", *Commentary* (now *Journal of the Market Research Society*), summer.

Young, J.W. (1963) *How to Become an Advertising Man*, p. 69. Chicago: Advertising Publications Inc.

The Retail Revolution gets Underway

By Andrew Seth, Chairman, Plum Baby

An introduction to:

17.1   What's New about the New Advertisers?

In 1978 a scruffy, down-at-heel retailer called Tesco mounted a survival operation in its stores called "Checkout". It was to change a lot of things in their favour. Engagingly Stephen notes that retailer advertising had risen from 1.6% of "all expenditure" to 3.3% (!) – scarcely, he says, revolutionary progress but the beginnings of a trend that has by no means run out of steam three decades later. Stephen's far-sightedness did not end there.

He goes on to observe the growth of "service" advertisers in the UK economy. Remember that this was *before* the huge changes begun in the 1980s as manufacturing companies went to the wall and were gradually replaced by the new service businesses that dominate our British economic landscape today.

Stephen quotes the emergence of manufacturing's declining profit spiral, noting how while these companies were finding it much more difficult to make returns, the retailers were finding it a lot easier. He could not have foreseen how far this particular change would take us and how massive the shift in balance of power has been since then. Nor is it by any means exhausted yet.

In passing, Stephen notes other emergent but seminal changes in society as a whole. Despite perceived endemic economic weakness in the UK – recall that the 1970s was the decade that began with the 3-day week and finished with the IMF heavies taking Chancellor Healey firmly to task – Stephen describes Britain as experiencing "the new affluence" to which he adds the existence of a *new individualism*, based on new sets of individual and discovered values in which the better informed and more challenging members of society could revel.

And finally he makes the illuminating observation that late 1970 consumers appear to want brands that offer not just functional advantage but something called "enjoyment" as well. "Good heavens – what will they want next?" I hear him saying. Now we know that the great brands must marry emotional strength (the *affective charge* as it was sometimes called) to performance to succeed.

Four Predictions

I turn now to the heart of Stephen's *Admap* piece where he offered, in his usual gentle but reasoned way, four predictions.

Growth for Some (Heavily Supported) Mid Market fmcg Brands

The first was about fmcg or grocery brands. He forecast that there would be growth for a clutch of strong middle-market brands, with high repeat purchase levels, that would link product advantage (NB these still matter) to *added values* (a new idea in the 1970s, but one we named a business for in the 1990s) that were non-functional.

These pillar consumer brands which could unite purpose advantage with emotional strength would grow and would use consumer demand to resist the price-cutting requirement that the new retailers would want. Since advertising would exist to reinforce reputation and repeat purchase, it would be more difficult to measure. Has this prediction proved accurate? JWT's erstwhile portfolio of brands – Persil, Kit-Kat, Andrex and Mr Kipling – have shown pretty good evidence over time.

New Retailers Need to Balance Price and Brand Values

Next King looks at the new retailers. He observes that their model is partly product but also service. He notes with disarming clarity how no retailer has yet achieved a balance between operational and strategic communication: they either advertise range and pricing to build traffic, or they try to build brand values. But nobody does both.

Well, he says, this can't last. "*I forecast that soon we will see a grocery retailer invent a clear and practical service philosophy to do both.*" Through the 1980s I had the job of selling the Unilever brands to a formidable Sainsbury company where "good food costs less" and they made "the best butter in the world". For a long time they were an impregnable brand fortress until nimbler assailants came along and took their fine brand clothes away.

Entertaining Advertising

King's third area concerns another group of new advertisers where he admits to some surprise that they have so far not really taken advantage of the advertising opportunities in front of them. He wonders why hotel groups, holiday and travel companies, and entertainment industries are unwilling to investigate what advertising could do for them.

Stephen's surprise wouldn't have to last much longer and what he might think of the inhabitants of the airwaves in the early twenty-first century is anyone's guess. One feels the trends have outstripped even his vivid imagination. Not only are these categories now huge spenders in their own right, but the more conventional advertisers like automobiles or beer have felt the need to present their brands in entirely entertainment styles of communication. The intrinsic product differences, if there are any, are submerged in a farrago of consumer entertainment which all competitors appear to regard as the required passport of entry for brands in these categories.

Perhaps this prediction has gone farther than Stephen felt it ever would; perhaps indeed it has gone farther than it should. Is it generating effective returns for these advertisers; do they try to measure what it's doing? I wonder. It doesn't always look like it.

The Evolution of the Corporate Brand

King's final prediction relates to what we now know as corporate advertisers – an assembly of "institutions desperate to explain themselves", as he engagingly describes this ill-assorted conglomerate medley. Politely Stephen recognizes them as "interesting and important" but sees their inherent problem.

Confronted by the "new individualism" (see above), these bodies were experiencing a need to explain themselves and their role, feeling, a shade plaintively, that "nobody understands them". Stephen is at his intellectually rigorous best when he describes what then happens. "Ah" says the Chairman (Minister, senior Public Official) "we need some advertising to explain our corporate viewpoint. Then they'll understand us."

Stephen describes the ensuing processes as essentially "primitive", the objectives are "fuzzy", target group setting is "naïve", the style "insulting", and any research done was usually "superficial". You'll conclude that he doesn't think much of the approaches and summarizes most of the advertising effort as "ill considered".

His prediction – generous in the extreme, given his own forthright analysis – is that the groups involved will learn how to make this kind of communication work, and that it will be a key growth area for both existing but also many new advertisers. The second part of his prediction has been accurate but I'm a lot more doubtful about what's been learned, particularly given the questionable use that official and business bodies of all kinds now make of corporate communications technique and messages.

The accuracy and wisdom contained in Stephen's article on the New Advertisers, is a typically studied and perceptive review of the way ahead for the best advertising practitioners for whom he was so profound a personal influence. I feel privileged to have known and worked with him.

Chosen Areas

Stephen made his predictions in 1979. Here in his four chosen areas are tentative forecasts for 2007 onwards. They are unlikely to stand scrutiny as well as his originals!

1. *The pre-eminence of strong and durable mid-market brands will continue.* There are less today in the UK than when Stephen was writing, partly because companies lack the determination to create and maintain such brands and partly because, in a global world, some great brands are now global. The capacity of UK companies to build great brands for tomorrow's market remains doubtful. Asia – China and India – will be a principal source for tomorrow's brands, as Europe and notably the USA have been in the second half of the twentieth century.
2. *Retailer power is today's norm and will continue.* The UK balance of power between manufacturer and retailer has shifted permanently. Retailing is consolidating globally and a handful of players now dominate. One is Britain's Tesco, but USA's Wal-Mart leads the way. The collective dominance of a few will persist. However, niche players can develop their franchises since consumer preferences are shifting. This will encourage a renaissance of local – high street – shopping. The threatened environment will strongly influence consumer preferences; its effect on shopping is significant and accelerating.
3. *Entertainment brands will grow even more rapidly.* Immense markets will spring up providing new exciting entertainment for consumers of all ages. Markets will come and go with breathtaking rapidity. Technology is the key component; its development means that changes will happen at greater speed. But conflicting influences still exist. Consumers communicate personally in new ways with each other, with the internet as support. Second, the need to limit global warming instils responsibility; business and governments will need to respond.

4. *Corporate communication will be more rational and strategic.* Public sector investment defeats all attempts to trim the growth as central government takes more control. More corporate advertising does not necessarily increase consumer understanding. Companies appreciate that *the brand is the business*, adopting a business model that communicates unified values behind a single corporate brand. Governments and the public sector happily adopt marketing techniques, often at the expense of coherent policies. Given the waste and irrelevance inherent in current corporate activity, a saner world should seek to trim corporate advertising, relating investment to strategic priorities and becoming more measurable in the process.

17.1

What's New about the New Advertisers?*

By Stephen King

This article is based on Stephen King's article at the Admap Conference in Paris, but because it is particularly relevant in the context of the following four articles it appears in this section rather than with other conference papers.

It is fairly easy to conclude that *Admap*'s 1978 Conference "The Revolution in Advertising?' got its titles wrong – except for the question marks – and that there's nothing new at all about the new advertisers. Or that there wouldn't be anything new about them, even if there *were* any new advertisers. After all, there was advertising for retailers, financial services, audio equipment and records in Victorian times, and direct response was probably more important then than now.

But, while there seems to be no revolution, there have been changes in the balance between advertisers and in the roles for advertising. More important, I think we may be in some sort of transitional stage in advertising, just as we are in society as a whole. So what I'd like to do is speculate about the dynamics of the changes and about the effects they might have in future on the roles for advertising. And that means, by implication, on the way media will be used by advertisers.

First, a quick look at the broad changes in balance of advertising expenditure in the UK on press and TV in the 1970s (see Table 17.1). To add a little flavour to these very broad categories, there is also a short-list of high-fliers in (Table 17.2).

Taken with the decline in spending on food and household stores, these figures give a fairly good hint about the changes in society during the 1970s. One other thing is particularly striking

Table 17.1 Changes in UK advertising expenditure 1970–1977

Press and TV at constant prices	
Retail	+153%
Leisure equipment	+140%
Household equipment	+32%
Motoring	+27%
Industrial and Institutioinal	+18%
Food	−11%
Household stores	−39%

Source: MEAL, AA (These are MEAL figures, adjusted by the AA's separate indices for press and television rates)

*Published in *Admap*. January 1979. Reproduced with permission.

Table 17.2   Some high-fliers

Press and TV at constant prices	
Records	+1564%
Tape recorders	+725%
Perfume	+341%
Jewellery, watches, clocks	+82%
Banks	+79%
Photographic	+79%

Source: MEAL, AA.

about this list of high-fliers. In every case the balance of spending has shifted from press to television. In total, 14% of their expenditure was on television in 1970, 43% in 1977.

And to get the matter into proportion, Table 17.3 shows the changes in retailers' advertising.

While grocery retailers have more than doubled their expenditure in real terms, that is a smaller increase than for some of the other high-fliers and a great deal smaller than for department stores. Or, to look at it in terms of share of total advertising, grocery retailers moved from 1.6% in 1970 to 3.3% in 1977; an important change, but hardly revolutionary. Again, there was the swing to television, which accounted for 12% of retailers' advertising in 1970 and 27% in 1977.

Table 17.3   Changes in UK advertising expenditure 1970–1977

Press and TV at constant prices	
Retail	
Department and retail stores	+417%
Chain grocery and Co-op	+123%
Direct response, mail order, catalogues	+19%

Source: MEAL, AA

THE TRENDS BEHIND THE CHANGES

If we are to understand the nature of these changes in advertising expenditure, and if we are to make any reasonable predictions, we have to make some judgement about what lies behind them. There seem to me to be four social and economic trends of particular importance.

Freedom Through Technology

There is a tendency nowadays to treat the rapid advance of technology as some sort of threat. We forget how much freedom and enjoyment it brings to us as consumers. This is almost certainly going to be a continuing trend, and will greatly affect both the sort of things that are advertised and the roles for advertising.

Technology can make simple products simpler, cheaper and more reliable. At the mass-market end of the scale, they become less important and more disposable. The risks involved in buying them become less; if we make a mistake, it's not the end of the world. We've seen writing instruments and cigarette lighters become disposable over a long period; pocket calculators have become disposable over a few years. Already there are, for instance, cameras or watches or shoes that are cheaper to renew than to repair. They are already becoming more like "consumables" than "durables', and the real technological revolution has barely begun.

At the more expensive end of the scale, many products are becoming far too complicated for the ordinary buyer to understand – hi-fi, for example. And this means that all types of service are going to become more important – not just in their own right, but as an adjunct to many kinds of product.

All this has to be seen within the slow move from the agricultural society to the industrial society to the post-industrial or service society. I think it is making for two particular changes in relation to consumers and roles for advertising.

First, there is a limit to the application of standardized technology to services. In the immediate future there is a lot of scope. We shall certainly see quite dramatic changes in entertainment and probably in retailing. There is room for production-line methods in catering – look at the equipment and layout of McDonald's, for instance. But in the end there is a limit. Services will always depend on people as individuals, and happily we shall never see them wholly standardized.

The second major change lies in what people get out of products and services. Technology helps them to move from an era in which *survival* is everything to one in which it is most important that things *function* properly; and finally one in which function is taken for granted and *enjoyment* or satisfaction is what really matters. I think that we are in a very uneasy and transitional stage in this country between the function stage and the enjoyment stage. We seem to be rather rapidly leaving an industrial society without trying very hard to invent or enter a service or post-industrial society. The leaders of our economy still seem to be clinging to the purity of function, while consumers are already looking for enjoyment.

The Profit Spiral

There has been a fairly steady decline in the real rate of return on capital for manufacturing companies during the 1970s. Their average pre-tax real rate of return (net trading income as a percentage of net trading assets, at replacement costs after providing for stock appreciation) was 9.9% in the 1960s and the lowest annual figure was 8.5%. By 1977 it was down to 3.2%, having sunk as low as 1.4% in 1975. There could be some cyclical recovery in company profits, but because many of the causes of the decline are social and political, it is very hard to envisage any significant improvement in the near future.

This situation has apparently led to a vicious spiral, with low profits leading to low investment in all forms of production and product innovation and marketing – in turn leading to lower profits. The pressure from retailers has not by any means caused the profit spiral, but it has certainly sharpened the problem for packaged goods manufacturers and contributed to the "crisis in branding". The 11% decline in food advertising and 39% decline in household stores advertising since 1970 bears all the signs of manufacturers being caught up in the profit spiral. By contrast retailers, whose organization into large-scale enterprises came many years after that of manufacturers, are still in a moderately virtuous spiral with increasing profits leading to increased investment, in sites, stores and advertising, leading to increased profits.

One of the manufacturers' responses to these pressures over the past decade has been the self-protective merger, and many companies have got bigger and more bureaucratic. And that of course tends to clash with the third trend.

The New Individualism

There have been truly amazing social changes in the UK in the last 15 years. They can be measured easily enough in terms of education, married women in full-time jobs, mobility through access to cars, holidays abroad and so on. What is less easily measurable is much more important – a complete change in value systems. People seem to have moved from fixed and inherited values to individual and discovered values. They place increasing emphasis on the individual personality and individual creativity. They have wider horizons. They're more fully educated in the widest sense of the word; they know what's going on. In particular, they know what's going on in production, retailing, marketing and advertising. They are no more happy to see size and bureaucracy in manufacturers and standardization in their products than they are to see it in government departments, nationalized industries, local authorities or trade unions.

The New Affluence

With this new individualism and new technology has come a new affluence, which has provided the funds for the move from the functioning society to the enjoying society and from products to services.

We often seem to play down this new affluence in the UK. This is partly because we tend to think of the static consumers' expenditure of the last five years as an economic disaster rather than a plateau; and partly because there is such a political obsession with distribution and redistribution of income it's easy to forget to see how much there is. Table 17.4 shows how remarkable the changes have been.

If we take the households earning over £90 per week at 1976 prices (that is, over £30 per week in 1962 money), we can see that the standard of living that was possible for a small minority in the early sixties is now (bearing in mind the advances since 1976) possible for around 40% of households. This top group of course pays rather more in tax than it used to – 18% of income in 1962, 23% in 1976 – but it is still a very dramatic change.

Table 17.4   UK household income

At constant (1976) prices % of households with income of:	1962	1976
Over £90 p. w.	16.3%	37.6%
£60–90 p. w.	25.6%	23.9%
£30–60 p. w.	39.0%	22.0%
Under £30 p. w.	18.9%	16.5%

Source: Family Expenditure Survey.

NEW ROLES FOR ADVERTISING?

It is easy enough to see how these four trends have affected the sort of things that are advertised today – why advertising for tape-recorders, banks and jewellery has grown and for washing powders has declined. What is a little more subtle is the way in which they have affected the *roles* for advertising and the use of media. I think there are three main, interrelated dimensions which affect the role for advertising.

REPEAT-   UNIQUE-
PURCHASE   PURCHASE

Figure 17.1

1. **Scale of buying** (see Figure 17.1) – The first is to do with the nature of the goods and the buying process. Certain things we buy repeatedly, like packaged goods, so that most of what we think about them comes from repeated *direct* experience. At the other end of the scale there are things about which we know virtually nothing from direct experience, like a new house for instance. In the middle are things like cars, where we might have no experience of the model but a lot of experience of the manufacturer.

   Where goods or services come on this scale quite clearly affects the job that advertising has to do.

2. **Scale of responses** (see Figure 17.2) – As a result of that and other factors, there are differences in the directness of response that advertisers are trying to get. At the direct end, most classified advertising is trying to get an immediate response, usually for unique purchases. At the indirect end, a lot of advertising is aiming to reinforce long-established attitudes, usually for repeat-purchase brands. Most of the time, it's a matter of a blend – somewhere in the middle.

DIRECT   INDIRECT

Figure 17.2

3. **Scale of rewards** (see Figure 17.3) – Again, we can look at the role of advertising from the point of view of which of the rewards offered by goods and services should be most strongly featured – the functional rewards or the non-functional rewards. More often, of course, on which blend of them in the middle. And this is clearly related to the move from the functioning society to the enjoying society.

FUNCTIONAL   NON-FUNCTIONAL

Figure 17.3

These three scales seem to me to provide the link between the broad tren2ds that have affected marketing and the "new" tasks that advertising sets out to perform. There are four main categories of advertising in which I think it's possible to see changes that will become increasingly important – grocery goods, retailers, enjoyment products and services, and "institutions desperate to explain themselves".

GROCERY GOODS

Packaged goods sold in grocery shops have always accounted for a large proportion of total advertising, but with the 19% drop in real advertising expenditure on food and household stores, it has clearly been declining. I have a nasty feeling that in this whole category we have never really quite taken into account the sheer power of the four trends and their effects on products, marketing and advertising. (I would draw a distinction here between these grocery goods and, say, drink, tobacco and confectionery – which have different distribution systems, different degrees of tax interference and a different position on the survive/function/enjoy scale.)

In the more structured life of the early 1960s one could say that (symbolically) the latent demand for grocery goods was rather like that shown in Figure 17.4.

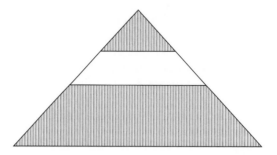

Figure 17.4

At the top there was a small demand for premium-priced, exclusive, high-quality, high margin goods. At the bottom there was a very large demand for low-priced, standardized, moderate-quality (not cheap and nasty), low-margin goods. But very little in the middle. The manufacturer could be either a small specialist, making up for low volume by high margins; or a mass-marketer, making up for low margins by high sales. To be in the middle was to be caught between two stools.

Two things have changed all that. First, technology has advanced a great deal more in retailing than in manufacturing. Today, with the greater concentration in retail organizations, economies of scale in distribution are at least as important as economies of scale in production. Retailers, though they have by no means taken full advantage of their position, are now in many product fields rather better placed to supply the demand at the bottom of the triangle than manufacturers are – just as Marks & Spencer did many years ago in the underwear market and are now doing in food; or as Boots are doing in cosmetics.

Secondly, the shape of latent demand has changed. The new individualism and the new affluence mean that there is now a mass market for fairly exclusive, fairly high-priced, high-quality, high-margin brands. The shape of demand is maybe more like that shown in Figure 17.5.

There is still, and surely always will be, a small demand for the super-exclusive and a large demand for the no-nonsense, cheap and cheerful, grocery goods at the bottom. What is different is the huge potential for manufacturer brands in the middle. There are already signs that some brand leaders have based their success on being "middle market" brands – for instance, Mr Kipling, Andrex, Imperial Leather, Chum, Whiskas, some of the ranges from Bird's Eye and Findus. (Indeed one could argue that the whole frozen food market fits in here.) What brands of this type tend to have in common is a high quality of product, clear product differences, a fair amount of product innovation and new variants; and a steady, if not necessarily spectacular, investment in packaging and advertising. They have got onto a more or

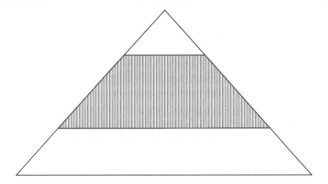

Figure 17.5

less virtuous spiral, and consumer demand is protecting them from having to give away all their profits in price-cutting. To put it another way, such manufacturers are specializing in what being a manufacturer ought to mean – making things better and more inventively than anyone else.

It is quite easy to see the scope for some changes in the role of advertising for such brands. They are clearly moving towards the repeat-purchase end of the scale of buying. In the past their premium price might have made them more a special occasion purchase, but no longer. The role for advertising becomes more one of reminder and reinforcement of an existing buying habit than one of getting people to relate the brand at all to their ordinary lives.

At the same time, compared with the cheap and cheerful brands, these middle market brands belong much more to the enjoying society than the functioning society. Advertising will clearly have to bring out the product differences that such brands should have, but is likely to be operating more at the non-functional than the functional end of the scale of rewards.

And on the scale of responses, there is likely to be a greater emphasis on indirect responses. Clearly, as for any repeat-purchase brand, there must be a short-term and direct response. But that is not to say much more than that the frequency of advertising will have to be kept up. Rather more important will be the long-term and indirect response to the *added values* of the brand, because it will be these – including basic quality and product differences – that allow the brand to keep up its margins and fight off the crisis in branding.

So my first prediction (speculation?) is that these middle market brands will be more important "new" advertisers, with the role for advertising moving towards the indirect and non-functional ends of the scales. And that will raise difficult questions for research, since it is so much harder to evaluate advertising of that sort. It should also make the press media think rather hard. In the past, one might have argued that high-quality brands, with small exclusive groups of buyers, were unsuited to television. Now that the new affluence has come to so many households, that argument is weaker. The real question now becomes: Which media contribute most to the non-functional (aesthetic, stylistic, psychological) values of brands? Television seems to be winning that battle. I don't think that there's anything inevitable about this, but can't help wondering what the press will be doing about it.

RETAILERS

In terms of the trends and scales we've been considering, retailers occupy a fascinatingly ambivalent position. For instance, they're partly product – that is, a physical entity with shelves full of goods; partly a service – that is, a selection of goods, sometimes advice to the consumer, sometimes a repair service; all run by imperfectly controllable people. Each shop in a chain is partly a standardized product, and partly a unique thing – in terms of its position and convenience for the individual consumer.

Equally it's partly a repeat-purchase product – in the sense that the consumer goes back to a shop again and again – and partly a unique purchase, in the sense that today's precise combination of goods on the shelf and their prices may not exist next week.

It is hardly surprising then that there is a fair diversity in the roles for the different retailers' campaigns. For instance, current advertisements for International Stores seem to me to be aiming to operate at the extreme functional end of the scale of rewards and the extreme direct end of the scale of responses. They simply show the prices at which a short list of manufacturer brands is available this week; there appears to be no attempt to bring to mind any of the other rewards there might be in shopping at International (say, quality of non-branded goods, style of store, attitudes of staff, company philosophy), and no hint of long-term benefits from establishing a habit of shopping there.

Towards the other end of the scale, Habitat advertising is offering long-term and non-functional rewards – a design selection service, as well as specifically priced goods available now. It is one of the relatively few examples of a middle market brand in retailing. In an area in which most people lack confidence – the choice of household style – Habitat is offering the long-term and non-functional assurance of consistent and coherent good taste.

There are many positions between these two. While most grocery retailers have roles for advertising fairly near to that of International, non-grocery retailers tend to lie somewhere in the middle. Clearly, where a retailer has mainly non-branded goods – as, for instance, a clothing store – it is easier to build a balanced brand from the store itself. But some retailers, such as Boots and W.H. Smith, even though they are directly competing with other retailers selling manufacturer brands, have made a good deal of progress in establishing a balance. The rewards featured in advertising are certainly the functional ones of availability and price, but they are also the non-functional ones of selection, advice and service.

Retailers seem to be beginning to face up to a very unpleasant dilemma. Their experience tells them that if they try to use their advertising solely to build up long-term values, they just do not get the short-term boost to store traffic that they get from the "low prices on these brands now" advertising. On the other hand, they are becoming uncomfortably aware that if they don't, either by store/service improvements or advertising, add *any* values, they will end up with their own crisis in branding and possibly bankrupt through loss of margins.

So far they have tended to attack the dilemma by adding to their traditional press advertising some television "image building" advertising. However, there is not much evidence from consumer research that any of it is yet doing much good. It may well be that the very use of the sloppy and misleading phrase "image building" is a pointer to lack of clarity about objectives – a hint that advertising is being used as a *substitute* for product or service improvements.

My second prediction is that one day soon a retail chain is going to invent a clear, specific and practical service (maybe based on the new technology) or a clear and specific service philosophy that positions it as a unique brand, and is carried through to all its activities. When that happens, there may well be a useful new role for advertising and a new use of media. Meanwhile, if retailers are using advertising mainly for direct and functional purposes, there seems to be a very strong case for putting a great deal more of it into local and regional press media.

ENJOYMENT PRODUCTS AND SERVICES

My third category of "new" advertisers is entirely predictable from the social and economic trends, and their use of advertising is fairly predictable too. The new affluence, the new individualism and the move from the functioning society to the enjoying society was bound to increase expenditure on and advertising for "enjoyment products and services". (The conventional phrase "leisure goods" has, I think, too many overtones of passive inactivity.) Obviously, too, the advertising tends to concentrate on the non-functional rewards. Even where, as in hi-fi, it is giving technical specifications, they work more by reassuring people than by leading to rational assessments of directly competitive equipment.

On the whole, enjoyment products are nearer the unique end of the buying scale. Goods like cameras or tape recorders, are not only too expensive to buy very frequently, but also constantly being improved and adapted, so that it is impossible to purchase the same model repeatedly. And most of the cheaper equipment products, like records, are part unique (the music) and part repeated (the singer or the record company).

Not surprisingly, therefore, there has been a growing emphasis on the direct end of the scale of responses. What has perhaps been fairly new to this country has been the combination of direct responses and non-functional values. Whatever the associations of the past, I cannot see any inexorable reason why goods sold directly should be cheap and nasty or should be presented as if they were. I would envisage considerable growth in "direct response" type advertising for high-quality enjoyment products, particularly on television. In the USA, with all the advantages of more and more local TV stations, this sort of advertising is booming; and I think it will here too, because of the contribution that television can make to non-functional values. Again, the press will have to take positive action if it is to defend its traditional preserve.

Surprisingly (to me) there has been very little growth in advertising for enjoyment services – hotels, holidays, travel, restaurants, entertainments, etc. I suspect this is due to the rather undeveloped organization of most of the services, and I feel sure that more organized marketing and advertising will come in time. There is scope for one particular "new" role for advertising. One of the problems that many large service organizations have is that they are geographically decentralized and depend, for both performance and reputation, on the behaviour of people of widely varying ability and personalities. How does the company get the quality and consistency in a service organization that people take for granted in products? Advertising can make a contribution by demonstrating to the staff how they are expected by customers to behave. It can give them standards to live up to. For instance, the Schreiber pledge about furniture delivery dates, which used to be featured in its advertising, was not only presenting a value to the public, but was also putting the whole production and distribution system for the company on its best behaviour. A recent offer from Ford dealers to "phone in and have your car's electrical system checked for only £1" was intended not only to get a direct response from the public but also to affect the way that customers were treated when they did phone in.

So my third prediction is a growth in advertising for enjoyment products and services, with an increased use of television and an important role for advertising in not only promoting services but controlling them.

INSTITUTIONS DESPERATE TO EXPLAIN THEMSELVES

In many ways, I think my last category of "new" advertisers is the most interesting, and may in the long run be the most important. All around us we can see examples of diseconomies of scale in manufacturing and service companies, government departments, the civil service, Quangos, the consumer protection industry, nationalized industries, local authorities and trade unions. As organizations get bigger and more stratified, so they clash with the new individualism. People get more and more angry with them, and they get more and more hurt and feel that nobody understands them. Eventually they're driven to using advertising to explain themselves.

This category covers most of what we have come to call "corporate advertising". (There are no doubt institutions who have taken up advertising for good and positive reasons, with clear and compelling objectives that have nothing to do with an irritation at being misunderstood; but I think they are still a minority.) It also covers a much wider field – such as trade unionists who feel that the public doesn't understand their side of a dispute; civil servants who think that people don't love them very much; Governments, from North Korea to South Africa, who think that the news about them is unfair; trade associations of otherwise competing companies who feel threatened by the advance of creeping corporatism.

In terms of the scales we have been considering, this really is a new form of advertising. For instance, it is usually trying to operate at the extreme indirect end of the scale of responses. As often as not, the response required seems to be one of "Oh, now I understand" or "They're not as bad as I thought" – very indirect in relation to the institutions' commercial or other objectives.

The rewards offered usually seem to be at the extreme non-functional end of the scale. In fact, it may be stretching it to try to use this scale at all, because the most striking thing about much of this sort of institutional advertising is that it isn't actually offering any rewards. It is not saying "Here's something for you". It's saying "Let me tell you about *me*". Prompting the response "Why on earth should I?"

What is really new about this sort of advertising is that most of it is amazingly primitive. The most charitable personal view of it or interpretation of qualitative research into it, leads to the conclusion that most of it simply hasn't been thought out properly. Here is a short-list of common faults:

- *Objectives:* Fuzzy – Not surprising, if the starting point is 'nobody loves us'. When the objectives are written down at all, I suspect they read something like this:

CORPORATE OBJECTIVES

To communicate to opinion leaders, the City and the public in general our corporate image as a dynamic, profitable and forward-looking company, yet one whose philosophy is deeply rooted in the best traditions of social and ecological concern.

Fine until you start wondering what it means and what to do with it.

- *Target groups:* Naïve – One wonders, when viewing some campaigns, whether anyone really considered the complex nature of the relationships that different groups have with an institution; how people can have more than one relationship; how the media overlap, and so on. Institutions often seem to think that they can at the same time tell one lot of people that they're big and successful, and another lot that they're small, local and concerned. Or that they can tell the investors that they're amazingly profitable and the trade unions that they have no spare cash. I wonder if they know what a high readership the *Financial Times* has among trade union leaders.
- *Style:* Insulting – I think that many corporate advertisements are still greatly under-estimating their audience's intelligence. They are still full of old clichés about serving the nation, building a better future and preserving our island heritage for tomorrow's generation. There

are still pictures of kiddies skipping into the sunset or grandiose irrelevancies in a sea of expensive white (or pink) space.

- *Research:* Superficial – Even the best companies (that is, those who try at all to measure the effects of their institutional advertising) seem to be content with plotting changes in the numbers mentioning the company in answer to questions like "Which of the companies on this list would you say were well-managed . . . innovative . . . serve the nation?" Fair enough maybe as a measure of awareness, but such research cannot hope to measure what really goes on in the relationship between an individual and an institution. (Not the fault of the research companies. They can only do what they're paid for, and no form of measurement will be satisfactory if the objectives are fuzzy.)

- *Role for advertising:* Ill-considered – Campaigns often fail to recognize that communication is about getting people to respond – not just telling them things. The immediate response of many people to most corporate advertisements is one of bafflement: "Why are you telling me all this?'" As a result, either they ignore them or impute to the companies all sorts of unworthy motives. In that sense, they can often make the original problem worse.

There are signs that gradually this sort of advertising is being tackled more systematically, especially on television. But there is one particular problem there. The very act of running a television campaign leads people to feel that there is a massive attempt to mould their opinions. As one man put it in a recent group discussion: "All they're saying, all of them, is 'We are good for you' " – and the group started talking about Big Brother and the lack of a personal touch and so on. There appeared to be problems of this sort even with advertising as well-made and sensibly aimed as that of ICI. Dunlop appears to have come nearest to solving these problems by having a clearly-perceived rationale, that of diversifying from tyres into general rubber goods and by removing any potential threat through use of witty and popular commercials.

In fact, I don't think the problems are anything like as difficult as they are made to seem, provided we refuse to accept as a brief "Nobody understands us; you must tell them how good we really are". For instance, the London and Scottish Clearing Banks *might* have given such a brief for their 1977 campaign, but they did not; they worked out clearly who didn't love them, why they didn't and precisely what had to be done about it. The main object of the campaign was very specific – to reinforce the views of "moderate" politicians that bank nationalization would be a certain vote-loser. The target groups were worked out in great detail, the overlap between them and the flow of ideas from one to another. The style of the campaign did not, I think, underestimate the intelligence of the audience.

It was not aiming to *tell* people, but to *ask* them: it was above all aiming for a response, not just a vague nod of approval. It certainly got an amazing response, and nobody ever said: "Why are you telling me all this?" – the purpose of the campaign was overt and accepted as entirely reasonable. And finally the research was related precisely to the original objectives. It does seem to be possible to overcome the common faults that I listed above.

My fourth prediction therefore is that we shall all learn how to do this sort of advertising better, and that it will become one of the main growth areas. Perhaps I'd even accept that it will provide us with new advertisers.

18
A Robust Defence of What Brand
Advertising is For

By Stephen Carter CBE, Chief of Strategy and Principal Advisor to the Prime Minister

An introduction to:

18.1   New Brands: Barriers to Entry?

Like a number of contributors to this book, I had the good fortune to work with Stephen King and to know him a little personally. Re-reading this article reminded me of how visionary a thinker Stephen was. How fortunate the advertising industry, and J. Walter Thompson in particular, was in the 1970s and 1980s to attract and retain some of the most original thinkers of the day on the longer term aspects of commercialization, competition and the role of communications.

By contrast, at the turn of the twenty-first century the advertising industry's clients and practitioners find themselves beset by bad news and challenge in equal measure. We see traditional broadcasting fragmenting from the mass channels of coverage and cultural dominance, to literally hundreds of niche channels that increasingly seem to better serve individuals viewing preferences. The large advertisers are questioning the value of broadcast television, radio, print display and classified advertising which inevitably changes the role of the agencies that provide them with strategic advice and creativity to exploit these channels.

The Challenge of Digital Underlines the Power of Advertising

This is leaving many traditional media owners and agencies (as well as their shareholders) wondering whether their business models will survive the transition to digital. Furthermore, if they do survive, will the margins be sufficiently attractive to justify the investment in content or people that is necessary to continue to differentiate them from their lower cost more accessible on-line competitors?

Conversely, the internet world is being fuelled by advertisers' enthusiasm for participating in the internet boom at a lower absolute entry price. In the United Kingdom alone, in the year ending June 2006, the published figures showed on-line advertising spending reaching £1.65 billion; a staggering 40%+ growth rate year on year. In particular, Google's click-through advertising revenue model, which allows users to follow up their interests, rather than interrupting them (as with display advertising), has created a global and local alternative to traditional media.

Given these trends in traditional and currently still labelled "new media", it would seem reasonable to suggest that the exponential increase in advertising spend on-line is not just evidence of advertisers' preference for a newer and often cheaper medium, but also hard evidence of one of Stephen's central points – namely, that advertising does in fact reward those companies and brands who take a longer term view of risk.

The 1980s: An Unexplored Terrain for Competition Policy

This contrary picture of the value and price of advertising may on first analysis make the notion of new brands, and their accompanying advertising as a barrier to market entry, seem more of a quaint notion, as opposed to "a dry and specialist topic" as the author describes it in a characteristically self-deprecating way.

However, its underlying thesis is an insightful and very understandable parley into competition policy. In the UK this is a relatively new area of jurisprudence and therefore commentary, and can suffer from a greater than usual lack of understanding between practitioners and academics.

The thesis of Stephen's argument, like much of his thinking, operates on a number of levels.

He succinctly argues that the lasting contribution of brand advertising is not in the launching of products or brands on unsuspecting new customers. Nor is its lasting contribution in spending to justify higher prices and margins. Instead, consistently effective advertising serves to efficiently remind customers who have tried a brand or product, and have not been disappointed, to do so again and again.

Thus advertising serves to maintain sales and/or minimize sales decline. In Stephen's own words *"Advertising can make all the difference between consumer sales being stable upwards, or stable downwards."* This is a simple but powerfully insightful view of the effective use of advertising expenditure. In my experience it is one that is too often ignored by clients and agencies to the cost of their businesses and brands.

In analysing whether advertising for new brands is a meaningful barrier to entry to marketing for new entrants, and therefore structurally anti-competitive, Stephen makes a point about the development of effective public policy, particularly in the area of competition policy. He argues that it is critically important for the theorists to understand the practice, and perhaps even more importantly, where the theory and the practice meet. Again this is particularly far-sighted.

Competition Policy has been Open to Broad Interpretations

In the United Kingdom, we have had to rely on fair trading legislation and broad principles to deal with competition issues for most of the last 30 years, leaving the United Kingdom out of step with European legislation. Our competition rules lack the severity of criminality or quasi-criminality that is now associated with pricing cartels and abuses of dominant market positions. Consequently, what is and what is not anti-competitive has been open to some broad interpretations.

It was not until 1998 that the Competition Act received Royal Assent, with many of its provisions not entering into force until the beginning of March 2000, in order to allow business some adjustment time. Equally the Enterprise Act did not receive Royal Assent until 2002, which in turn allowed for the current Competition Appeal Tribunal, which got its full powers in April 2003. These two pieces of legislation created a comprehensive framework both for dealing with specific abuses, and for more broad-ranging market investigations, where the relevant authorities were concerned about the feature, or features, of any particular market.

It is only recently that the United Kingdom has created the necessary statutory and judicial framework for an appropriately robust approach to both structural and specific competition abuses. It is not surprising, therefore, in the absence of such a framework in the 1970s, that some uninformed commentators may have turned to the profile of advertising and its relatively new and highly visible powers of persuasion and seen it as potentially anti-competitive.

Stephen was a passionate believer in the informed consumers' right to choose, and to do so in competitive markets. In that context, effectively regulated advertising has a critical role in providing information to inform that choice. Conversely, overly regulated advertising can have a distorting effect the other way.

So it is not difficult to imagine how, in the largely state-controlled 1970s, that a limited number of powerful private companies with strongly marketed popular brands could have created a presumption, that rather than contributing to effective competition, their use of advertising was in fact a barrier to innovation and therefore proper informed consumer choice.

How Markets Function in the Consumer Interest

On reflection this is perhaps not surprising. It was really only in the 1980s and the 1990s that we saw the rolling back of state control in favour of private ownership along with the de-regulation of financial services which allowed an increase in sophisticated financial products and greater access to capital and investment. The combination of these two things, underpinned by increasingly effective technology and the forces of globalization, has put the effective functioning of markets in the consumer interest under greater analytical scrutiny.

Like any good advertising man, profitability was always central to Stephen's view of the world. Without profit there is no reason for activity, and without activity there is no investment that ultimately creates businesses. Today, as we see more and more private capital seeking returns in the high twenties, rather than public capital living with returns in the high teens, we may be facing a situation where the appetite for investment and development risk is perversely reducing rather than increasing.

Stephen would, I suspect, find this particularly ironic given that the barriers he identifies and dismisses – distribution channels and capital costs of new technology – are less significant issues today (largely because of the internet) than they were as barriers to entry in the 1970s.

Above all, the article is a call for companies and their advisers to embrace informed and measured risk, and to use advertising selectively and consistently. Of all the points in the article, these last two are, I suspect the ones that would be closest to both Stephen's heart as well as his head.

How we have Moved on: The Relevance of the Argument Today

1. The 1970s and 1980s were a golden era not just of advertising but of *thinking* about advertising and communication.
2. Now media fragmentation challenges not just the economics but the cultural dominance of mass broadcasting.
3. New media brings new advertising models, new risks and new opportunities.

4. In any media, the lasting contribution of advertising is reminding customers to keep on buying.
5. Competitive markets and competition theory can be quite different things.
6. Recent legislation has given the UK competition authorities real teeth.
7. Freely available and accurate information is essential to the effective working of competitive markets.

18.1

New Brands: Barriers to Entry?*

By Stephen King

A look at what actually happens to the marketplace casts doubt on the Price Commission's theory.

Can heavy advertising by established brands reduce competition, by acting as a "barrier to entry" for new brands? The Price Commission believes that it can. Its report on Southalls (Birmingham) Ltd concluded that "... high levels of (advertising) expenditure act as a restraint on competition by presenting a formidable barrier to potential new suppliers".

The whole question of "barriers to entry" is much more complex than it sounds. It certainly cannot be sensibly discussed outside the wider context of developing and marketing new brands. Rather than attempt to examine the theoretical issues or to look at the role and effects of advertising in isolation, I would like to deal with *marketing practice*.

From the viewpoint of a manufacturer who wants to develop new brands of packaged goods, what are the main barriers? Is advertising by established brands one of them? If so, in what way is it a barrier?

In a rather simple way, there must *be* barriers, because so few new brands and new products succeed. Various studies have shown that some 60 to 70% of new products that are tried out in test markets are never extended to national marketing. And most of those that are launched nationally do not survive for very long. Of 400 new food products launched nationally in 1965, 49% had disappeared from the shops by 1969, 69% by 1973 and 78% by 1975 (Kraushar, Andrews & Eassie, 1976). The popular cliché that "9 out of 10 new products fail" remains a fair guide to reality for packaged goods. In fact, the first barriers to the manufacturer of packaged goods appear at the planning stage, before the decision has been made of what market to try to enter; and at this stage there is no doubt whatsoever that the biggest barrier to entry, both practically and psychologically, is low profitability in the market to be entered. If the existing companies in the market do not seem to be making much profit, is it likely that a newcomer could?

It is not hard to see why this has become such a barrier. Figure 18.1, from figures published in *Trade and Industry*, September 1978, shows the real rate of return on capital in the food, drink and tobacco industries. To put it starkly, the manufacturer thinking of entering the "average" market would be facing a prospect, with his proposed new brand, of a 1-in-10 chance of earning around 5% on his capital. This barrier certainly rules out markets that are not well above average for profitability.

A second major barrier at this early stage is the need in many markets for heavy capital investment. It is not that it is particularly hard to raise the finance; it is simply a matter of *risk*.

*Published in *Advertising*, Spring 1979. This article is a shortened version of a much longer booklet published by the Advertising Association in 1980 called *Advertising as a Barrier to Market Entry*. Reproduced with permission.

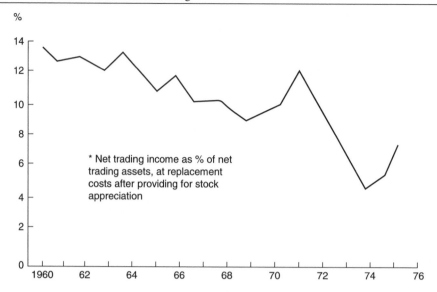

Figure 18.1 Companies' real rate of return on food, drink and tobacco
Source: Trade & Industry, September 1978

Though something can be done with laboratory and pilot plant work, the capital investment and indeed all forms of start-up costs usually have to be incurred before there is anything but a fairly speculative idea of whether the new brand will succeed. If the brand fails, current expenditure can be switched off and some return can usually be retrieved before the brand is finally withdrawn. But the capital expenditure and start-up costs are rarely recoverable.

Sadly, risk-taking seems to be becoming rarer. As companies feel, and individuals feel, increasingly that there are penalties for failure, but few rewards for success, playing safe becomes the norm. It may at times be a self-induced barrier, but it is certainly a very important one.

A third specific barrier at the planning stage is patents. They are often very formidable and require persistence and considerable time to overcome. Kodak's introduction of an instant camera was delayed for many years by the complexity of Polaroid's patents, and even then it was a matter of an expensive court case.

This is a very obvious sort of barrier; but there is an important principle involved too, one that has a bearing on many issues of the true interest of the public. There is no doubt that from a narrow and short-term point of view the public suffered from Polaroid's patents. They were deprived for many years of Kodak's technology and were forced to pay the higher prices that resulted from Polaroid's monopoly of instant cameras. (One has only to look at the drop in UK prices since the introduction of Kodak's instant camera in the UK to see the effects of competition.)

But the broader and long-term view comes to a different and more sensible conclusion. This is that, without the protection of patents, Polaroid could never have got onto the market at all. In the long run the protection of patents has brought about more innovation and more competition, by giving inventors more secure rewards.

Let us say, however, that our manufacturer has overcome all these barriers at the planning stage. He has chosen a market that looks reasonably profitable; he can manage the costs and risk of investment; and there are no patent problems. He has developed a new brand for the chosen product field, and is ready to put it into the market. What are the barriers that face him now?

Barrier No. 4 is the natural scepticism of retailers. Good distribution is vital to success, as common sense suggests and as Nielsen (1969, 1970) have convincingly demonstrated.

Consumer research makes its importance clear too. For instance, JWT's *New Housewife Survey* (1967) asked young housewives how they found out about new products they had recently tried: 42% said they had seen them in a shop; 12% mentioned recommendations from retailers: 13% other recommendations; 18% advertising; 9% free samples; and 8% gave other answers.

It might seem a little surprising that only 18% of the sample mentioned advertising. Our surprise comes partly because we tend to think of shops and recommenders in physical terms; while we usually talk of advertising expenditure in abstract and collective terms, with apparently huge sums of money involved. When the advertising is translated into practical terms it seems a lot less. Let us imagine, for instance, that our manufacturer has decided to spend £1/2 million on television advertising, including the costs of the commercials, during those first critical four months. (That is what the average brand from the top 10 advertisers spent over the whole of 1977.) What does that mean in practical terms?

The average housewife is exposed to about 3,000 television commercials over four months. That is, the set would be switched on and she would be in the room during the screening of 3,000 commercials. If our manufacturer spent £1/2 million, then just eight of those 3,000 commercials would be for his new brand. It is hardly surprising that advertising does not emerge as the most important communication medium in making people aware of the existence of new brands.

In any case, all the evidence is that simple awareness is only the first step. Important as it is, the successful launch of a new brand (the first four months of distribution and sales) is not the only, or even the most critical, factor in its success. The point is illustrated by the typical pattern of consumer buying of a new brand. Figure 18.2 shows the norm for packaged goods

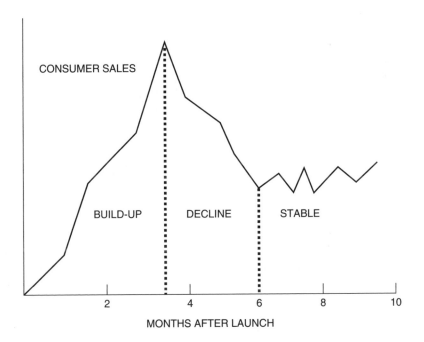

Figure 18.2 Typical pattern of consumer sales for new brands (44 market tests)
Source: BMRB Retail Audit

as shown by an analysis of 44 test markets. First there is a build-up to a peak, in line with the growth of distribution. Then there is a decline, as the distribution curve flattens out and as some consumers, having tried the new brand once, either lose interest or decide not to buy it again. Finally, after quite a short time – on average about six months after launch – a relatively stable level of sales is reached.

Advertising has important roles in two of these stages, though they are very different roles. First, in the build-up stage, advertising and sales promotion, by contributing to the initial excitement of the launch, can affect the height of the peak. What happens at the second stage, the decline, is almost entirely due to the degree of satisfaction given by the new brand to its buyers. The evidence is that the percentage drop from the peak to the stable level is directly related to the brand itself; for instance, it is much the same in each area of the country, irrespective of weight of advertising. The role for advertising at the third stage, when sales are more or less stable, is particularly important. It is the role of maintaining and building the brand, reminding those who have tried it to buy it again. Advertising here can make all the difference between the consumer sales being stable-upwards or stable-downwards.

Consumer panel data confirm this picture, and in particular illustrate how new brands usually fail. The typical pattern is one in which enough households try the brand to make it a success, but simply do not go on buying it often enough.

These findings are the result of very extensive research, (Davis, 1964; Parfitt and Collins, 1968) and cast much light on the realities of entry into new markets. In particular, they illustrate two fundamental points: The first is that advertising has a part to play in the initial launch of a new brand, but is probably less important than getting distribution. (The two are of course interrelated, since it would be difficult to get distribution without the promise of advertising.) This phase is of very short duration, about three to four months, and is the *relatively* easy part of breaking into a market. A far more important role for advertising comes after the initial launch, and trial of the brand by households. It is the *maintenance* of the new brand, keeping up the rate of repurchase by reminding buyers to buy again. This is the hard part.

The second consideration is the buyer's satisfaction with the brand. It governs the level of the "stable" sales and the rate of repurchase. Very few new brands are actively disliked; the problem is far more often one of indifference. There is a very strict limit to what advertising can achieve in building a brand, if people are totally apathetic towards it.

The crucial importance of the buyer's satisfaction brings us to the fifth barrier, which is quite simply the need for the new brand to be *better and different*. There have been many analyses, post-mortems and research studies to show why successes are successes and failures are failures; and they nearly all come to the same basic conclusions. The figures in Table 18.1 are representative of such findings, and come from a very thorough analysis (Davidson, 1976) of 100 new grocery brands, covering 38 product categories, launched in the UK between 1960 and 1970. Fifty were successes and 50 were failures; the figures compare the two groups.

New brands tend, not unexpectedly, to be rather more expensive than established brands. But the evidence here is that price is not a very critical factor in success or failure. The four new brands that were lower in price were all successful, but there is very little difference between the two groups in terms of same-priced new brands and higher-priced new brands. By contrast, better performance and distinctiveness are highly associated with success in new brands.

Getting a better performance than existing brands and producing a new brand that is radically different from them is a very great deal easier said than done. It calls for considerable

Table 18.1   Success and failure in new brands

Feature	50 successes	50 failures
Price:		
Higher price than competitors	26	25
Same price	20	25
Lower price	4	—
	50	50
Performance:		
Better performance than competitors	37	10
Same performance	13	30
Worse performance	—	10
	50	50
Distinctiveness:		
Dramatically very different from competitors	34	15
Marginally different	6	19
Similar	10	16
	50	50

speculative expenditure on research and development; great efficiency; meticulous consumer research. Above all – the really hard part – it requires skills of intuition, inventiveness and interpretation; and the tact and energy needed to guide and force through the new ideas, which are nearly always disruptive to the existing production, finance, marketing and sales departments.

In many ways, therefore, we have to conclude that the only really important "barrier to entry" for new brands after the planning stage is the *need to produce a better and distinctive brand*. But that is surely a rather curious use of the phrase "barrier to entry". Most manufacturers would put it another way. They would say that producing a better and distinctive new brand was simply an essential part of the process. And that is how they would describe their own advertising for the new brand – it is an essential part of the process of efficiently launching, maintaining and building the brand. They would describe the selling, display, sales promotion, warehousing, distribution and transport activities in exactly the same way.

So far I have not mentioned the advertising of established brands as a "barrier to entry", and I doubt if many manufacturers would think of it in that way. In fact, there seems to be only one way in which one could include it at all, and that is by naming as the sixth barrier the *efficiency of competitors*.

Obviously, it is much harder to succeed with a new brand if it faces competitors who have efficient production, quality control, reliability; who innovate regularly with design improvements and new variants; who have up-to-date and efficient distribution systems; who have efficient cost-control systems and competitive pricing; who use advertising efficiently; and so on. In that sense, efficiency of competitors is a "barrier to entry" for a new brand. But it is a fairly bizarre way to think of it. It is unlikely that there will be a call for inefficient companies, in order to promote new competition.

Manufacturers of new brands almost invariably look on the advertising of established brands as a perfectly normal part of the process of bringing them to the consumer. Typically, it might account for between one-tenth and one-fifth of the cost of that total process, which covers warehousing, transport, selling, sales promotion, display, advertising, retailer's costs and retailer's profits. But even if the process of bringing existing brands to the public is regarded as normal rather than a "barrier to entry", there is little doubt what the major protection is for the existing brands. It is the satisfactions of consumers with what they are already buying. That is why it is so necessary for the newcomer to be better and/or different. If the new brand is no better, why should the consumer bother to change to it?

There is no doubt, either, that one of the most important roles for advertising for an established brand is to remind people of those satisfactions. It is an essential part of the maintenance of a brand. It is reinforcing people's existing buying habits.

The view has often been put forward that advertising is therefore acting as a form of "unfair competition"; that by building "brand loyalty" it is *unfairly* reinforcing buying habits; and that it is therefore acting as an *unreasonable* barrier to the new brand. Unfortunately, the term "brand loyalty" is one of several that are widely used in marketing but which have very imprecise meanings. The realities tend to be rather different from the oversimple theory. True "brand loyalty" (that is, sticking to just one brand over a long period) is rare. As a rough guide, over a one-year period about 10% of the buyers of a brand buy that brand alone; and they tend to be particularly light buyers of the product type. This whole area has been very extensively investigated (e.g. Ehrenberg, 1972), and the general conclusion reached is that in most consumer goods markets most people have a short-list of brands which they find acceptable, and they buy the individual brands from this short-list in an irregular way at differing frequencies. The main role for advertising in such markets is to bring a brand to the top of people's mental short-list or to try to keep it there. In other words, the task is one of *competitive maintenance*.

A very clear-cut example of the need for maintenance came from extensive research into the effectiveness of advertising for the wearing of seat-belts. Use of seat-belts is a benefit that costs nothing (the law prescribes the original investment costs) and which most people favour. The research showed that when about £2 million a year was spent on advertising, some 33% of drivers on the road wore seat-belts. When £1/4 million or less was spent, about 28% wore them. If reminder is needed in this non-competitive area to persuade this "captive market" to continue doing something that they already approve of, it seems clear that most manufacturers in competitive markets will need to remind their consumers, simply in order to stay in business.

But the implication of the "brand loyalty" argument is that advertising's role goes beyond simple reminder of the *existence* of a brand; and this is perfectly true. It is reminding consumers not only of the brand's existence, but its *values* to them – whether those values are functional, economic or psychological (more likely, a blend of all three). Its purpose is to show the brand to be worth its full price, so that it will not have to be sold at a cut-price. In this way it aims to keep up a reasonable *profit margin* for the manufacturer.

But does not that mean that advertising puts up prices? The fairly clear answer – maybe surprising from a superficial viewpoint – is that over time it tends to have the opposite effect. The best way to see this comes from looking at reality rather than considering theory. Figure 18.3 shows the results of a study of the price movements of heavily-advertised brands of processed food, compared with the movements of the Retail Price Index for all food. The "heavily-advertised brands" were all the food brands spending over £1/4 million on press and television advertising in 1977 which were also on the market in 1964. (Bread and butter were excluded, as having been particularly subject to official controls.) Their prices were built into a weighted index.

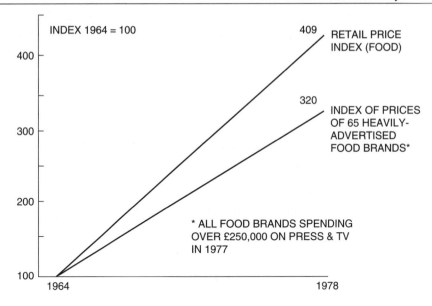

Figure 18.3   Increase in prices, 1964–1978

Despite all the qualifications that have to be made about any price index, the differences are so marked that the only possible conclusion is that "heavily-advertised" food brands go up less in price than food in general.[1] The reason for this is fairly clear, if rather hard to prove. It lies in the contribution of advertising to the *efficiency* of the manufacturer's operation, and relates to the main roles for advertising identified above. The first of these is in competitive maintenance of demand, by reminding consumers. It acts as a control mechanism, enabling the scale of all operations to be reasonably predictable. This affects economies of scale in production – not only in scale *per se*, but also in efficient plant utilization. More strikingly, it can affect economies of scale in distribution (in which, being a more decentralized operation, the scope for inefficiency is greater). Perhaps most of all, it can cut down the total costs of the process of "bringing the brand to the consumer". A major new study of branded goods markets by Dr Duncan Reekie (of the University of Edinburgh) shortly to be published by the Advertising Association, shows clearly that where there are relatively high advertising costs they tend to be more than offset by the lower retail margins needed.

The second way in which advertising acts to keep prices down is a more long-term one, and even harder to demonstrate. It relates to advertising's role in keeping up profit margins; that leads to more investment and innovation, hence greater efficiency in the long run. There can be no doubt that declining profit margins tend to put manufacturers into a vicious spiral; they start cutting back on those very activities which are designed to protect and build the company's long-term prosperity. In general, under profit pressure, there is often a tendency to see survival rather than progress as the top priority, and to retreat into a sort of siege mentality.

The decline of efficiency of established UK companies that could result from this sort of vicious spiral would of course act to break down one of the "barriers to entry" in their markets. Unfortunately, those established companies would be too busy defending their own markets,

---

[1] Results were much the same in the earlier study, "*What Puts the Prices Up?*" by the J. Walter Thompson Company in 1965.

and too much under threat, to want to take the risks themselves of entering new markets. The main beneficiaries of the breaking of the efficiency barriers would be new imported brands.

While this description of the vicious spiral might seem a little oversimple, and maybe overstated, no one viewing the UK market dispassionately today could doubt that import penetration from new foreign brands is one of the country's main economic problems. Most people who believe in competition and free trade will oppose *unfair* "barriers to entry"; but to reduce barriers by reducing the efficiency of UK companies would surely be suicidal.

The evidence seems to point fairly unequivocally to two general conclusions. Advertising for established brands is not a barrier to entry in the sense of an *unfair restraint* which prevents new manufacturers from *trying* to enter a market. On the contrary: by building reasonable profit margins in the market, it makes the idea of entry more attractive to them. However, in the sense of contributing to the *efficiency* of established brands, advertising means that the new brand must be efficient too. It must be better and/or different in order to succeed. Part of this "barrier" of efficiency is the contribution that advertising makes over time to restraining price increases on existing brands.

REFERENCES

A.C. Nielsen Company (1969) *Researcher*, January/February.

A.C. Nielsen Company (1970) *Researcher*, January/February.

Davidson, J.H. (1976) "Why most new consumer brands fail", *Harvard Business Review*, March/April.

Davis, E.J. (1964) "The sales curves of new products", Market Research Society Conference.

Ehrenberg, A.S.C. (1972) *Repeat Buying: Theory and Applications*, North-Holland. [The bibliography of this book has well over 100 entries.]

Kraushar, Andrews & Eassie (1976) *New Products in the Grocery Trade*. Based on Shaw's Price List.

Parfitt, J.H. and Collins, B.J.K. (1968) "The use of consumer panels for brand share prediction", *Journal of Marketing Research*, May.

The Train to Strawberry Hill

By Hugh Burkitt, Chief Executive, The Marketing Society, UK

An introduction to:

19.1   Has Marketing Failed, or was it Never Really Tried?

Stephen King's definition of "Real Marketing" and his picture of the ideal marketer remain entirely contemporary. But my answers to the questions he poses about marketing – *Has Marketing Failed, or was it Never Really Tried?* – are more positive.

Then and Now

Stephen's concern about the grim marketing performance of many British manufacturing companies in the 1970s and 1980s is understandable. British Leyland sold what it could make in the brief periods when it was not on strike. Unfortunately this was a line of dodgy motors that broke down more often than Japanese ones. It is not surprising to find 20 years later that Toyota is the biggest car company in the world and British Leyland's successor – Rover, despite regular government bungs – has gone bust.

But since the mid-1980s, the British economy has been through an astonishing transformation. Then, three million people were out of work and our manufacturing exports were in free fall. Instead, we have been through an unprecedented export boom, we have the fifth largest economy in the world and we are drawing in armies of energetic young workers from the new EU countries of the old eastern bloc.

Our dark satanic mills have become fashionable offices and luxury apartments in the knowledge based economy. The former headquarters of the National Coal Board is the home of Britain's leading hedge fund. We make our national living by moving money silently in and out of the City, exporting The X Factor, and importing the world's best footballers so that we can sell Premier League matches and Manchester United shirts to fans all round the globe.

But can "Marketing" Take any Credit for This?

I would argue that much of this success dates from our willingness to free up markets in the Thatcher era. The Big Bang occurred in London in October 1986, and the City now accounts for 17% of our national income. There are freer markets for consumers in banking, transport, utilities and telecommunications. UK businesses generally have prospered by following the customer and the money and either getting out of manufacturing altogether, or getting it done abroad.

Even James Dyson – one of the most celebrated proponents of British design and engineering – gets his vacuum cleaners made in Malaysia. Many economists have argued that, today, national economic success depends on being as open as possible to the global economy and avoiding manufacture because global competition keeps pushing down the cost of production. The big business successes of the modern era are "platform companies", who sell everywhere but make nowhere, choosing the cheapest place to source their brands – like Dell and L'Oreal. That sounds like good marketing to me.

Marketing Concepts are being Adopted by Government

As our manufacturing subsided, so did support for the unions and the Labour Party. The New Labour brand was a brilliant marketing response. Starting with focus groups, the Labour Party was re-engineered to serve the consumers rather than the workers. Thatcher's privatizations had aimed to provide customers with more choice, and this principle has not been seriously questioned during a decade of government by New Labour.

On a macro level the NHS has endless targets to deliver better service to patients, and on a micro level some interesting work has also been going on which suggests greater customer orientation. Hospital trusts in Kent and Lancashire have been studying Toyota's "Lean Management" philosophy, with the aim of improving patient flow in their A&E departments. Lessons from Toyota have been discussed in Rapid Improvement Workshops in the NHS which encourage staff themselves to design changes in handling patients.

The government's aim for "personalized learning" to be standard practice in state schools by "the end of the next decade" may be jeered at by political cynics, but it demonstrates an important principle. Someone is trying to think about the output of schools from the perspective of their individual customers rather than treating all pupils in schools as one mass-production line.

The public services still have a long way to go and I may now be betraying signs of demented optimism. But I do believe that the Departments of Health and Education are gradually getting the idea that customers are the reason for their existence. Indeed, they get the concept of marketing as described by Peter Drucker 50 years ago: *"Marketing is not a specialised activity. It is the whole business seen from the point of view of its final result, that is, from the customer's point of view".*

However, I was told recently by a senior executive in the Government Communication Network that the word "marketing" is not used in polite civil service circles, because in their minds it is inextricably bound up with the vulgar business of advertising. There is still some work to do in lightening the darker corners of public service.

The Gap Between Marketing as a Philosophy and Marketing as a Function

Stephen was much exercised by this. His view of marketing people may be slightly jaundiced as a result of dealing with them as clients – a role in which they often disappoint. But whatever criticism may be hurled at today's marketers, they understand that marketing is a bigger concept than just the name of their department.

In the Marketing Society's book entitled *Marketing Excellence*, there are 34 case histories and they come from 29 different companies. This provides heartening evidence that marketing is alive and well in the UK. It would have been hard to predict in the mid-1980s that the most outstanding company in the book would be a giant retailer – Tesco.

However, an outstanding team of marketers has turned Tesco into a fine example of *Real Marketing* in action. When the chairman, Sir Terry Leahy, gave the Marketing Society's Annual Lecture a few years ago he spoke of the point in the 1990s when Tesco changed from being *"a company with a marketing department to being a marketing company"*. They have not only learned to listen continually to what their customers want, they do that difficult thing that Stephen valued so highly – they act on it.

Stephen would particularly approve of Tesco's Core Purpose: *"To create value for customers to earn their lifetime loyalty."* Tesco's marketing department is described by marketing director, Tim Mason, as "small, creative and entrepreneurial". They also have an awesome database to which to market. The Tesco Clubcard gives them the full buying pattern of 15 million customers and they make 12 million different mailings to that database. The fabled era of one to one marketing has almost arrived.

Two other retailers who had no truck with marketing in the mid-1980s – Marks and Spencer and the John Lewis Partnership – have both been doing well, with strong marketers in key roles. Marks and Spencer's IPA Effectiveness Award winner "Your M&S" campaign has been led by the Society's Marketer of the Year for 2006. The turn round of the John Lewis Partnership from laggard to leader in the last 15 years also owes much to improved marketing.

The CEO as Brand Manager

Stephen was right in seeing the CEO as the ideal Brand Manager. Although the greatest number of CEOs still come from an accounting background, there is some evidence from research by PA Consulting that CEOs from marketing deliver a higher rate of return for shareholders. The Marketing Society's own research suggests that CEOs understand *Real Marketing* because they are keen to create top-line growth, but often find their own marketers inadequate. They say they want their marketers to be more accountable, more innovative, and more collaborative: a challenge to both hiring practices and training.

A Journey, not a Destination

Marketers now have to face the challenge that the unfettered stimulation of consumer demand is environmentally unsustainable. Climate change has become "An Inconvenient Truth" that we can no longer ignore. But shrewd companies led by King-style enthusiasts will surely see this as an opportunity, not a problem.

Each morning that I travel out to the Society's offices, I take the train to Strawberry Hill and get off one station earlier at Teddington. I am told that if I stayed on the train and stopped at Strawberry Hill I would find that there are, alas, no strawberries and no hill.

One of our fellows said to me when I became Chief Executive, that the Marketing Society is a journey, not a destination. I like the sound of Strawberry Hill, and as I trundle towards it, I continue to travel hopefully.

19.1
Has Marketing Failed, or was it Never Really Tried?*

By Stephen King

Maybe one can tell the state of the art in any subject by analysing the themes of its conferences. Conferences on textile design or machine tools or frozen food distribution are all about practical and purposive issues. Conferences on marketing are apt to be about bridging the gap between theory and practice. We are all constantly aware that there are gaps of various sorts. What is not so easy is to understand why; and if we do not understand why, we will never succeed in doing anything about it.

This article attempts to attack the question from the practical end. Through working in an advertising agency I have had close contact with marketing practice in many companies in consumer goods and services. My knowledge of the theoretical end is a lot patchier. I have had no formal marketing training, though I have read a good deal of the literature and have often been much helped by it. On the other hand, I have scanned certain marketing periodicals for 25 years with despairing incomprehension, failing entirely to derive any benefit from them at all. And I see people emerging from various institutions with qualifications in marketing, but cannot imagine how some of them are remotely suited to any of the jobs that I know about.

In the UK, marketing has always been like this. Its whole history has been something of a paradox.

It arrived in the 1950s, travelling over from the USA and alighting at Newcastle. It spread from Procter and Gamble, and has gone from strength to strength. More and more manufacturing companies got themselves Marketing Managers; and the Marketing Managers got themselves bigger staffs, bigger salaries, bigger offices and bigger company cars. University graduates found a new career to aspire to, and the Marketing Society was founded in 1959. The whole thing has been a huge success.

The UK's marketing *achievement* over these 30 years is rather less impressive. In fact, it has been the worst period of decline in our share of market since the Industrial Revolution. In 1950 the UK had a 26% share of world exports of manufactured goods. By 1979 it was down to 9.5% (see Figure 19.1). (The Americans, from whom we learned our marketing, did almost as badly, going from 27% to 16%). During most of the period profits and employment in manufacturing have declined too.

The performance of UK manufacturers in the home market has been even worse than in export markets, particularly in the last 10 years – during which the import penetration of manufactured goods went up from 17% to 26%.

There have of course been marked differences between industries. Chemicals and packaged consumer goods have done well; cars, durables and machine tools badly. But on the whole

*Published in *Journal of Marketing Management*, 1(1), 1985. Reproduced with permission.

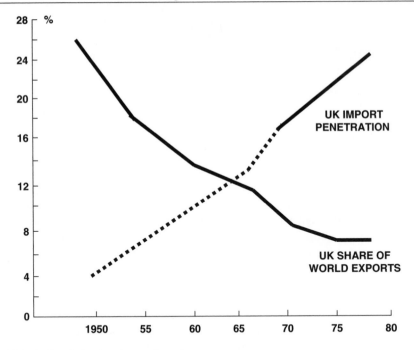

Figure 19.1   UK trade in manufactured goods

you could say that our espousal of marketing has come at the very time that our marketing performance has been most dismal.

Is this just a coincidence? Or has marketing, as practised by most UK manufacturers, been a failure? Or, alternatively, has it never really been tried – is it really an effective principle which has never been properly carried out?

There are of course a great many different causes of weakness in British manufacturing performance – historical, social, economic, political. But increasingly people are expressing doubts about *marketing*, as it is practised, or, as some would say, as it isn't (Bell and Emory, 1971; Newbould and Jackson, 1972).

The export performance is not too hard to explain. Its root cause is a long failure to adjust to the switch from the "soft" markets of the Empire and Commonwealth to the more sophisticated industrialized markets. As NEDO (the National Economic Development Office) put it:

> The long-term fall in the UK export share appears to be associated with a fall in the relative quality or sophistication of UK exports, i.e. their non-price competitiveness, rather than with a decline in their price competitiveness.

You could certainly call that a failure of marketing or of market analysis. But the UK share of exports of goods has stabilized at a fairly reasonable level since we joined the EEC; we remain strong in exporting services; and the value of our exports as a percentage of Gross Domestic Product is still higher than that of Germany, Japan, France and the USA. There are, in fact, signs that we are gradually sorting out the export problems.

The loss of share of our own market is a much more worrying reflection on marketing performance, and that is where I want to concentrate in this article. If we can see where the differences lie between marketing successes and marketing failures, we may get a better idea of whether gaps between theory and practice are to blame.

THE CONTEXT FOR MARKETING

To judge the performance of marketing we must first look at the context in which it has been operating over the last 30 years. I think there are four major trends that are relevant – two to do with the manufacturers and two to do with the consumers. Since the first two are problems and since they conflict with the second two, which are opportunities, we can begin to see what it is that has gone wrong.

The first manufacturer trend is the Producer Bureaucracy. Organizations have got bigger; and that has inevitably meant more hierarchies, more rulebooks and more playing safe. The proportion of UK manufacturing output accounted for by the 100 biggest companies has doubled in the 30-year period, from about 22% to about 44%. Eight companies now employ over 100,000 people each, and six public corporations over 150,000. Eleven trade unions have over a quarter of a million members. There are over one million people, including 90,000 civil servants, working in the health and social security services.

But the producer bureaucracy is more than mere size and cumbrousness. As these institutions get bigger they get less responsive. They look inwards rather than outwards. Their motto becomes: "The customer comes second." All their zeal and effort goes towards perpetuating and caring for themselves.

For instance, planners and architects seem to have put up the tower blocks *they* want to build, not necessarily what people want to live in. Schools seem to be run for the benefit of the teachers, hospitals for the benefit of the porters. British Shipbuilders seem to feel they have a divine right to be paid taxpayers' money in order to build, at a loss, ships that no one much wants to buy. The producer bureaucracy was perhaps best summed up by the local authority that ran, in the Midlands, the Bagnall to Greenfield bus service. They faced complaints that bus drivers were "speeding past queues of people with a smile and a wave of the hand". Deeply hurt by this cruel attack, the authority replied that "it is impossible for the drivers to keep to timetables if they have to stop for passengers".

Manufacturers are not as bad as the public sector, but there is no doubt that producer bureaucracy has often affected their approach to marketing.

The second trend that has affected manufacturers has been the Profit Spiral. Their real rate of return on capital has declined steadily from 13.1% in 1960 to 3.7% in 1979 (Figure 19.2). Inevitably the decline leads to lower investment and particularly lower investment in risky ventures.

All the popular villains have been blamed – managements, unions, economists, bankers, the public sector and the Government. Though few of them have much to be proud of, the real cause is the growth of competition and the progressive removal of protectionism. Rationing went in the early 1950s. Tarriff barriers and Commonwealth Preference went in the 1950s and 1960s. The EEC was joined in 1973. And the present Government is busy trying finally to kick away the crutches, while we all wait with bated breath to see whether the patient will walk or will fall to the ground moaning and calling for a disability pension. In fact, the signs are just beginning to emerge that this "new realism" will work.

The producer bureaucracy and the profit spiral, have been such serious problems inhibiting manufacturers' performance that many of them have failed to notice the dramatic opportunities in the two consumer trends.

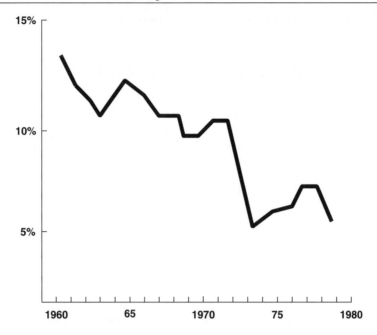

Figure 19.2   UK manufacturing industry real rates of return on capital employed

First, the New Individualism. In the UK, as in the USA and most of Europe, research shows that there have been huge changes in people's interests, tastes and aspirations. They have moved from fixed and inherited values to individual and discovered values. Their horizons have widened in many ways, but especially in a desire for self-expression and self-determination. People want to own their own houses, to decorate and furnish them in their own particular style. The same goes for their cars and clothes and cooking. They want to explore and experiment, to be individuals.

The producer bureaucracies are inevitably ill designed to meet that desire, even when they notice it.

Secondly, the New Affluence. While companies have been suffering from the profit squeeze, most consumers have been doing fairly well (Figure 19.3). However much the media have concentrated on gloom and disaster, consumer spending has grown by about 25% in real terms in each of the three decades. House ownership has risen from 30% to 55%, car ownership from 15% to 60%. In the last 10 years 40% of homes have acquired a freezer and 70% a colour television set; holiday visits abroad have gone up by two-thirds and real spending on radio and electrical goods has more than doubled. Even the current recession is not a recession in consumer spending in real terms – it is more a pause in growth.

What this means is that the new individualism has been able to express itself in increased buying of exciting and stylish goods and services. Despite the doctrinaire views of certain mis-guided economists and quangos, customers have been turning away from the cheap and nasty. It is abundantly clear that what they are looking for is quality, value and style. Unfortunately, they have been increasingly finding them in imported goods. Is British marketing to blame for this?

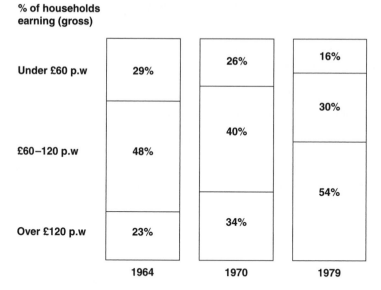

% of households earning (gross)

	1964	1970	1979
Under £60 p.w	29%	26%	16%
£60–120 p.w	48%	40%	30%
Over £120 p.w	23%	34%	54%

Figure 19.3   Changes in household income (at 1979 prices)
Source: Family Expenditure Survey

FOUR ROUTES TO FAILURE

Of course, that raises the question of what we mean by marketing, and that is probably the most fundamental issue of the gap between theory and practice. In the literature there are a great many definitions of marketing, most of them rather abstract. They tend to strain hard to be comprehensive and cover all eventualities. As a result, however well thought out they may be, they usually do not trip very readily off the tongue, and are received by practical marketing men with a surge of apathy. The approach among the practitioners is very different. They tend not to define anything at all. They act first and give it a name afterwards. As a result, there is a wide spread of activities which are called marketing, and many of them seem to have failed.

Let me pick out four of these "marketing" routes to failure.

1. Thrust Marketing

Thrust Marketing is what happens in companies when the Sales Manager decides to change his title to Marketing Manager, though not his function. (As such it is an aspect of the growth of the producer bureaucracy.) It can often happen too when a small entrepreneur feels he's expanded enough to take on his first marketing manager, but can't afford a sales manager too.

Thrust Marketing is the sort of marketing that concerns itself only with that part of the total process that lies between the factory door and the retailer's shelves or, for industrial goods, the factory door and the cheque book. It does not concern itself with what the product or brand is, its design, quality and purpose. Nor is it interested in the final consumer's needs, wants, desires, aspirations or product experience. As long as the link in the middle is made, the Thrust Marketer reckons he's done a good job.

The entrepreneur, who has taken on his first marketing man, might well be very impressed when presented with a purposive "six-point" Marketing Plan like this:

MARKETING PLAN

1. Up-weight 2p-off flashbacks to 80% of throughput.
2. Increase over-riders to selected multiples.
3. Re-motivate sales forces with incentive plan.
4. Initiate tailor-made in-store merchandising with dealer-loaders.
5. Increase stock levels to create product-push, by means of a retailer competition.
6. Launch a countrywide back-to-back coupon drop to create consumer-pull.

In fact, this sort of activity may be pretty close to what the general public and the media mean by "marketing".

It may take our entrepreneur some time to realize that this is an all-purpose Thrust Marketing Plan, which can be trotted out on all occasions, since it takes no account of either product or consumer. It may indeed work fairly well for a time, but it tends to fall apart when a competitor comes forward with a better brand that is more in line with what the customer wants. The problem of Thrust Marketing is that essentially its only weapon is price and price-cutting. It assumes that what people are looking for is cheapness; it fails because what they are really looking for is value.

Thrust Marketing has almost been the norm in many of the heavy industries. Take, for instance, textile machinery. This has long been a special area of British domination, so that in 1955 the UK still had a 30% share of world trade – with Germany next at 20%. Twenty years later, Germany's share of textile machinery exports was up to 33% the UK's down to 12%. There is a clear hint of why this happened in the unit price of the exported machines: the British machines averaged $4760; the German ones, at $6310, were about a third more expensive. Thrust Marketing had struck again. And it affected the home market too, in that the average machine imported into the UK cost 20% more than the average British machine exported. A survey showed that during this period 89% of British textile manufacturers bought foreign machinery (Figure 19.4), and the reasons they gave for doing so show clearly enough why Thrust Marketing fails: it takes no account of what the customer really wants and his constantly rising aspirations. (Pavitt, 1980)

2. Marketing Department Marketing

The weaknesses of Thrust Marketing soon became clear, but what was not so obvious was that Marketing Department Marketing often suffered from some of the same faults. Companies recognized that selling and marketing were not the same and set up their marketing departments. Marketing Department Marketing recognized the importance of the final customer, and started studying consumers' behaviours, attitudes and buying habits. Unfortunately they were both victims and supporters of the producer bureaucracy. The Marketing Department was simply bolted onto the standard company organogram, with all its hierarchies and reporting lines and rigid department barriers. Naturally the Marketing Department busily developed its own arcane mysteries and impenetrable techniques. Marketing must be the jealously guarded province of the Marketing Department, just as production was of the Production Department or R&D of the R&D Department.

One of the Marketing Department's more successful ventures in strengthening its position on the organization chart was the development of the brand manager. This new breed of bright young men rapidly disguised their lack of experience in the real word, and impressed their managements with talk of brand-switching matrices, multi-variate analysis,

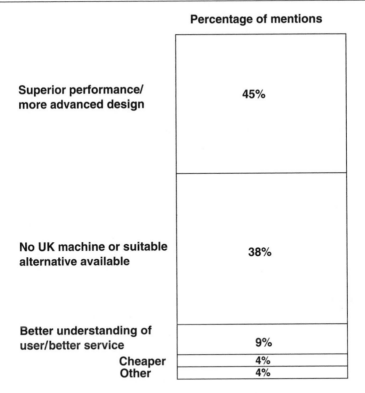

Percentage of mentions

Superior performance/
more advanced design — 45%

No UK machine or suitable
alternative available — 38%

Better understanding of
user/better service — 9%

Cheaper — 4%

Other — 4%

Figure 19.4   Why did 95 UK textile manufacturers buy foreign-made machinery? 1970–1975

competitive pre-talk of preference scores, socio-economic segmentation, n-dimensional concept space, day-after recall and similar gibberish. The Production Manager felt that discussion of the worn bearings on No. 3 machine couldn't really compete; he suffered considerable loss of prestige and confidence in his own skills and judgements about what sort of products he ought to be making. The R&D Manager went on dreaming of being a Real Scientist and winning a Nobel Prize. Departmental barriers were significantly strengthened.

So the marketing men gained in prestige and salary, and attracted bright undergraduates. They understood that the company's success depended on studying the consumer's wants, and genuinely made progress in doing so. But all too often they were given little real authority and, because of these departmental barriers, were not able to do much about *meeting* those wants. For instance, there were marketing men and consumer surveys around in the British motorcycle industry in the 1950s, when Vespas and Lambrettas became popular. They pointed out that styles and tastes were changing, and the market wasn't made up solely of ton-up tearaways and Dad taking Mum for the day by the sea in the sidecar. But they couldn't get through to the production men who knew what they wanted to make. Today the last remnants of the British motorbike manufacturers are still making heavy, basic, over-engineered monsters, while the Japanese have mopped up the market with elegant machines that have self-starters and wing-mirrors and style.

The UK motor industry has market research coming out of its ears; the marketing men know well enough what people want. But it doesn't help them much when they cannot do anything, for instance, about quality control. Research done by ADAC Stressenwecht (the German equivalent of the Automobile Association) shows that the average number of breakdown calls per 1000 registrations (in cars up to two years old) for the top five Japanese makes was 6.2. For British Leyland cars it was 38.3. In fact, Marketing Department Marketing has worked well enough in a stable environment, for instance, in the packaged food market, where product improvements tend to be gradual and not very complicated. But it has been a resounding failure in markets where foreign competitors attack with radical product innovation.

3. Accountant's Marketing

Even in the stable packaged goods markets, there has been a new type of marketing failure – Accountant's Marketing. The producer bureaucracy has played its part here too, as companies get bigger and bigger, through mergers and acquisitions. Gradually the accountants drift to the top of the organization, replacing those whose experience has been in either the company's products or its customers (Hayes and Abernathy, 1980). (In the USA, the number of accountants at the top of the top 100 companies has gone up by 50% in the last 25 years, the number of technical people down by 15% and marketing men down by 20%.)

The result has been that manager's objectives – including Marketing Managers – have increasingly been set in simple terms as the bottom-line figure on a profit-and-loss statement. They have been made to feel that their personal progress depends on turning in good quarterly profit figures. A recent study (Webster, 1981) of the views of chief executives and operating officers in 30 major US corporations suggests that they have, maybe rather late in the day, recognized the results of Accountant's Marketing: "They . . . suspect that they have been guilty of giving conflicting signals to the marketers in their organizations because they, the top executives, have not resolved the complex trade-offs between short-term and long-term measures of financial performance."

Even in the fairly successful world of packaged consumer goods this has led to a "crisis in branding" (King, 1978). The pressure was put on by the profit spiral and the recession of 1974/75, but even more by increased concentration in the retail trade. In 1973 the top five UK grocery chains did about 40% of the business; by the end of 1980 their share was nearer 60%. But their profit margins had halved, and this profit squeeze was passed on to the manufacturers, under the threat of the retailers' massively increased buying power.

To see the practical results of this I looked at the old-established "flagship" brands of the 1970s (King, 1980). There were 67 food brands that had been on the market since 1964 and were also spending at least £250 000 on press and television advertising in 1977. The key to their progress in the 1970s was their retail-selling price.

Between 1964 and 1978 the Retail Price Index for food went up by 308%. But the prices paid by consumers for these flagship brands went up only by 211%. In other words, if they had kept up with the prices of food in general they would have been retailing at about 30% more than they actually were in 1978. That is a huge gap.

Profit margins in the food industry declined over the period, but not by very much – from 6% to 4%. No doubt there were also some improvements in production and distribution efficiency. But neither of these factors could account for more than a small part of that gap.

It is clear that, under Accountant's Marketing, the gap was mainly closed by sacrificing the long-term health of brands – their essential *branding* – to short-term profits. Price-cutting (the weapon of the Thrust Marketer) was the main marketing activity, because it affected volume in the short-run; and that had to be funded by cuts elsewhere. So there were cuts in all forms of expenditure to do with distant returns – R&D, product quality, product improvement, process improvement, innovation generally, consumer research and advertising.

The only one of these that was measured on a regular basis was advertising expenditure, but all the circumstantial evidence suggests that the other aspects of branding suffered to. By 1978 the advertising expenditure on the 67 flagship brands was 36% lower in real terms than it had been in 1970, and in 1979 (when it was affected by the TV strike) it was 52% lower. Much more important, there were signs in many market sectors that the general level of product quality had actually declined in the 1970s. Some old-established brands were no longer beating private label brands in blind product tests. And all this, in the era of the New Individualism and the New Affluence.

The pattern seems to have been much the same in industrial goods (with some notable exceptions in the chemical and electronic industries). Between 1967 and 1975 real spending on industrial R&D declined by 10% in the UK, while it grew by about 50% in France and Germany and 90% in Japan (Schott, 1981). The USA, with a growth of 20% did only a little better than the UK, and the survey of chief executives commented:

> Several respondents expressed the opinion that the financial management orientation that tended to dominate corporate strategy in the 1970s may have created a relatively short-term orientation that left firms in a somewhat weakened position to meet market conditions of the 80s.

The danger was that many manufacturers were getting into a vicious spiral. They weren't earning enough to invest in the improvement of brands that would meet the customers' aspirations and bring in the sales and profits of the future. And it is a great deal harder to get out of a vicious spiral than to avoid getting into one. Accountant's Marketing has been something of a disaster.

4. Formula Marketing

Even where companies have avoided Accountant's Marketing, they have often succumbed to a close relative, Formula Marketing. This is a form of marketing in which control is held to be more important than innovation. (It is a result of both the producer bureaucracy and the profit squeeze.) It is much safer to be static than dynamic; and who is going to take risks when his whole future depends on turning in the results that his distant boss is calling for? The older people at the top of the hierarchy do not entirely trust the young people at the bottom; so they keep handing them heavy bibles of rules, filled with tried and tested formulae for success in marketing.

While chief executives are largely responsible for formula marketing, this does not prevent their complaining about it. The survey of US chief executives reported that a common view was that

> product managers used to come from many areas within a firm – sales, manufacturing, engineering and others – as well as from outside. Today in contrast the standard source is the top 20 or 30 MBA programs in leading universities ... MBAs all tend to think alike, to approach problems the same way, to obscure a problem with excessive number crunching and analysis, to want to move into general management too quickly, to be unwilling to stay in a position long enough to develop competence and learn the details of the business ... marketing managers do not like to take risks and are unable to approach problems in an innovative and entrepreneurial fashion.

There is a heavy reliance on consumer research and testing. On the face of it that is very proper. The trouble is that consumer research can really only tell you about the post. It can tell you what people did and thought at one point in time; it can't tell you *directly* what they might do in a new set of circumstances. For instance, the first estimate of the market for electronic computers in 1945 projected worldwide sales of 10 units. Today the mass media have advertisements for Sinclair home computers selling at under £70, and worldwide some 400 000 have been sold.

The trouble about Formula Marketing is that it tends to produce safe middle-of-the-road brands which, at best, are modestly improved from time to time. They are deeply vulnerable from both ends. Retailers have proved that they can usually market copies of safe packaged goods brands more economically than the original manufacturers, and the pressure of private label and generic brands is unlikely to diminish. And in many other product fields the retailers are likely to dominate the market before the manufacturers really establish brands at all.

Equally Formula Marketers are vulnerable, as we have seen, to technical innovation in imported goods – particularly in the heavy industries.

The record for innovation and new brands is probably better in the grocery trade than elsewhere, but it is hardly very satisfactory. A recent analysis showed that of 585 new advertised food brands, in 31 product categories, launched between 1969 and 1976, 310 were off the market by 1978 (Figure 19.5).

Of the survivors only 21 had sales in 1978 of over £4 million at RSP. Practically all were from food manufacturers staying very close to their existing businesses, and indeed about half of them were really range extensions rather than new brands. Clearly manufacturers are right to develop range extensions, but where are the flagship brands of the future to come from? If some of the costs of the new brand failures and of tending the walking wounded had been put into genuine innovation, it is hard to believe that the results would not have been better.

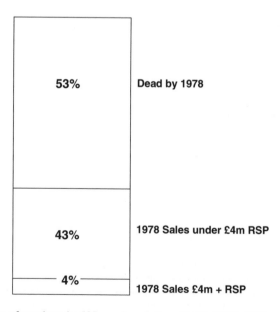

Figure 19.5   The fate of new brands: 585 new brands launched in 1969–1976

Recent performance has been symbolized by the two product types, which between them won no less than six places in lists of the Top Ten new product launches of 1978 and 1979. At a time when the new individualists were experimenting with exciting recipes, providing increasing variety in their own entertaining and seeing luscious presentations of inventive dishes in their weekly magazines, the top new brands were of instant custard and instant noodles. In each sector there was one originator and at least three me-too brands. There was certainly some valuable new technology and they were ingenious lines from a convenience point of view. But it would be very hard to argue that they were keeping up with consumers aspirations, or indeed that many of the manufacturers involved have the making here of a solid long-term business.

WHAT HAS SUCCEEDED?

It's always easy to pick out the failures. But what lies behind the many successes there have also been? Most people would agree that Thrust Marketing, Market Department Marketing, Accountant's Marketing and Formula Marketing have been pretty unsuccessful. But they would argue that these aren't real marketing at all. So what is Real Marketing – the sort that does work?

I believe that it's helpful to have looked at the four types of false marketing, because it makes it possible to pick out, by contrast, four essential aspects of Real Marketing.

1. Starting with the Customer

Starting with and aiming to satisfy the customer is the converse of Thrust Marketing, and is the essence of any definition of Real Marketing. The distributive and pricing elements are usually a necessary condition for success, but never a sufficient one.

Real Marketing's starting point is designing a product or service to meet the wants of a group of customers. It is *adding values* to the raw materials to meet the totality of those wants, both physical and psychological. So it embraces suitability for purpose, quality, design, brand personality, style, availability, after-sales service, ease of repair and all other aspects of a customer's relationship with a brand.

Since it always operates in a competitive environment, that means meeting customers' wants better than competitors do – which cannot be achieved without putting considerable resources into understanding people and the changes in their values and aspirations.

Three quick examples: Mr Kipling cakes were launched nationally in 1970. The brand was very firmly based on the public's desire for better quality in bought cakes, a trend towards informal eating (hence small personal cakes rather than large shared cakes), and a general move towards premium-priced goods and a sense of style. By 1975, Mr Kipling was brand leader, and today it turns in a profit of well over £5 million.

The UK hosiery market was not an easy one in the 1960s and 1970s. There was a huge over-capacity, a growth in supermarket sales, a threat from cheap imports, private label and price-cutting in a fragmented, low-profit industry. Yet Pretty Polly managed to quadruple its market share, keep out imports, become brand leader and one of the top half dozen producers in the world, while substantially and continuously increasing profits. The secret lay in regular heavy investment in the latest machinery and a single-minded approach to brand building – all based on satisfying what the customer wanted in the way of efficiency, fashion and style.

The Volkswagen Beetle is one of the most successful brands of car there has ever been. At exactly the right time it recognized and met a desire among a section of car buyers for a no-nonsense, rugged, economical, small family car. What distinguished it from other "People's

Cars" is that it recognized too the need for a brand personality: that what the customer is looking for is a great deal more than just a means of transport.

2. Working Over Time

In contrast with Accountant's Marketing, Real Marketing sets out to work over time. The whole point of branding – that is, in simple terms, designing something special and putting one's name on it – is to make it a little easier to be successful in the future than at present. Its most fundamental purpose is to identify a unique article or service, and remind people of the satisfaction that they or others have had from it in the past.

This means that Real Marketing cannot be divorced from product quality, product improvement, process improvement and manufacturing productivity. All those are an essential ingredient of satisfying customers over time. It is possible, if there is a crisis, to stop investing for the future and to exploit the accumulated goodwill in a brand's added value – just so long as there is a return to the long-term investment called for by Real Marketing as soon as the crisis is over.

Perhaps the most encouraging sign in the UK economy today is that, under pressure of severe profit squeeze and industrial recession, manufacturers of consumer goods have not taken the easy way out, the method of Accountant's Marketing, cutting the marketing budget. They have grasped the nettle and improved manufacturing efficiency, often with painful effects on employment. As Figure 19.6 shows, the traditional link between profits and advertising expenditure has been dramatically broken.

Lever Brothers treatment of Persil is a fine example of Real Marketing working over time. Persil is one of the most amazing post-war brands in the UK. In 1950, it was market leader in

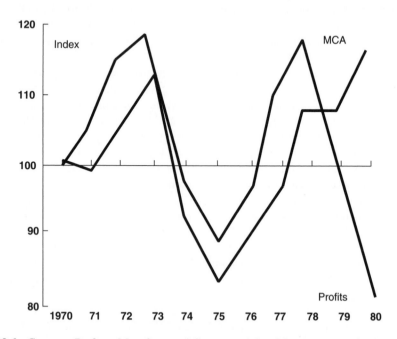

Figure 19.6   Company Profits v. Manufacturers' Consumer Advertising (constant prices)

washing powders, with a brand share of about 30%. But it was a soap powder, and everywhere else the non-soap detergents were taking over. Since then Persil has faced new competition from Tide, Surf, Daz, Omo, Fairy Snow, Ariel, Ariel Automatic, Radiant and Bold. It fought back via Real Marketing – a regular series of product improvements, inducing investment in processing, a number of minor process improvements, and crucially the addition, long before automatic machines were really established, of a low-suds variant, Persil Automatic. Perhaps most striking has been the consistency of its brand personality, based on a fundamental understanding of what consumers really want in their washing powders (which is a good deal more than plain efficiency). Today Persil and Persil Automatic together have nearly 40% of the market.

3. Using All the Company Resources

It becomes increasingly clear that Real Marketing cannot be thought of as a department activity. It is a matter of harnessing *all* of the company's resources to satisfy customers, and of linking what the customer wants with what the company is (or can become) uniquely available to provide so that it can prosper by doing so. The question is: who is in a position in the company – who has the skills, influence and authority – to do that job?

The answer in small entrepreneurial companies is easy enough: it's the boss. In large struc-tured companies, it's not so simple. Very often no single person has both the power and the knowledge effectively to mobilize all the company resources. The clear implication is that in such companies Marketing Department Marketing should be replaced by a *group* representing the necessary skills. In my view, the basic group for marketing management would be one of three people: the Chief Executive, to represent company policy and allocation of resources, including finance; the Manufacturing Director, representing production, design and R&D; the Marketing Director, representing customers, distribution and communications (Figure 19.7). I don't see how Real Marketing can be done without mobilizing and coordinating all those

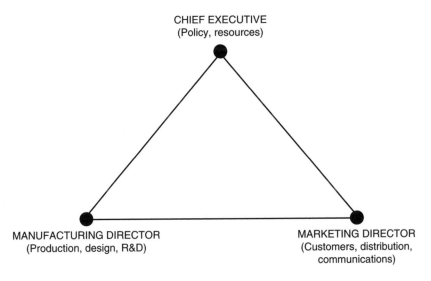

Figure 19.7   The Real Brand Management

resources and skills, and in large companies I don't see how it can be done without setting up this sort of group.

It goes rather further than that. Real Marketing requires a link between the customer and the *corporate personality*. This is where entrepreneurs have a great advantage and why they are so often better at marketing than large companies. Not only do Freddie Laker and Terence Conran have a real instinct for what their customers want and a real knowledge of what they themselves offer; but also everything they do is governed by their own personalities – the style is unmistakable. (Laker has of course also demonstrated the dangers of one-man entrepreneurism, but the amazing public response to his collapse showed what he had previously achieved.)

There is no real reason why large companies shouldn't have clear-cut corporate personality too, and the best of them do. Think of ICI, IBM, Kellogg's, Sainsbury's, Marks and Spencer's, Sony, Ford, Guinness. It requires a clear sense of direction, adhered to over a long period of time: and it seems to be an essential part of Real Marketing.

4. Innovating

The fourth essential element of Real Marketing is innovation – the antithesis of Formula Marketing. Real Marketing can never be safe and static. It is always fighting against competitors; even monopolies have to face substitutes. And it is always aiming to please customers, whose ideas and aspirations are constantly changing.

There can be little doubt that the marketing failure of the UK since the war in heavy industries is fundamentally a failure to change and innovate (Pavitt, 1980). Equally, the record in new brands of consumer goods is really rather depressing, when every serious analysis has come to the same conclusion: that success in new brands depends on being "better and different" (Davidson, 1976).

What Real Marketing is calling for is more resources devoted to innovation than normally happens, and it requires a different attitude of mind. But what is perhaps not sufficiently understood is that the organization and methods that work best for steadily improving routines are by no means the best for innovation. Hierarchies, systems, rulebooks and formulae work pretty well for controlling and improving the efficiency of repeated actions. They are hopeless for inventing, experimenting with and developing something that has never happened before (King, 1973).

If marketing is to succeed – and become Real Marketing – it has got to come to grips with the more flexible methods of group work and project management, with qualitative research and lateral thinking with judgement and risk-taking.

SO HAS MARKETING FAILED?

What emerges is that Real Marketing is a broad and quite complex business philosophy. Its essence is:

- Putting the customer first – not the distribution system
- Giving satisfaction over time – not just profits this month
- Using all the company resources – not just one department's
- Innovating – not just sticking to formulae.

Where it is followed, it seems to work. But we have to admit that there are far too many instances where it has never really been tried. Absence of Real Marketing emerges as a central cause of economic failure in Britain over the past 30 years (Spurrell, 1980). I do not think that marketing education can be completely absolved from blame, if the practitioners sometimes fail to see the difference between Real Marketing and Thrust Marketing, Marketing Department Marketing, Accountant's Marketing or Formula Marketing. (One of the lessons we learn early in the advertising business is that if an audience fails to receive an idea, it is the fault of the sender, not the receiver.)

It is not necessarily that marketing theory is bad theory, though no doubt it sometimes is. It seems to me much more that the theory has been allowed to become too complicated and too diffuse. Maybe the best way of bridging the gaps would be to concentrate on a small number of them that seem to be particularly destructive. Here is my short-list:

1. We must make much clearer the distinction between marketing as a philosophy or business principle and marketing as a discrete activity carried out by people who are not in finance or production or R&D or general management. What is needed for managing Real Marketing is polymaths, people who understand production and simple accounting as well as consumers and distribution. Marketing education needs to stress that the job is one of mobilizing all the resources in the company. That clearly means considerable semantic difficulties, and no doubt some inter-departmental squabbles within Business Schools, but unless such problems are given a high priority the most fundamental of gaps between theory and practice will remain.

2. I doubt if quite enough emphasis is put on the forms of organization that are most likely to be innovative, or indeed on innovation as the basis of Real Marketing. Left to themselves, most producer bureaucracies will form into hierarchical organizations with rigid departmental barriers. Marketing education must call more strongly for group work, project management and venture management. It must get people to recognize that getting things done in any organization is often a great deal harder than knowing what to do. Marketing directors have to be evangelists first, technocrats second.

3. Time-scale has become a great deal more important in marketing than it used to be. I believe that marketing education must concentrate more on the genuine conflicts that there are between the short term and long term. A generation of top managers calling for profits this week and of brand managers aiming for a quick flashy success before moving on could bring almost any company to its knees. Marketing educators have to learn how to warn against this without always apparently offering jam tomorrow.

4. I think that marketing education has to be brave enough to emphasize that judgement will always be more important than technique in marketing. The data which is marketing's raw material will always be dodgy, consumers will always be irrational, cause and effect will always be partly impenetrable, competition will always ensure that rules are there to be broken. As the commentary on the US chief executives study put it:

> Marketing is different from finance and production, the other areas of management decision making where operations research and econometrics have been applied so forcefully and effectively.... Yet marketers aspire to the same degree of rigor that has characterized the analysis of their colleagues in these other functions. The result may have been a significant sacrifice of relevance.

The overriding impression that one gets from marketing periodicals and some marketing books is that technique is all-important. Partly this is caused, particularly in the USA, by the pressure to publish. (It appears not to matter too much *what* is published – never mind the quality, feel the width.) Perhaps a more important cause is a feeling of inferiority, of not being a proper profession – a view of marketing shown by surveys to be shared by MPs and the general public. But it seems to me that there are perfectly respectable professions which are equally dependent on judgement: historians, for instance, are constantly developing hypotheses based on incomplete and inaccurate data, in order to produce explanations of cause and effect, by judgement and an understanding of people's motives.

Maybe some of the time spent by some teachers on producing unreadable esoterica would be better used in listening to consumers, watching practical marketing men in action and, if possible, having a go at it themselves.

REFERENCES

Bell, M.L. and Emory, C.W. (1971) "The faltering marketing concept", *Journal of Marketing*, 35, 37–42.

Davidson, J.H. (1976) "Why most new consumer brands fail", *Harvard Business Review* 54(2), 117–122.

Hayes, R.H. and Abernathy, W.J. (1980) "Managing our way to economic decline", *Harvard Business Review*, 58(4), 67–77.

King, S.H.M. (1973) *Developing New Brands* (pp. 40–48). London: Pitman.

King, S.H.M. (1978) *Crisis in Branding*. London: J.Walter Thompson Co Ltd.

King, S.H.M. (1980) *Advertising as a Barrier to Market Entry* (pp. 28–30). London: The Advertising Association.

Newbould, G.D. and Jackson, A.S. (1972) *The Receding Ideal*. Liverpool: Guthstead Limited.

Pavitt, K. (ed.) (1980) *Technical Innovation and British Economic Performance*. London: Macmillan.

Schott, K. (1981) *Industrial Innovation in the UK, Canada and the US*. London: North America Research Association.

Spurrell, D.J. (1980) "Business strategy in the United Kingdom – the challenge from abroad", *Nat West Quarterly Review*, 3, 35–44.

Webster, F.E. (1981) "Top management's concerns about marketing: Issues for the 1980s", *Journal of Marketing*, 45, 9–16.

A Challenge to Change Behaviour

By Neil Cassie, Founding Partner, The Cassie Partnership

An introduction to:

20.1   Brand Building in the 1990s

My aim in this introduction to Stephen's article "Brand Building in the 1990s" is to highlight the challenge I believe he was actually laying down for marketers and those of us in the world of marketing services.

In the midst of what are astonishingly far-sighted predictions of: "More Confident Consumers", "New Concepts of Quality", "The Competitive Screw Tightening", "Side Effects of Technology" and more, Stephen made his real point.

He was challenging us – agencies and marketing clients alike – to *behave* differently so that together we could grow the value of the brands in our care. In fact, in the final section of what was his last published article he asks us to enjoy starting again from first principles and using *ourselves* and our experience as a research source.

As his thinking and arguments develop towards the concept of the company brand, the second element of his challenge was laid down. He asks of us to stop using the old classic fmcg brands as the models to which we should aspire.

And as Stephen looked at a future apparently so opaque to others, he laid down the third element of his challenge. He envisioned a future where consumer choice would be based, not on classic product or even service discriminators, but on the *people* of the company that provided these products or services. In fact, the discriminator would flow from the culture that their "collective being" stood for.

A Call for New Styles of Leadership

He knew that companies would have to transform themselves because he saw that discriminators would be built on people within organizations, not on the things the company produced. A new calibre of leadership, new qualities of communication and new skills and roles would be required. The core management competence would become an ability to embrace, galvanize and inspire the *intangible* human capital of the business.

He also saw what would *not* be needed: hierarchy, silos, chains of command and control infrastructure.

In the article you will find that Stephen uses the terminology of brands and branding to describe what he means by this new type of company environment. I feel he was suggesting that we apply the philosophies and principles of brand building, rather than be constrained by the deadening language of conventional organizational structures.

And, therein lay his core challenge at the beginning of the 1990s: would this actually happen?

The answer, from the perspective of the first decade of the twenty-first century, is that some changes *have* happened. Corporate brands are increasingly common but few companies have really grasped the challenge.

This is why what Stephen wrote 15 years ago is so valuable 15 years later.

From "Push" to "Pull"

So much of what Stephen predicted came true, but to a large degree, increasing wealth, stable economies, globalization, technology and mergers and acquisitions ensured that demand for products and services remained relatively constant in the 1990s.

This allowed companies to retain their somewhat rigid, highly structured, top-down approach to business. To meet predictable demand, process, systems, centralized decision making and command and control prevailed.

Today, however, we have moved beyond the "push" economies of the 1990s to the "pull" economies of the twenty-first century. As we rush at headlong speed from predictable "push" to non-predictable "pull" demand, people are replacing processes at the heart of modern business.

We are seeing dramatic shifts from hierarchical, silo organizations to innovative, fluid human organisms. Within these new dynamic environments, talent marketplaces are being created where the talent of the business can flow to the point of greatest need at a moment's notice.

In this new business paradigm, success is defined by the inherent, personal value of each individual being aligned with the vision and values of the organization.

At its most successful, this alignment and fluidity has the potential to create a culture of productivity, innovation, localized decision making, learning and trust. The recognition of the need to move to this "ideal state" is now widespread among global business leaders (as it was to Stephen 15 years earlier).

What can Marketing Services do?

The questions they are asking are:

- Who can help us to make the transition from the tangible to the intangible while still ensuring the growth of our business?
- Who can help us to break out of our rigid, process-driven approach to place people at the heart of our value creation?
- Who can help us to link inextricably the growth of our people with the growth of our company?

Had the marketing and advertising fraternity paid more heed to Stephen's advice at the time, I believe that companies would not be looking so hard now for the suppliers/partners with the right skill set to help them to succeed.

Marketing and advertising people *do* have the inherent skill set to meet these redefined client demands. But the question remains, do they have the will to break out of their own conventions?

Many have taken the luxury of ignoring Stephen's parting advice and, over the past years, have been facing the consequences. From where I sit with my clients every day, it is clear that the time to act is now. Otherwise the large global management consultancies will eventually acquire the necessary skills and further displace advertising and marketing from the top table.

Stephen laid out his challenges in the article you are about to read, but was generous enough through his own behaviour, words and ideas to give us plenty of clues as to how to proceed in order to meet them. No better time than now to begin that journey.

I was struck by the relevance of a Brian Andreas story from his book *"Mostly True"* (Berkeley, 1993). In this context, it is the most appropriate epitaph to Stephen I can think of:

> *He wrote secret notes to*
> *people he hadn't met yet.*
> *Some of them aren't even*
> *born, he said, but we live*
> *In a strange neighbourhood &*
> *they will need help*
> *figuring things out & I*
> *won't always be around*
> *to explain it to them.*

"Secret Notes," Brian Andreas: *Mostly True*

Some Practical Advice

1. The first thing you can do is read up on the subject. I recommend "From push to pull: The next frontier of innovation", *McKinsey Quarterly*, 2005; "Authentic leadership development: Getting to the root of positive forms of leadership," *The Leadership Quarterly*, 16, 2005. These articles represent only one from each publication and there are many more that are worth reading.

2. The second and perhaps more important thing to do is to question your own behaviour and in particular the limitations you place upon yourself.

   Really think about your personal, inherent value. Answer the question "Why me?". What is it that differentiates you from your peers? How can you bring that unique value into work most of the time? What are the challenges you will face and what are your plans to overcome them?

   Think of all this in the context of your "story so far". Then project forward into your ideal world and write your "story to come". Share both stories with those close to you professionally and personally. See how your stories affect them and also how they affect you.

   Shape the company you work for around you, not the other way around.

3. Practise that behaviour and manage its implications and you will be in a position to advise your clients in response to their new demands, and be well beyond the confines of your existing role.

20.1

Brand Building in the 1990s*

By Stephen King

NEW PRESSURES

It's always easy to drift on with the old ways of doing things, simply because social and economic movements are gradual and it never seems the right day to make a change. A new decade (and we can still just about think of the 1990s as that) can at least prod us to look again at our marketing methods and maybe revise the textbooks. I think we need to.

However gradually they've grown, the pressures on companies during the past decade have become formidable, and they seem likely to intensify in the 1990s. Let me pick out six of them: three to do with people and three to do with the companies themselves.

1. More Confident Consumers

In almost all markets, consumers have become more confident, readier to experiment and trust their own judgement. They're less tolerant of products and services that don't contribute to their own values. By the end of the 1990s they'll be more mature (roughly 10% more over-35s and 10% fewer under-35s in Europe). They'll have more disposable income and wealth and be more worldly-wise. They'll have an even greater understanding of marketing, advertising, public relations and direct response. They'll ensure that customers in business-to-business marketing become more demanding too.

Underlying this new confidence is rampant individualism. Despite all the talk about "globalism", there has rarely been a time when people have been more aware of the tribes to which they belong. The individualism is likely to transcend national cultural differences: there will be more differences, say, within Germany than between the "average" German and the "average" Briton.

2. New Concepts of "Quality"

People will still be looking for high quality and personal added values, variants, style and fashion changes. But their interpretation of "quality" seems to be changing quite fast. It's increasingly based on what they feel are *real values* – not superficial styling. They are searching for the "full life"; one in which they find meaning and culture in everything they do and buy. There are certainly excesses in much that currently surrounds "greenism", but it's an indication of a growing social awareness. People are increasingly willing to pay a little extra for a clear conscience.

*Published in *Journal of Marketing Management*, 7(1), 1991. Reproduced with permission.

3. Shortage of Skills

A combination of demographic changes (especially in Germany) and a weakness in educational and training systems (most notably Britain's in the intermediate vocational area) means that there is likely to be a severe shortage of the skills needed to meet these new demands for quality.

4. The Competitive Screw Tightens

Competition is intensifying in almost all fields, typified maybe by Japanese investment in Europe, up by some 350% over four years. In 1989 the number of Japanese companies with plants in Europe went up by 23% to over 500. The real pressures from all this investment have yet to come, but it is clear that there will be over-capacity in many markets.

At the same time, there are stirrings in the European retail trade, as the most national of companies start looking outside their traditional boundaries. Some of the international but decentralized companies, such as Auchan or Tengelman, are looking at centralizing their buying. Pan-European buying groups are emerging. Aldi has invaded the UK, sending out some ominous signals about price wars. All the signs are that the balance of power between manufacturers and retailers is still going the retailers' way.

5. Side-Effects of New Technology

New technology has perhaps been talked about more than it has actually affected brand building so far. But that will surely change in the 1990s. There will be shorter product and service life-cycles and faster technological leapfrogging, with more discontinuities than we've seen before, via new materials, electronics and biotechology. Constant innovation will be a necessary part of normal commercial life, but few companies will be able to rely on having any *demonstrable* product or service advantage for more than a few months.

Retailers will get better at using the power of the data on turnover, stocks and profit that scanning has put at their fingertips. So far, this information has been used mainly as just another weapon in the long bouts of arm-wrestling with their suppliers. Now the more innovative retailers, such as Vons in California and Generale Supermercati in Italy, are using the detailed information they have about individual local customers to develop more accurately tailor-made services for them. There is a huge opportunity in new technology for retailers to become the consumer's friend and helper in a way that few manufacturers will be able to match.

6. Restructuring

In just two years, takeovers of the really big companies (those worth over 1 billion ECUs) have gone up by two and a half times. There has been a wave of mergers, takeovers, MBOs, LBOs, bundling, unbundling and all sorts of barbarians at the gates. There may now be a temporary pause for breath, but the process will surely start up again. John Harvey-Jones has suggested that at least half the companies in Europe will disappear by the mid-1990s. Even when company structures are left unchanged, there are often huge corporate alliances – such as Philips/Thomson in high-definition TV, Sumitomo/Yuasa/Lucas in car components, Volkswagen/Ford in the development of a vehicle to challenge the Renault Espace.

Many organizations and people must be wondering who they are, to whom they owe loyalty and what their corporate culture is.

BRAND BUILDING

In such times of pressure and rapid change, how are companies to ensure that they stay on the right side of John Harvey-Jones's dividing line? How are they to retain and build their customer base and their margins? If they are constantly being restructured in some way, how are they to succeed in building any enduring link with their consumers?

Most people in marketing would agree that success will depend critically on developing skills in *brand building*. That is, on using all the company's particular assets to create unique entities that certain consumers really want; entities which have a lasting personality, based on a special combination of physical, functional and psychological values; and which have a competitive advantage in at least one area of marketing (raw materials/sourcing, product/design/patents, production systems, supply/sales/service networks, depth of understanding of consumers, style/fashion, and so on).

Most would say (e.g. Doyle, 1989) that brand building is the only way in these circumstances:

- to build a stable, long-term demand
- to add the values that will entice customers and consumers
- to build and hold decent margins
- to provide a firm base for expansion into product improvements, variants, added services, new countries, etc.
- to protect the company against the growing power of intermediaries
- to transform an organization from a faceless bureaucracy to a company that is attractive to work for or deal with.

All this is hardly new. Does it simply mean that the message for the 1990s is exactly the same as for the 1980s? For some brands, the answer must be "yes". For the "classic" brand leaders in packaged grocery products (such as Coke, Pepsi, Marlboro, Ivory, Lux Toilet Soap, Persil, Oxo, Bovril, Mars, Kit Kat, Andrex), it will be the mixture as before. There seems no reason why such brands should not prosper more or less indefinitely, given adequate tender loving care. If they can be given consistent branding and marketing expenditure, regular innovation and extension, based on sensible economies of scale and cost control, they will surely be brand leaders in 20 years' time, just as most of them were 20 years ago. The evidence is overwhelming that their sort of market share, based on high product quality and supported by a high proportion of advertising in the marketing mix, is linked to a high return on investment (Abraham, 1990; Buzzell and Gale, 1987; The Ogilvy Center, 1989).

But with the changes that are coming in the 1990s, it seems to me that such brands will become steadily rarer and a smaller part of consumers' expenditure than we have been used to. It's been clear for many years that nowadays successful new single-line brands are a great rarity (Madell, 1980; Tauber, 1988), and indeed that many of the classic brands would simply never have made it if they had been launched in today's circumstances. We can get a hint of what's been happening by looking at which brands spend most on press and TV advertising. In 1969, of the 25 top-spending brands in the UK, 19 were repeat-purchase packaged goods; in 1989 it was just one.

We are going to have to get out of the habit of using the old classic brands as the models to which we should aspire. I believe that brand building in the 1990s, is entering a new mode. It is not simply a matter of these more demanding pressures, but also that the long-promised "service economy" seems genuinely to be happening in the new Europe. (Or at least that it will burst forth after the next period of recessionary battening down of the hatches.)

People are increasingly valuing non-functional rewards more, even if the style of those rewards may be changing somewhat from one of glitz and designer everything to one of authenticity and greenism. White-collar service is now the employment mode of the majority. More people work in IT and entertainment and communications and financial services, less in satanic mills. The norm in Europe is adding values, not basic production.

We must get better at recognizing the key marketing implication of this sort of economy. It is not simply that more of people's money will be spent on "services" rather than on "products". It is more that virtually everything we buy is a combination of product and service (Foxall, 1985). And that, for a brand to be successful, the service element is going to have to become more dominant (Christopher, 1985).

This in turn will imply, in an era of rapid technological leapfrog, that increasingly the *company brand* will become the main discriminator. That is, consumers' choice of what they buy will depend rather less on an evaluation of the functional benefits to them of a product or service, rather more on their assessment of the people in the company behind it, their skills, attitudes, behaviour, design, style, language, greenism, altruism, modes of communication, speed of response, and so on – the whole company culture, in fact.

In essence, brand building in the 1990s will involve designing and controlling all aspects of a company, leading people and activities well beyond the traditional skills of the marketing department and the agencies that it employs. It will be a lot closer to the marketing of services (such as airlines, hotels, retailers, building societies) than to the brand building of the classic brands.

But the problem is that the whole idea of branding in services is relatively new. There is no very well-established body of either readable academic findings or practical folklore. Conferences on service marketing tend to treat it as a specialist subject rather than as the new centre of brand building. And many service companies, especially those in financial services, have rushed into a quick purchase of the brand managers, methods and communication media of the classic repeat-purchase brand companies – sometimes with rather unhappy results.

There's a lesser but still obstructive problem of language. Most managers outside marketing (and indeed some in it) are not used to thinking of companies as "brands" – the world has been linked too firmly in their minds with trivial things in packages in grocery stores. The term "corporate identity" is used by many to mean roughly what I mean by "company brand"; but since it's even more widely used to mean the company logo, it seems to me to be a dangerous (as well as a cumbersome) phrase.

There is still a lot to do in simply establishing what will be new about brand building in the 1990s.

WHAT'S DIFFERENT ABOUT A COMPANY BRAND?

In fact there are some fairly obvious differences between the classic brands and the "new" service-based company brands.

The Consumers are Different

When the classic brands were launched, people looked to authorities for their opinions. Attitudes were inherited and respect was shown. Such people as teachers, doctors, bank managers, lawyers, MPs (maybe even journalists and financiers) were looked up to. A classic brand could become the authority in its own field, and mass marketing was quite feasible. Today, there's not a great deal of respect for any authority, and marketing companies face not an admass but a lot of people who want to be treated as individuals.

Most Service-based Products Can be Readily Copied

Most of the classic brands had a good run before copies came onto the market and had time to establish themselves. Many of them were based on genuine product inventions, sometimes patents. This is simply not true of today's service-based products: think of the many "products" produced by banks and building societies. However ingenious, they can be quickly and easily copied, and usually are.

The Points of Contact for a Company Brand are More Diverse

For the classic brand, some of the traditional marketing rules of thumb (like, for instance, the 4Ps) work well enough. If product, packaging, pricing, distribution and advertising are more or less right, it is likely that all will be well. Final consumers and retailers make up the only really important points of contact for the brand.

When the company is the brand, there are clearly far more points of contact. They range from the closest to home (employees) to the furthest distant (the community in general) – with, in between, shareholders, Government departments, institutions (The City, Trade Unions, etc.), journalists, experts, MPs, suppliers, customers, retailers, pressure groups and consumers of the company's products/services. These groups are by no means self-contained: the trade unionist negotiating a wage claim is probably a reader of the advertisement in the *Financial Times* proclaiming the company's 14th consecutive year of record profits.

Because of this diversity of contact, there is far greater diversity of communication media used. For the classic brand, advertising and packaging are overwhelmingly important. For the company brand, it can range from the most personal (face-to-face) to the most impersonal (general publicity) via the telephone, demonstrations, print material (both personal and broadcast), design in general, packaging, promotions and advertising. Anything up to half-a-dozen departments, with jealously guarded budgets, can be responsible for important communications on behalf of the brand.

It's clear that coordinating all this, so that the company brand is presented coherently and consistently, is a far harder task than anything faced by a classic brand. Many companies have barely started dealing with it.

Discriminators are Based on People, not Things

The classic brands had tangible products that stood out from their variable competitors. Most gave instant sensual satisfaction and the consumers knew immediately whether they liked them or not. Even when it was copied, the unique personality of a brand was based ultimately on the product. The source of success for these brands was repeat-purchase of a standard article, based on the familiarity and consistent quality of an old friend. They became a habit; they were one more agonizing decision that didn't have to be made.

Consumers repeat-buy the company brand too and they compare it with competitors (Brouillard Communications, 1988), but it is no standard article. The discriminator is a changing collection of people, values, styles and behaviour. What binds the people together is very intangible – a complex set of norms, conventions, methods, examples, organizational patterns, rules and personalities.

With such major differences in consumers, products, points of contact, media use and discriminators, we may have to abandon the marketing rules derived from the classic brands and go back to basics in our approach to brand building. This is no dreary solemn duty: the opportunities opened up are extraordinarily stimulating.

BUILDING THE COMPANY BRAND

In fact we may have to take a new look at every aspect of brand building. But let me here just pick out four that seem to be particularly important:

1. The Staff as Brand-builders

The idea that the employees of a company will be the key element in brand building and a major communication medium in the 1990s is a liberating one. To take just a few of the implications:

- *The role of the Personnel Director.* Maybe he/she should be thought of primarily as a marketing person and should have direct experience in it. At the moment, there tends to be an almost complete barrier between personnel and marketing departments; there are different strands of theoretical background, consultants, research agencies, communication methods – and this is surely wrong. The criteria used for selection and evaluation of employees should certainly take into account individuals' skills in reflecting, contributing to and presenting the corporate brand.
- *Expressing company strategies.* There clearly should be a full programme of explaining brand (i.e. company) strategies to *all* members of the staff and indeed of using the staff's reactions at times to modify the strategy. For many companies the discipline of explaining could make a useful test of whether the strategy makes sense.
- *Training, motivation, leadership.* There are some clear lessons from the best companies – for instance, McDonald's with their Hamburger University; Sainsbury's, completion of whose training course is accepted as one-third of a university degree; British Airways, whose staff training was central to its turnaround. But there are plenty of black spots too. For instance, some research has shown that about half the people who take a test drive in a car end up by buying it; yet other research suggests that only in 10% of cases do salesmen in franchised car dealers offer the enquirers a test drive. Another recent "mystery shopper" survey showed that, when cashiers were asked for information on their bank's (brand's) mortgage services, most handed out leaflets, but only 15% took the enquirer's name and address. Not the staff's fault – just a symptom of thoughtless training and leadership.
- *Internal communications.* Some companies do it well enough, some not so well. But relatively few programmes of employee communications derive from brand building and the planning of the company brand values. The editor of the house journal should be an important member of the brand building team.

2. Organization

It's arguable that in a competitive situation getting the company branding right is the most important job for the management. Equally, it's clear that not many companies have organized their management structures with that in mind. The companies behind the classic brands are not by any means a good model (indeed they may be increasingly wrong for their own purposes). They tend to rely too much on the traditional "family tree" type hierarchy. That means they

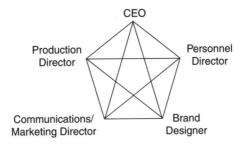

Figure 20.1   The New Brand Management

are too split by function to lead naturally to the innovation and imagination that any brand constantly needs. Decisions tend to be made too tactically, too low down in the organization, with too little guidance from the top.

The right organization for a company brand implies that brand management should reside right at the top. And since inventive organizations tend to be based on small, flexible, interactive, multidisciplinary working groups, I think that our model (at a symbolic, rather than organization chart, level) should be something like Figure 20.1.

The skills needed for this management working group would be those of *production* (the organization and efficient running of the company's products/services); *personnel* (recruitment/training/inspiring of the people who make up the corporate brand); *communications* (all aspects of communications, marketing and consumer/customer research); and possibly as a separate skill that of *brand designer* (a new type of animal, concerned with design in its broadest sense (Lorenz, 1986), from R&D to adding services to products and vice versa, with a passion for the totality of the brand). The whole group to be led by the CEO – he's the real brand *manager*.

However such a model is translated into reality, it seems to me that many companies need to take a new look at their organization charts, with brand building in mind. Most authorities (e.g. Pascale and Athos, 1981; Doyle *et al.*, 1990) seem to agree that there will have to be a more flexible and less hierarchical approach, with more informal networking, in order to get the rapid response and to attract the rare skills that a successful company brand needs.

It clearly goes a lot further than organization. What the best company brands represent is a common culture – common aims, standards, language, approaches and style. A common personality, rather than a book of rules. This may sound a little abstract and qualitative, but it is what consumers value in company brands (IBM, ICI or Marks & Spencer, for instance) that puts an enormous premium on sheer leadership from the top (Hamel and Prahalad, 1989). A company brand cannot succeed if the individuals doing the detailed work are zombies who aren't allowed to take any initiatives. Equally, it will not be a brand at all if there are no common links or if they don't know how they're expected to behave.

3. Common Methods for Communicating Brand Values

Charisma will not do the whole job. If the brand is to be established as a coherent and consistent entity, there must be a common approach to the strategies and tactics of communication. This common approach will have to be followed both by those in the company and by the specialist outside agencies. At the same time it has to be established without constricting the imagination, which is the basis of all effective communication.

Precisely how that's done will differ by company, but these seem to me to be the areas in which there should be common methodology and common language:

- *Consumers' buying systems.* Ways of analysing the processes and cycles by which people buy and use and re-buy the company's products/services, as a basis for deciding what methods of communication are best for what purpose at each stage.
- *Brand audit.* Auditing where the company brand stands in people's minds, compared with competitors, and why.
- *Brand positioning and brand personality.* Clear and evocative expressions of *what* the brand should be seen to offer and *who* it should be seen to be.
- *Brand strategy.* What at the strategic level is to be done to the products and the brand to bring them nearer to the desired positioning and personality.
- *Briefing.* Methods of briefing that aim to ensure that the brand is always presented consistently and in line with these strategic decisions, while allowing the maximum of inventive freedom at the tactical level.

It's an extremely demanding and time-consuming job to establish such working methods and common languages, and even more so to get them followed. But I think it will be both easier and more effective than trying to break up the empires and budgets of all those in the company who are communicating in some way about the brand. Rigid centralization and hierarchical line of command are not really options for communications.

4.1 The Brand Idea

Many of the best of the classic brands are famous at least partly because they have had a vivid and enduring advertising idea. By contrast, research (Biel, 1990; Gordon and Ryan, 1983) has shown that people are scornful of the more hackneyed themes and campaign types, especially on television – the musical wallpaper, the side-by-side comparisons, the talking heads, the computer graphics, the miracle-everything-slashed-unique-opportunity sales. They are equally aware of some very entertaining advertising for some brand whose name has temporarily slipped their mind. The value of a good advertising idea linked inexorably to a brand is enormous. It is clear that this would be even more valuable to a company brand, because its products/services are likely to be even less distinguishable from the competitors' and because its contacts with consumers are likely to be even more diverse. It would have to have something broader than an advertising idea, simply because of the wider range of communication vehicles used.

It's easier to recognize a good idea years later than to see it at the time or to describe it. But on the whole a good communication idea for a company brand would be an *original metaphor for the brand's personality.* That is, the brand would be borrowing from the outside something with the same personality characteristics; which could be *uniquely* associated with it; that could be reasonably long-lasting; and that in some way illuminated and enhanced the brand itself.

There are many examples from the advertising of classic brands:

- *Marlboro*: the cowboy – The individual facing the elements.
- *Esso*: the tiger – Graceful, powerful, aggressive.
- *Andrex*: the puppy – Soft, durable, wholesome.
- *Persil*: mother love – Metaphor for taking care of clothes.
- *Mr Kipling*: the voice – Tone of voice as metaphor for traditional craftsmanship.

Of course it is a very great deal harder to find an adequate metaphor for the personality of a whole service-based company, usable in a much wider range of media than advertising. It's not easy to think of many examples – there is Lloyds Bank's black horse, Legal & General's brolly, the Prudential's Rock of Gibraltar, Merrill Lynch's thundering herd. Some companies have used the personality of the founder for a brand idea (Habitat, Laker, The Body Shop, Next) but of course that can mean a rather dangerous impermanence. There are some good "brand gestures" (some public policy designed to symbolize a company's personality), such as Marks & Spenser's no-quibble exchange of goods or John Lewis's no-quibble return of cash if shown to be undersold. But on the whole there seem to be a lot of missed opportunities for company brand ideas.

FUN FOR ALL

The intriguing thing is that if one accepts these basic notions of what brand building will be like in the 1990s – the move from the model of the classic brand to that of the service-based company brand – there is no shortage of ideas on what to do about it: quite the reverse. New research methods are merging too (Baird *et al.*, 1988). And in this area I think we can be less shy about using ourselves and our experiences as a research source. It is clear that many people in companies and many teachers of marketing will be able to have a very enjoyable time starting again from first principles.

REFERENCES

Abraham, M. (1990) *Fact-based Design to Improve Advertising and Promotion Productivity.* 2nd ARF Advertising and Promotion Workshop.

Baird, C., Banks, R., Smith, P. and Morgan, R. (1988) *The SMART Approach to Customer Service.* Market Research Society Conference.

Biel, A.L. (1990) "Love the ad. Buy the product?", *Admap*, September.

Brouillard Communications (1988) *The Winning Edge.* New York: Brouillard Communications.

Buzzell, R.D. and Gale, B.M. (1987) *The PIMS Principles.* New York: The Free Press.

Christopher, M. (1985) "The strategy of customer service", in *Marketing in the Service Industries.* London: Frank Cass.

Doyle, P. (1989) "Building successful brands: The strategic options", *Journal of Marketing Management*, 5(1), 77–95.

Doyle, P., Saunders, J. and Wong, V. (1990) "Competition in global markets: A case study of American and Japanese competition for the British Market", *Journal of Marketing.*

Foxall, G. (1985) "Marketing *is* service marketing", in *Marketing in the Service Industries.* London: Frank Cass.

Gordon, W. and Ryan, C. (1983) *How do Consumers Feel Advertising Works?* Market Research Society Conference.

Hamel, G. and Prahalad, C.K. (1989) "Strategic intent", *Harvard Business Review*, May/June, pp. 63–76.

Lorenz, C. (1986) *The Design Dimension.* Oxford: Blackwell.

Madell, J. (1980) "New products: How to succeed when the odds are against you", *Marketing Week*, 22 February.

The Ogilvy Center for Research & Development (1989) *Advertising, Sales Promotion and the Bottom Line.* The Ogilvy Center.

Pascale, R.T. and Athos, A.G. (1981) *The Art of Japanese Management.* New York: Simon & Schuster.

Tauber, E.M. (1988) "Brand leverage: Strategy for growth in a cost-control world", *Journal of Advertising Research*, August/September, pp. 26–30.

Resumé of Stephen King's Life

1. *Born:*
   25 February 1931 in Melton Mowbray.

2. *Educated:*
   Oxford University, 1951–55.
   MA degree in Greats (philosophy and ancient history)

3. *Business career:*

1955–57	Publicity Assistant, Mond Nickel Co., London.
1957	Marketing Department, J.Walter Thompson Ltd, London.
1964	Set up and ran Advertising Research Unit, JWT.
1965	Set up and ran New Product Development Unit, JWT.
1967	Chairman of JWT Research and Development Committee.
1968	Set up and ran Account Planning Department, JWT.
1969	Appointed Board Director, JWT.

1976   Set up and ran Development Group, JWT.

1979   Appointed Chairman of newly-formed market research group, MRB International.

1989   Non-executive Director of WPP Group.

1992   Non-executive Director of Henley Centre.

4. *Clients worked with:*
Associated Biscuits, Beechams, Berger Paints, British Nutrition Foundation, Bowater-Scott, Committee of London Clearing Bankers, Findus, Golden Wonder, Guinness, Kraft, Kellogg's, John Harvey & Sons, Lever Brothers, Mr Kipling, Oxo, RHM, St Ivel, Schweppes, Taunton Cider, TSB, Windmill Bakery.

5. *External Activities:*

1970   Member of IPA Marketing Committee (Chairman of Advertising Evaluation Working Party)

1977–78   Member of Ministry of Agriculture's JCO Working Party on the Scientific Basis of Food Choice.

1979–81   On panel of judges for Market Research Society's Special Award

1980–84   On panel of judges for IPA Advertising Effectiveness Awards

PUBLICATIONS

1964   *Pin-Pointing the Affluent Household.* London: JWT.
How Many Nations? A study of regional differences in spending. London: JWT.

1965   "How useful is proposition testing?", *Advertising Quarterly*, No. 6.

1967   "Can research evaluate the creative content of advertising?", MRS Conference, winner of MRS Coglan Award, and *Admap*, Vol. 3, No. 6.

1967   "Sharpening up creativity", *Advertising Management*, June.

1968   "What can pre-testing do?" *Admap*, Vol. 4, No. 3.

1968   "Selective perception and Advertising", *Admap*, Vol. 4, No. 9.

1968   "Advertising research for new brands", *JMRS*, Vol. 10, No. 3.

1969   "Inter-media decisions: implications for agency structure", *Admap*, Vol. 5, No. 10.

1969   "Identifying market opportunities", in *Long-range Planning for Marketing and Diversification*, BIM and University of Bradford Management Centre. (Later, in *Creating and Marketing New Products*, eds. Wills, Hayhurst and Midgley. London: Crosby Lockwood Staples, 1973; and *Analytical Marketing Management*, eds. Doyle, Law, Weinberg and Simmonds, London: Harper & Row, 1974.)

1969   "Advertising effectiveness research: A short bibliography", *IPA Forum*, No. 25.

1970   "Development of the brand", *Advertising Quarterly*, No. 24.

1971   *What is a Brand?* London: JWT.

1972	*Tomorrow's Food* (with Jeremy Bullmore). London: JWT.
1973	*Developing New Brands*. London: Pitman.
1975	"Who positions brands, and what do they want to know?", in *Brand Positioning*, eds. Green and Christopher. MCB (European Marketing and Customer Studies) Ltd.
1975	"Practical progress from a theory of advertisements", *Admap*, Vol. 11, No. 10.
1976	"The coming of the cool customer", *Advertising Quarterly*, No. 48.
1976	"The new order", in *Consumer Change in the mid-70s*, ed. King. London: JWT.
1977	"Improving advertising decisions", *Admap*, Vol. 13, No. 4.
1978	*The Bank Nationalisation Debate, 1975–1978*. London: Committee of London Clearing Bankers.
1978/79	"Public response – the key to corporate advertising", *Advertising*, Winter.
1978	*Crisis in Branding*. London: JWT.
1978	"Branding: How to beat the crisis in packaged goods", *Campaign*, 27 October.
1979	"What's new about the new advertisers?", *Admap*, Vol. 15, No. 1.
1979	*Public versus Private Opinion*. Brussels: ESOMAR.
1979	"Opinion research in democratic society", *British Public Opinion*, No. 1
1979	"Testing the official view", *Financial Times*, No. 59.
1980	"Presentation and the choice of food", in *Nutrition and Lifestyles*, ed. Turner. London: Applied Science Publishers.
1980	"A look at the 1970s with quiet dissatisfaction", *The Grocer*, 19 April.
1980	"Conflicts in democracy: the need for more opinion research", *Advertising*, No. 65.
1980	*Advertising as a Barrier to Market Entry*. London: Advertising Association.
1980	*The Recession: Prospects for Consumer Goods*. London: JWT.
1980	"Growth with brands", *Retail & Distribution Management*, September/October.
1981	"How the public see banks", in *The Banks and the Public*. London: Institute of Bankers.
1981	*Eating Behaviour and Attitudes to Food, Nutrition and Health*. London: British Nutrition Foundation.
1981	"Conflicts between public and private opinion", *Long-Range Planning*, Vol. 14, No. 4.
1982	"Has marketing failed, or was it never really tried?", in *Marketing Education Group Proceedings*, ed. Thomas. University of Lancaster.
1983	"Trends in meal planning and eating habits", in *Food and People*, ed. Turner. London: John Libbey.
1983	"Applying research to decision-making" in *MRS Newsletter*, No. 208, June; *London Business School Journal*, Winter; *Marketing Intelligence & Planning*, Vol. 1, No. 3.

1984   *Developing New Brands* (with new introduction). London: JWT.

1984   "Setting advertising budgets for lasting effects", *Admap*, Vol. 20, No. 7/8 (also as "Quale budget pubblicitario per l'efficacia a lungo termine", *Media Forum* III, Italy).

1985   "The British meal", *Admap*, Vol. 21, No. 10.

1989   "The anatomy of account planning", *Admap*, Vol. 25, No. 11 (November).

1989   "Branding opportunities in financial services", *Proceedings of the 6th Annual Advertising & Marketing Financial Services Conference*.

1989   *International Business Communications Ltd*, July.

1989   "The financial evaluation of brands", in *The Longer and Broader Effects of Advertising*. IPA.

1991   "Brand building in the 1990s", *Journal of Marketing Management*. Vol. 7 (January), pp. 3–13.

1991   "Tomorrow's research", *Admap*, Vol. 26, No. 9, pp. 19–24.

Index

Index compiled by Liz Granger